Critical Praise from the States Where the Events Described in this Book Took Place

NEW ENGLAND
"By using imagination, a novel approach, and an excellent prose style, the authors have made a fascinating book."

—*New England Quarterly*

"This is the best account we have of this two-year period, and should prove to be a nearly definitive study."

—*Boston Herald*

NEW YORK
"A brilliant interpretation . . . a challenging work."

—*New York Historical Society*

"Impressive! . . . The authors have given us a searching account of the crisis and provided some memorable portraits of officials in America impaled on the dilemma of having to enforce a measure which they themselves opposed."

—*The New York Times*

PENNSYLVANIA
"This book fills a major gap in the historical literature of the pre-Revolutionary period. . . . It will be read both for information and pleasure."

—*The Pennsylvania Magazine of History and Biography*

VIRGINIA
"A brilliant contribution to the colonial field. Combining great industry, astute scholarship, and a vivid style, the authors have sought 'to recreate two years of American history.' They have succeeded admirably."

—*The William and Mary Quarterly*

THE STAMP ACT CRISIS

PROLOGUE TO REVOLUTION

Edmund S. Morgan
Helen M. Morgan

NEW, REVISED EDITION

COLLIER BOOKS, NEW YORK
COLLIER MACMILLAN LTD., LONDON

For

E. M. M.

Preface to the First Edition

THE BOOK BEFORE you is an attempt to recreate two years of American history. If the attempt is successful, it will be apparent that these years were decisive ones in the several colonies that later became the United States. In a book dealing with so brief a span of time it might have been possible to furnish the reader with a comprehensive account of what happened in each of these colonies. To have done so, however, would have meant repeating a dozen times a train of events in which the variations had only local significance. Such tedious reproduction of a pattern would have robbed the story of its movement and given it the deceptively static quality of a wall-paper print. On the other hand to have described the pattern in purely general terms would have been to lose contact with actual persons and places.

Our solution has been to see general issues so far as possible through the eyes of particular men. The large attention given these men is not meant to magnify their individual importance. To be sure, they did play important roles in the crisis, but they have been singled out because their experiences exhibit most strikingly the impact of the crisis on human beings.

A word about our collaboration—the original conception of the book and the actual writing of it have been carried out by Edmund S. Morgan, but both the structure of the thought and the final expression have been the product of so close a cooperation that it would be misleading to assign the book to a single author. We have considered and reconsidered every word so often that the book has become ours far more completely than if each of us had written separate parts of it.

We wish to express our gratitude to the other people who have helped us: to Professor Donald Fleming of the History Department at Brown University who read the manuscript and offered many valuable suggestions, and to the librarians at the John Hay Library, the John Carter Brown Library, the William L. Clements Library, the Henry E. Huntington Library, the Harvard College Library, the Yale University Library, the Boston Public Library, the New York Public Library, the Library Company of Philadelphia, the Library of Congress, the New Hampshire Historical Society, the Massachusetts Historical Society, the Massachusetts Archives, the American Antiquarian Society, the Rhode Island Historical Society, the Newport Historical Society, the Connecticut Historical Society, the New York Historical Society, the Historical Society of Pennsylvania, the American Philosophical Society, the Maryland Historical Society, the Virginia Historical Society, and the South Carolina Historical Society. The last two of these societies we did not visit, but their librarians furnished us with copies of documents.

Finally we owe a debt of gratitude to Brown University, where a genuine respect for scholarship, on the part of faculty, students, and administration, has been a constant encouragement and inspiration.

E. S. M.
H.M.M.

Preface to the Second Edition

In the ten years since the appearance of the first edition of this work, several books and articles relating to the subject have appeared, and we have become aware of a number of deficiencies in our treatment which we have attempted in some measure to correct in this new edition. We are grateful to everyone who has called our attention to errors, and especially to David S. Lovejoy and Bernhard Knollenberg, two scholars whose erudition is matched by their generosity.

The book nevertheless remains substantially as it was, for none of the changes affects its major themes or theses. Among these the one which has aroused most controversy is the one that seems to us to be the least controversial: that the colonies in objecting to the Stamp Act did not distinguish between internal and external taxation but did distinguish between taxation and legislation and placed the limits of Parliament's authority in the colonies between these two functions. In the book we sought to describe and explain this latter distinction. But we did not include (except in the note following Chapter VII) and have not now included a detailed demonstration that the colonies, with few exceptions in 1764 and none in 1765, objected to all Parliamentary taxes and not merely to internal ones. The evidence for this fact has been presented in an article (E. S. Morgan, "Colonial Ideas of Parliamentary Power," *William and Mary Quarterly*, 3d ser., 5 [1948], 311-341 and 6 [1949], 162-170); and many of the documents cited in the article are now assembled in E. S. Morgan, *Prologue to Revolution: Sources and Documents on the Stamp Act Crisis 1764–1766* (Chapel Hill: University of North Carolina Press, 1959). Anyone wishing to examine the evidence can find there all the formal protests against the Stamp Act issued by colonial assemblies in 1765, as well as selections from newspapers and pamphlets. For the convenience of those wishing to check our statements against these sources, we have placed citations to *Prologue to Revolution* in the appropriate footnotes of the present edition.

One other word of explanation is called for. We deliberately singled out for special attention men who (with the exception of Daniel Dulany) were not leaders of colonial resistance to the Stamp Act but sufferers from that resistance. There are two reasons for this apparent one-sidedness: one is that the Stamp Act crisis affected most drastically the lives of persons who opposed the resistance to it; the other is that in the main body of the narrative we have been primarily concerned with displaying the ideas and actions of the resisters. The attention to Bernard, Robinson, Hutchinson, Ingersoll, and Hughes is designed to show the other side of the picture and thus achieve a kind of balance.

E. S. M.
H.M.M.

September 1962

Contents

PART IV
Revolution Delayed

PART I

ABSOLUTE AUTHORITY AND
INALIENABLE RIGHT

Chapter I

Prologue

THE PLACE WAS something out of a fairy tale, a ghost town in the wilderness, empty houses lining the street on one side, savage plants creeping toward them to recover their domain, and on the other side—an enchanted castle, where a gentleman lived with his wife and her young sister. They might have been king, queen, and princess, and the two tame deer which wandered about the house were doubtless a lord and lady transformed by some magic into their present shape. There was a rich meadow, surrounded on three sides by a winding river, and shady lanes which led past a marble fountain, and a covered bower where the princess sat and bewailed the suitor who did not come.

This was Germanna, on the Rapidan River in Spotsylvania; the king was Colonel Alexander Spotswood, former Governor of Virginia, and the queen was the wife whom he had brought from London to live in this improbable paradise. The empty houses had once been the homes of the German settlers whom Spotswood had planted there but who had since deserted him. In September, 1732, the place was visited by a traveller who, like the Spotswoods, would have looked more at home on Regent Street than on the frontier of Virginia. William Byrd had come to consult with the Colonel about iron-mining, but he had a gift for recording scenes and conversations, and in his journal he snatched the whole episode out of time and left it to us, complete with Spotswood's oracular pronouncements not only on iron-mining, but also on tar-burning, hemp, the Spaniards, the post office, and British politics.[1] In this fantastic setting, so far from the civilized world, far it might seem from the world at all, Spotswood spoke of events in London or Boston as though

[1] J. S. Bassett, ed., *The Writings of "Colonel William Byrd of Westover in Virginia"* (New York, 1901), 356-470.

he could abolish at will the desert of woods and water that separated him from them. He told Byrd how the British government had demanded that the people of Massachusetts settle a standing salary upon the governor whom the King appointed for them. The New Englanders had refused, and now, said Spotswood, the Ministry were receding from their demand. "He said further," Byrd recorded, "that if the Assembly in New England would stand Bluff, he did not see how they cou'd be forct to raise Money against their Will, for if they shou'd direct it to be done by Act of Parliament, which they have threaten'd to do, (though it be against the Right of Englishmen to be taxt, but by their Representatives), yet they wou'd find it no easy matter to put such an Act in Execution."[2]

It was a prophecy delivered in the wilderness, and those magic words "the Right of Englishmen," which more than once had measured the tread of marching feet, would continue to lay their spell long after Spotswood was in his grave and his castle in ruins. But this book is concerned with history, and though history may sometimes take on the guise of a fairy story, as it did on the banks of the Rapidan in 1732, it must shortly come back to earth. In sober fact, Spotswood's prophecy need not be ascribed to second sight, for he had been Governor of Virginia, and he knew from bitter experience how jealously a colonial assembly guarded its right to levy taxes. In 1715 the House of Burgesses had refused to grant the supplies necessary for defense against the Indians, because they thought that he had called some of their prerogatives in question. He had denounced them and finally dissolved them, but he had not beaten them.[3] And he knew that any attempt by Parliament to beat them would have met with doubled resistance.

In 1732 the Assembly of Massachusetts "stood Bluff," as the Virginia Assembly stood in 1715, and the Ministry did

[2] *Ibid.*, 365-366. The episode is treated in L. W. Labaree, *Royal Government in America* (New Haven, 1930), 359-366.

[3] H. R. McIlwaine, ed., *Journals of the House of Burgesses of Virginia, 1712–1714, 1715–1718, 1720–1722, 1725–1726* (Richmond, 1912), 121-170.

recede from their demand. For a generation thereafter, as for three generations before, New Englanders and other Americans went about their business unhampered by Parliamentary taxes. Yet the assemblies did not relax their vigilance, and wise governors avoided so far as possible any conflicts which might prompt a discussion of rights. They knew, as Edmund Burke was to say, that when people begin to define their rights, it is "a sure symptom of an ill-conducted state."

During the first six decades of the eighteenth century Britain allowed her children to grow in their own way: though the internal quarrels of the colonies were constant, there were only occasional points of friction with the mother country, such as the episode which Spotswood discussed with Byrd; and before the colonists had time to formulate a definition of their rights, the British receded—without any disclaimer of their own right—and the colonists went about their business of catching fish or growing tobacco without further philosophizing. The happy result of this policy was that by 1760 the British Empire was the strongest and most prosperous power and British subjects the freest inhabitants in the western world. A less propitious result was that the rights of the colonists in relation to the mother country had never come up for close examination, and hence no one knew exactly what they were.

The colonies had been founded under the authority of the King but had taken advantage of three thousand miles of ocean to achieve a considerable independence of him and of the royal governors he sent to rule them. From a comfortable distance they watched Parliament assume the same powers in Great Britain that their assemblies were assuming in America. The growing impotence of the King was the symbol of their freedom, for it separated them effectively from the real power of the British government. As long as Parliament continued to deal with them through the King, as long as its power reached them in the diluted form of royal instructions, they need fear no interference. To be sure Parliament did direct the operation of their commerce in the Acts of Trade and Navigation, but except in this area British authority was exerted through the King and through the Board of Trade, which he had established in 1696 to assist him and his Councilors in formulating colonial policy. The colonies in turn devised an informal method of keeping England informed of their views: they appointed agents to represent their interests in London, and these agents could go to the Secretary of State or the Board of Trade and offer petitions or explain the effects which might be expected from any measure affecting the welfare of their clients.

To persons with tidy minds an empire which required such handymen to keep it running might seem in need of overhauling. But the British Empire had the great advantage of success. The structure might not appeal to an architect, but it seemed adequate to most of the people who lived in it. So long as they did not have to decide who had what rights and what authority, they could get along well together. Early in 1764 it became apparent that they would have to decide. Governor Spotswood had not predicted what would happen if a dispute should arise in which both Parliament and the colonies "stood Bluff." The ensuing pages try to tell what did happen.

Chapter II

Francis Bernard, Royal Governor

WHEN ENGLISHMEN and Americans finally found themselves quarreling about the rights of Englishmen, anyone could look back and see that the trouble had been brewing ever since Colonel Washington surrendered his force of Virginians to the French at Fort Necessity in the summer of 1754. For five years after that skirmish, through disaster and defeat, Englishmen and Americans fought the French in North America. After the enemy crumbled on the Plains of Abraham in 1759, England joined America in rejoicing, but at the same time Englishmen looked at their possessions across the ocean with new eyes. When they counted the cost in blood and money of the victory at Quebec, they could not fail to see that most of the blood and most of the money had come from England, and they naturally asked what they would gain from the sacrifice. The colonies had benefited enormously by their attachment to England. What could England expect in return?

Once the question was put, the answer was bound to follow, that the colonies ought to contribute more to imperial support than could be found in the records of the Treasury. Quebec had scarcely fallen before short-sighted ministers began to talk of a colonial tax. At Whitehall and Westminster there was little comprehension of the effect such an innovation could have in America, and the ignorance was even greater in Parliament and among the people at large. But here and there a clear-headed individual who had had experience with bumptious Americans anticipated their antagonism if Parliament should try to tax them before settling its right to do so. Instead of forcing such a premature measure it would be wiser to proceed at once to reorganize the colonies. Most of them had been founded before the vindication of Parliamentary supremacy in England, and a careful reconstruction to make this new authority as clear in the forests of America as in the streets of London must be accomplished before any foolhardy attempt at taxation should crystallize colonial sentiment against it. Unfortunately the Ministry was so occupied with winding up the war and playing politics inside Parliament that it had little time to examine its authority in territories three thousand miles away. Consequently, while statesmen and politicians pulled and hauled to hold their parties together, the problem of taking up the slack in the British Empire was ignored except by a few zealous men, mostly on the outer fringes of government, who cried out in vain for reform.

Best known, perhaps, was Thomas Pownall, the former Governor of Massachusetts. His plans for reorganization were published in a book called *The Administration of the Colonies*. Through six editions, each larger than its predecessor, he urged his schemes and died without finding a receptive audience.[1] Less conspicuous than Pownall was his successor in Massachusetts, who also perceived from the vantage point of New England that the empire needed remodeling. Francis Bernard's plans were clearer, simpler, and more concise than Pownall's, and though he too failed to make himself heard in Whitehall, his efforts to do so and the forces which frustrated him are a part of the story this book attempts to tell.

Bernard was an altogether improbable man to become the architect of a new British Empire, and it seems likely that the defects of his character and birth led his superiors to underestimate the merit of his proposals. The son of a country rector, he had gone through Oxford, the Middle Temple, and twenty years as a barrister in Lincolnshire by the time Washington surrendered at Fort Necessity.[2] His only qualification for a place in the colonial service was the fact that he had managed to marry a cousin of Lord Barrington, one of the most remarkable politicians of the age. From 1755 until 1778, while other cabinet officers came and went, Lord

---

[1] London, 1764, 1765, 1766, 1768, 1774, 1777.
[2] On Bernard's early life see the *Dictionary of National Biography* and E. A. Jones, *American Members of the Inns of Court* (London, 1924), 17-18.

Barrington stayed in office, mostly as Secretary at War. There were those who inferred that he was able to hold his post because he was not troubled by principles, but the fact that he held it was indisputable.

From the day of his marriage in 1741 Bernard cultivated a close acquaintance with his wife's cousin. During seventeen years, while Mrs. Bernard bore him a succession of children, he went about his legal business, contenting himself with the small honors of serving as local steward or receiver or recorder. By 1758, when he was forty-six years old, his family had grown to eight children, and the cost of bringing them up in the manner to which he had become accustomed was beginning to exceed his income. For assistance he turned to his influential relative. In eighteenth-century England gentlemen of power frequently showed their affection for needy friends and relations by finding them comfortable positions in the pay of the government. The position which Barrington found for Bernard was no sinecure. In 1759 when General Wolfe was taking Quebec, Bernard had been royal Governor of New Jersey for a little more than a year.

It must have been a considerable wrench for a small city lawyer with a large family to pull up stakes and head for America. The salary which rewarded this move was £800 a year, an attractive sum, but Bernard had to pay £400 in fees for his commission, and it cost him £1200 to bring his family and furnishings across the ocean.[3] After a year's service he could count a net loss of £800. Money meant a lot to him, and he worried about it as he tried his hand at governing an American colony. He worried, in fact, about a great many things. Essentially a parvenu, he was always afraid that people were not treating him with the proper respect. He never knew when to leave a matter alone but must constantly take up his pen to complain about some injury, real or imaginary. He did not know how to deal with people, and the mantle of authority only magnified his difficulty. In view of these handicaps his success as Governor

---

[3] Bernard to John Pownall, January 13, 1761, to Barrington, January 17, 1761, Bernard Papers, I, 289-295, Harvard College Library.

of New Jersey was remarkable. Shrewdly perceiving that the Quakers held the balance of power in the colony, and that they had been badly treated by the former governor, he courted their support and was rewarded by an unprecedented harmony in his dealings with the Assembly.[4] So well did he show up in this situation that after two years Lord Barrington was able to get him transferred to the stormy, intractable, and important colony of Massachusetts Bay.

Bernard was happy with the promotion, for his new salary would be £300 a year larger. He was still badly in debt and anxious to increase his income by every possible means, so much so that he made a fool of himself trying too hard to sell his house and various knickknacks to his successor in New Jersey.[5] The move to Massachusetts temporarily embarrassed his finances still further: besides the cost of moving there was again the £400 in fees on his new commission. On top of this came the death of King George II, a real disaster, for it meant that he must renew the commission, at the cost of still another £400.[6]

But the government of Massachusetts would bring other than monetary rewards, and Bernard, though no longer a young man, was ambitious and fired by the possibilities he saw before him. He had been as impressed as his superiors by what he took to be his political abilities in governing New Jersey; and in Massachusetts he would have more room to exercise them. In Massachusetts he might also expand his perspective to view the colonies as a whole; eventually, who could tell, he might rise from a provincial governor to an imperial statesman. As he entered the colony and received the plaudits of the citizens, he already took a larger view of things than he had at Perth Amboy or in Lincolnshire. In New Jersey he had rested his policy on an alliance with the Quakers. Here he would rise above the sordid bickerings of

[4] Bernard to Bishop of Bristol, January 7, 1760, to John Taylor, October 12, 1759, to Halifax, July 18, 1760, Bernard Papers, I, 190-192, 212, 266-271.

[5] Bernard to Boone, June 3, 10, 1760, Bernard Papers, I, 252-259, 261.

[6] See note 3.

provincial politics and found his administration "on the broad bottom of the people in general."[7]

Such a course might have been possible for a man with the Olympian character to carry it out. Bernard had already persuaded himself that he had such a character and continued to believe during the next few years that he was displaying it. But the fundamental insecurity of his temperament betrayed him. Even before he left New Jersey his trivial troubles preceded him to Massachusetts. A servant girl who was preparing his Boston residence ran off with a man who had already seduced two of his maids at Perth Amboy, and Bernard could not forbear writing tedious letters to people in Boston complaining of the rascal.[8]

From first to last there was always someone abusing him. After a gratifying welcome by the people of Massachusetts he was disappointed to find the merchants combining against him. He consoled himself that this was the consequence of his dutiful attention to the Laws of Trade. He was sure too that the merchants were encouraged by a few designing politicians, particularly James Otis, Jr., who bore him an undeserved grudge for not appointing the elder Otis to the bench of the Superior Court.[9] There were also some unscrupulous customs officers siding with the merchants, and the plot reached serious proportions late in 1761 when John Temple, the new Surveyor General of the Customs, not only upheld this insubordination but himself failed to accord the proper respect to His Majesty's Governor. This was insufferable, and Bernard wrote petulantly to England of all the insults he had borne. "There never," he cried, "was a governor so ill treated by a subject of the government, since the Colonies were first planted."[10] Even the British Navy joined the conspiracy when

[7] Bernard to John Pownall, May 12, 1761, Bernard Papers, I, 317.

[8] Bernard to Andrew Oliver, June 15, 1760, Bernard Papers, I, 262-263.

[9] Bernard to John Pownall, January 19, February 21, July 6, 1761, to Thomas Pownall, August 28, 1761, Bernard Papers, I, 296-298, 322-323; II, 9.

[10] To John Pownall, May 6, 1765, Bernard Papers, III, 288. The first three volumes of the Bernard Papers are full of letters

Admiral Colville claimed Bernard's share of vessels condemned in Massachusetts for violating the Laws of Trade.[11]
On every hand heartless men were scheming to deprive him
of the dignity and profit that were rightly his.

To all of these trials Bernard responded by dashing off letters to England, complaining of his persecutors and protesting that the mass of the people loved him. Perhaps because
of the bad judgment he too evidently displayed, the Board
of Trade and the Privy Council paid little attention to the
other letters he was writing. Though he deluded himself
about the popularity of his administration, Bernard did have
the vision and the perspective and the insight to see that the
American governments must be reformed in order to secure
colonial submission to Parliament's unlimited authority. In
New Jersey he had become acquainted with the deficiencies
of imperial control in the middle colonies. At Boston he discovered that Massachusetts was constitutionally incapable of
functioning effectively as part of the empire, and that nearby
Connecticut and Rhode Island were no better than independent republics. A reform of colonial administration was
glaringly needed, and by December of 1761 he knew who
ought to direct that reform. On the fifteenth of the month
he wrote to Lord Barrington that "when a Revisal and settlement of the political state of North America should have a
place in the British Councils, I might possibly be of some
service."[12] During the next two years he sent over a barrage
of letters informing everyone who might be interested that he
was ready at a moment's notice to take sail for England and
advise the Ministry on the proper procedure for reorganizing
the colonies.[13]

---

dealing with Bernard's troubles with the merchants and customs
officers. See especially I, 315-320; II, 24-26, 30.

[11] Bernard to Colville, April 25, 1764, to Halifax, February
18, 1764, Bernard Papers, III, 39, 141-144.

[12] Bernard Papers, II, 21-23; Edward Channing and Archibald
Cary Coolidge, eds., *The Barrington-Bernard Correspondence*
(Cambridge, 1912), 42-45.

[13] See letters to Charles Townshend, May 18, 1763; to Richard
Jackson, May 21, 1763, and August 3, 1763; to Lord Shelburne,
July 25, 1763; Bernard Papers, II, 60-62, 65-68, 92-94, and 84-85,
respectively.

After the peace treaty with France had been signed in February, 1763, Bernard's eagerness quickened. His friend Richard Jackson, agent of the colony of Connecticut, Member of Parliament, and intimate of George Grenville, wrote that the Crown was considering a union of Rhode Island, Connecticut, and Massachusetts in one government. Though Jackson indicated his own coolness to the suggestion, Bernard jumped at it. The government of Connecticut was a "monster in politicks," he said, and both Rhode Island and Connecticut must be made more dependent upon the mother country. He continued with a measure of political philosophy: "I consider Government not to be a Right but a trust, and that the Royal Grants of Jurisdiction in America either to private persons or Corporations are no more than temporary provisions untill the Parliament that is the whole Legislature, shall settle the Government, . . ." This was strong medicine. According to Bernard, the charters of Connecticut and Rhode Island, dating from 1662 and 1663 respectively, and that of Massachusetts, dating from 1691, were temporary trusts and could be revoked by Parliament at will. Perhaps he realized that these ideas would go down in New England like chopped hay, even though they should come from so popular a man as he considered Francis Bernard to be. He encouraged himself by adding, "Surely this is law now, whatever it was before the Revolution," which might be translated as "I think this is law now, even though many will deny it."[14]

In spite of his easy dismissal of colonial charters Bernard did not intend to oppress the Americans. He had no grudge against the people he governed. What he had was an orderly mind that foresaw trouble in the imperfect subordination of the colonies to Parliament. His diagnosis of the difficulty was doubtless assisted by the fact that Parliament's position in the colonies closely resembled his own position in the world. Both were insecure and untried. The insults he received or fancied were a token of the larger ones Parliament received daily in colonial violations of the Laws of Trade. Through the office he held, Bernard saw his personal sufferings transfigured: an

[14] Bernard to Jackson, August 2, 1763, Bernard Papers, III, 89-92.

insult to Francis Bernard, Governor of Massachusetts, became an insult to Parliament; and his personal anxiety and ambition were exalted to anxiety and ambition for the empire. What he wanted for himself was wealth, distinction, and perhaps power; what he wanted for Parliament was a benevolent despotism over the colonies. The two aims were fused in his vision of a new colonial empire of which he should be the guiding genius, or in which at least his own dignity would be firmly established under the aegis of a supreme Parliament.

In the spring of 1764, while events of the greatest importance for him and for the colonies were preparing in England, Bernard was in Concord, Massachusetts, where he had convened the Assembly in order to avoid the small-pox at Boston. Here in the country air that later generations would also find congenial to health and to writing, he began to put his ideas on paper. With characteristic tidiness he reduced them to a set of propositions numbered consecutively from one to ninety-seven, beginning with principles he considered self-evident and proceeding relentlessly until the necessary steps for reorganization were plainly marked out.[15]

Bernard began by defining the sovereignty of Great Britain, which he placed in the King, acting with the advice and consent of Parliament. This was the axiom which all British subjects took for granted. It was not necessary to point out that Parliament was the final authority in any conceivable contest with the King. The propositions went on to distinguish the areas under the control of the sovereign power into Great Britain herself and the external dominions which, together with Great Britain, made up the empire. The American colonies, were, of course, a part of these external dominions. As such they were subject to the King in Parliament just as much as Great Britain was herself. And Bernard went on with the ideas he had already expressed to Jackson, that the colonial governments with their representative assemblies were simply convenient temporary arrangements which Parliament

---

[15] The propositions were not printed until 1774 in *Select Letters on the Trade and Government of America, and the Principles of Law and Polity, Applied to the American Colonies* (London, 1774).

could alter at will. He did not shrink from the conclusion that this line of reasoning led to: "The rule that a *British* subject shall not be bound by laws, or liable to taxes, but what he has consented to by his representatives, must be confined to the inhabitants of *Great Britain* only; and is not strictly true even there."[16] Parliament, in other words, had every right to tax and legislate for the colonies, although they were unrepresented in it. And yet why should they not be represented? Bernard thought they should: though it was impracticable for all parts of the empire to send members to Parliament, it was not, in his opinion, impracticable for the Americans. He could foresee no detrimental consequences for the mother country; and though the Americans could not properly claim representation as a right, to make them a gift of it would effectively quiet their protests when Parliament began to exercise its authority more broadly over them.

Coming to the colonial governments themselves, Bernard insisted on uniformity. Their constitutions varied as widely as the different times and conditions of their founding. But now that they had reached maturity, it was improper for the people of one colony to have fewer rights and privileges than those of another, since all were subject to one King and one law and all equally fit for one form of government. It was unfair, for example, for the people of Rhode Island and Connecticut to elect their own governors, who permitted them to ignore the Acts of Trade, while the faithful royal governor of Massachusetts kept his people within the law.[17] All colonies should have royal governors. And all should retain their assemblies, which were still convenient arrangements for conducting local affairs but the assemblies must be altered to provide for an independent upper house, to be neither the tool of the lower house nor yet an executive council of the governor. In Parliament the independence of the upper house rested on the hereditary succession of the Lords. Bernard

16 *Ibid.*, 75.
17 This point was made by Bernard in letters to William Pitt, October 3, 1761, to Lord Egremont, October 25, 1763, to John Pownall, February 10, 1764, and to Lord Halifax, December 14, 1764, Bernard Papers, II, 14-16; III, 99-100, 130, 200.

thought the new colonial governments should resemble England's as closely as possible, and though he believed that America was not yet ready for the establishment of a hereditary nobility, still "A *Nobility* appointed by the *King* for life, and made independent, would probably give strength and stability to the *American* governments, as effectually as an hereditary *Nobility* does to that of *Great Britain*."[18]

With a royal governor and an influential house of nobles in every colony, both ready to support the power that created them, Parliament would be in a better position to exercise its authority over the Americans. But though Bernard granted Parliament's unlimited authority, he recommended that in the matter of colonial taxation it confine itself to duties on trade. Taxes, he felt, should be levied on those who benefited most from them. Since the protection of trade was the most expensive part of imperial defense, Parliament, as the imperial legislature, might appropriately tax trade to pay for it. The expenses of local government, on the other hand, should be met by internal taxes, and these could best be left for the local representative assemblies to levy. Parliament might establish a "civil list," naming the offices of government and the salaries required for each, but it need not step in unless the colonists failed to raise the requisite amount. In this way royal officials would be freed from servile dependence on the assemblies, but at the same time a colony's internal economy would not be disrupted through unwise taxes levied by a Parliament unacquainted with local conditions.

Bernard wrote as an Englishman brought up on the doctrine of Parliamentary supremacy; but he knew, as few Englishmen did, the pitfalls waiting in America for the minister who should attempt to wield Parliamentary authority there in the existing political chaos. His plan aimed at complete recognition of Parliament's authority. To secure this without unduly antagonizing the Americans he was willing to continue their privilege of raising their own internal taxes and in addition to allow them representation in Parliament.

It is remarkable how closely Bernard's ideas conformed to those of the men who were to become his bitter enemies.

[18] *Select Letters*, 83.

While he was writing his *Principles of Law and Polity, Applied to the Government of the British Colonies in America* (the title he gave to his ninety-seven propositions), James Otis, who also attended the meeting of the Assembly at Concord, was writing *The Rights of the British Colonies Asserted and Proved*.[19] Otis's pamphlet was a passionate denial of Parliament's right to tax the colonies, either internally or by duties on trade, but though he differed from Bernard on the question of right, he agreed, in part at least, that the remedy was to grant the colonies representation in Parliament. Unfortunately Parliament offered the two men no opportunity to work together for this reform, but forced them to take their respective stands on the question of right.

As Bernard and Otis were agreed on the desirability of colonial representation in Parliament, Bernard and John Adams were agreed on the necessity of an independent, aristocratic upper house in a properly constituted legislature. The principle of "balanced" government—and Bernard used the word "balanced" to describe it—was John Adams's great contribution to the governments of the independent United States. In 1764, before Adams began to stress the idea, Bernard fully understood it and wished to see it established throughout America. If his recommendations had been accepted in London, it is not impossible that Adams and Otis might have been found by his side in supporting the reformation of colonial government.

Even as it was, Bernard felt that he could count on the backing of many influential colonists. In Massachusetts he was sure that the most prudent men were behind him, in spite of the grumbling at his strict attention to the Laws of Trade. In at least three other colonies he knew there were strong elements in favor of reform. The situation in Pennsylvania was familiar to him from his service in nearby New Jersey. During his years there he had written to Lord Barrington that the government of Pennsylvania must be taken over by the Crown and the governor made independent of the people. "Till these things are done," he had said, "there

[19] Boston, 1764.

will be no restoring peace to that distracted province."[20]
Now, he heard, the most enlightened Pennsylvanians were
taking the matter into their own hands: a petition had been
circulated asking the King to revoke the governmental powers
of the Penn family and make Pennsylvania a royal colony.
The Assembly approved it and sent it to Bernard's friend
Richard Jackson for presentation. Bernard, following the
whole affair in the newspapers, admired the masterly manner
in which it had been brought to a crisis and recognized the
hand of his friend Benjamin Franklin behind it.[21] In November, 1764, Franklin himself left for London to further it.[22]

Similarly from Rhode Island came news that the sensible
people were sick and tired of the corruption and quarreling
in the popular government there. The *Boston News-Letter*
for May 3, 1764, reported from Newport that "Many of the
Inhabitants seem desirous of an alteration of their present
Form of Government, and are willing to be on the Footing
which the Inhabitants of Pennsylvania have requested, viz.
to be a Royal Government." How many inhabitants of Rhode
Island favored such a change may be questioned, but some of
them had indeed drafted a petition to the King, asking for
a revocation of the charter. By October their petition was
on its way to England, and they wrote to Benjamin Franklin,
urging him to support it along with his own.[23]

In Connecticut too signs of readiness appeared. The quarrel there between the "Old Light" and the "New Light" factions of the Congregational Church had sent moderately disposed members in disgust to the Anglican Church. And the
feeling of the Anglican ministers about the Connecticut charter was no secret. They had been pushed around for years

[20] Bernard to Barrington, May 23, 1759, *Barrington-Bernard
Correspondence,* 4-6.
[21] Bernard to [Richard Jackson] April 7, 1764, Bernard Papers,
III, 229-230.
[22] On the Pennsylvania petition see below, ch. XIV.
[23] Martin Howard to Benjamin Franklin, November 16, 1764,
and May 14, 1765; Thomas Moffat to Benjamin Franklin, May
12, 1764. Franklin Papers, I, 108; II, 127; I, 88, American Philosophical Society.

by a government which supported only the established Congregational Church. In letters to their headquarters in London they had more than once suggested that the only salvation for the colony would be a royal governor and an Anglican bishop, and when Samuel Johnson, a leader of the Church in Connecticut, heard that Franklin was off for London to apply for royal government, he wrote to him, "Would to God you were charged with pleading the same cause in behalf of all the governments that they might all alike be taken into the King's immediate protection. It would certainly be best for us all to be under one form of government, and I beg that your best influence may be so directed that the government at home, when they take yours in hand may make one work of it."[24]

The men backing these pleas for reorganization were undeniably some of the most substantial citizens of the new world—men of property, influence, and judgment. There was one point in Bernard's program which would probably attract them as much as it attracted him: the American nobility. Resounding titles appeal to men in any age, and this was an age when aristocracy had not yet had to do battle with the philosophy of social equality. Even in America, ten years before the Declaration of Independence, scarcely anyone doubted the rightness and desirability of social distinctions. Though Boston was soon to see mobs roaming the streets, they would not be seeking to haul down the banners of aristocracy. In fact one of the mortifying scenes about to be enacted before Governor Bernard was that in which gentle-

[24] Undated, Herbert and Carol Schneider, *Samuel Johnson, President of King's College: His Career and Writings* (4 vols., New York, 1929) I, 349. The letter was undoubtedly written late in 1764 or early in 1765. See also letters by Samuel Johnson, April 14, 1751, and July 13, 1760, in Francis L. Hawks and William S. Perry, eds., *Documentary History of the Protestant Episcopal Church . . . containing Numerous Hitherto Unpublished Documents concerning the Church in Connecticut* (New York, 1863), I, 278, 312, and a letter signed "Ecclesanglicus," dated New London, August 10, 1764, which says, "Great God incline his Majesty and Privy Council to send us a Bishop for his church, and a Governor for the Colony." Chalmers Papers, Harvard College Library.

men, who should have known better, disguised themselves in working-men's clothes and led the mob in attacking officers of the King's government.

An American nobility was by no means a fanciful idea in 1764, and might have served to forestall some of the troubles which were close at hand. Bernard would not have found it difficult to name suitable candidates in the colonies of his acquaintance. In every northern colony there were the merchants, those of large fortune, that is, and with wide investments, who could be expected to weather the storms of depression and shipwreck which made colonial commerce a matter of large risks and large returns. Besides the merchants in the north and the correspondingly wealthy planters in the south, there were professional men, lawyers and doctors, and the more important officials in the customs service or government. In Massachusetts the Lieutenant-Governor, Thomas Hutchinson, was an obvious candidate: dignified, conservative, and prudent; so were Andrew Oliver, Secretary of the province, and Colonel Israel Williams of Hatfield and the other so-called "River Gods," who dominated the western part of the colony. Then of course there was Francis Bernard.

In Connecticut, despite its present "republican" form of government, there were some properly qualified men, like Jared Ingersoll, the New Haven attorney, and Joseph Harrison, the Customs Collector there, who was on intimate terms with the Marquis of Rockingham, and Thomas Fitch, who did as good a job as could be expected of an elected governor. Even in Rhode Island, the most disgracefully radical and lawless colony, there were gentlemen on whom a title would sit becomingly, those for example who were petitioning for a royal government. Martin Howard, Jr., an attorney, was a man of proper sentiments, and so was Doctor Thomas Moffat, a Scotch physician who had come to Newport in the wake of Bishop Berkeley and who maintained a distinguished library and collection of paintings. John Robinson, the recently arrived Collector of the port, was a likely person also, though Bernard was soon to find him too much under the influence of the Surveyor General of the Customs, John Temple. Temple was one of those pushing people who might well be left out of any colonial aristocracy.

If proper candidates for an aristocracy could be found in Rhode Island and Connecticut, they could surely be found in every colony. The fact that Benjamin Franklin was taking the lead for royal government in Pennsylvania was a good omen, for Franklin had already demonstrated his influence by getting his son William appointed Governor of New Jersey. It was possible that Franklin himself would be the first royal governor of Pennsylvania,[25] and he would doubtless be glad to have his government supported by a local peerage, made up of his abler and more well-to-do friends, like John Hughes and Joseph Galloway.

All in all, the prospect seemed favorable for realizing Bernard's scheme. Not only were there influential colonists who might support it strongly in hopes of gaining a seat in the new aristocracy, but people in general appeared reconciled to some kind of reorganization. Although alarmed by new restrictions on their trade and impending Parliamentary taxation, they showed no particular concern about reports that the structure of the colonial governments would be altered. The newspapers printed rumors from London of boundary readjustments for the northern colonies: "It is said there will be but four, viz. Nova Scotia, Province of Main, New Hampshire and New York—the Massachusetts Rhode Island and Connecticut are to be divided between New York and New Hampshire."[26] The likelihood of a colonial representation in Parliament was also suggested and even the establishment of an American nobility.[27] The Boston newspapers which expressed themselves with greatest vehemence on the taxation of the colonies printed these items without comment.

The succession of rumors must have been provocative to a man of Bernard's ambition. He knew that his analysis of the situation was a penetrating one and that the Ministry in England would profit by studying it. He saw the mood for reorganization ripe in both England and America, and he

[25] See William Allen to Thomas Penn, March 11, 1765, Penn Correspondence 1765–1771, Historical Society of Pennsylvania.
[26] Boston Gazette, April 22, 1765.
[27] Boston Post-Boy and Advertiser, February 25, 1765; Boston Gazette, supplement, May 27, 1765.

felt strongly that it was now or never. The concluding paragraphs of his ninety-seven propositions were prophetic:

96. The people of *North America*, at this time, expect a revisal and reformation of the *American* Governments, and are better disposed to submit to it than ever they were, or perhaps ever will be again.

97. This is therefore the proper and critical time to reform the *American* governments upon a general, constitutional, firm, and durable plan; and if it is not done now, it will probably every day grow more difficult, till at last it becomes impracticable.[28]

Filled with the urgency of the situation Bernard sent a copy of his plan to Lord Barrington as soon as it was finished and asked him to show it to Lord Halifax and Lord Hillsborough, each of whom might be expected to have a hand in the coming reorganization.[29] Three weeks later he sent copies to Richard Jackson. Jackson could show it to other persons of influence in the administration and if they approved its sentiments might have it printed.[30]

Jackson apparently did not find it advisable to publish the piece, but Bernard continued to press advice on him.[31] On November 9, 1764, he finally abandoned the indirect approach and wrote to Lord Halifax himself, now Secretary of State for the Southern Department and charged with control of the colonies.[32] Barrington had told him that Halifax praised the ninety-seven propositions as "the best thing of the kind by much that he ever read."[33] Taking this as a license to open correspondence on the subject, Bernard plunged in with a ten-page letter amplifying some details of his scheme. In the ninety-seven propositions he had recommended that colonial boundaries be redrawn to conform better to physiog-

[28] *Select Letters*, 84-85.
[29] June 23, 1764, *Barrington-Bernard Correspondence*, 75-77.
[30] July 9, 1764, Bernard Papers, III, 237-238.
[31] October 22, 1764, Bernard Papers, X, 230-236.
[32] Bernard Papers, X, 238-247.
[33] Barrington to Bernard, October 3, 1764, *Barrington-Bernard Correspondence*, 81.

raphy. What he proposed now was a union of Massachusetts, Rhode Island, and eastern Connecticut, with western Connecticut attached to New York. In this enlarged government of Massachusetts a governor's council and a separate upper house of the legislature should both be appointed by the King, the former for life, the latter during his pleasure. The reform should be brought about by act of Parliament. This was not the complete colonial reorganization he envisaged, but it was at least a beginning.[34]

Bernard never had the opportunity of observing the reaction of New England to such an act or to any other act for reorganizing the colonies. Lord Halifax may have been sympathetic with his schemes, for he himself had long felt the need of reform in colonial administration, but no one in England sensed the urgency of the situation as Bernard did. British statesmen had not experienced the insults of uncouth Americans and might have dismissed them with the assurance of birth and breeding if they had. Yet they would have been wise to listen to Bernard, for however secure they might be in rank and fortune, they were conducting a government whose position in the colonies was no more secure than Francis Bernard's. When their government finally felt the sting of colonial insubordination, it would respond with the same petulance that Bernard had shown to the insults of James Otis and John Temple, but it would be unable to translate its sense of injury into a larger scheme of colonial reform. Now, instead of undertaking the reorganization Bernard was urging, they sent him two revenue acts to enforce. These were the premature measures he had feared, acts which he had expressly urged the Ministry not to pass. In the repercussions that followed, his wishful identification with Parliament became a reality, for the colonists struck at royal officers with a violence that Parliament could not fail to resent. But the fulfillment, coming as it did, reduced the would-be imperial statesman to a provincial pariah and reorganization of the colonies to a hopeless dream.

[34] November 9, 1764, Bernard Papers, X, 238-247.

Chapter III

The Sugar Act

THE MINISTERS AT Whitehall who neglected the advice of the royal governor of Massachusetts Bay were not as reckless as they seemed from across the water. Although the acquisition of Canada sharpened the imperial vision of men like Bernard, it also presented the British government with problems that could not wait for an answer. It was all very well to draw up schemes for reorganizing the colonies—Bernard was not the only one doing that—but to get a plan accepted by Parliament and into operation might be a long and ticklish business. In the meantime the empire must be administered and protected. The problem was not new, but to the men responsible for balancing the British budget, it looked a great deal more difficult than it had before the war.

In the black years when Englishmen fought with their backs to the wall, they gave freely of blood and money, and succeeded in winning the war. They did not succeed in paying for it. The arrival of peace found the national debt rising at a perilous rate; it had grown from £72,289,673 in 1755 to £122,603,336 in 1763 and to £129,586,789 in 1764.[1] Merely to pay the interest would require a heavier burden of taxation than had been known before, but besides increasing the debt, the war had fastened a great new peace-time expense on the budget. Though Canada and the Mississippi Valley were doubtless a glorious addition to the empire, in terms of pounds and shillings they were a long-term investment. They might pay off heavily in the distant future when filled by the prolific, burgeoning people of the American colonies, who

[1] *Journals of the House of Commons,* XXVII, 167; XXIX, 432, 760. Grenville told Parliament that the debt had risen from £67,000,000 to £140,000,000 (Jasper Mauduit to the Speaker of the Massachusetts House of Representatives, April 7, 1764, Massachusetts Archives, XXII, 361-363, and Israel Mauduit, *Mr. Grenville's Offer to the Colony Assemblies to raise the Supply Themselves,* n.p., n.d.), but this was apparently an exaggeration.

doubled their numbers every twenty-five years. For the present they were a liability: until the Englishmen outnumbered the hostile French and Indian population, there would be constant danger of repossession by France in a future war. It was essential therefore that the British maintain a standing army in America. What greater folly than to expend blood and money in the conquest of Canada only to give it up because of the high cost of defense? No one was surprised when the government decided to maintain 10,000 regular troops in America,[2] and its wisdom was demonstrated when an Indian uprising under Pontiac in 1763 threatened to drive the British back to the coast. Troops there must be in America whatever the cost.

The cost was not small. The annual expense of 10,000 troops was estimated at more than £220,000.[3] Other peacetime expenses, quite apart from interest on the national debt, had also increased,[4] so that the problem of making ends meet was desperate. Obviously new sources of revenue must be found, and obviously the new world was the place to look for them. In all fairness the Americans should help support the army protecting them. Though an American tax would be a novelty, few members of Parliament would doubt their authority to levy it, nor, considering the circumstances, its equity. It might be more judicious to proceed by the old method of sending requisitions to the colonial governors, requests for a contribution, but that method had proved unreliable even in wartime. The Treasury needed money at once, and if requisitions were sent, there would be delay after delay in getting a response and perhaps nothing to show for it in the end. Likewise if taxation were postponed until a

[2] *Journals of the House of Commons*, XXIX, 506, 530 (March 7, 1763). See Clarence W. Alvord, *The Mississippi Valley in British Politics* (Cleveland, 1917), ch. 4.

[3] *Journals of the House of Commons*, XXIX, 681. Grenville said that American expenses had risen to £350,000 (see references cited in note 1), but this figure included other expenses than the military. Actual disbursements for the military were only a little over £200,000. Treasury Papers, Class I, Bundle 433, f. 404, Public Record Office, Library of Congress transcripts.

[4] See the figures in *The Annual Register . . . for the Year 1764*, 155-163.

colonial reorganization smoothed the way, years might pass before anything was accomplished. Reorganization, like the settlement of Canada, was a gradual and long-range matter. The gaping hole in the British Treasury demanded immediate action.

The man who undertook to balance Britain's budget was George Grenville, brother-in-law of the great William Pitt, but a man with a mind and will of his own. George Grenville was nobody's fool. Although he thought Americans grossly undertaxed by comparison with Englishmen, he had no intention of saddling them with any part of the interest charges on the British national debt.[5] He did not even intend to assign them the whole expense of the new standing army,[6] for their protection was an imperial concern as well as a local American one. Yet something they must pay.

On taking office in the summer of 1763, Grenville found laws already on the books which offered the possibility of some income from the Americans. Some of the Acts of Trade made use of customs duties to regulate the flow of colonial commerce for the advantage of the mother country. The returns from these duties demonstrated equally the success of the American smugglers and the failure of the royal customs collectors. Surely the latter ought to be collecting more than the ridiculous sum of £1800 a year.[7] Too many of

[5] "Mr. Grenville, after the kindest expressions of regard to the Colonies, assured my brother, that whatever were the distresses bro't upon the revenue by the extravagant Expences of the War, they did not mean to draw anything from America for the relief of them." Jasper Mauduit to the Speaker of the Massachusetts House of Representatives, February 11, 1764, Massachusetts Historical Society, *Collections*, 74 (1918), 146n.

[6] Thomas Whately, *The Regulations Lately Made concerning the Colonies and the Taxes Imposed upon Them, Considered* (London, 1765), 101-103. This pamphlet, though written by Whately, was widely attributed to Grenville and doubtless represented his views, for Whately was one of his secretaries in the Treasury Department. The third edition of the pamphlet bore Grenville's name on the title page. See Massachusetts Historical Society, *Collections*, 6th ser., 9 (1897), 77.

[7] W. L. Grant and James Munro, eds., *Acts of the Privy Council of England, Colonial Series* (London, 1908–   ), IV, 569; Whately, *Regulations Lately Made*, 57.

them sat placidly in England enjoying their large salaries, while their ill-paid and irresponsible deputies collected bribes instead of customs in America. Grenville promptly ordered the office-holders to perform their duties in person or forfeit their jobs; and in order to check on them and facilitate their work he instructed colonial governors to report regularly on contraband trade, and the Navy to patrol American ports and inlets for smugglers.[8] Now perhaps the customs returns would begin to look respectable. But Grenville did not wait to see, for even if strictly enforced, the existing laws were inadequate. The customs duties had been designed to regulate the flow of trade rather than fill the Treasury. To obtain a satisfactory revenue from them, he would have to get Parliament to revise them with this purpose in view. While customs officers hurried to their posts and naval officers took up stations along the Atlantic coast, he was already preparing recommendations and by March 9, 1764, had them ready. On that day and the days following, his suggestions were presented to an attentive House of Commons in a series of resolutions. He himself introduced the first proposals, covering a new schedule of duties.[9]

The proposals would affect many branches of colonial commerce. Madeira, the staple of trade with the Wine Islands, was for the first time to bear a duty, £7 a ton. Drawbacks (customs duties refunded on re-exportation) on European and Asian textiles exported from Great Britain to the colonies were to be discontinued, and new duties placed on coffee, pimiento, foreign indigo, and foreign sugar. Lumber and iron bound for Europe must be shipped first to England. Foreign rum was to be prohibited. Most important of all, the duty on foreign molasses was to be reduced from 6d. to 3d. a gallon.

Two days after proposing these alterations in duties the

[8] Treasury Papers, Class I, Bundle 430, ff. 332-334; *Acts of the Privy Council, Colonial*, IV, 570-572.

[9] *Journals of the House of Commons*, XXIX, 934-935. Accounts of Grenville's speech may be found in a letter of Edward Montague April 11, 1764, quoted in *Virginia Gazette* (Purdie & Dixon), October 3, 1766; and in a letter of Israel Mauduit, March 10, 1764, Massachusetts Archives, XXII, 357.

Ministry called for an amendment in the means of collecting and enforcing them.[10] Violators were to be detected through an elaborate system of bonds and cockets which would reveal exactly what a vessel was carrying and where she had previously called. More important, once a violation had been detected it should be prosecuted in the admiralty courts. These courts, operating without juries, had been deciding maritime cases in the colonies since 1697, but their jurisdiction in some colonies had been contested by the common-law courts, and in others the judges had fallen under the influence of local merchants. As a result, smugglers had frequently been acquitted by sympathetic judges or juries. Customs officers had pleaded for a strengthening of the admiralty courts and an extension of their jurisdiction; and Lord Colville, the admiral in charge of American waters, supported them. Colville thought the remedy for local influence was to have violations of the Acts of Trade tried at Halifax, where his flagship was stationed.[11] Grenville agreed. He recommended that Parliament give the admiralty courts clear jurisdiction over the Acts of Trade; and he arranged for an order in council to establish a new court at Halifax with original jurisdiction over cases that customs officers in any colony chose to bring before it.[12] To free the customs officers still further from local pressures, he recommended giving them immunity from retaliatory damage suits by merchants. If a collector seized a ship but failed to prove his case against her, he should not be liable for his error, provided the judge was satisfied there had been a probability of guilt.[13]

[10] *Journals of the House of Commons*, XXIX, 940.

[11] Colville to Philip Stephens, October 25, 1763, Admiralty Secretary In Letters 482, Public Record Office, Library of Congress transcripts.

[12] *Acts of the Privy Council, Colonial,* IV, 663-664. C. M. Andrews, *The Colonial Period of American History* (New Haven, 1934–1938), IV, 222-271; Carl Ubbelohde, *The Vice-Admiralty Courts and the American Revolution* (Chapel Hill, 1960).

[13] These measures will be found in the Act as passed, 4 George III, c. 15, Danby Pickering, ed., *The Statutes at Large . . .* (Cambridge, 1762–1807), XXVI, 40-52. They were apparently not embodied in specific resolutions beforehand. For the terms of the act see E. S. Morgan, *Prologue to Revolution: Sources and Documents on the Stamp Act Crisis* (Chapel Hill, 1959), 4-8.

If Parliament was at all interested in reforming the administration of the colonies, here was a profitable place to begin.[14] If not, the Ministry could defend its recommendations on more familiar ground: though designed to raise money, the new duties, like the old, would regulate colonial trade for the welfare of the mother country. They would, in fact, bring new benefits to British merchants and manufacturers. The heavy duty on Madeira was designed to break the monopoly which that Portuguese product had acquired over the colonial wine market. American ships carried pipe staves and provisions to the Azores and had hitherto returned with pipes of Madeira in the hold duty free. As a result Madeira was plentiful in America, and the colonists had grown fond of it. Though they would still be able to buy it—at a price— they were expected to shift to cheaper wine, obtainable from English merchants. The abolition of the drawback on foreign textiles (a luxury for which the rich could well afford to pay a higher price) would cause the colonies to buy more British textiles. British linens might not be as good as French, but they were adequate and would improve with the encouragement thus given them. To be sure, the high prices might lead the Americans to set up linen manufactures themselves, but the possibility seemed remote, since labor was so dear in the colonies. If the Americans for any reason should attempt to embark on such a manufacture, the drawback could be restored.

The reduction of the molasses duty was also designed to benefit both trade and Treasury. Duties on foreign molasses, whether large or small, were an advantage to the British sugar planters. But in order to benefit the Treasury, the duties must be set at a figure which, though high enough to yield a good income, would not be so high as to stop the flourishing trade and hence the revenue. Grenville had received a good deal of advice, asked and unasked, on this question, and

[14] The official ministerial defense was offered by Thomas Whately in *The Regulations Lately Made*, which seems to have followed the lines laid down by Grenville in his speech of March 9. The ensuing two paragraphs are based largely on *The Regulations Lately Made*, 58-87. A selection from the pamphlet is in *Prologue to Revolution*, 17-23.

had finally concluded upon 3d. a gallon as the figure likely to bring in the largest revenue. Governor Bernard and Jasper Mauduit, the agent of Massachusetts, had both warned that 3d. was too much,[15] but he did not agree with their reasoning. It was well known that the cost of smuggling molasses had ranged from less than ½ d. to 1½ d. a gallon, the price for which collectors agreed to look the other way. The trade, having grown to its present strength with this sum as one of the fixed costs, could surely bear a little more now. Grenville and his advisers calculated that a 3d. duty would not reduce the trade by more than 22%. If they levied only 1d., as Jasper Mauduit had urged, trade might continue unabated, but the total revenue would be less.[16] Grenville therefore stuck to his figure, and Parliament accepted it without a murmur.

The only resolution that did not call for immediate action by Parliament was the fifteenth, which provided that "towards further defraying the said Expences, it may be proper to charge certain Stamp Duties in the said Colonies and Plantations."[17] Grenville evidently doubted that the revenue from the new duties would be as much as he wanted from the colonies. By the fifteenth resolution he simply announced his intention of levying a stamp duty—that is, an excise tax on various documents and articles made of paper—sometime in the future. With the exception of this resolution, which called

[15] Bernard to Jackson, August 3, 1763, Bernard Papers, Harvard College Library, III, 93-94; Jasper Mauduit to the Lords of the Treasury, read February 27, 1764, Treasury Papers, Class I, Bundle 430, ff. 204-205.

[16] Treasury Papers, Class I, Bundle 434, f. 52. These calculations were, of course, not borne out by events. Grenville's measures did put the customs service on a paying basis, so that a net total of about £20,000 was extracted from the North American colonies between September 29, 1764, and October 10, 1765 (Treasury Papers, Class I, Bundle 430, f. 228), but of this amount the duty on molasses probably accounted for less than £5000 (*ibid.,* Bundle 434, f. 53). Later, when the duty was reduced to 1d. a gallon, it netted a much larger amount (*ibid.,* Bundle 434, f. 70). See also O. M. Dickerson, Letter to the Editor, *William and Mary Quarterly,* 3d ser., 6 (1949), 353. On the cost of smuggling see Bernhard Knollenberg, *Origin of the American Revolution* (New York, 1960), 139, 339.

[17] *Journals of the House of Commons,* XXIX, 935.

for no action, and with minor revisions, his proposals were drawn into a bill, and enacted into law—the Sugar Act of 1764, it was usually called, because the part of it which drew most attention was the three-penny tax on molasses.

Although the new law was formally a revision in the regulations of trade, there was no attempt to conceal its main purpose: it was offered as a revenue act, and the preamble affirmed that it was "just and necessary, that a revenue be raised, in your Majesty's said dominions in *America.*"[18] The colonists were at last to be taxed.

From the very beginning the colonies greeted the attentions of George Grenville with consternation. Of his first effort to enforce existing customs regulations Governor Bernard reported that "the publication of orders for the strict execution of the Molasses Act has caused a greater alarm in this country than the taking of *Fort William Henry* did in 1757 . . . the Merchants say, There is an end of the trade in this Province. . . ."[19] The Act had been due to expire in a few months, but now the colonists correctly surmised the intention of the Ministry to continue it.[20] If they could no longer evade the duty on molasses, the future of some colonies would be dismal indeed. Probably none of the Acts of Trade had been universally complied with, but in the case of the Molasses Act violation had been wholesale, for by their own admission New England merchants could not have obeyed it and stayed in business.

The Americans blamed both the establishment and the enforcement of the sugar duties on the influence of the British West Indian sugar planters. These nabobs, who drew huge incomes from the labor of their slaves, were able to spend their lives in England, where a judicious use of their wealth

[18] *Statutes at Large,* XXVI, 33; *Prologue to Revolution,* 4-8.
[19] *Select Letters on the Trade and Government of America* (London, 1774), 9.
[20] The House of Commons, in March of 1763, had actually voted a bill to extend it, but the final reading had been postponed and never resumed. *Journals of the House of Commons,* XXIX, 623. When the Sugar Act was passed, it contained a provision extending the old duties until the end of September, 1764, when the new ones were to take effect.

secured legislation favoring their interests above those of the mainland colonies, in fact above those of England herself.[21] To defeat this sinister power, the colonists relied on the good sense of the mother country. They could not believe that, if awakened to the facts, she would allow her trade with a whole continent to be sacrificed to these grasping plutocrats.

The Assembly of Rhode Island, that colony which sometimes seemed to regard itself as the ally, rather than the subject of Great Britain, put the case in a remonstrance to the Board of Trade.[22] Rhode Island, they pointed out, consumed £120,000 sterling of British manufactures every year and herself produced little more than £5000 worth of exports. Only the profits from the molasses trade enabled the colony to pay for her consumption of British goods. As the British sugar islands could supply less than a fifth of the molasses that poured into Rhode Island's thirty distilleries, the other four-fifths must be French and subject to duty, the collection of which would entail a prohibitive increase in price and put an end not only to the molasses trade but to the distilling industry, the African trade in rum, and the sale of fish and produce in the West Indies, and consequently to the profits which British manufacturers were drawing from Rhode Island. A memorial to Parliament from New York rehearsed these same arguments but with more impressive figures: the preponderance of New York's imports over her exports amounted to nearly £470,000 sterling, all of which was made up through the trade deriving from French molasses.[23] The New York memorial was not approved by the House of Representatives until April 20, 1764, when the Sugar Act— though news had not yet reached America—had already passed both houses of Parliament; nor unfortunately had the Rhode Island remonstrance and one from the Massachusetts

[21] Bernard, *Select Letters,* 9. The North Americans seem to have credited the West Indians with greater influence in England than they actually possessed. See L. B. Namier, *England in the Age of the American Revolution* (London, 1930), 271-279.

[22] John R. Bartlett, ed., *Records of the Colony of Rhode Island and Providence Plantations* (Providence, 1861), VI, 378-383.

[23] *Journal of the Votes and Proceedings of the General Assembly of the Colony of New York* (New York, 1766), II, 740-744.

Assembly[24] reached England by March 9, when Grenville introduced his resolutions for revision and continuation of the molasses duty.

Even though the colonies had surmised the Ministry's intention to continue some duty,[25] when news arrived early in May, 1764, that Grenville had called for 3d. per gallon, they were taken by surprise. Rumor had led them to suppose that the figure would be 1d. or 2d. a gallon.[26] It was conceivable that the trade might have borne a 2d. duty, though even this would have caused hardship. A 3d. duty would be as prohibitive as a 6d. one, and would entail all the disastrous consequences described in the protests that had gone to England.

Although the duty on molasses was the most distressing provision of the Sugar Act, it was by no means the only one to cause alarm in the colonies. The new restrictions on the export of lumber threatened to ruin a branch of business almost as vital as that based on molasses. America's forests were one of her greatest economic assets, and colonial merchants had built up a substantial lumber trade at several European ports. Now it was forbidden to land colonial lumber in any part of Europe except Great Britain. Though from there it could be reshipped, the increased costs might well destroy the trade. The new wine duties, while drying up the consumption of Madeira as intended, would also shrink the profitable island market for American provisions. The abolition of drawbacks on foreign textiles would curb another branch of commerce.

[24] On the Massachusetts protest, see *Journal of the Honorable House of Representatives* . . . (Boston, 1763), 132; Connecticut Historical Society, *Collections,* 18 (1920), 261-273. Jasper Mauduit, the agent, failing to receive the protest in time, drew up a petition to the Lords of the Treasury himself (Treasury Papers, Class I, Bundle 430, ff. 204-205; see also Massachusetts Historical Society, *Collections,* 74 [1918], 144n., 146n.), but it evidently had no effect. No petition against the bill reached Parliament.

[25] A committee of the Massachusetts General Court appointed to consider the question, conjectured that the policy of enforcing the 6d. duty had been adopted in order to secure acquiescence in the renewal at a lower figure. Thomas Cushing to Jasper Mauduit, January, 1764, Massachusetts Historical Society, *Collections,* 74 (1918), 145.

[26] *Massachusetts Gazette and Boston News-Letter,* May 26, 1763, March 29, April 5, 1764.

Thus all the minor avenues of trade, through which the colonists might have recovered from the ruin of their molasses business, were also blocked. Furthermore the old solution of smuggling was no longer practical, for the risk of seizure was so great that the added cost of smuggling would have the same effect as the payment of duties.

The terms of the Sugar Act undoubtedly caused genuine distress to colonial merchants, but this was heightened by a number of circumstances not directly connected with the Act itself. Most annoying, perhaps, was the literal-mindedness of naval officers. The Navy lives in a world of its own, and when the commanders of ships in American waters received instructions to assist in collecting the customs, they went about the business with no regard whatever for the facts of economic life. It is not likely that Parliament intended the new restrictions to apply to every dory that crossed an American river, but the Navy thought it necessary to exact the full measure of obedience from everything that floated, especially since the officers claimed a share of the prize money on every seizure they made.[27] By November of 1764 William Allen, the Chief Justice of Pennsylvania, was complaining to a business correspondent in London, that "even the Intercourse between here and New Jersey is, in a great Measure interrupted, which was carried on in Flats and small Boats, and the produce of the Western part of that Colony shipped off from this City, but now, one of those poor fellows cannot take in a few Staves, or Pig Iron, or Bar Iron, or Tar &c. but they must go thirty or forty Miles, or more to give Bond, the Charge of which and his travelling, make the Burthen intollerable. It never was the intention of the Legislature at home to destroy this little River-Trade, which is carried on in a kind of Market Boats, but their Regulations

---

[27] This was a matter of dispute between the Navy and the colonial governors, the latter maintaining that the share claimed by the Navy should go to the governor of the colony where the ship was seized. See letters of Lord Colville to Philip Stephens, November 24, 1763, September 22, 1764, Admiralty Secretary In Letters 482, Public Record Office, Library of Congress transcripts; Francis Bernard to Lord Colville, April 25, 1764, to J. Pownall, December 29, 1763, and to Lord Halifax, February 18, 1764, Bernard Papers, III, 39, 119, and 141-144 respectively.

were only for Sea Vessels. This is a general Complaint all over the Continent."[28] Allen was right. Not merely in Philadelphia, but in Boston, Newport, Charles Town, and the other centers of shipping, merchants found that the men-of-war were so completely unbending that, as one Boston merchant said, "no vessel hardly comes in or goes out, but they find some pretence to seize and detain her."[29]

To be sure the merchants fought back. They boycotted pilots who brought naval vessels into port,[30] offered mates and midshipmen higher wages than the Navy was allowed to pay,[31] and raised howling mobs when the Navy consequently had to impress seamen to fill out its crews.[32] In Boston, where people had already had a good deal of practice in minding their neighbors' business, they even wrote anonymous letters to the authorities in England complaining of the "immodest women" that the naval officers brought with them.[33] But these tactics probably served to make the Navy more determined in carrying out what it took to be its duties.

Another circumstance adding to colonial irritation was that Parliament followed the Sugar Act almost immediately by an act prohibiting the issue of paper money as legal tender.[34] A similar prohibition had already been applied to

[28] William Allen to D. Barclay & Sons, November 20, 1764; Lewis B. Walker, ed., *The Burd Papers: Extracts from Chief Justice William Allen's Letter Book* (n.p., 1897), 65.

[29] *Massachusetts Gazette*, May 17, 1764. See also *Newport Mercury*, June 10, 1765. Governor Bull of South Carolina wrote to Charles Garth, the colony's agent, complaining of the Navy's treatment of "Decked Pettiaugers and Schooners in their Necessary Coasting Voyages." Charles Garth to Committee of Correspondence of the South Carolina Assembly, December 23, 1765, South Carolina Historical Society.

[30] Lord Colville to Philip Stephens, November 9, 1764, Admiralty Secretary In Letters 482.

[31] Lord Colville to Philip Stephens, November 9, 1764, and August 8, 1765, *ibid.*

[32] For an example see ch. IV.

[33] Lord Colville to Philip Stephens, August 8, 1765, Admiralty Secretary In Letters 482.

[34] 4 George III, c. 34, *Statutes at Large*, XXVI, 103-105. Jack P. Greene and Richard M. Jellison, "The Currency Act of 1764 in Imperial-Colonial Relations," *William and Mary Quarterly*, 3d ser., *18* (1961), 485-518.

New England in 1751; now it was extended to all the American colonies. Although the use of paper money had sometimes resulted in inflation, with hardship for creditors, the lack of it would be a hardship to almost everyone. The balance of trade with England prevented the colonies from acquiring a supply of hard money there, and the new restrictions on trade would prevent them from acquiring it elsewhere, so that without paper money they would be without any medium of exchange with which to carry on business. Economic life would be reduced to bartering. As one Philadelphia merchant expressed it, "the Inhabitants will be reduced to the necessity of primitive Times in this Place, of going to Market for the Provisions of their Families with Rum Sugar Melasses Ozenbrigs &c &c instead of Money. . . ."[35] The effect on commerce, in combination with the Sugar Act, was obvious. Samuel Rhoads, Jr., another Philadelphian, wrote to his business correspondents in England: "If you will deprive us of all Medium of Trade among ourselves, we shall not be able to export Provisions &c. in the same Degree as formerly, and if we are not on any Terms allow'd a Trade to get Money from abroad, we shall have none to pay you for Goods, and then unless you will send them Gratis our Dealings must end."[36]

The final and most serious circumstance aggravating the burden of the Sugar Act, was a post-war depression. The initial depression probably had no connection with the Sugar Act. Colonial credit had expanded during the war, and the post-war contraction brought a number of large-scale bankruptcies. From Philadelphia Chief Justice Allen wrote in May, 1765, "I think we have a gloomy Prospect before us, as there are of late some Persons failed, who were no way Suspected, and a probability of some others, as the whisper goes, . . ."[37] In Boston there was the most alarming failure in the history of the town, when Nathaniel Wheelwright stopped payment on

---

[35] November 9, 1765, Daniel Roberdeau to Meyler & Hall, Roberdeau Letter Book, Historical Society of Pennsylvania.

[36] June 22, 1764, *Pennsylvania Magazine of History and Biography*, 14 (1890), 423.

[37] William Allen to D. Barclay & Sons, May 19, 1765, *Burd Papers*, 67.

January 16, 1765. According to James Otis, this event gave as great a shock to credit in Massachusetts as the collapse of the South Sea Bubble did in England. Wheelwright had been heavily engaged in war contracts for the government in England, and had consequently acquired "such an undue Credit that he became next to the Treasurer, Banker General for the province and almost for the Continent." His failure carried a wave of lesser failures in its wake, and "such was the Consternation for some little time that people appeared with pale Horror and Dread, and when a little recovered run about the City. Widows and Orphans that are ruined can only bewail their fate, the more resolute have been pulling and hauling, attaching and summoning to secure themselves, but it was too late to shut the Stable door, . . ."[38] Wheelwright's failure could not be attributed directly to the Sugar Act, but the accompanying depression could be and was. When merchants found themselves in a tight spot and prevented from extricating themselves because of the Sugar Act, it was natural to blame the Act for everything.

The colonists were unwilling to die an economic death without a struggle and threw themselves into a fight for repeal. Their most effective weapon was the fact that such a large part of English industry and commerce was supported by the American market. An impoverished America would be unable to buy English manufactures. The assemblies of New York, Rhode Island, and Massachusetts had pointed this out to Parliament; the colonial merchants now impressed it on their British business correspondents. Upon learning of Grenville's resolutions, Samuel Rhoads, Jr., wrote, "I need not say much of future Dealings, because I fear that all our Trade with you must come to an End, for nothing can be more certain than its Intirely ceasing if your Legislature will carry into Execution those Resolves. . . ."[39] William Allen likewise warned that the Sugar Act must put an end to all

[38] James Otis to George Johnstone et al., June 27, 1765, Massachusetts Historical Society, Proceedings, 43 (1909), 204-207. Governor Bernard told the Board of Trade that Wheelwright's failure "was like an Earthquake . . . and a general Bankruptcy was apprehended for a time." April 8, 1765, Bernard Papers, III, 203-204.

[39] Pa. Mag. of Hist., 14 (1890), 423.

remittances from America to England, a fact which would "soon be perceived by the London Merchants, and by all the Manufacturers in England."[40]

Time alone would have proved the truth of these warnings, and probably soon with the assistance of the post-war depression, which was also being felt in England; but the colonists knew that a determined boycott of English goods would further hasten the day. They urged one another to replace British manufactures with American.[41] Widows and widowers should stop wearing the costly mourning clothes fashionable at the time and stop handing out fancy gloves and scarves to other mourners at funerals.[42] Such luxuries must be foregone until American manufacturers could supply them. American thirst should be quenched with American brew,[43] and American ladies should set aside "gaudy, butterfly, vain, fantastick, and expensive Dresses brought from Europe" and appear in "decent plain Dresses made in their own Country."[44] In New York a society for the promotion of colonial manufactures was established which offered bounties for the production of articles generally imported from England.[45] In Philadelphia the several volunteer fire companies pledged themselves to eat no more lamb and to drink no imported beer, in order to encourage the local brewing industry and the raising of wool.[46]

This was language which merchants and manufacturers could understand, a sure means to enlist their support in the fight for repeal. And Parliament would have to listen when they spoke up. If exports to the colonies fell off sharply, the cries of distress throughout the kingdom would drown out the

[40] *Burd Papers,* 65-66.

[41] *Massachusetts Gazette and Boston News-Letter,* July 5, 1764; *Boston Post-Boy and Advertiser,* October 1, 1764. See A. M. Schlesinger, *The Colonial Merchants and the American Revolution, 1763–1776* (New York, 1918), ch. 2.

[42] *Boston Post-Boy and Advertiser,* October 1, 8, 29, 1764; *Newport Mercury,* August 20, 1764.

[43] *Pennsylvania Journal,* August 23, 1764; *Massachusetts Gazette and Boston News-Letter,* September 6, 13, 1764.

[44] *Pennsylvania Journal,* August 23, 1764.

[45] *London Chronicle,* January 26-29, 1765; *Pennsylvania Journal,* December 27, 1764; Schlesinger, *Colonial Merchants,* 64.

[46] *Pennsylvania Gazette,* February 28, March 7, 1765.

voice of the West Indies planters and be heard inside the House of Commons.

Undoubtedly the drastic economic effects the colonists anticipated from the Sugar Act prompted the alarm they felt, but it was natural for them to inquire into the right of the matter. The whole structure of constitutional government had grown out of resistance to the unwise or irresponsible use of authority, and the colonists were following the example of their English ancestors when they asked whether a measure which threatened such disastrous consequences could be enacted of right. They found the answer too in the constitutional principles which Englishmen had fought for on a hundred battlefields. Examining the Sugar Act, they saw that it curtailed the right of trial by jury, and they saw that the British Parliament was assuming the authority to tax them. Here was the ground upon which they could challenge the body that threatened them, the very ground on which that body had fought and gained its own supremacy over the King.

They had heard rumors of a colonial tax for some time, a tax to support a standing army in America. Ever since Wolfe captured Quebec this had been in the air,[47] and when in 1763 an army of 10,000 was definitely decided on, the rumors of taxation multiplied. Joseph Sherwood, the Rhode Island agent, wrote on August 4 that the colonies would be expected to bear the whole expense of the troops, and this was also reported in the newspapers.[48] There were assorted

[47] See Cecilius Calvert to Horatio Sharpe, January 19, 1760, *Archives of Maryland,* XXXI, 527.

[48] John R. Bartlett, ed., *Records of the Colony of Rhode Island and Providence Plantations* (Providence, 1861), VI, 368. Thomas Hutchinson wrote to Israel Williams, November 17, 1763, that "A revenue from the Colonies will certainly be attempted the next Parliament sufficient at least to support the troops to be kept up here." Bancroft Transcripts, New York Public Library. *The London Chronicle* reported in the issue of March 5-8, 1763, just after Parliament had voted to establish the troops (*Journals of the House of Commons,* XXIX, 506, 530, March 7, 1763), that they were "to be paid the first year by Great Britain, but afterwards by the colonies." This item was copied in colonial newspapers, e.g. *Pennsylvania Journal,* May 12, 1763. See also *Annual Register . . . for the Year 1763,* 21.

theories of how the money would be raised: by a poll tax,[49] by a stamp tax,[50] by a tax on imports.[51] These advance rumors elicited no extensive reaction, perhaps because they were too uncertain to form the basis of a protest; but there was no uncertainty left after the resolutions for the Sugar Act appeared. England intended to raise a revenue by taxes on trade and probably by a stamp tax. The passage of the Sugar Act, if we may believe James Otis, "set people a thinking, in six months, more than they had done in their whole lives before."[52] And what they thought about was the rights of Englishmen. The incantation of those potent words was heard from Portsmouth to Savannah.

In Massachusetts, the town of Boston, exhibiting what was to become a characteristic colonial attitude, detected the entering wedge of a movement to deprive the colonists of all their rights. The instructions prepared on May 24, 1764, for Boston's representatives in the General Assembly declared:

> But what still hightens our Apprehensions is that those unexpected proceedings may be preparatory to new Taxations upon us: For if our Trade may be taxed why not our Lands? Why not the produce of our Lands and every Thing we possess or make use of? This we apprehend annihilates our Charter Right to Govern and Tax ourselves.—It strikes at our British Privileges which as we have never forfeited them we hold in common with our Fellow Subjects who are Natives of Britain: If Taxes are laid upon us in any shape without ever having a Legal Representation where they are laid, are we not reduced from the Character of Free Subjects to the miserable state of Tributary Slaves?[53]

[49] Cecilius Calvert to Governor Sharpe, March 1, 1763. Sparks Mss. 9, f. 46a, Harvard College Library; *Archives of Maryland,* XIV (1895), 92.

[50] *Newport Mercury,* May 30, 1763.

[51] Governor Sharpe to Cecilius Calvert, June 4, 1763, Sparks Mss. 9, f. 52; *Boston Post-Boy and Advertiser,* May 14, 1764.

[52] *The Rights of the British Colonies Asserted and Proved* (Boston, 1764), 54.

[53] *A Report of the Record Commissioners of the City of Boston, Containing the Boston Town Records, 1758 to 1769* (Boston, 1886), 121-122.

It was also about this time that James Otis, one of the assemblymen from Boston, wrote his *Rights of the British Colonies Asserted and Proved*.[54] Otis insisted that a Parliament without American representatives, though supreme in authority, could have no more right to tax Americans than to make two plus two equal five. He explicitly rejected a distinction which Bernard was simultaneously setting down in his ninety-seven propositions, that external taxes on trade be levied by Parliament and internal taxes by the colonial assemblies. Otis affirmed flatly (had he and Bernard perhaps argued this together at Concord?) that "there is no foundation for the distinction some make in England between an internal and an external tax on the colonies."[55] Parliament had no right to levy either.

Before publishing his pamphlet and perhaps before writing it, Otis drew up a briefer statement of colonial rights, arguing that nature and the English Common Law entitled the colonists to the same rights as Englishmen in England and that it was beyond the power of Parliament to abridge those rights. The Massachusetts House of Representatives listened while Otis's statement was read and read again. Then they voted their approval and sent it to their agent in London with a letter further developing their views along the same lines.[56] By October they had drawn up and approved a petition to the King, informing him too that "we look *upon those Duties as a tax* [i.e. the duties imposed by the Sugar Act], and which we humbly apprehend ought not to be laid without the Representatives of the People affected by them."[57] The petition drafted by the House of Representatives so firmly denied Parliamentary authority that the Council feared it would give offense in England and do more harm than good. Under the leadership of Lieutnant-Governor Hutchinson they met in conference with a committee of the Representatives and

[54] Boston, 1764.

[55] *Ibid.*, 42.

[56] *Journal of the Honourable House of Representatives . . .* (Boston, 1764), 53, 66, 72-77. Otis printed his briefer statement as an appendix to his *Rights of the British Colonies Asserted and Proved*, 70-80.

[57] Oxenbridge Thacher Papers, Massachusetts Historical Society, and Massachusetts Archives, XXII, 414.

pleaded so successfully that the House withdrew their strong words in favor of tamer ones submitted by the Lieutenant-Governor.[58] The new document was directed not simply to the King but to the House of Commons, a significant recognition of that group's authority. Omitting entirely the question of rights, even the word, it asked instead for continuation of the "privilege" which the colonies had hitherto enjoyed of levying their own internal taxes. This argument was aimed at the proposed stamp tax. The Sugar Act itself was condemned on the familiar economic grounds. The address was such a model of restraint and loyalty that Governor Bernard himself endorsed it.[59] The members of the House of Representatives, though they accepted it, were not so enthusiastic. Their Speaker advised the agent that they

> were clearly for making an ample and full declaration of the exclusive Right of the People of the Colonies to tax themselves and that they ought not to be deprived of a right they had so long enjoyed and which they held by Birth and by Charter; but they coud not prevail with the Councill, tho they made several Tryalls, to be more explicit than they have been in the Petition sent you . . . You will therefore collect the sentiments of the Representative Body of People rather from what they have heretofore sent you than from the present Address.[60]

In Rhode Island where the whole government was popularly elected, no conservative politicians hampered the preparation of a spirited protest. Governor Stephen Hopkins himself stated the colony's objections to Parliamentary taxation in a pamphlet entitled *The Rights of Colonies Examined*.[61] Though Hopkins rehearsed all the woeful effects on trade to

[58] Alden Bradford, ed., *Speeches of the Governors of Massachusetts from 1765 to 1775* . . . (Boston, 1818), 21-24. On Hutchinson's role, see Governor Bernard's letters to Lord Halifax, John Pownall, and Richard Jackson, November 17, 18, 1764; Bernard Papers, III, 181-187, 189, 260-264.

[59] Bernard Papers, III, 181-187; *Select Letters*, 13-22.

[60] Massachusetts Historical Society, *Collections*, 74 (1918), 170-171.

[61] Providence, 1764, reprinted in *Records of the Colony of Rhode Island*, VI, 416-427.

be expected from the Sugar Act, his principal concern, as the title indicated, was rights, and he reserved his specific arguments on this head for the proposed stamp tax. This, he said, would be "a manifest violation of their [the colonists'] just and long enjoyed rights. For it must be confessed by all men, that they who are taxed at pleasure by others, cannot possibly have any property, can have nothing to be called their own; they who have no property, can have no freedom, but are indeed reduced to the most abject slavery."[62] The Assembly approved the Governor's pamphlet and sent it to the agent along with a petition to the King, which they had drawn themselves. This concluded with the request "that our trade may be restored to its former condition, and no further limited, restrained and burdened, than becomes necessary for the general good of all Your Majesty's subjects; that the courts of vice admiralty may not be vested with more extensive powers in the colonies than are given them by law in Great Britain; that the colonists may not be taxed but by the consent of their own representatives, as Your Majesty's other free subjects are."[63]

Both Rhode Island and Massachusetts, in demonstrating the unconstitutionality of Parliamentary taxation, concentrated their constitutional objections on the proposed stamp tax. In spite of the preamble which clearly announced the Sugar Act as a revenue measure, they skirted the question of right and protested it only as a crippling regulation of trade —unwise but within the authority of Parliament. It remained for the Assembly of New York, the colony which later became the stronghold of loyalism, to tell Parliament flatly that the Sugar Act violated colonial rights. On October 18, 1764, in petitions to the King, the House of Lords, and the House of Commons, the New Yorkers claimed an absolute exemption from taxes not granted by their own representatives.[64] The people of New York, they said, "nobly disdain the thought of claiming that Exemption as *a Privilege.—They*

---

[62] *Ibid.,* 423.
[63] *Ibid.,* 414-416.
[64] *Journals of the Votes and Proceedings of the General Assembly of the Colony of New York* . . . (New York, 1766), II, 769-779. *Prologue to Revolution,* 8-14.

found it on a Basis more honourable, solid and stable; they challenge it, and glory in it as their Right."[65] New York, like other colonies, had no quarrel with Parliament's power to regulate their trade. They would not, for example, ask for liberty to import woolens from France. But they demanded that regulations of trade be regulations of trade. Parliament could "model the Trade of the whole Empire, so as to subserve the Interest of her own, . . . But a Freedom to drive all Kinds of Traffic in a Subordination to, and not inconsistent with, the *British* Trade; and an Exemption from all Duties in such a Course of Commerce, is humbly claimed by the Colonies as the most essential of all the Rights to which they are intitled, . . ." The exemption from duties in all commerce not detrimental to the mother country was essential, in the opinion of the Assembly, to a proper enjoyment of the right of self-taxation. Any distinction between different kinds of taxes was futile, for,

> since all Impositions, whether they be internal Taxes, or Duties paid, for what we consume, equally diminish the Estates upon which they are charged; what avails it to any People, by which of them they are impoverished? Every Thing will be given up to preserve Life; and though there is a Diversity in the Means, yet, the whole Wealth of a Country may be as effectually drawn off, by the Exaction of Duties, as by any other Tax upon their Estates.
>
> And therefore, the General Assembly of *New-York*, in Fidelity to their Constituents, cannot but express the most earnest Supplication, that the Parliament will charge our Commerce with no other Duties, than a necessary Regard to the particular Trade of *Great-Britain*, evidently demands; but leave it to the legislative Power of the Colony, to impose all other Burthens upon it's own People, which the publick Exigences may require.
>
> Latterly, the Laws of Trade seem to have been framed without an Attention to this fundamental Claim.[66]

[65] *Ibid.*, II, 777.
[66] *Ibid.*, II, 778.

The Sugar Act by this reasoning infringed colonial rights not only by extending the jurisdiction of admiralty courts but by imposing duties on branches of colonial commerce which did not conflict with British interests. The molasses duty might be beneficial to the West Indies planters but certainly not to the commerce or manufactures of the mother country. It was therefore an abuse of the Parliamentary power to regulate trade.

North Carolina was the only other colony which took the Sugar Act squarely for what it was, a revenue act. The North Carolina Assembly, in a message to Governor Dobbs, on October 31, 1764, objected to the "new Taxes and Impositions laid on us without our Privity and Consent, and against what we esteem our Inherent right, and Exclusive privilege of Imposing our own Taxes."[67] The rest of the colonies, depending to some extent on how it would affect them, either ignored the Act or, like Massachusetts and Rhode Island, argued against it on economic grounds. But the colonies were not therefore ignoring Grenville's challenge to their rights. Several of those that failed to take issue with him over the Sugar Act, raised their voices against his resolution for a stamp tax: Connecticut, Pennsylvania, Virginia, and South Carolina sent their protests and denials that Parliament had the right to enact it into law.[68]

The remarkable thing about these various remonstrances both against the Sugar Act and the proposed stamp tax is that, except in Connecticut, their denial of Parliament's right to tax the colonies was wholesale and unqualified. Governor Thomas Fitch, writing for Connecticut, focused his strictures on internal taxes. But Hopkins in Rhode Island did not specify that one kind of tax would be more acceptable than another. Otis's pamphlet specifically rejected any distinction between

[67] William L. Saunders, ed., *The Colonial Records of North Carolina*, (Raleigh, 1886–1890), VI, 1261.

[68] J. H. Trumbull and C. J. Hoadly, eds., *Public Records of the Colony of Connecticut* (Hartford, 1850–1890), XII, 651-671; *Pennsylvania Archives*, 8th ser., VII (1935), 5643–5645, 5678–5682; J. P. Kennedy, ed., *Journals of the House of Burgesses of Virginia, 1761–1765* (Richmond, 1907), liv-lviii, 302-304; R. W. Gibbes, *Documentary History of the American Revolution* (New York, 1855), I, 1-6. *Prologue to Revolution,* 14-17.

taxes on trade and internal taxes. New York, of course, rejected "all Taxes not granted by themselves."[69] Pennsylvania instructed her agent to prevent the stamp tax "or any other Impositions or Taxes on the Colonists from being laid by the Parliament, inasmuch as they neither are or can be represented, under their present Circumstances, in that Legislature," and because such taxes would "have a Tendency to deprive the good People of this Province of their most essential Rights as British Subjects."[70] Virginia, in three petitions to King, Lords, and Commons, declared it a fundamental principle of the British constitution "that the People are not subject to any Taxes but such as are laid on them by their own Consent, or by those who are legally appointed to represent them."[71] North Carolina claimed the "Exclusive privilege of Imposing our own Taxes,"[72] and South Carolina the "inherent right of every British subject, not to be taxed but by his own consent, or that of his representative."[73]

With such a universal denial of Parliament's right to tax, it is surprising that the protests against the Sugar Act did not emphasize the question of right more than they did. Most colonies chose to regard it as a regulation of trade, which it was, rather than a revenue measure, which it also was. Because of its dual purpose they hesitated to question Parliament's authority to pass it, for it could always be defended as a mere regulation of trade. Only North Carolina, New York, and Massachusetts dared raise the question, and even they might have been content to overlook it had the duty been set at 1d. a gallon instead of 3d. In any event George Grenville did set the duty at 3d., and he did announce his intention of levying a stamp tax. This would be a naked and indisputable act of taxation. By these two steps he plunged the empire into the discussion of colonial rights which earlier ministers had been able to avoid, and which later ministers were unable to halt.

[69] Journal of the Votes and Proceedings, II, 776.
[70] Pennsylvania Archives, 8th ser., VII (1935), 5643–5645.
[71] Journals of the House of Burgesses, 1761–1765, lv, 302. Prologue to Revolution, 14-17.
[72] Colonial Records of North Carolina, VI, 1261.
[73] Gibbes, Documentary History, I, 2.

Chapter IV

John Robinson, Collector of Customs

THE OLD ROAD from Dighton, on Narragansett Bay, to the town of Taunton, Massachusetts, was eight miles, not too long for an afternoon's walk if you liked walking, and not unpleasant to travel as it wound past farms and fields, a trifle too muddy perhaps in April, and as full of holes and stumps as other American roads, yet not unpleasant. It was not the road that bothered the tight-lipped man stumbling along it on Friday afernoon, the twelfth of April, in the year 1765. It was not the road or the weather or the countryside, but the company. No one could enjoy walking eight miles beside a jeering mob and an impudent sheriff, with Taunton jail at the end of the road. The procession that afternoon would have been fitting for an enemy of society, a murderer perhaps. But John Robinson was no murderer. John Robinson was the man whom George Grenville had sent to collect His Majesty's customs in Narragansett Bay, and his only crime was enforcing the Laws of Trade.

Robinson had left England a little more than a year before, with only a hazy idea of what to expect from his new post. He knew of Rhode Island's bad reputation, for the other colonies hopefully propagated the idea that all smuggling was carried on from there. He knew that Newport, a town of eight or nine thousand inhabitants, was an appropriate place for the custom-house he was to occupy, for it was strategically located on an island commanding the entrance to Narragansett Bay. Beyond this he was innocent. His predecessor could not have told him much, because that happy individual had never seen the shores of Narragansett. Thomas Clift had acted by deputy, and when Grenville ordered all customs officers to their posts, he was one of those who thought the comforts of home in England more valuable than the profits of office in America.[1] His loss was John Robinson's gain, if anything could be called a gain that led a man along the road to Taunton with the sheriff by his side. As he tramped along, ignoring the insults hurled at him, ignoring the sword which one of his tormentors brandished over him, Robinson had to admit that his present predicament was not surprising after his experiences of the past year.

His education in the tribulations of American customs officers must have begun before he reached his post, for he had come by way of Boston[2] and undoubtedly learned from John Temple, the Surveyor General of Customs for the Northern District (New Jersey northward) what had occurred only a few months before, when a new Comptroller of Customs was installed in Rhode Island. The Governor of the colony, by instruction from the Assembly, had refused to administer the oaths of office, and Temple himself had been obliged to go to Providence for the ceremony. There, under his very nose, a vessel had landed a cargo from Surinam, without so much as a look in the direction of the customs officers. He had immediately ordered her seized, but that night a crowd of people with blackened faces boarded her, loaded an export cargo, and put her to sea before morning. Temple was pained, but not surprised, to discover that the ship belonged to a judge of the Rhode Island Superior Court.[3]

Thus forewarned and filled with misgivings about the people he was to live among, Robinson could hardly have been prepared for the civilized, almost sophisticated community that he found in Newport. People still talked of Bishop Berkeley, who had once lived there, and the Redwood Library furnished a meeting place for the gentlemen who continued to inhabit the intellectual world which he represented. The town was filled with fine houses, only a few of brick or stone, but

[1] Samuel G. Arnold, *History of the State of Rhode Island and Providence Plantations* (3d edn., New York, 1878), II, 246.

[2] Ezra Stiles, *Extracts from the Itineraries and other Miscellanies of Ezra Stiles,* Franklin B. Dexter, ed. (New Haven, 1916), 204; *Providence Gazette,* May 26, 1764.

[3] Francis Bernard to John Pownall, February 10, 1764, Bernard Papers, III, 130, Harvard College Library; Ezra Stiles to John Hubbard, January 30, 1764, Stiles Papers, Yale University Library.

many showing a taste that would not be complained of in London. Some were surrounded by the elaborate landscaping that was now regarded by Englishmen as one of the fine arts, and the farms that covered the rolling countryside were laid out in neat and prosperous fields, divided by beautiful stone walls that even England could not have matched. In May, when Robinson arrived, the whole island was a thing of beauty, rippling meadows, gardens ablaze with tulips, white sails and blue water glittering in the harbor. Any man would have been impressed, for Newport was truly one of the most delightful spots in eighteenth-century America.

After finding quarters with a British Army officer who had retired to this haven, Robinson settled down to business and found at once that the white sails were doing dirty work. The Newport merchants, whose houses looked so dignified and respectable, had fingers sticky with French molasses upon which they had paid no duties. With the zeal of a good housewife, he set about to scrub things clean. The merchants, he found, would be glad to make a bargain with him as they had with former customs officers, seventy thousand pounds per annum colonial currency, in return for freedom to take their ships in and out as they pleased.[4] But John Robinson preferred the hard way: backed by the new Sugar Act, he was confident he could collect duties as the law demanded. With the assistance of the royal Navy and of his subordinate customs officers he quickly began to catch Rhode Island ships in the act of smuggling molasses. It was not until he brought his prizes to the Admiralty Court for legal condemnation that he discovered what he was up against: the Rhode Island merchants knew more than one way to outwit a customs officer. Both the Judge and the Advocate (prosecuting attorney) of Rhode Island's Admiralty Court were natives of the place and sympathetic, to say the least, with the merchants. The Judge called trials on short notice in Providence at times when he knew that the Collector was occupied by his duties at Newport, and the Advocate frequently failed to appear at all, so that merchants and ship captains who had been caught redhanded were dismissed on the pretext of a lack of evidence.

[4] Ezra Stiles, *Extracts from the Itineraries,* 204.

If ever a smuggler had to be convicted and his ship consequently forfeited, the Court assumed the right of selling the vessel in the name of the King and generally did so at a trifle of her real value, perhaps to the culprit himself. Thus in one way or another the Sugar Act was evaded in the Admiralty Court as easily as the old Molasses Act had been in the common-law courts. To be sure, Robinson could take his cases to the Court at Halifax if he wished, but Halifax was several hundred miles away. If all his cases were to be tried there, he would never have time for his official duties in Rhode Island.[5]

The only real assistance that Robinson obtained was from the Navy. Two or three naval vessels were generally to be found in Newport Harbor, and under the new regulations some of their officers were commissioned as deputies to assist in the collection of customs duties. This did not make it any easier to win a case in Rhode Island's Admiralty Court, but it did make the initial seizure of smugglers possible. Unfortunately the assistance given him by the Navy added to the unpopularity he was winning only too rapidly by himself, for the British Navy was not welcome in American ports. The press gangs which came ashore from British warships to recruit sailors for the service had always aroused bitter resentment. In 1747, the people of Boston had greeted a press gang with a riot lasting three days.[6] But even if there was no attempt to impress American seamen or to enforce the Acts of Trade, there was apt to be friction whenever the Navy met up with civilians. A typical example was reported in the *Newport Mercury* on December 10, 1764. The officers of the *Cygnet* and the *Jamaica*, both men-of-war, had boarded a passenger ship running from Newfoundland to Boston and engaged in an altercation with the passengers. The incident concluded with a lieutenant running his sword through the

[5] John Robinson and John Nicoll to Governor Ward, February 22, 1766, in Gertrude S. Kimball, ed., *The Correspondence of the Colonial Governors of Rhode Island, 1723–1775* (Boston, 1903), II, 376-381; *Records of the Colony of Rhode Island*, VI, 457-459.

[6] Thomas Hutchinson, *History of the Colony and Province of Massachusetts Bay*, L. S. Mayo, ed. (Cambridge, 1936), II, 330-333.

belly of one of the passengers. When the *Cygnet* arrived in Newport Harbor a week after the news of this episode, she could scarcely have had a friendly reception. The newspapers failed to report, and probably few people ever learned, the part of the story which Robinson doubtless heard from Captain Leslie: the lieutenant's sword had come into play only after he was attacked with a broad axe and after several of his party had been thrown overboard by the passengers, who were suspected of being deserters from British warships.[7]

Such conflicts were by no means unusual. During Robinson's first year of residence the Rhode Islanders fought more than once with the men of the Navy. In fact he had been in Newport less than two months when he witnessed a most shocking incident. The naval schooner *St. John* had been impressing men in and around Narragansett Bay and had also seized a brig loaded with molasses. These actions, though legal, were cause enough for indignation in Rhode Island. The inhabitants of Newport found an opportunity to make their indignation righteous when three men from the schooner came ashore and stole some pigs and chickens. The indignation and its righteousness grew as the Sheriff, rowing out to arrest the offenders, was prevented from boarding the ship. Then, on the same day, one of the impressed seamen, having escaped, showed himself on shore in plain view of the *St. John*. Her commander lowered a boat with a contingent of armed men to capture him, for he was now regarded as a deserter. On shore a mob was assembling. As the boat touched land they seized the officer in charge and rained a shower of brickbats on his men, who quickly pushed off again without him. Meanwhile the Sheriff had reported to the civil authorities that he had not been allowed to serve his warrant. Two of the Governor's Council therefore gave orders to the gunners at Fort George in Newport Harbor that the *St. John* should not leave the harbor. When she got under sail late in the afternoon, the fort hailed her, and upon her refusal to answer, opened fire. About eight or ten shots were sent, none of which

[7] Lord Colville to Philip Stephens, February 16, 1765, Admiralty Secretary In Letters 482, Public Record Office, Library of Congress transcripts.

took effect, and the *St. John* came to safely under the stern of the *Squirrel* man-of-war, which was anchored outside the harbor. In the next few days the thieves were delivered to the authorities, but the incident had resulted in colonial guns firing upon a ship of His Majesty's Navy.[8]

People who dared fire on a ship of the royal Navy would dare—who could say what they would dare do to a mere customs collector? As John Robinson made his forced march to Taunton he must have realized that he could expect even worse treatment than he was now getting. The episode that landed him in Taunton jail began as a routine check on a suspicious cargo. The sloop *Polly* had sailed into Newport on April 2, 1765, after a voyage to Surinam. Her home port was Taunton, Massachusetts, which because of its location off Narragansett Bay was included in the jurisdiction of the custom-house at Newport. The captain reported a cargo of sixty-three casks of molasses, and Job Smith of Taunton, the owner, came to Newport and paid the 3d. a gallon tax required by the Sugar Act. The vessel then proceeded up the bay.[9]

Two days later John Robinson, looking over the record, decided that sixty-three casks of molasses was a surprisingly small cargo for a sloop the size of the *Polly* to be carrying. He communicated his suspicions to Captain Antrobus of the *Maidstone* man-of-war, and the two men, accompanied by Robinson's servant, Daniel Guthridge, and by Nicholas Lechmere, a minor customs officer, set off in a boat to have another look. They overtook the *Polly* at Dighton on April 6, and upon boarding her found double the reported quantity of molasses. In the name of the King they seized the vessel, together with the undeclared part of her cargo.

The next step was to have their prize brought to Newport for safekeeping until she could be properly condemned in

---

[8] *Records of the Colony of Rhode Island*, VI, 428-430; *Newport Mercury*, July 16, 1764; *Acts of the Privy Council, Colonial*, VI, 374-376, 384-387.

[9] The account which follows, except as otherwise noted, is based on the documents in Treasury Papers, Class I, Bundle 442, Library of Congress transcripts. Some of these are listed in *Acts of the Privy Council, Colonial*, VI, 382-383.

court, but no one in Dighton would serve the King on such a voyage. Leaving the vessel in charge of Guthridge and Lechmere, Robinson and Antrobus returned to Newport in search of a crew and sent them off on the morning of April 8. By this time Guthridge and Lechmere were on their way back with a sad story.

On Sunday afternoon, April 7, after Robinson and Antrobus had left, the two custodians grew thirsty and rowed to an enticing tavern which stood on the shore less than a hundred yards away. While they refreshed themselves, their boat was carried away, and darkness falling they saw some forty men in old clothes and blackened faces hurrying to the waterside. In boats and scows the mob swarmed aboard the *Polly*, and quickly carried away her whole cargo and everything else they could pry loose. Guthridge and Lechmere were given to understand that it would not be healthy to interfere. The next morning when they applied for aid to Colonel Richmond, a local justice of the peace, he told them darkly that earlier the same morning a party of men with guns, cutlasses, and blackened faces had come by looking for customs officers, and had dispersed only when he convinced them that Antrobus and Robinson were not at hand. There was no telling when they might assemble again. Lechmere and Guthridge decided that prudence lay in the direction of Newport and departed.

When they heard this story, Robinson and Antrobus set off at once for Dighton with a party of thirty marines and forty armed sailors. They soon met the crew they had despatched, returning without the *Polly* after a warm send-off by about a hundred people. And on reaching Swansea they were approached by Colonel Richmond, who did his best to discourage them from going farther, because "the handfull of men they had with them would be nothing against a whole Country." They replied by asking him and another justice of the peace for writs of assistance—warrants empowering them to search any building for suspected goods—but the justices held that only the Superior Court could grant such writs, and so the royal officers pressed on toward Dighton, giving no attention to the silent hostility of the farmhouses they passed. At Dighton they found that the mob had done its job well.

The *Polly* had been run aground at a spring tide, her sails, rigging, cables, anchors, and entire cargo carried away and her bottom bored full of holes. Robinson again took possession of his devalued prize in the name of the King and went ashore to see what could be done about recovering the stolen goods. He had no doubt that they would be found somewhere in the possession of Job Smith.

No sooner had he landed than a sheriff appeared with a warrant for his arrest in an action brought by Job Smith: Smith wanted £3000 damages for seizure of the *Polly* and her cargo. Though Robinson could surmise that Smith had recovered everything but the hull already, he was obliged to submit; and so he found himself slogging through the mud, listening to the curses of the country people who now lined the road to watch him pass. He might well have been suffering more than verbal insults, had not Captain Antrobus sent along some of his men to accompany the procession, for a number of the "incensed Rabble" were armed, among them the son of Job Smith. Antrobus himself remained in Dighton to guard the *Polly*.

Upon arrival in Taunton, Robinson immediately sent messages to John Temple, the Surveyor General, but since he had no friends in the town to stand bail for him, he had to spend the night in custody. But John Robinson was not the man to be intimidated by a lawsuit, or by sore feet, or even by a mob. The letter he wrote to Temple showed that he had no intention of giving up. "My Antagonist," he said, "by his Friends has made several Overtures for an Accomodation but as it is no more my Inclination than it is in my Power, to favour a Wretch deserving of the severest Treatment that the Law can inflict, I continue Inflexable, and ready to suffer anything that their malice and Wickedness can suggest, tho' happy in the Consolation that the whole is the Effect of my doing my Duty,"—brave words, written no doubt for transmittal to appreciative eyes in Whitehall, but the words of a man who was not afraid to do things the hard way. This was Friday, April 12; it was not until Sunday evening that a messenger arrived from the Surveyor General to bail him out. During the interval Job Smith and his friends had plenty of time to hide their molasses. The local justices of the peace had shown no disposition to help in recovering it. Rather, it seemed to Robinson, they offered every possible obstacle. And Samuel White, a local attorney and former Speaker of the Massachusetts Assembly, refused to give him any legal advice, on the ground that he had already been retained on the other side of the case. By the time Robinson was able to search buildings for the lost molasses, he could discover only eight hogsheads. These he sent to Newport, and Captain Antrobus after much difficulty floated the *Polly* and brought her back too. The prize had been plucked bare, but Robinson had at least maintained his dignity and in some measure the authority of the British government. He went at once to Boston to confer with the Surveyor General and to protest against the failure of the justices of the peace to assist him. On Temple's advice he decided to have the case of the *Polly* tried by the new Admiralty Court at Halifax.[10] The move would further aggravate the local feeling against him, but what of that? Popularity was not among the rewards which a customs officer could hope for.

The whole experience had been a trying one, and even though it had occurred in Massachusetts it must have made Robinson sympathize strongly with the aims of a group in Newport with whom he was becoming friendly. This was a small club of men, probably not more than fifteen or twenty, who had become thoroughly disgusted with the licentiousness of Rhode Island politics and wished to see a royal government established there.[11] Most of them were Anglicans and prob-

[10] Francis Bernard to Lord Halifax, May 11, 1765, *Bernard Papers*, III, 211-215.

[11] The membership of this group can be inferred from the events discussed below. In particular, however, consult *Providence Gazette*, September 15, 1764, February 23, 1765; James Otis, *Brief Remarks on the Defence of the Halifax Libel* (Boston, 1765); and Carl Bridenbaugh's discussion in his *Peter Harrison, First American Architect* (Chapel Hill, 1949), 124-126; *Cities in Revolt* (New York, 1955), 309; and *Mitre and Sceptre* (New York, 1962), 217. See also David S. Lovejoy, *Rhode Island Politics and the American Revolution 1760–1776* (Providence, 1958), 48-51, 68-69, 81; and E. S. Morgan, *The Gentle Puritan: A Life of Ezra Stiles* (New Haven, 1962) chs. 13 and 14.

ably would have looked with favor on the establishment of a bishop, too. It is not possible to identify all the members of the group, but probably one was Benjamin Wickham, the officer who shared bachelor's quarters with Robinson and who may have introduced him to the other members. The winter of 1764–1765 in Newport was unusually severe,[12] with the harbor frequently clogged by ice, so that Robinson had plenty of time to sit by the fire and enjoy the company of his new friends. There was George Rome, an agent sent by the English firm of Champion and Hayley to collect debts owed them in Rhode Island. Rome had come to Newport only in 1761, but other members of the group were residents of long standing: Peter Harrison, the amateur architect who had designed the Redwood Library, Dr. Thomas Moffat, who had come in the 1730's to enjoy the company of Bishop Berkeley, Martin Howard, Jr., the son of a respected citizen of the town, and perhaps Augustus Johnston, another native, who was Attorney General of the colony. These men were of conservative temper and united in their distaste for the popular form of government which prevailed under Rhode Island's charter of 1663. Since the election of 1757 the annual contest for the governor's chair had degenerated into a political feud between Samuel Ward of Newport and Westerly and Stephen Hopkins of Providence. Each side battled for votes with all the tricks known to politics, with polemic, bribery, flattery, slander, and even the devastating truth. The results were discouraging to those who thought that stability and decorum were essential attributes of good government. To the members of the Newport club the disorderly character of these elections was one more indication that the Rhode Islanders had more freedom than they knew how to use.

The cause and the cure for this unhappy situation they agreed on: "the colonies have originally been wrong founded. —They ought all to have been regal governments, and every executive officer appointed by the King. Until that is effected, and they are properly regulated, they will never be beneficial

[12] *Newport Mercury*, January 7, 28, February 4, 1765.

to themselves nor good subjects to Great-Britain."[13] So wrote
George Rome to Doctor Moffat in 1767, after the group had
been scattered far and wide by the events which were approaching when John Robinson returned from Taunton. But
Rome's views in 1767 could not have come as a surprise to
his correspondent, for the club had been doing their best to
make them a reality ever since 1764. Doctor Moffat and
Martin Howard, Jr., had taken the lead in the attempt to have
the charter of Rhode Island revoked and the government of
the colony placed in the hands of the Crown. The campaign
began on April 23, 1764, with a letter signed Z.Y., printed on
the front page of the *Newport Mercury*. The writer (probably
Moffat or Howard) lamented the evils of party contention in
Rhode Island and urged as a solution an act of Parliament
revoking the colony's charter and establishing royal government. The letter was too straightforward. Had the conservatives been more experienced in the political maneuvering they
despised so much, they would not have tipped their hands so
early in the game. Perhaps they were overconfident, because
they believed that the change they were suggesting was in the
cards. Like Bernard they had noticed the reports that Parliament was going to overhaul the colonial governments, and
surely their own would be one of the first to require attention.
The letter of Z.Y. showed what the conservatives were expect-
ing when it concluded, "Upon the whole, I hope every honest
man in the colony will seriously think of these things, and
join to facilitate and hasten that general reformation of the
colonies, which, we have reason to think, is now under the
consideration of our rulers at home." The letter gladdened
the heart and quickened the pulse of Francis Bernard in
Boston, but to most Rhode Islanders the proposal to revoke
their charter must have come as a shock. And the next move
in the conservative campaign was no more subtle. On June 11
the *Mercury* carried, by request of "some of our Customers,"
a copy of the commission which Charles I had issued to

[13] *The Representations of Governor Hutchinson and Others,
Contained in Certain Letters Transmitted to England* . . . (Boston,
1773), 53.

Archbishop Laud and others in 1634, with power to revoke all colonial charters. This was presumably intended to suggest that a similar move by George III would not be a novel one; but in a country which had not been sorry to see Charles I lose his head and perhaps had harbored the regicides, the suggestion was ill designed to win sympathy. Not until August 20 did the conservatives begin to clothe their sentiments in more appealing colors. On that date the *Mercury* began the first of a series of letters signed "O.Z. &c. &c." They were published over the next seven months and aimed principally at encouraging local industry, particularly the growth and manufacture of flax, hemp, and wool. Home industries were already popular with the most ardent local patriots as a possible means to turn British public opinion against the Sugar Act and the proposed Stamp Act, but the conservatives had no such end in view. They were not interested in bringing pressure to bear on Parliament but rather in diverting their countrymen's energies away from disloyal protests against its enactments. O.Z. and his colleagues discovered new reason for satisfaction with the policies of the mother country. "We cannot repress our filial Gratitude," they said, "when we consider that at the same Time Molasses is reduced to Three Pence per Gallon Duty, a Bounty of £8 Sterling per Ton is granted for Hemp raised in the Colonies. The Benefits the Colonies receive, we think, overbalance the Impositions supposed to be laid upon them."[14] There followed much good advice about the methods of growing hemp.

Mingled, however, with the sober information about husbandry were occasional sarcastic jabs at the truculent pamphlets against the Sugar Act printed at Boston and the insubordinate petitions sent home by New York. There were also persistent hints that Rhode Island would be better off under a royal government. In commending a humble attention to home industry the writers would be led to attack the pride of their countrymen and from there to a suggestion that neither the people nor the government of Rhode Island were so nearly perfect as to be incapable of improvement. "If we

[14] *Newport Mercury*, September 17, 1764.

are so vain as to think either ourselves or our government too perfect to need an ammendment, it is a sure mark that we are in a reprobate state."[15] (No pious New Englander could ignore that warning!) The legislature of Pennsylvania was commended for seeking to have that colony's charter revoked, and Benjamin Franklin was hailed as "the friend of liberty and of mankind," for going to England with their petition.[16] Though the Rhode Island charter was corporate, and not proprietary like that of Pennsylvania, nevertheless "undue power and influence, in whatever mode it appears, should be opposed, when it breaks the harmony or destroys the equilibrium of government." Obviously in Rhode Island the undue power and influence were in the hands of the people.

In singing the praises of Franklin and the Pennsylvanians the Newport group were slyly complimenting themselves. Though they could not hope that the Rhode Island Assembly would imitate Pennsylvania's, they had already prepared a private petition of their own, asking for royal government. Joseph Harrison (formerly a member of the group but now Collector of Customs at New Haven) obliged his friends by taking the petition with him on a trip to London in October, 1764, and Martin Howard, Jr., wrote to Franklin urging him to forward the good cause for Rhode Island as well as Pennsylvania.[17] Franklin was no stranger to the Newport group, for both Howard and Moffat had corresponded with him before, and evidently found reason to believe that he would be sympathetic with their aims. Only the preceding May, Moffat had informed him that Rhode Island was agitated with rumors about the abolition of charter governments and that "The (few) Friends to regular and good Government are wishing for a deprivation [of the charter] while the Herd deplore it as a Calamity."[18] So confident were the Newport royalists of Franklin's support that Howard wrote him of Rhode Island, "it is now nothing but a Burlesque upon Order

[15] *Ibid.*, November 19, 1764.
[16] *Ibid.*
[17] Martin Howard, Jr., to Benjamin Franklin, November 16, 1764, Franklin Papers, I, 108, American Philosophical Society.
[18] *Ibid.*, I, 88.

and Government, and will never get right without the Constitution is altered, I have not time to enlarge and indeed your thorough knowledge of the subject would anticipate all and more than I could say."[19]

Whether Benjamin Franklin actually did sympathize with the aims of Moffat and Howard and their friends is a question to which that shrewd philosopher left no answer, but there was no doubt about the attitude of the "herd," and of a good many people who could not be included in that category, in Rhode Island. They had not been taken in by the O.Z. letters in spite of the current popularity of home industries, and the revelation that the authors were also behind a petition for royal government was enough to damn them completely. On September 15 a correspondent of the *Providence Gazette* who signed himself "I ***" had attacked the motives of O.Z. and charged "that some, if not all, of the Members of this wonderful club are at this Time actually conspiring against the Liberties of the Colony, and that they have, with other Enemies of the Colony, formed a Petition, and sent it to the King, praying that our most valuable Charter Privileges may be taken away, notwithstanding their specious Pretences in the News-Papers of promoting the Welfare of the Government." Governor Hopkins confirmed the charge in a message to the Assembly on November 4, 1764,[20] and shortly thereafter published his *Rights of Colonies Examined*,[21] which included a diatribe against those who were ready to surrender colonial liberties.

Hopkins' pamphlet was no mean performance, and Martin Howard, Jr., felt obliged to answer it with a new appeal for submission to the authority of Parliament. In February, 1765, he published anonymously *A Letter from a Gentleman at Halifax to his Friend in Rhode Island*,[22] a point-by-point reply to Hopkins, written in a haughty, condescending tone. The title deceived no one. Everybody knew that the gentleman at Halifax was Martin Howard, Jr., just as everybody

[19] November 16, 1764, *ibid.*, I, 108.
[20] *Records of the Colony of Rhode Island*, VI, 414.
[21] Providence, 1764, reprinted in *Records of the Colony of Rhode Island*, VI, 416-427.
[22] Newport, 1765.

knew, beyond much doubt, that Martin Howard, Jr., and Dr. Moffat were the authors of the O.Z. letters and the leaders in the anti-charter petition.

Governor Hopkins answered Howard's Halifax Letter in the *Providence Gazette*,[23] but James Otis, the Boston patriot, gave a more stinging rebuttal in a pamphlet entitled *A Vindication of the British Colonies against the Aspersions of the Halifax Gentleman in his Letter to a Rhode Island Friend*.[24] And when Howard came back with *A Defense of the Letter from a Gentleman at Halifax*,[25] Otis replied again with *Brief Remarks on the Defense of the Halifax Libel*.[26] This last pamphlet lowered the controversy to a level that had hitherto been approached but never quite reached. The other pamphlets had confined themselves mainly to a discussion of principles; Otis struck at persons. Though he lived in Boston, he had relatives in Newport and was well acquainted with the situation there.[27] He branded the Newport conservatives in words that had just enough truth in them to lend plausibility to his most extravagant charges. He accused them of drinking toasts to the pretender and concluded: "Such is the little, dirty, drinking, drabbing, contaminated knot of thieves, beggars and transports, or the worthy descendents of such, collected from the four winds of the earth, and made up of Turks, Jews and other Infidels, with a few renegado Christians and Catholics, and altogether formed into a club of scarce a dozen at N—p—t. From hence proceed Halifax-letters, petitions to alter the colony forms of government, libels upon all good colonists and subjects, and every evil work that can enter into the heart of man."[28] Scurrilous as these remarks were, they expressed a growing bitterness that was shared by many Newporters against the band of royalists in their midst.

[23] *Providence Gazette,* February 23, March 2, 9, 1765, and *Providence Gazette,* postscript, April 8, 1765.
[24] Boston, 1765.
[25] Newport, 1765.
[26] Boston, 1765.
[27] Major Jonathan Otis of Newport, one of the Sons of Liberty there, was a relative of Otis's. Ezra Stiles, Stamp Act Notebook, Stiles Papers, Yale University Library.
[28] *Brief Remarks,* 5.

Besides his damnation of the club as a whole, Otis had some special epithets for the two men who were recognized as its leaders. Howard he called Martinus Scriblerus, and Moffat was variously Dr. Smallbrain, Dr. Murphy, or "that mawgazeen of knowledge Dr. Mumchance." Referring to the O.Z. letters, Otis advised Howard to find better ways of spending his time, "instead of teaching people to spin and manufacture wool before they know where to get it, as he and the Dr. have been employed for these 12 months, with regard to the good people of R——— Island."[29] Otis had nothing to say about John Robinson, but Robinson's association with the club, his vigorous collection of duties, and his employment of the Navy to assist him rendered him one of the most hated men in Rhode Island. With the approach of November, when the Stamp Act was to go into effect, an explosive situation was developing in Newport; and though Robinson would have no immediate part in enforcing the Act, he was as obvious a target for popular wrath as the other members of the group when the pent-up hatred finally broke loose. Four years later, when the smoke had cleared a little, he would have occasion to remember, and to avenge, the contribution which James Otis had made to the terror which struck at him and his friends only a few months after his return from Taunton.

[29] *Ibid.*, 28.

Chapter V

The Stamp Act[1]

WHEN GEORGE GRENVILLE tightened up the administration of the colonial customs service and revised the rates to make them produce a revenue, he knew that he was only beginning, that the colonies could and should contribute more to the cost of their defence. During the summer of 1763 he had already begun to consider the possibility of a stamp tax, and had assigned two different individuals to prepare drafts of an American Stamp Act. When these were presented to him on September 30, 1763, and October 10, 1763, respectively, he found neither satisfactory. The men who drew them up simply did not know the details of American judicial procedures well enough to name and describe the documents upon which a tax should be collected. In fact it is unlikely that anyone in the offices at Whitehall knew enough. Consequently, although Grenville was anxious to increase the revenue as rapidly as possible, a stamp tax would have to wait until the necessary information could be gathered.[2]

Since he could not present Parliament with an American Stamp Act in the spring of 1764, why did Grenville offer his resolution that one might be proper in the future? Why not wait until he had it ready, before introducing the subject? Unfortunately he left no answer to this question, and we can only infer his motives from things he did and said. From these one fact emerges: Grenville was worried, though probably not greatly, about the reaction to a stamp tax both in Parliament and in the colonies. When introducing the

[1] I have treated parts of this subject in greater detail in an article entitled "The Postponement of the Stamp Act," *William & Mary Quarterly*, 3d ser., 7 (1950), 353-392.

[2] Additional Mss., 35910, ff. 136-159; 35911, ff. 17-37; 36226, f. 353, British Museum, Library of Congress transcripts. Cf. George Bancroft, *History of the United States* (Boston, 1834–1874), V, 151.

resolution, he affirmed, a little too confidently, that he "hoped that the power and sovereignty of Parliament, over every part of the British dominions, for the purpose of raising or collecting any tax, would never be disputed. That if there was a single man doubted it, he would take the sense of the House, having heard without doors hints of this nature dropped."[3] No one in Parliament rose to this challenge, and it is doubtful that a majority ever would have disavowed the authority to tax the colonies. Legislative bodies are not fond of setting limits on their own competence, and Parliament had long since accustomed itself to the idea of its own omnipotence. Yet Grenville had heard hints dropped outside Parliament. Perhaps he knew that his great brother-in-law did not share the general view, and a view which William Pitt did not share was possibly not so general after all. One way to establish its acceptance, however, was by a Parliamentary resolution. Once Parliament agreed that it had the right to levy stamp duties in the colonies, it was not likely to reverse its opinion when asked to exercise the right. An assertion of the right, in such a resolution, would be more acceptable if unencumbered with the details of any immediate application; and the application, in the bill he was preparing, would be more acceptable if the question of right had already been settled.[4]

There was also the question of how a stamp act would be received in the colonies. Grenville saw a way to take care of

[3] Edward Montague, letter of April 11, 1764, quoted in *Virginia Gazette* (Purdie & Dixon), October 3, 1766. Cf. Eliphalet Dyer to Jared Ingersoll, April 14, 1764, New Haven Colony Historical Society, *Papers,* 9 (1918), 291, "Mr. Grenville strongly urg'd not only the power but the right of Parliament to tax the colonys, and hop'd in Gods Name as his Expression was that none would dare dispute their Sovereignty."

[4] It was implied in one newspaper report (see *Pennsylvania Gazette,* May 10, 1764) that Parliament had previously debated the constitutionality of taxing the colonies and had determined the question in the affirmative. This does not seem to be supported by the records, though it is clear that a stamp tax had been suggested many times during the eighteenth century and as recently as the previous year. See *Newport Mercury,* May 30, 1763; cf. Bancroft, *History of the United States,* V, 88n.

this problem too with his advance resolution: when introducing it to Parliament he managed to maneuver the colonists into a position where a stamp act would appear to be the result of their own failure to come to the assistance of the mother country in an hour of need. Although he had almost certainly made up his mind to have the tax enacted at the next session of Parliament, he gave the impression that the colonies might avert it if they took proper action during the intervening year. There is no official record of what he said in Parliament on March 9, 1764, and in the several accounts by private hands most of the space is devoted to his remarks on the deplorable condition of English finances and his explanation of the resolutions which were to form the basis of the Sugar Act.[5] With regard to the fifteenth resolution (which affirmed that a stamp tax might be necessary), the accounts are meager, but a few facts stand out: Grenville announced that he wished no action on this subject until the next session, that his reason for delay was a desire to consult the ease, the interest (or the quiet), and the good will of the colonies, and that the colonies might take advantage of the delay to offer any objections they might have to the tax, or to suggest some more satisfactory tax, or—and here was the most misleading suggestion—to raise the money themselves in any way they saw fit. Two accounts of the speech clearly affirm that Grenville offered the colonies this alternative of raising the money themselves. Jasper Mauduit, the agent of Massachusetts, was not present when the speech was delivered, but his brother Israel was, and on the basis of Israel's report, Jasper transmitted to the Massachusetts Assembly on March 13 copies of the resolutions which had been passed, with comments upon them. Of the fifteenth resolution he wrote, "The Stamp duty you will see, is deferr'd till next Year. I mean the actual laying it: Mr. Grenville being willing to give to the Provinces their option to raise that

---

[5] Besides the accounts cited in note 3, see *Archives of Maryland*, XIV (1895), 144; *Connecticut Courant*, September 16, 1765; New Haven Colony Historical Society, *Papers*, 9 (1918), 294; Massachusetts Historical Society, *Collections*, 6th series, 9 (1897), 20; Massachusetts Archives, XXII, 359.

or some equivalent tax, Desirous as he express'd himself to consult the Ease, the Quiet, and the Goodwill of the Colonies."[6] Here Mauduit speaks in the first two sentences as though the tax was certain to be passed the next session, but then he adds that the colonies have an "option" to raise some other tax, presumably through their own assemblies.

The report by Edward Montague, the agent of Virginia, stated even more explicitly that Grenville had given the colonies this alternative: "Mr. G—— then suggested that this [his?] great object, being the relief of this kingdom from the burthen which in justice America should bear, it would be as satisfactory to him if the several provinces would among themselves, and in modes best suited to their circumstances, raise a sum adequate to the expense of their defence."[7]

According to these two accounts Grenville definitely proposed in his speech of March 9, that the colonies might avert the stamp tax. If they would prefer to tax themselves rather than be taxed by Parliament they had a year in which to take action. Having made this magnanimous gesture, Grenville put in motion the machinery for drawing up a stamp bill to present to the next session of Parliament. For reasons that will become apparent Grenville was probably certain that the colonies would do nothing, and he wanted to have his bill ready by 1765. He gave to Thomas Whately in the treasury office the task of preparing it,[8] and Whately wrote to persons he knew in America to get the necessary information. He wrote to Jared Ingersoll of Connecticut, asking, "Would it yield a considerable Revenue if the Duty were low upon

[6] Massachusetts Archives, XXII, 359.

[7] *Virginia Gazette* (Purdie & Dixon), October 3, 1766; *Virginia Magazine of History and Biography*, X (1903), 8-9.

[8] This is clearly established in Additional Mss., 35911, ff. 17-37, British Museum. See also Additional Mss., 35910, ff. 311-323. The two previous drafts of a Stamp Act had been drawn by Henry McCulloh and Thomas Cruwys. See note 2. Charles R. Ritcheson in "The Preparation of the Stamp Act," *William and Mary Quarterly*, 3d ser., 10 (1953) argues that the draft we have attributed to Cruwys was written by John Tabor Kempe. For the reasons why Kempe could not have written it, see the letters by E. S. Morgan and Bernhard Knollenberg, *Ibid.*, 11 (1954), 157-160, 512-513.

mercantile Instruments, high upon gratuitous Grants of lands and moderate upon Law Proceedings? Would the Execution of such a Law be attended with great Inconveniencies, or open to frequent Evasions which could not be guarded against?"[9] He asked more detailed questions of John Temple at Boston:

> I know there has been a stamp act in your Colony [referring to a Massachusetts stamp act of 1755]. I should be glad to know what was its product and on what articles it chiefly produced. What difficulties have occurr'd in executing it? What objections may be made to it, and what additional provisions must be made to those in force here? The greatest difficulty will be to ascertain the law proceedings that ought to be stampt. I should be much obliged to you if you could procure me the names of your several courts and of the respective instruments and proceedings used therein, which any lawyer of your acquaintance can readily furnish you with. Have you any fines and recoveries? Have you any inferior Courts that hold plea to a certain sum only? What appeals have you from one Court to another? And are your writs the same as are mentioned in our stamp acts? It will be a principal object of attention here to make this tax as little burthensome as possible, but for this purpose it will be necessary to know whether the same duties as are imposed in England on obligations, instruments of conveyance, and indentures of apprenticeship would be too heavy on the Colonies. Which of the English duties will be burthensome? which should be omitted? and which lighten'd and why? I should also be glad to be inform'd whether you use stampt cards and dice, how many newspapers are circulated in the Province, and what may reasonably be expected to be the produce of a stamp act, should the duty be laid at an average in any given proportion to that imposed in England.[10]

[9] New Haven Colony Historical Society, *Papers*, 9 (1918), 294.
[10] Massachusetts Historical Society, *Collections*, 6th series, 9 (1897), 22-23.

Whately did not have to rely wholly on information obtained informally from his friends. On August 11, 1764, the Earl of Halifax, Secretary of State for the Southern Department, sent a circular letter to the colonial governors announcing the resolution for a future stamp tax and asking for "a list of all instruments made use of in public transactions, law proceedings, grants, conveyances, securities of land or money within your government, with proper and sufficient descriptions of the same, in order, that if Parliament should think proper to pursue the intention of the aforesaid resolution, they may thereby be enabled to carry it into execution, in the most effectual and least burdensome manner."[11] On the basis of the various reports he received Whately drew up a tentative schedule of duties, and most of his recommendations were accepted in the bill that was eventually laid before Parliament. In general the American rates were lower than the corresponding English ones. They could be raised after the colonists were used to the tax. In a few cases, however, the American charges were higher at the outset. If any incipient American democrats had seen Whately's report, there would surely have been howls of rage when they read that "the Duties upon Admissions to any of the professions or to the University degrees should certainly be as high as they are in England; it would indeed be better if they were raised both here and there considerably in order to keep mean persons out of those situations in life which they disgrace."[12] Accordingly the colonial tax was set at £2 for matriculation and the same amount for a degree, though in England it was two shillings for one and two shillings, sixpence for the other; admission to the bar in America was £10, in England £6; and taxes on admission to minor public offices were also slightly higher in America.[13]

While Thomas Whately was busy preparing the Stamp Act, the colonial agents, to say nothing of the colonists, were puzzling over the meaning of the alternative proposal that

[11] *Records of the Colony of Rhode Island*, VI, 404.

[12] Additional Mss., 35910, ff. 317-318, British Museum.

[13] *Ibid.*, ff. 167-203, lists conveniently the English duties at the time, which may be compared with those of Grenville's Stamp Act in *Statutes at Large*, XXVI, 179-204 (5 George III, c. 12).

Grenville had made in his speech of March 9. For a reason which is obvious enough if we assume that Grenville had already made up his mind to have a stamp tax, he had not communicated the proposal to the colonial assemblies through the channel normally used. Had he really intended to allow the colonies a chance to raise the money themselves, he would have made his offer in the regular manner by having the Secretary of State for the Southern Department write to the governors of the colonies. He had had Halifax write for the information about colonial judicial transactions needed in draughting the Stamp Act, but he made no communication on the subject of letting the colonial assemblies tax themselves. There was a good deal of justice in a complaint published later in the *Boston Gazette*, after the Stamp Act had become a law:

It has been said the Stamp Act was put off a year, that the colonies might have notice to object and give their reasons against it. What notice the other colonies had, I know not. The Massachusetts never had a line about it from one of the public offices. Mr. Jasper M-ud-t indeed told them, that his brother Israel told him, that Mr. Gr-v-ll haughtily told him, to tell his brother to tell his constituents, that if they would not stamp themselves, he would have them stamped, or very nearly to that effect.[14]

Yet in spite of the fact that Grenville did not make the offer in proper form, he did make it, and the agents did report it to their constituents—Israel did tell Jasper, and Jasper did tell the Massachusetts Assembly. It was only a short time after the speech, however, before the agents realized that the terms of the proposal they had communicated to the colonies were not entirely clear. Grenville had said that if the colonies would raise among themselves an adequate sum or sum equivalent to that expected from the stamp tax, he would accept it in lieu of a stamp tax. But how much was an "adequate" or "equivalent" sum? If the colonies were to lay an equivalent tax themselves, they would have to know either how much was needed in all, or else what were the intended

[14] *Boston Gazette*, January 20, 1766.

taxable items and rates. Without this information it would be impossible for them to act upon Grenville's proposal. The agents, before they could have had time to hear from their constituents about it, decided to have a talk with the Minister. He met them on May 17, 1764, in a conference which was afterwards described in some detail by three of the participants.[15]

Grenville opened by stating that he had not changed his mind, but he then proceeded to propose something he had not so much as mentioned in his speech.[16] The agents were trying to find out "the sort of proposition, which would probably be accepted from them to Parliament,"[17] in other words how much he wanted the colonies to raise. But Grenville, rather than stating the sum he wanted from them, now proposed that they assent in advance to the Parliamentary tax and thereby set a precedent for being consulted about any future taxes! He also spoke strongly of the difficulties which "would have"[18] attended any scheme of letting them tax themselves, as though that issue were closed. But he did not expressly repudiate his offer; and the agents, although they could not help seeing that he was discouraging action by the colonies, apparently did not recognize that he was precluding it. They did not, however, press for a statement of the exact sum with

15 By Jasper Mauduit, whose brother Israel attended the conference for him, in a letter to the Speaker of the Massachusetts House of Representatives, May 26, 1764, Massachusetts Archives, XXII, 375; Massachusetts Historical Society, *Collections,* 74 (1918), 147n.; by Charles Garth in a letter to the Committee of Correspondence of South Carolina, June 5, 1764, *English Historical Review,* 54 (1939), 646-648; and by William Knox, in *The Claim of the Colonies to an Exemption from Internal Taxes* (London, 1765), 31-33. *Prologue to Revolution,* 27-28, 96-97.

16 But Grenville may have discussed it with some of the agents or other friends of the colonies, for Thomas Penn, one of the Proprietors of Pennsylvania, wrote from London on March 9, 1764, that a stamp tax had been proposed, but "we have endeavoured to get this last postponed, as it is an internal Tax, and wait til some sort of consent to it shall be given by the several Assemblys, to prevent a Tax of that nature from being laid without the consent of the Colonys, . . ." Penn Correspondence, VIII (1763–1766), 33, Historical Society of Pennsylvania.

17 *Claim of the Colonies,* 31-32.

18 *English Historical Review,* 54 (1939), 647.

which the colonies might satisfy him. Grenville had steered the conference beyond that subject, and they probably feared to upset his evident good humor by insisting on a matter so obviously distasteful. They must prolong the conference and find out, if possible, the terms of the act he expected to bring in if the colonies did not raise the money themselves. They must know the terms, one of the agents explained, "in order that our respective constituents might have the whole, both substance and form under their deliberation, when they would be far better able to determine whether or how far, to approve or disapprove."[19] But the details of the act were, of course, unknown to Grenville himself, for it had not yet been drawn up. Israel Mauduit pointed out that to ask the colonies to assent in advance to a bill without giving the provisions of it was asking them "to assent to they did not know what."[20] To this Grenville answered simply that it was not necessary to bother with details, "That everyone knew the stamp laws here; and that this Bill is intended to be formd upon the same plan."[21] He did agree to consult with the agents on this matter just before the meeting of Parliament, provided that in the meantime the colonial assemblies should signify their assent to the general idea of a stamp tax. He warned that any protests based on the financial inability of the colonies to pay would carry little weight in Parliament. In his speech of March 9 he had already made it plain that he would listen to nothing which called in question the right of Parliament to levy the tax, so that he left the colonies very little room either for criticism or for constructive action.

It is evident from this conference that Grenville was determined upon a stamp tax. Though he was willing to make magnanimous gestures, he had no intention of allowing the colonies to prevent passage of his measure either by objections to it or by raising an "equivalent" sum. They would not thwart him by levying a substitute tax themselves: by withholding the necessary information he made sure of that. Nor would he be troubled by their objections: thanks to his foresighted resolution he could safely predict Parliament's unsympathetic re-

[19] Ibid., 646-647.
[20] Massachusetts Archives, XXII, 375.
[21] Ibid.

action here. Grenville must have felt comfortably satisfied with all his maneuvers. He had made it useless for the colonies to attempt any action to avert the tax, and yet he had carried out his interview so smoothly, and expressed his affection for the colonies so convincingly, that the agents did not perceive, nor inform their clients, of the hopelessness of their efforts.

It was only when a colony set about to tax itself that the hollowness of Grenville's offer became apparent. Massachusetts made the attempt. Though Governor Bernard was convinced that the Ministry really intended to let the colonies raise all internal taxes themselves, yet when several members of the Assembly approached him in the summer of 1764, asking for a special session in order that the colony might tax itself to avoid being taxed by Parliament, Bernard refused, because he saw that nothing could be done without more information from Grenville. He related the entire incident to his friend Richard Jackson, in a letter dated at Boston, August 18, 1764:

Dear Sir

Yesterday the members for Boston came to me to signify that it was the desire of many Members of the House that the Assembly might meet as soon as possible, that proper measures might be taken to prevent an inland parliamentary Taxation. That their Agent had wrote word that Mr. Grenville had told him that such a taxation might be prevented, if they would tax themselves to the same purposes as were intended by the former. That they were desirous of immediately setting about such taxation themselves or at least of doing something to prevent a parliamentary tax.

I told them that in the present state of things I did not see that they could do anything more than they might have done last session: that is to signify their desire that they might be allowed to tax themselves and not be taxed by the parliament. That it was impossible at present to proceed to an actual taxation, untill the demands of the ministry should be further explained. That If every province was to be left to raise the Money in what manner they pleased, the particular sum expected from each province as their proportion must be first ascertained. That if a stamp Duty was to be imposed by provincial Acts as forming of itself a proportion of charge, the Duties themselves must be first settled, as they ought to be the same in every province; otherwise they will not be a proportional charge. That neither of these things can be done by the provinces themselves, they must be settled by some authority that can mediate between the Provinces and moderate their partialities for themselves. That in regard to the Provinces preferring to tax themselves rather than to be taxed by Parliament, there can be no doubt of that being the desire of the Ministry. The Friends of the Provinces had been long aware of that preference; you had particularly urged it: and I had wrote upon the same subject. In short it could never be doubted but that if the parliament should require certain sums of the provinces, It is of no little Consequence to them that such sums should be raised by provincial Acts. For thereby the forms of their priviledges (which are no little part of them) are kept up, tho' the Substance is impeached, as it frequently must be in Subordinate Governments, whose relation to the Sovereign power has never been formally settled nor is generally understood.

But I promised them that I would Call the Assembly together about the middle of october, when there would be time enough to send instructions to the agent before this business could be brought on in parliament. However, if the Ministry should be settling their plan before hand, I wish you would interpose on the behalf of the province that they may at least have the liberty of enacting internal taxations themselves: which I have no doubt, but that they will readily do, when it shall be positively required of them. I am Sir

your most faithfull and obedient servant.[22]

This letter shows plainly enough why the colonies did not take advantage of Grenville's offer to let them tax themselves. Not only was the offer never made them in a regular manner by letters from the Secretary of State, but it was never

[22] Bernard Papers, III, 248-249, Harvard College Library.

couched in terms that were definite enough to permit of action. Several colonies signified their willingness to contribute if requested in a regular manner for a specific sum,[23] but such a request was never made.

What the colonies did do was to take up the challenge which Grenville had thrown to Parliament and which Parliament had endorsed and passed on to them. The Americans read the fifteenth resolution correctly, as a declaration of Parliament's right to tax them.[24] And since the challenge was no more than a declaration, albeit by a body which regarded its own declarations as final, they replied in the mode, infuriating to omnipotence, of talking back. In the petitions to Parliament and letters to their agents that we have already examined, they denied that Parliament had any right to tax them. This denial was by no means limited to the dusky halls of legislative assemblies. The people at large were as much concerned over the measure as their representatives. Jared Ingersoll, in answer to Thomas Whately's inquiries, warned the man who was drafting the Stamp Act, that the minds of the people "are filled with the most dreadfull apprehensions from such a Step's taking place, from whence I leave you to guess how Easily a tax of that kind would be Collected; tis difficult to say how many ways could be invented to avoid the payment of a tax laid upon a Country without the Consent of the Legislature of that Country and in the opinion of most of the people Contrary to the foundation principles of their natural and Constitutional rights and Liberties. Dont think me impertinent, Since you desire Information, when I tell you that I have heard Gentlemen of the greatest property in Neighbouring Governments say, Seemingly very Cooly, that should such a Step take place they would immediately remove

[23] Pennsylvania included such a statement in instructions to her agent, *Pennsylvania Archives*, 8th ser., VII (1935), 5678-5682, and so evidently did other colonies, for according to Charles Garth the agents decided later to acquaint Grenville with the fact that "most of the Colonies had signify'd their inclinations to assist their Mother Country upon proper requisitions from hence." *English Historical Review*, 54 (1939), 649.

[24] In referring to the fifteenth resolution Americans frequently spoke of it as an assertion of Parliament's right to tax the colonies, e.g. *Records of the Colony of Rhode Island*, VI, 422.

themselves with their families and fortunes into some foreign Kingdom."[25] Ingersoll also told Whately, much as Bernard had told Jackson, that "If the King should fix the proportion of our Duty, we all say we will do our parts in the Common Cause, but if the Parliament once interpose and Lay a tax, tho' it may be a very moderate one . . . what Consequences may, or rather may not, follow?"[26]

With his two secretaries, Jackson and Whately, receiving communications of this kind, and with other colonial agents spreading petitions and pamphlets to the same effect around London, Grenville could see for himself that the champions of colonial reorganization were right in crying that the authority of Parliament in America needed bolstering, but he did not therefore agree that reorganization would provide the best reinforcement. The way to get authority recognized was to exercise it, and Grenville was prepared to do just that with his stamp tax. Twenty-three years before, in 1742, Sir William Keith had proposed such a tax precisely because he thought it would establish among the Americans "a more just and favourable opinion of their dependency on a British Parliament, than what they generally have at present."[27] And doubtless Thomas Whately voiced Grenville's own view when he called the Stamp Act "the great measure of the Sessions . . . on account of the important point it establishes, the Right of Parliament to lay an internal Tax upon the Colonies."[28]

If Parliament was not as aware as Grenville that its authority in America needed support, the colonists themselves completed the awakening. As the protests from across the ocean poured into England, Parliamentary hackles rose, and the Minister could rejoice, for, as he had calculated, the members reacted to the denial of their authority with the wrath of injured dignity. The unfortunate colonial agents, fighting frantically to stave off the coming blow, saw that because

[25] Ingersoll to Whately, July 6, 1764, New Haven Colony Historical Society, *Papers,* 9 (1918), 299-300.

[26] *Ibid.,* 299.

[27] Additional Mss., 33028, British Museum.

[28] Thomas Whately to John Temple, February 9, 1765, Temple-Whately Letter Book, Stowe Collection, Huntington Library.

of their clients' declarations the battle was being transformed into a test of Parliament's authority. The main issue was no longer raising a revenue, but putting the Americans in their place. The agents knew that Parliament would refuse to hear any arguments calling its authority into question, and yet they had specific instructions, or else petitions to present, which required them to contest the bill on the question of right. A few of them, led by William Knox of Georgia, thought that all the agents should unite in a petition of their own, leaving out offensive expressions against Parliamentary authority. It would at least get a hearing and thereby establish a precedent in Parliament for receiving petitions from the colonies before taxing them, whatever that might be worth. The petition was drawn up, but most of the agents did not feel free to sign it, and the project was dropped.[29]

Some of the agents tried to enlist the aid of the merchants. The colonial non-importation movement, combined with the depression, was making itself felt in England, but though they were generally opposed to the stamp tax, the merchants had not yet become sufficiently alarmed to mobilize and concert their opposition. As Jasper Mauduit put it in a letter to the Massachusetts Assembly on January 16, 1765, "The Merchants talk much, but cannot bring them to Act."[30]

By this time the situation was becoming desperate. Parliament was due to open, and though a good deal of propaganda had been published, most of it probably at the instigation of the agents, there was no organized opposition in the House of Commons to contest the bill when Grenville should bring it in.[31] The agents decided to make one last attempt to stop the tax at its source and deputed four of their number to call on the Minister again and point out to him that most of the colonies had expressed their willingness to contribute to the British Treasury if called upon to do so in a regular, constitutional manner. The agents who met with Grenville on February 2, 1765, were Charles Garth, agent of South

[29] Knox, *Claim of the Colonies,* 35.
[30] Massachusetts Archives, XXII, 426.
[31] See Fred J. Ericson, "The Contemporary British Opposition to the Stamp Act," Michigan Academy of Science, Arts, and Letters, *Papers,* 29 (1943), 489-505.

Carolina and Member of Parliament for a borough in Wilt-
shire, Richard Jackson, agent of Connecticut and now also of
Pennsylvania and Massachusetts, also Member of Parliament
for Weymouth and secretary to Grenville, Benjamin Franklin,
who had recently come over to urge a royal government for
Pennsylvania, and Jared Ingersoll, who had also just arrived,
on private business. Ingersoll left the most complete account
of the conference in a letter to Governor Fitch, dated
February 11, 1765. He wrote:

> The Agents of the Colonies have had several Meetings,
> at one of which they were pleased to desire Mr. Franklin
> and myself as having lately Come from America and know-
> ing more Intimately the Sentiments of the people, to wait
> on Mr. Grenville, together with Mr. Jackson and Mr. Garth
> who being Agents are also Members of Parliament, to
> remonstrate against the Stamp Bill, and to propose in Case
> any Tax must be laid upon America, that the several
> Colonies might be permitted to lay the Tax themselves.
> This we did Saturday before last. Mr. Grenville gave us
> a full hearing—told us he took no pleasure in giving the
> Americans so much uneasiness as he found he did—that it
> was the Duty of his Office to manage the revenue—that he
> really was made to believe that considering the whole of the
> Circumstances of the Mother Country and the Colonies, the
> later could and ought to pay something, and that he knew
> of no better way than that now pursuing to lay such Tax,
> but that if we could tell of a better he would adopt it. We
> then urged the Method first mentioned as being a Method
> the people had been used to—that it would at least seem to
> be their own Act and prevent that uneasiness and Jealousy
> which otherwise we found would take place—that they
> could raise the Money best by their own Officers &c &c
>
> Mr Jackson told him plainly that he foresaw [by] the
> Measure now pursuing, by enabling the Crown to keep up
> an armed Force of its own in America and to pay the
> Governours in the Kings Goverments and all with the
> Americans own Money, the Assemblies *in* the Colonys
> would be subverted—that the Governors would have no
> Occasion, as for any Ends of their own or of the Crown,

to call 'Em and that they never would be called together in the Kings Goverments. Mr. Grenville warmly rejected the thought, said no such thing was intended nor would he beleived take place.[32]

One may doubt whether Grenville's judgment on this last point was as acute as Jackson's. Though Grenville himself may have had no intention of subverting the colonial assemblies, the colonial governors would have been glad to free themselves from the control of those bodies, and if Parliament were to collect taxes in the colonies, the assemblies might very well lose the power of the purse entirely.

The conference up to this point was no more than what could have been expected: the agents had urged that the colonies be allowed to tax themselves, and the Minister had urged that a stamp tax levied by Parliament was preferable. But now the meeting took a new turn. In answer to the request that he let the colonies raise the money in their own assemblies, Grenville asked the agents if they "could agree upon the several proportions Each Colony should raise."[33] A more fatuous question can scarcely be imagined, and if the agents had not been so soothed by the Minister's personal charm, they would probably have shown some indignation at his asking it. Grenville himself, in his speech of March 9, had been the first to propose that the colonies raise the money themselves but had failed to provide them with the details of how much was wanted from each or from all. When the agents had sought these details in the conference of May 17, he had refused them and had made a different proposal, that the colonial assemblies assent in advance to a tax by Parliament, but even in this connection he had not offered the details of the bill he wanted them to assent to. The colonial assemblies had ignored this second proposal, which would have meant resigning the very function for which they existed; yet they had stated their willingness to comply with any requisition made in the normal, constitutional manner. Now the agents were asking once more that the colonies be

[32] Connecticut Historical Society, *Collections*, 18 (1920), 324-325. *Prologue to Revolution*, 31-34.

[33] *Ibid.*

allowed to do so. Grenville's answer was to ask the agents if they were empowered to do what he himself should have done in the first place, namely to set the proportion of a total sum which each colony should bear. "We told him no," says Ingersoll, "He said he did not think anybody here was furnished with Materials for that purpose. . . ."[34]

If Grenville did not think that anyone in England was furnished with information to set the proportion for each colony, who did he think was furnished with it? It was his business, or the business of his Secretary of State, to have this information, and the Board of Trade existed to provide him with it. The colonies had no connection with one another except through the British government. They could not have settled the proper proportions except by an inter-colonial congress, but such a congress could not properly have been called without authorization from Great Britain, and could not have acted anyhow without knowing the total sum expected from the colonies.[35] When members of the Massachusetts Assembly wished to take up Grenville's offer by taxing themselves, Governor Bernard had rightly told them that they could do nothing until the Minister gave them more information. The Minister now wanted to know whether the colonial agents could provide the information which *he* should have given *them*.

When the conference of February 2 was over the agents must have realized at last that Grenville's offer had never been made in good faith, that a year ago, even while making the offer, he had already made up his mind to levy a stamp

[34] *Ibid.*

[35] Benjamin Franklin discussed the possibility of such a congress with Richard Jackson (Carl Van Doren, ed., *Letters and Papers of Benjamin Franklin and Richard Jackson, 1753–1785,* Philadelphia, 1947, p. 175), but there is no indication that Grenville ever suggested calling one. When the Stamp Act Congress was held, after passage of the Stamp Act, Parliament refused to receive its communications, because, among other reasons, the Congress "partook too much of a federal Union assembled without any Requisition on the Part of the Supreme Power." Charles Garth to Ringgold, Murdoch, and Tilghman, February 26, 1766, *Maryland Historical Magazine,* VI, 282-287. This indicates how Parliament might have treated the proceedings of a congress assembled without authorization from England.

tax. The willingness he had then expressed to let the colonies tax themselves or offer objections was nothing more than a rhetorical gesture, designed to demonstrate his own benevolence. In the conference of February 2, 1765, he even told the agents that "he had pledged his Word for Offering the Stamp Bill to the house."[36] What he had given the colonies was not an opportunity to tax themselves but an opportunity to refuse to tax themselves.

In the time that was left the agents continued their preparation for the ensuing battle in Parliament, but the impudence of the Americans had so irritated the law-makers, that the issue was a foregone conclusion. One member wrote to a friend that the insubordinate declarations against Parliamentary right were going to be examined, "but first it is thought proper to establish that Right by a new execution of it, and in the strongest instance, an internal Tax, that of the Stamp duty."[37] On February 6, when Grenville reminded the House of their resolution of the preceding year, there followed a lively debate, but though a great deal was said in demonstration of Parliament's right to levy the tax, no one argued the other side of the question. Even the most eloquent opponents of the tax spoke in terms of equity and expediency and did not venture to deny the absolute authority of Parliament.

The staunchest supporter of the colonies in this first debate was Colonel Isaac Barré, a veteran of the French and Indian War. According to one observer, "He most strongly recommended that if there must be a tax laid, tho' he could wish there was to be none, that the Provinces might be indulged with the liberty as heretofore of furnishing their quotas of any sums required and colecting it in their own modes."[38] Barré, in other words, advocated the proposal that Grenville himself had first made but failed to carry through. Charles Townshend, author-to-be of the Townshend Duties, spoke

[36] Connecticut Historical Society, *Collections,* 18 (1920), 325.
[37] Edward Sedgwick to Edward Weston, February 14, 1765, Charles Fleetwood Weston Underwood Mss., Historical Manuscripts Commission, *Tenth Report,* [pt. 1] (1885), 382.
[38] John Nelson to John Temple, n.d., Massachusetts Historical Society, *Collections,* 6th ser., 9 (1897), 46.

with some warmth in the debate, asking on one occasion: "And now will these Americans, Children planted by our Care, nourished up by our Indulgence untill they are grown to a Degree of Strength and Opulence, and protected by our Arms, will they grudge to contribute their mite to relieve us from the heavy weight of that burden which we lie under?" To this Barré answered with words that would soon make him famous throughout the American Colonies:

They planted by your Care? No! your Oppressions planted em in America. They fled from your Tyranny to a then uncultivated and unhospitable Country—where they exposed themselves to almost all the hardships to which human Nature is liable, and among others to the Cruelties of a Savage foe, the most subtle and I take upon me to say the most formidable of any People upon the face of Gods Earth. And yet, actuated by Principles of true english Lyberty, they met all these hardships with pleasure, compared with those they suffered in their own Country, from the hands of those who should have been their Friends.

They nourished by *your* indulgence? they grew by your neglect of Em: as soon as you began to care about Em, that Care was Exercised in sending persons to rule over Em, in one Department and another, who were perhaps the Deputies of Deputies to some Member of this house—sent to Spy out their Lyberty, to misrepresent their Actions and to prey upon Em; men whose behaviour on many Occasions has caused the Blood of those Sons of Liberty to recoil within them; men promoted to the highest Seats of Justice, some, who to my knowledge were glad by going to a foreign Country to Escape being brought to the Bar of a Court of Justice in their own.

They protected by *your* Arms? they have nobly taken up Arms in your defence, have Exerted a Valour amidst their constant and Laborious industry for the defence of a Country, whose frontier, while drench'd in blood, its interior Parts have yielded all its little Savings to your Emolument. And beleive me, remember I this Day told you so, that same Spirit of freedom which actuated that people at first, will accompany them still.—But prudence forbids me to explain myself further. God knows I do not at this Time speak from motives of party Heat, what I deliver are the genuine Sentiments of my heart.[39]

Even Barré's eloquence, which did not, after all, deny the authority of Parliament, could not alter the determination of the members to prove their unlimited authority by taxing the colonies. With regard to the ability of the colonies to pay, Grenville had figures ready at hand to show that their total public debts amounted to only about £900,000, all of which was scheduled to be paid off before the year 1769.[40] The per capita indebtedness of the colonists was thus only a fraction of that in England. The sentiment in favor of the tax was so strong that the opposition, instead of bringing the matter to a vote on the immediate question, tried to get through a vote to adjourn. Mr. Beckford, a former West Indian, made the motion, and Colonel Barré seconded it, remarking that he "should with greater pleasure second a motion that it might never be bro't on the carpet again."[41] The motion was lost by a vote of 245 to 49, taken at about midnight, and on the following day the House of Commons passed, without a division, the fifty-five resolutions which formed the basis of the Stamp Act.[42]

Grenville, having thus secured the approval of Parliament, brought in the bill itself on February 13. It received its first reading then and its second on February 15.[43] This was the crucial reading, and the opposition prepared to present petitions against it. After the debate of February 6, Charles

[39] Connecticut Historical Society, *Collections,* 18 (1920), 322-323. *Prologue to Revolution,* 32.

[40] Treasury Papers, Class I, Bundle 433, f. 402; Charles Garth to Committee of Correspondence of South Carolina, February 8, 1765, *English Historical Review,* 54 (1939), 649-650. For a comparison of the public debt in the various colonies with that in England, see L. H. Gipson, *The British Empire Before the American Revolution* (New York, 1936–1961) 10, 53-110.

[41] Massachusetts Historical Society, *Collections,* 6th ser., 9 (1897), 46.

[42] *Journal of the House of Commons,* XXX, 97-101.

[43] *Ibid.,* 131, 148.

Garth, agent for South Carolina, had written to his clients that "the power of Parliament was asserted and so universally agreed to, that no petition disputing it will be received."[44] Accordingly he had drawn up a petition in which he tried to avoid the question of Parliamentary authority. Since he was a Member of Parliament, he could not sign it himself, but he secured the signatures of a few South Carolinians who happened to be in London. It was to no avail, because Parliament refused to hear any petitions against the bill. When Sir William Meredith presented the petition from Virginia, two reasons were given for refusing to consider it: first, that it was contrary to the custom of the House of Commons to hear petitions against money bills, second and more important, that it cast doubt on the authority of Parliament. According to Garth, "The House declared they would not suffer a petition that should hint at questioning the supremacy and authority of Parliament to impose taxes in every part of the British Dominions."[45] In spite of his efforts to avoid the contentious subject Garth's own carefully contrived petition on behalf of South Carolina met the same fate. He was called upon to state its contents, "Which done, the House were of opinion it tended to question the right of Parliament to exercise this power of taxation, and being likewise against a Money Bill, was also refus'd."[46] Richard Jackson had no better success with the petitions from Connecticut and Massachusetts, which were likewise denied a hearing.[47] The one from New York was couched in such strong terms that no Member of Parliament could be persuaded to present it.[48]

The refusal of Parliament to hear these petitions did not pass without debate. General Conway, another veteran of the late war though not of the American branch of it, was the principal defender of the colonies at this juncture. He made

[44] *English Historical Review*, 54 (1939), 650.

[45] *Ibid.*

[46] *Ibid.*, 651.

[47] *Ibid.*, and Connecticut Historical Society, *Collections*, 18 (1920), 341. It is possible that the petition from Massachusetts was never formally presented. See Jared Ingersoll's account, *ibid.*, 334-335.

[48] *Ibid.*, 335.

a telling point when he reminded the members that they had postponed the Stamp Act the preceding year in order to give the colonies time to send messages representing their objections to it. "This time has been given," said Conway. "The Representations are come from the Colonies; and shall we shut our Ears against that Information, which, with an Affectation of Candour, we allotted sufficient Time to reach us? . . . from whom, unless from themselves, are we to learn the Circumstances of the Colonies, and the fatal Consequences that may attend the imposing of this Tax?"[49]

Conway's plea on February 15 was no more effective than Barré's had been on February 6. The bill survived the second reading without even a division. The third reading was a mere formality, and by March 22 the Stamp Act was a statute of the realm.[50]

The printed text of the act occupied some twenty-five pages and prescribed taxes for: fifteen classes of documents used in court proceedings (including the licenses of attorneys), the papers used in clearing ships from harbors, college diplomas, appointments to public office, bonds, grants and deeds for land, mortgages, indentures, leases, contracts, bills of sale, articles of apprenticeship, liquor licenses, playing cards, dice, pamphlets, newspapers (and advertisements in them), and almanacs. All these would now have to be written or printed on paper carrying a stamp embossed by the Treasury Office. The user would obtain the paper already stamped from the distributor; and stamped paper was loaded aboard ships for delivery in the colonies during the summer and fall.

The highest tax, £10, was placed as Whately had recommended on attorneys' licenses. Other papers relating to court proceedings were taxed in amounts varying from 3d. to 10s. Land grants under a hundred acres were taxed 1s. 6d., between 100 and 200 acres 2s., and from 200 to 320 acres 2s. 6d., with an additional 2s. 6d. for every additional 320

---

[49] *Maryland Gazette*, June 13, 1765. *Prologue to Revolution*, 34-35.

[50] *The Parliamentary History of England* (London, 1806–1820), XVI, 40.

acres. Cards were taxed a shilling a pack, dice ten shillings, and newspapers and pamphlets at the rate of a penny for a single sheet and a shilling for every sheet in pamphlets or papers totaling more than one sheet and fewer than six sheets in octavo, fewer than twelve in quarto, or fewer than twenty in folio (in other words, the tax on pamphlets grew in proportion to their size but ceased altogether if they became large enough to qualify as a book). The amounts had to be paid in sterling, not in colonial currency, but the administration did not propose thus to draw hard money out of the colonies. The proceeds of the tax were to be expended in America in procurement of supplies for the troops stationed there.[51]

Although the amounts charged would not in most cases impose severe hardships, they would remind colonists in their business transactions of the authority that Parliament claimed over them. And those who read the act carefully would notice, quite apart from the taxes themselves, two ominous features. One was the provision for taxes on documents in courts "exercising ecclesiastical jurisdiction." This could mean simply the special probate courts which in the colonies adjudicated the testamentary matters that were handled in England by ecclesiastical courts. But it could also mean that England was contemplating the establishment of bishops in America; for ecclesiastical courts were presided over by bishops, whose prerogative it was to exercise jurisdiction not only in testamentary cases but also in moral offenses. To colonists whose ancestors had fled from the jurisdiction of English bishops and who had never seen an ecclesiastical court themselves, the prospect of American bishops was anything but welcome.

The hint contained in the Stamp Act that such a prospect might be in store for them coincided with rumors to the same effect and with renewed efforts by Anglicans in the northern colonies to secure the appointment of a bishop. The efforts of this small minority, which did not win the support of southern Anglicans, had already alarmed the Congregationalists, Presbyterians, and other non-Anglican denomina-

[51] *Statutes at Large,* XXVI, 179-204; *Prologue to Revolution,* 35-43.

tions who constituted a majority of the population in the northern colonies; and the hostility which the Stamp Act was to meet in America was probably heightened by this circumstance.[52]

The other ominous provision of the Act was not a matter of speculation. On its way through Parliament, the Act had been amended to provide for enforcement, at the election of the prosecutor, either in common-law courts or in admiralty courts. Since the Sugar Act had already set the precedent for trying colonial revenue cases in admiralty courts, it probably seemed a logical extension of this principle to give the admiralty courts jurisdiction over cases arising out of violations of the Stamp Act. It was a principle, however, that Englishmen had successfully resisted in the past and that could not have been applied in England itself without raising a storm of protest. Admiralty courts in England, operating as in the colonies under Roman law and without juries, were confined to cases arising on the high seas and below the first bridge on navigable rivers. The Sugar Act and the Navigation Acts could conceivably be interpreted as falling within this definition (though the Navigation Acts were *not* so interpreted in England, where violations were tried in common-law courts). But by no stretch of the imagination could the Stamp Act be so interpreted.[53]

As they read the Stamp Act, then, the colonists would find themselves taxed without consent for purposes of revenue, their rights to common-law trial abridged, the authority of one prerogative court (admiralty) enlarged, and the establishment of another (ecclesiastical) hinted at.

[52] Bridenbaugh, *Mitre and Sceptre*, 230-259.

[53] On the significance of this extension of admiralty jurisdiction see David S. Lovejoy. "Rights Imply Equality: The Case Against Admiralty Jurisdiction in America, 1764–1776," *William and Mary Quarterly*, 3d ser., 16 (1959), 459-484. Cf. Ubbelohde, *Vice-Admiralty Courts*, 75-76.

Chapter VI

Daniel Dulany, Pamphleteer

WHEN NEWS REACHED America that the Stamp Act had passed, anger erupted first in a torrent of words. Of these millions of words which the Act provoked and which found their way into print, probably none were more widely read or more universally approved than those of a Maryland lawyer, Daniel Dulany, in a pamphlet called *Considerations on the Propriety of imposing Taxes in the British Colonies, for the Purpose of raising a Revenue, by Act of Parliament.*[1]

When his pamphlet appeared, Dulany was already an outstanding provincial lawyer and politician. He was one of those able sons of an able father, who by starting life with the accumulated advantages of their parents' brains and industry, are able to use their own brains and their own industry to maintain and increase the family fortunes and prestige. Dulany's father had come to Maryland a penniless immigrant.[2] By hard work and shrewd investments he had built himself a fortune and won a place in the confidence of Lord Baltimore, the Proprietor of the colony. When his son Daniel was ready for serious schooling, he was able to send him to England to study successively at Eton, Cambridge, and finally the Middle Temple. The father, who had himself earned a place on the Maryland bar and had even returned to England to study at Gray's Inn, decided early that his son too should be a lawyer, and Daniel acquiesced readily.[3] At Eton and

[1] First edition, North America [Annapolis], 1765; second edition, Annapolis, 1765. I have used the second edition. A selection is in *Prologue to Revolution*, 77-88.

[2] On the elder Dulany, see the article by Newton D. Mereness in *Dictionary of Amer. Biog.*, and Aubrey C. Land, "Genesis of a Colonial Fortune," *William and Mary Quarterly*, 3rd ser., 7 (1950), 255-269.

[3] Daniel Dulany, Sr., to Peter Goddard, 1741, Dulany Papers, Maryland Historical Society.

Cambridge he lived frugally[4] and studied the "law of Nature and Nations," a step which his father endorsed as good preparation for his future calling.[5] At the Middle Temple in London he went through the regular training of a lawyer,[6] so that when he returned to Maryland in 1746 to take up the career which his father had laid out for him, he was as well equipped to practice as any English barrister and far better equipped than most Americans.

Daniel Dulany was admitted to the bar in Maryland in 1747 and quickly made a name for himself, not only in the law but in politics as well. By 1751 he had been elected to the Assembly and was earning a reputation similar to his father's as a defender of the Proprietor.[7] At this time, as always in Maryland's colonial history, the Assembly was divided between the friends of the Proprietor and those who wanted to curb his lordship's political power and to reduce the quitrents which he collected on the lands in the province. Daniel Dulany became so closely associated with the proprietary party that in 1754 Lord Baltimore apologized for not appointing him to the Governor's Council (a more distinguished position than that of an elected member of the Assembly), on the grounds that he was needed in the Assembly to protect the proprietary interests there.[8]

But Dulany was no mere tool of Lord Baltimore. Though he recognized the Proprietor's legal rights and was ready to defend them, he was not afraid to defend the rights of the people as well, whenever the occasion should arise. After he was finally appointed to the Governor's Council in 1757, the Governor found him somewhat too independent, and wrote to the Proprietor's secretary that "he is fond of being thought a Patriot Councillor and rather inclined to serve the People

[4] Daniel Dulany, Sr., to Mr. Hyde, June 7, 1747, says that his son's expenses at Eton "did not Exceed £50 a year and seldom reached it." *Ibid.*

[5] Daniel Dulany, Sr., to Peter Goddard, 1741, *ibid.*

[6] Jones, *American Members of the Inns of Court*, 68.

[7] Daniel Dulany, Sr., to Cecilius Calvert, December 26, 1752, Dulany Papers.

[8] Cecilius Calvert to Daniel Dulany, April 17, 1754, *ibid.*

than the Proprietary."[9] Though Dulany, as it turned out later, was no demagogue, and finally lost his popularity in Maryland by supporting the interests of the Proprietor, in this early period at least, before 1765, he kept a sharp eye on contests in which popular rights seemed to be at stake. Through books and newspapers he maintained an interest in political events in England as well as America, and in May, 1764, he read in the *Maryland Gazette* that the House of Commons in England had debated the question of its right to tax the colonies and had decided in favor of such a right.[10]

As far as Dulany was concerned the Parliamentary resolution did not settle the question. He had been thinking about the matter himself for some ten years, and he had come to the conclusion that there were colonial rights involved which could not be overthrown simply by the fiat of Parliament. When he had first considered the idea of a Parliamentary tax, it had not seemed entirely unreasonable to him. In 1755, at the beginning of the French and Indian War, the rumor had gone around that Parliament might tax the colonies. At that time Dulany had written a friend that it was reasonable for the mother country to expect a contribution from the colonies toward the expense of the war and that a Parliamentary tax appeared to be necessary, but even this early he went on to say that "so many things are to be considered in making a regulation of this sort just and effectual, that I dread the consequence of the Parliament's undertaking it."[11] By summer of 1764 the consequences had come to appear even more dreadful, and Dulany must have given the problem increasing attention as he read in the newspapers not only that Parliament would lay a tax of some sort but that there would be a general reorganization of the colonial governments, that boundaries would be adjusted, and that proprietary titles would be

[9] Governor Sharpe to Cecilius Calvert, May 8, 1764, *Archives of Maryland*, XIV, (1895), 160.

[10] *Maryland Gazette*, May 17, 1764; *Considerations*, 33. The debate referred to in the *Maryland Gazette* may have been simply the debate over the fifteenth resolution of March 10, which was evidently regarded as an assertion of Parliamentary right. See ch. V, n. 4.

[11] *Pa. Mag. of Hist.*, 3 (1879), 148.

returned to the Crown. He did not know of the sweeping changes which Governor Bernard was advocating in private letters, but he did receive from his bookseller in London a number of pamphlets and books which advocated a thorough overhaul of colonial affairs and which denied, almost in advance of colonial protests, that the colonists were exempt from Parliamentary taxation.

One of the most substantial of these, Thomas Pownall's *Administration of the Colonies*,[12] struck Dulany as a pompous piece of work. Pownall apparently thought himself the only person in the world with sufficient experience of colonial affairs to direct the management of them. Dulany thought otherwise. He could remember that Pownall had come to the colonies only a dozen years ago, as a mere secretary to the new governor of New York, Sir Danvers Osborne. After Osborne hanged himself in a fit of despondency Pownall by a series of intrigues raised himself from one post to another and now paraded on the title page of his book as "Late Governor and Commander in Chief of his Majesty's Provinces, Massachusetts-Bay and South-Carolina, and Lieutenant-Governor of New-Jersey." Dulany could think of another title given him in a satirical piece published in Boston four or five years before called *Proposals for Printing by Subscription the History of the publick life and distinguished actions of vice-admiral Sir Thomas Brazen*.[13] Dulany had read this piece of invective and thought that the label "Brazen" suited admirably the character of the man who had written *The Administration of the Colonies*. Dulany's views were perhaps prejudiced, but he may have been particularly irked by the fact that Pownall suggested, with no apparent concern for the violation of colonial rights, that a stamp tax was a suitable mode of raising money in America.[14]

[12] The first edition was published in March, 1764, the second edition in March, 1765.

[13] Boston, 1760; see *Considerations,* 13. Dulany may have been in Boston or nearby when this pamphlet, attributed to Samuel Waterhouse, was published. One of his few surviving letters indicates that he was in Rhode Island September 21, 1760. Dulany Papers.

[14] First edition, pp. 66-67; second edition, pp. 90-92.

In the spring of 1765, probably along with news of the passage of the Stamp Act, Dulany received three anonymous pamphlets which disposed of colonial rights even more cavalierly than Pownall had done. *The Objections to the Taxation of our American Colonies by the Legislature of Great Britain briefly Considered*[15] Dulany recognized, by what means is hard to say, as the work of one of the Lords of Trade.[16] The author was Soame Jenyns, a man who fancied himself a wit and who affirmed the absolute authority of Parliament without any salvos whatever to the rights of Englishmen or Americans. Jenyns denied unequivocally the principle that an Englishman cannot be taxed without the consent of his representatives and disposed of all objections with such flourishes as this: "The Liberty of an *Englishman* is a Phrase of so various a Signification, having within these few years been used as a synonymous Term for Blasphemy, Bawdy, Treason, Libels, Strong Beer, and Cyder, that I shall not here presume to define its meaning; but I shall venture to assert what it cannot mean; that is, an Exemption from Taxes imposed by the Authority of the Parliament of *Great Britain;* . . ."[17] Dulany was nettled but thought that such fuming scarcely deserved an answer.[18]

Another piece which affirmed the Parliamentary right to tax was *The Claim of the Colonies to an Exemption from Internal Taxes imposed by Authority of Parliament, Examined.*[19] The author, as one might learn from the context, was one of the colonial agents in London (William Knox of Georgia), and it was clear that this agent had succumbed to Grenville's charms. He had nothing but praise for the fairmindedness of the Minister who had inaugurated the Stamp Act and even implied that he had given the colonists an opportunity to avert it. Dulany knew well enough what kind of opportunity the colonists had actually had; he knew that no requisition had been sent in the regular form, no re-

[15] London, 1765.
[16] *Considerations*, 35.
[17] *Objections to Taxation*, 9.
[18] *Considerations*, 35.
[19] London, 1765.

quest made of the colonial assemblies before this naked act of power.

These pamphlets were irritating, because the authors all seemed unworthy of the great question they had undertaken to discuss. But there was a fourth publication, which could not be dismissed so lightly—the pamphlet entitled *The Regulations Lately Made concerning the Colonies and the Taxes Imposed upon Them, considered*.[20] This was evidently written by someone close to the Ministry. Dulany, like other Americans, attributed it to Grenville himself. Though the author was actually Thomas Whately, one of Grenville's secretaries, there can be little doubt that it represented Grenville's views.[21] Because of the source from which it came and the seriousness of its approach this was a much more important piece of work than the others which Dulany had seen, but it was full of pious self-congratulation on the wisdom of the present Ministry. Dulany could not help reflecting that the members of the present Ministry had formerly shown little enthusiasm for the great additions made to the empire in the last war by William Pitt but that now they seemed to regard themselves as the only ministers who had ever given attention to the empire.[22]

The Regulations Lately Made devoted most of its space to demonstrating the wisdom of the Sugar Act of 1764 as a means of directing the trade of the American colonies into proper channels; but in its last pages the author took up the question of Parliament's authority to tax the colonies and supported it with a plausible line of reasoning, all the more irritating because of the assurance with which it was delivered. After reading this and the other pamphlets and the accounts in the newspapers of the small opposition which the

[20] London, 1765.

[21] See ch. III, n. 6. For evidence that other Americans as well as Dulany, attributed the pamphlet to Grenville, see James C. Ballagh, ed., *The Letters of Richard Henry Lee* (New York, 1911), I, 7-10; article signed "Freeman," reprinted from *New York Gazette* in *Maryland Gazette*, August 1, 1765: and article signed "Colonus" in *Providence Gazette Extraordinary*, August 24, 1765.

[22] *Considerations*, 18-19. The quotation on these pages is compounded from pp. 5-15 of *The Regulations Lately Made*.

Stamp Act had met in Parliament, Dulany's indignation rose in the same way that the indignation of other Americans was rising all over the continent. Finally he set pen to paper and, with just enough anger to make his words bite, undertook to answer some of the specious contentions of the British pamphleteers and to prove to the satisfaction of both Englishmen and Americans that Parliament had no right to tax the colonies.

In the various apologies for Parliamentary taxation that had come into his hands during the preceding six months Dulany had been particularly struck by the absurdity of the argument for "virtual" representation. He could read in the *Pennsylvania Gazette* (May 16) in an extract of a letter from London that the Ministry had argued for the Stamp Act in Parliament on the ground "that the colonies were all virtually represented in Parliament, in the same manner as those of the subjects in Great Britain, who did not vote for representatives."[23] That the Ministry were founding their right to tax the colonies on this ground was evident also from the last pages of *The Regulations Lately Made.*

In reading this pamphlet Dulany could not have failed to perceive that Grenville had admitted that no British subject could be taxed without the consent of his representatives. Grenville had argued that Parliament had authority to tax the colonies only because they were represented in Parliament, not represented to be sure by delegates whom they themselves had chosen, but virtually represented by the delegates chosen in England. Grenville (speaking through Whately) had said:

. . . they [the colonies] claim it is true the Privilege, which is common to all *British* Subjects, of being taxed only with their own Consent, given by their Representatives; and may they ever enjoy the Privilege in all its Extent. May this sacred Pledge of Liberty be preserved inviolate, to the utmost Verge of our Dominions, and to the latest Page of

[23] The letter was designated as coming from a gentleman in London to his friend in Charles Town, South Carolina. Actually it was written by Charles Garth, the London agent of South Carolina, to the Assembly's Committee of Correspondence and is quoted in full in *English Historical Review*, 54 (1939), 649-650.

our History! but let us not limit the legislative Rights of the *British* People to Subjects of Taxation only: No new Law whatever can bind us that is made without the Concurrence of our Representatives. . . . For the Fact is, that the Inhabitants of the Colonies are represented in Parliament: they do not indeed chuse the Members of that Assembly; neither are Nine Tenths of the People of *Britain* Electors; . . . The Colonies are in exactly the same Situation: All *British* Subjects are really in the same: none are actually, all are virtually represented in Parliament; for every Member of Parliament sits in the House not as Representative of his own Constituents, but as one of that august Assembly by which all the Commons of *Great Britain* are represented. Their Rights and their Interests, however his own Borough may be affected by general Dispositions, ought to be the great Objects of his Attention, and the only Rules for his Conduct.[24]

Grenville went on to argue that not only the majority of the people of Great Britain but most of the land itself was represented in Parliament only by virtual representation; for there were many large towns, like Birmingham and Leeds, which elected no members. Later Grenville and his followers would drop this admission that the right to tax rested on the representative character of Parliament and rest the right simply on the all-powerful sovereignty of Parliament.[25] But in this pamphlet and in their arguments for passage of the

[24] *Regulations Lately Made,* 104-109.

[25] Dulany called attention to the shift when it took place. In a letter to General Conway, c. 1766, he wrote, "this idea of the Right to tax the Colonies by Statute, tho' they are not represented in Parliament, in any manner, has, it should seem, occurred since the Stamp Act, for if the right to tax and the right to regulate had been imagined by Mr. Grenville to be inseparable why did he task his ingenuity to find out a virtual Representation. Why did not some able friend intimate to him his Hazard on the Slippery ground, he chose, when the all powerful Sovereignty of Parliament might have afforded so safe a footing?" Sparks Mss., 44, Harvard College Library. Cf. the similar views expressed in a letter to Walter Dulany, c. 1766, in *Maryland Historical Magazine,* 14 (1919), 381.

Stamp Act, they upheld the principle for which the colonists would be contending during the next ten years, that a legislative body can tax only those persons who are represented in it. Dulany must have discerned that Grenville's whole position could be destroyed by showing that the colonies were not represented, either virtually or actually, in the British Parliament. If he did not perceive this obvious fact, a newspaper article, appearing first in the *New York Gazette,* and reprinted both in the *Pennsylvania Journal* (June 13, 20, 27) and in the *Maryland Gazette* (August 1) pointed it out to him. The author of this article, signing himself "Freeman," observed:

> that it was admitted in Parliament, even by the greatest Enemies to the Colonies, that they had in the fullest Sense, a Right to be Taxed only by their own Consent, given by their Representatives, but it was said by these Gentlemen, that the Colonies were *virtually* represented in the *English* Parliament—Here let the Reader note well, That the Minister grounds his Pretence of the Parliament's Right to Tax the Colonies, entirely upon this, *that they are* virtually *represented in Parliament:* If therefore he fails in the Proof of their being so Represented, he must, by his own Argument, give up the Point, and allow that the Parliament has no Manner of Right to tax the Colonies.

Dulany knew that it would be easy to convince his fellow-Americans that they were not virtually represented in Parliament. Not only was the idea repugnant to their interests, but it was repugnant to their whole conception of representative government. Within a week after he had written and published his pamphlet, and probably before they had read it, the people in Anne Arundel County declared in instructions to their members in the Maryland Assembly that "The MINISTER'S *virtual Representation* adduced argumentatively, in Support of the TAX on us is fantastical and frivolous."[26] In this declaration the people of Anne Arundel denied

[26] October 24 supplement to *Maryland Gazette,* October 10, 1765.

the idea of virtual representation not only by the substance of their statement but by their very manner of making it, in an instruction to their assemblymen, for the idea of virtual representation assumed that a legislator was not bound to his particular constituents or subject to their directions after his election, but that he represented the whole nation. Actually it had not been common for the electors in the southern colonies to direct their representatives because of the inconvenience of gathering the people of a whole county in order to draw up instructions. In the northern colonies, where representation in the assemblies was by town, the town meeting frequently instructed its delegate, not only on local matters but on general questions as well. The representative, in other words, was regarded as the agent of his constituents, and this conception prevailed in the southern colonies as well as the northern, even though the southerners could not readily act upon it. Consequently the idea of a virtual representation, in which the legislator acted for nobody in particular but everybody in general, was indeed "fantastical and frivolous" to the colonists.[27]

Dulany knew, however, that the idea had vogue in England. The great Algernon Sidney himself, in his *Discourses Concerning Government*, had affirmed that the members chosen for the various counties and boroughs were representatives of the whole nation, "and tho it be fit for them as Friends and Neighbors (so far as may be) to harken to the Opinions of the Electors for the Information of their Judgments, and to the end that what they shall say may be of more weight, when every one is known not to speak his own thoughts only, but those of a great number of men; yet they are not strictly and properly oblig'd to give account of their Actions to any, unless the whole Body of the Nation for which they serve, and who are equally concern'd in their Resolutions, could be assembled."[28] Perhaps Dulany remembered a debate that took place in Parliament in 1745 while

[27] See Kenneth Colegrove, "New England Town Mandates," Colonial Society of Massachusetts, *Publications*, 21 (1911), 411-449. Cf. *Colonial Records of North Carolina*, VII, 249-252.
[28] *Discourses Concerning Government*, sec. 44.

he was a student at the Middle Temple. Thomas Carew had argued for annual elections to the House of Commons in order that members might be kept in closer contact with their constituents, but Sir Thomas Yonge had ridden the bill down with a speech in which he pointed out that a member of Parliament after his election is "the attorney of the people of England, and as such is at full freedom to act as he thinks best for the people of England in general. He may receive, he may ask, he may even follow the advice of his particular constituents; but he is not obliged, nor ought he to follow their advice, if he thinks it inconsistent with the general interest of his country."[29]

This was the general belief in England by 1765. Within a few months William Blackstone reaffirmed it in his famous *Commentaries*,[30] and nine years later Edmund Burke gave it classic expression in his *Address to the Electors of Bristol*.[31] Thomas Whately and George Grenville in 1765 were simply extending the idea to cover the whole empire. Probably most Americans thought it had been stretched beyond the elastic limit in reaching Leeds and Birmingham. Dulany, however, was willing to concede all of Great Britain to the Ministry; he drew the line at the Atlantic Ocean, and he believed that he could demonstrate in terms irresistible to Englishmen as well as Americans, that the colonists were not represented in Parliament in the way that Englishmen were.

In a preface to his pamphlet Dulany acknowledged that "It would, now, be an unfashionable Doctrine, whatever the ancient Opinion might be, to affirm that the Constituent can bind his Representative by Instructions." The reason why instructions were not generally considered binding in England was that, as Grenville said, each member was considered the representative of those who did not participate in choosing him as well as of those who did. But this idea, despite its currency, had never been defined or carefully scrutinized. Dulany, accepting it as far as England was concerned, attempted to determine the meaning, and the only way in which he could

[29] *Parliamentary History*, XII, 1078.
[30] Bk. I, ch. 2, sec. 2.
[31] *Works* (4th edn., Boston, 1871), II, 94-98.

make sense of it was to assume that a dual representation was involved, whereby those who could participate in elections represented those who could not. In this way the members of Parliament actually represented the voters and virtually represented the non-voters. When this supposition was applied merely to England, it could be defended with some pretense of reason: it could be argued, for example, that voteless Leeds and Birmingham were adequately represented in a Parliament containing members from other industrial boroughs with similar interests. To extend the concept to the whole empire, however, was to reduce it to absurdity; to say that the voters of England had similar interests to the colonists' was so far from true that in the matter of taxation the very reverse was true. The author of *The Claim of the Colonies* admitted that it would be advantageous to both the Parliament and the people of Great Britain to load America with taxes, for every shilling that came to the Treasury from the colonies meant one shilling less to be collected at home.[32] A tax raised in England would affect the legislators who voted for it and the electors who chose them as well as the non-voting population, but a tax raised by Parliament in America would affect the people who levied it only by reducing their total tax bill. In this situation to say that the Americans were virtually represented in Parliament was ridiculous.

It was not true, moreover, that there was a great deal of English land not represented in Parliament. Grenville, in maintaining this proposition, had been thinking only of the borough representation. It was well known that this was based on a distribution of population which had long since changed, leaving empty shells of towns with representatives while newly risen industrial centers had none. But in addition to borough representatives Parliament contained two members from each county, so that every square foot of English land was represented, if not by a special borough member, then at least by the two county members. No English property-holder, therefore, was in the same situation as an American, who

---

[32] *Claim of the Colonies*, 28-30; cited in *Considerations*, 11.

could not participate in the election of any member. Not one acre of American ground was represented in Parliament; not one acre of English ground was unrepresented.

Dulany pursued these arguments to show that Americans were not represented in Parliament even by the standards of virtual representation, but he did not leave the matter there. He knew, whatever might be said about the representative's independence of his constituents, that in practice many members did follow instructions. Twenty-two years before, in 1743, just after he had taken his chambers at the Middle Temple, there had been a remarkable series of instructions sent by various boroughs to their members. In fact there was still among the family papers a letter he had written to his good father at the time, remarking that "The People are very bold in their instructions to their representatives, and insist very much upon having their Grievances redressed, before they grant any Supplies."[33] Dulany could agree with Sidney and with Sir Thomas Yonge, that the representatives were not bound by these instructions, but what representative, facing re-election, would be apt to ignore them? Even the most ardent advocates of virtual representation, as the conception had been defended before Grenville's time, had admitted the propriety of a member's hearing and possibly heeding the advice of his constituents and the right of his constituents to replace him at the next election if he did not. But to what member of Parliament could the Americans give advice? What member could they replace at the next election for violating their wishes? Instead of giving instructions they must appear as petitioners, humbly begging for favors. How could it be said, then, that Americans were represented in Parliament in anything like the way that Englishmen were?

Having demonstrated that virtual representation, as applied to America, was a fantasy, Dulany might have rested his case. He had shown that Grenville's policy of taxation was unwarranted by Grenville's own principles. But he had more to say. Like other Americans he was full of indignation at the

[33] January 22, 1743, Dulany Papers.

easy gestures with which English writers dismissed colonial rights. Something must be said on that score. Moreover, he did not want to leave the statement of the colonial position with a mere refutation of the idea of virtual representation. In a sense, if one accepted Grenville's avowed position, that no laws whatever could be made for Englishmen (including Americans) without the consent of their representatives, then a mere proof that Americans were not represented in Parliament would prove too much, for it would leave Parliament with no authority whatever in America, and such a result did not accord with Dulany's own views. What he wanted to do was to ascertain the limits of Parliament's authority, not to dissolve it utterly.

Dulany was careful to point out near the beginning of his essay that he was concerned with propriety and not with power.[34] Like other Englishmen and Americans he acknowledged that the power of Parliament was supreme: there was no institution or authority superior to Parliament which could legally call it to account. And yet there were admittedly things that it could not with propriety do. That excellent newspaper article by "Freeman" had pointed out: "No Parliament can alter the Nature of Things, or make that good which is really evil. If they could do this, then they might alter the whole Frame of the Constitution where they are chosen—They might make themselves independent on their Constituents, and be perpetual Dictators—or they might do any Thing— But this cannot be: There is certainly some Bounds to their Power, and 'tis Pity they were not more certainly known."[35] Englishmen were constantly sounding out the limits of Parliament's power in England, but in America, where that power had been so seldom exercised, the limits had not been ascertained. Dulany must have read "Freeman's" article, and he agreed that bounds should be prescribed beyond which Parliament could not with propriety wield its power over

[34] *Considerations*, 7.
[35] *Maryland Gazette*, August 1; *Pennsylvania Journal*, June 13, 20, 27.

Americans. This was necessary not only to arouse the colonists against Parliament's transgressions but also, he felt, to prevent the development of extravagant colonial claims of the type that were already beginning to appear, to the effect that Parliament had no power at all in America.

On May 30, for example, the *Maryland Gazette* had reprinted a piece from one of the northern newspapers in which the author maintained that the only relation between the people of England and those of the colonies was "that we are all the common subjects of the same King; and by any Thing that hath been said in the present controversy, I cannot find that the Inhabitants of the Colonies are *dependent* on the *People* of *Britain*, or the *People* of *Britain* on them, any more than *Kent* is on *Sussex*, or *Sussex* on *Kent*." Before the controversy was over the newspapers would be filled with shrill assertions that Parliament had "no more Legislative Authority over us than those that lived before the Flood."[36] On this basis even the Acts of Trade and Navigation would be unconstitutional, and indeed one writer in New York affirmed that the colonists had submitted to them only because of their expediency and not because of their legality.[37] This kind of talk, in Dulany's opinion at least, went a good deal too far. He was ready to acknowledge a dependence on Parliament; the question was how much, for it seemed to him perfectly reasonable that the colonists should be dependent without being reduced to the status of slaves. To be sure one English pamphleteer had maintained that any line between absolute dependency and independence was "a whimsical Imagination, a chimerical Speculation against Fact and Experience." This

[36] *Pennsylvania Journal*, February 6, 1766; *Maryland Gazette*, February 20, 1766; *Boston Gazette*, February 24, 1766. *Prologue to Revolution*, 71-77.

[37] *Considerations upon the Rights of the Colonists to the Privileges of British Subjects* (New York, 1766), 11. For other statements of the view that Parliament had no authority in the colonies and that the only connection between England and the colonies was a common King, see *Providence Gazette*, August 18, 1764; *Boston Gazette*, March 17, 1766.

assertion, said Dulany, contained "more Confidence than Solidity," and he determined to disprove it.[38]

Dulany was a lawyer, and he set about establishing the bounds of Parliament's authority with a lawyer-like regard for tradition and precedent. Other spokesmen for the colonial cause had already begun to argue in terms of the natural rights of man,[39] but Dulany knew that however such arguments might appeal to Americans, they would carry small weight in the British Parliament. The question, as he saw it, did not hinge so much on natural rights as it did on constitutional rights. As long as the colonists had the constitution on their side—and he was sure that they had—it would be best for them to ground their arguments upon it.

On the other hand Dulany did not make the mistake of supposing that the British constitution was so exact a body of principles that its interpretation could be left to the determination of legal experts. He could remember several opinions of legal experts employed by ministries in the past, opinions on American affairs, and they all declared that to be legal which the Minister for the time being deemed to be expedient. Dulany knew that the law was a fallible instrument, and when it came to deciding what was constitutional and what was not, the opinion of a lawyer was to be trusted only insofar as his arguments were convincing. In deter-

[38] *Considerations*, 14. I have not been able to identify the quotation which Dulany refers to. In citing his opponents' arguments Dulany generally stated what he took to be their position, sometimes quoting word for word, more often summarizing or paraphrasing, but always including the whole in quotation marks as though it were an exact transcription. Most of his quotations can be traced to one of the pamphlets discussed above, but this one has eluded me.

[39] For the statements of natural rights during the Stamp Act period, see James Otis, *The Rights of the Colonies Asserted and Proved*, 34; the New York Assembly's Petition to the House of Commons of October 18, 1764, *Journal of the Votes and Proceedings . . .* (New York, 1766), II, 776-779; Pennsylvania Resolves and Massachusetts Resolves of 1765, cited in Chapter VII; articles in *Boston Gazette*, November 18, 1765, December 2, 1765; *Boston Post-Boy and Advertiser*, December 30, 1765; and resolves by Sons of Liberty in various towns, cited in Chapter XI.

mining the bounds of Parliament's authority in the colonies, therefore, Dulany made no pretense of relying upon bare legal precedents but sought to rest his case upon what he took to be acknowledged principles of the constitution and upon the manner in which those principles had hitherto been applied in English and American history.

The fundamental principle of the British constitution, as Dulany understood it, prescribed a mixed government, compounded of monarchy, aristocracy, and democracy, represented respectively by the King, the House of Lords, and the House of Commons. This was not a peculiar belief of Dulany's but rather a commonplace of political theory at the time. In the threefold division, Dulany observed, the levying of taxes was generally considered "the Province of the House of Commons as the Representative of the People."[40] Taxation was regarded, in other words, not as an act of sovereign power by the whole legislature, but as a free gift of the people by their representatives. In support of this statement he had only to point out that the House of Commons alone could originate a bill of taxation and the other branches of the government were allowed merely to assent to it without modification. This procedure embodied the principle which Grenville had acknowledged, that no British subject could be taxed except by the consent of his representatives. Though the American colonists were British subjects, they were not represented in Parliament but only in their colonial assemblies. Therefore the colonial assemblies could tax them, but Parliament could not. Parliament had authority to tax only those persons who were represented in the House of Commons, namely the people of England, Scotland, and Wales.

Dulany, though insistent that Parliament's right to tax was limited, upheld its right to legislate for all British subjects, including the Irish and the Americans, who were not represented in it. He saw no inconsistency here, because for him taxation and legislation were two separate functions, the former associated with the representative character of the

House of Commons, the latter with the supreme authority of Parliament. Parliament was entitled to legislate for both mother country and colonies, because its legislative power derived not from its representative character (as Grenville apparently believed) but from its sovereignty over the whole empire.

Since Dulany was concerned about the issue of Parliamentary taxation rather than Parliamentary legislation, he did not define the latter except on points where confusion between the two might arise. For instance, while admitting that the colonies by their very nature were dependencies of their mother country and that "the supreme authority vested in the King, Lords, and Commons may justly be exercised to secure, or preserve their Dependance whenever necessary for that Purpose,"[41] he hastened to deny that this implied a right to tax. As Dulany put it, "tho' the Right of the Superior to use the proper Means for preserving the Subordination of his Inferior is admitted, yet, it does not necessarily follow, that he has a Right to seize the Property of his Inferior when he pleases."[42] And again, "The Right of Exemption from all Taxes *without their Consent*, the Colonies claim as *British* Subjects. . . . On the other Hand, they acknowledge themselves to be subordinate to the Mother-Country and that the Authority vested in the supreme Council of the Nation, may be justly exercised to support and preserve that Subordination."[43]

What Dulany meant by supporting and preserving the subordination of the colonies he made clear in several places: he meant that Parliament might regulate the trade of the empire, as it had done in the Acts of Trade and Navigation, in order to insure that the colonies subserve the economic interests of the mother country. He even admitted that regulations of trade might take the form of import or export duties levied in the colonies and that such duties might produce an "incidental Revenue," but he put those words in italics and followed them by a demonstration that regulations

[41] *Ibid.*, 15.
[42] *Ibid.*, 15.
[43] *Ibid.*, 28.

of trade in the past could not be regarded as taxes, for they had clearly not been made with an intention of producing revenue.[44] This he could prove readily by evidence which Grenville himself had provided. In *The Regulations Lately Made* Grenville had supplied figures on customs duties in America which indicated that the average annual remittance from such duties during the past thirty years had been less than £2000, while the cost of collecting them had been £7600. Duties which cost four times as much to collect as they produced might well be justified as regulations of trade, but they could scarcely be regarded as taxes levied for the purpose of revenue.[45]

The gist of Dulany's whole argument was that taxation formed no part of the authority which Parliament enjoyed as the supreme power in the empire. Taxation was the function of representative bodies, and the only representative bodies in America were the colonial assemblies, so that an American could "give his Consent in no other Manner than in Assembly."[46] In maintaining this position Dulany was unable to refrain from lashing out in digression after digression against various absurdities he had found in the British pamphleteers. He was too angry to keep his remarks entirely on the high level of constitutional theory; and he found occasion to make effective use of a number of ideas and episodes that had been rankling in his mind. Remembering, for example, that the stamp tax had been levied ostensibly to help defray the expense of the troops stationed in America, he made sarcastic reference to an episode he had read of in the newspapers: some of the troops stationed in Canada, displeased with the judgment of a civil court in sentencing one of their officers to prison, had entered the judge's house and cut off his ears and slit his nose.[47] Was money needed in the British exchequer, Dulany asked, so that troops could be "employed in the national Service of Cropping the Ears, and Slitting the

[44] *Ibid.*, 34-35.
[45] *Regulations Lately Made*, 57; *Considerations*, 35.
[46] *Considerations*, 29.
[47] *Maryland Gazette*, July 18, 1765.

Nostrils of the Civil Magistrates, as Marks of Distinction?"[48]
Sometimes in these slashing attacks Dulany hit below the belt,
as when he attributed to Thomas Pownall views which the
latter had never held.[49] Nevertheless, fair or unfair, his blows
struck home, and in spite of all digressions he hammered out
his main point, that Parliament's authority in the colonies had
limits this side of the right to tax.

It was only when he came to discuss the question of what
steps the colonists ought to take if Parliament overstepped
its bounds, that Dulany touched a note of moderation. Even
here he spoke as though he meant to propose a vigorous resistance. "Instead of moping, and puling, and whining to
excite Compassion; in such a Situation we ought with Spirit,
and Vigour, and Alacrity, to bid Defiance to Tyranny, by
exposing it's Impotence, by making it as contemptible, as it
would be detestable."[50] How then were the colonies to make
tyranny contemptible? "By a vigorous Application to Manufactures."[51] The colonists must go to their looms and spinning
wheels and make Britain tremble for the loss of her colonial
customers. Even this measure Dulany thought would be improper for the colonial assemblies to direct, but the assemblymen might at least set an example: "The Sight of our Representatives, all adorned in compleat Dresses of their own
Leather, and Flax, and Wool . . . would excite, not the Gaze
of Admiration, the Flutter of an agitated Imagination, or the
momentary Amusement of a transient Scene, but a calm,
solid, heart-felt Delight."[52]

This was something of a comedown from the warm words
with which Dulany had blasted Grenville and his adherents.
After arguing that virtual representation did not extend to
America, Dulany seems to have found no inconsistency in
recommending a course of action which assumed that it did.
By reducing purchases of British manufactures, he thought,
the Americans would be able to alarm the British merchants

[48] *Considerations,* 42.
[49] *Ibid.,* 13.
[50] *Ibid.,* 47.
[51] *Ibid.,* 47.
[52] *Ibid.,* 48.

and enlist their support in Parliament. He apparently did not see that the success of such procedure might serve as a partial refutation of his argument that American interest could not be felt by a Parliament elected entirely in Great Britain. Actually economic pressure was already being applied before his recommendations appeared, and did help to bring about repeal; but by that time it was no longer necessary for him to explain his inconsistency, for Parliament had ceased to justify its authority over the colonies by the doctrine of virtual representation. Virtual representation had become a dead issue, and Dulany had helped to kill it.[53]

Meanwhile Dulany's pamphlet was bought by his countrymen as they had scarcely bought any pamphlet before. Its articulation and justification of their own instinctive view of colonial rights delighted them. Already before its publication they had begun in their assemblies to do what Dulany did, to draw a line between Parliamentary authority and American rights. When they had done with argument and debate, it appeared that the united determination of Americans from Georgia to New Hampshire agreed with the private opinion of Daniel Dulany.

[53] See below, chs. XV, XVI, and above, n. 25.

Chapter VII

Resolution

PARLIAMENT HAD NOT rejected the American petitions; Parliament had simply refused to consider them at all, and thereby made painfully clear how much its members cared for the rights of the colonies. The early news reports showed that the Ministry had not only swept aside the colonial petitions but had pushed through the Stamp Act with no opposition worthy of the name. Had the members been satisfied with Grenville's fatuous talk about virtual representation? Had they supposed that the colonists would submit tamely to an act which violated the very basis of constitutional government? Had they thought that by refusing to hear the petitions they could silence two and a half million voices? Evidently they had. It would be necessary, then, to show them that Americans would not be satisfied with virtual representation, would not submit tamely, would not be silent.

In Williamsburg, Virginia, the House of Burgesses was going through the routine business of the May session—bills for building roads, docking entails, selling surplus military supplies, offering bounties on wolves—when news arrived that the petitions over which the Assembly had labored the previous year had not received a hearing and that stamp duties would be collected in America.[1] The Burgesses left no

[1] According to Edmund Pendleton, writing in 1790, the news of the Stamp Act came in a letter from Edward Montague, the Virginia agent, toward the end of the session, after many members had already gone home. E. S. Morgan, "Edmund Pendleton on the Virginia Resolves," *Maryland Historical Magazine,* 46 (1951), 71-80. It may be that Montague's letter took from early February until late May to reach Virginia, but the news it contained was printed in the *Pennsylvania Gazette* on April 18, the *Maryland Gazette* on April 25, and the *Georgia Gazette* on May 2. Copies of the *Virginia Gazette* for these months are not extant, but it is inconceivable that the news did not reach Virginia before the end of May.

record of what they thought about the treatment of their petitions, but one may guess that they felt the same indignation that other colonists expressed. For example, William Smith, Jr., one of the authors of the New York petitions, wrote to a friend in England:

When the Americans reflect upon the Parliament's refusal to hear their Representations—when they read abstracts of the speeches within doors [inside Parliament], and the ministerial pamphlets without, and find themselves tantalized and contemned, advantages taken of their silence heretofore, and Remonstrances forbidden in time to come; and above all, when they see the prospects of innumerable loads arising from this connection with an overburdened nation interested in shaking the weight off of their own shoulders, and commanding silence in the oppressed Beast on which it is cast; what can be expected but discontent for a while, and in the end open opposition. The boldness of the Minister amazes our people. This single stroke has lost Great Britain the affection of all her Colonies.[2]

But William Smith did not propose immediate opposition, and similarly the men who had drawn up Virginia's petitions do not appear to have felt the need for replying at once to the Ministry's challenge. Most of the Burgesses, when the calendar of routine business was nearing completion, packed their bags and left the heat of Williamsburg for the comfort of their plantations. It was not the authors of the petitions but a new member who insisted on translating them without delay into a declaration of rights. Most of the old members had already departed when Patrick Henry, who had been admitted to the House only nine days before, rose to introduce a series of resolutions against the Stamp Act.

What Henry said and what the Burgesses did are clear in legend but cloudy in history. Thirty-nine Burgesses were present in the Chamber, and several spectators were watching in the lobby, but so far as we know today only one, a visiting stranger, wrote down any part of what he heard and saw. The

[2] Massachusetts Historical Society, *Collections*, 4th ser., 10 (1871), 570-571.

first newspaper to report what happened was some five hundred miles away. The first attempt to reconstruct the event was twenty-five years and a revolution later, and the second attempt was forty to fifty years later and only succeeded in giving form to a legend. James Madison made the first attempt in 1790, by writing to Edmund Pendleton, one of the authors of the petitions of 1764. Pendleton answered as best he could, but it turned out that he was one of those who had already left for home when it happened and could only reply with dimly remembered hearsay.[3] Madison did not pursue the inquiry further, and by the time that William Wirt took it up in 1805, there were only two or three old men who could remember. Of these Thomas Jefferson, who had watched from the lobby, had the most vivid recollection, but forty-year-old recollections, however vivid, are apt to be compounded of fact and fantasy; and when Wirt put together his findings in a life of Patrick Henry, he drew a picture which merely perpetuated the legend that had already developed.[4]

The legend was one of Patrick Henry pouring forth torrents of sublime eloquence and bidding defiance to the shouts of "treason!" which rang from all corners of the House. The legend in all its appealing and dramatic simplicity still lingers for the schoolboy, but is now denied to adults, for in 1921 a contemporary eye-witness account turned up in the journal of an unknown French traveler, who had stood with Jefferson in the lobby of the House of Burgesses on May 30 and 31, 1765. Of all the spectators and of all the thirty-nine Burgesses, this anonymous stranger was the only one who left a message for future historians, and though his account contains at least one recognizable error of fact, it is the only direct road that we can follow back to those critical days when Virginia pointed the way to freedom.

May the 30th. Set out Early from halfway house in the Chair and broke fast at York, arived at williamsburg at 12, where I saw three Negroes hanging at the galous for have-

[3] *Maryland Historical Magazine,* 46 (1951), 74.
[4] *Sketches of the Life and Character of Patrick Henry* (Philadelphia, 1817).

ing robed Mr. Waltho of 300 ps. I went imediately to the assembly which was seting, where I was entertained with very strong Debates Concerning Dutys that the parlement wants to lay on the american Colonys, which they Call or Stile stamp Dutys. Shortly after I Came in one of the members stood up and said he had read that in former times tarquin and Julus had their Brutus, Charles had his Cromwell, and he Did not Doubt but some good american would stand up, in favour of his Country, but (says he) in a more moderate manner, and was going to Continue, when the speaker of the house rose and Said, he, the last that stood up had spoke traison, and was sorey to see that not one of the members of the house was loyal Enough to stop him, before he had gone so far, upon which the Same member stood up again (his name is henery) and said that if he had afronted the speaker, or the house, he was ready to ask pardon, and he would shew his loyalty to his majesty King G. the third, at the Expence of the last Drop of his blood, but what he had said must be atributed to the Interest of his Countrys Dying liberty which he had at heart, and the heat of passion might have lead him to have said something more than he intended, but, again, if he said any thing wrong, he beged the speaker and the houses pardon. some other Members stood up and backed him, on which that afaire was droped.[5]

This account gives us a ringside seat in the House of Burgesses for long enough to deflate the legend of Henry's daring. Unfortunately it fails to tell us exactly what he proposed that the Burgesses do about the Stamp Act. From the official records we can discover that they passed four resolutions on that afternoon, and if we are to believe Henry himself and the recollections of Pendleton and Jefferson, Henry was arguing for the passage of these resolutions in his famous speech. In the printed Journals of the House they stand as follows:

Resolved, That the first Adventurers and Settlers of this his Majesty's Colony and Dominion of *Virginia* brought with them, and transmitted to their Posterity, and all other his Majesty's Subjects since inhabiting in this his Majesty's said Colony, all the Liberties, Privileges, Franchises, and Immunities, that have at any Time been held, enjoyed, and possessed, by the people of *Great Britain.*

Resolved, That by two royal Charters, granted by King *James* the First, the Colonists aforesaid are declared entitled to all Liberties, Privileges, and Immunities of Denizens and natural Subjects, to all Intents and Purposes, as if they had been abiding and born within the Realm of *England.*

Resolved, That the Taxation of the People by themselves, or by Persons chosen by themselves to represent them, who can only know what Taxes the People are able to bear, or the easiest Method of raising them, and must themselves be affected by every Tax laid on the People, is the only Security against a burthensome Taxation, and the distinguishing Characteristick of *British* Freedom, without which the ancient Constitution cannot exist.

Resolved, That his Majesty's liege People of this his most ancient and loyal Colony have without Interruption enjoyed the inestimable Right of being governed by such Laws, respecting their internal Polity and Taxation, as are derived from their own Consent, with the Approbation of their Sovereign, or his Substitute; and that the same hath never been forfeited or yielded up, but hath been constantly recognized by the Kings and People of *Great Britain.*[6]

Was this, then, the action which Henry urged upon the Burgesses? Or was this a compromise representing something less than he asked for? Or was it perhaps more? The printed record is silent, and the manuscript record has disappeared, but a letter from Governor Fauquier to the Board of Trade, on June 5, indicates that the four resolutions in the Journals must originally have been followed by a fifth:

[6] John Pendleton Kennedy, ed., *Journals of the House of Burgesses of Virginia, 1761–1765* (Richmond, 1907), 360. This and the other documents relating to the Virginia resolves are in *Prologue to Revolution,* 46-50.

On Wednesday the 29th of May, just at the end of the Session when most of the members had left the town, there being but 39 present out of 116 of which the House of Burgesses now consists, a motion was made to take into consideration the Stamp Act, a copy of which had crept into the House, and in a Committee of the whole House five resolutions were proposed and agreed to, all by very small majorities. On Thursday the 30th they were reported and agreed to by the House, the numbers being as before in the Committee; the greatest majority being 22 to 17; for the 5th Resolution, 20 to 19 only.[7]

What was this fifth resolution which passed by so narrow a majority and which is missing from the records? When Patrick Henry died, he left behind a paper on which five resolutions were written, four of them (with slight verbal alterations) as they stood in the Journal, the fifth one reading:

> Resolved Therefore that the General Assembly of this Colony have the only and sole exclusive Right and Power to lay Taxes and Impositions upon the Inhabitants of this Colony and that every Attempt to vest such Power in any other Person or Persons whatsoever other than the General Assembly aforesaid has a manifest Tendency to destroy British as well as American Freedom.[8]

This resolution, it may be, was the fifth one, which passed by so slender a margin. Though it does not differ much from the others, it is more specific in its assertions and may therefore have earned fewer votes. We have the Frenchman's word for it that the debates were "very strong," and Jefferson even forty years later recalled that the debate on the fifth one was "most bloody."[9] Jefferson also remembered how Peyton Randolph walked into the lobby afterward exclaiming, "by God, I would have given 500 guineas for a single vote."[10]

[7] *Ibid.,* lxvii.
[8] *Ibid.,* frontispiece.
[9] *Pa. Mag. of Hist.,* 34 (1910), 389.
[10] *Ibid.* Nine years later Jefferson recalled it as 100 guineas, *ibid.,* 399.

A single vote would have divided the house evenly on the fifth resolution, and Randolph knew that John Robinson, the Speaker, would then have been called to cast the deciding vote and would have voted against it.

Why Randolph, Robinson, Robert Carter Nicholas, and even Richard Bland and George Wythe, all of whom are said to have opposed the resolutions, should have been so hostile to them is not apparent. Most of these men had been active in drawing up the petitions of the preceding year, and Henry's resolutions did little more than paraphrase the petitions. George Wythe, who had drawn the petition to the House of Commons, told Jefferson that his first draft had required toning down because the other members of the committee thought it treasonable.[11] And Richard Bland was soon to express in print a view of Parliament's authority which was at least as restricted as that taken in the resolutions.[12] The argument of the opposition, if correctly recalled by Jefferson and Edmund Pendleton, was that the petitions of the preceding year were a sufficient statement of the colonial position and that no further step should be taken until some answer was received to these. But this argument was specious, for the Burgesses knew that the petitions had not received a hearing. In all probability, the opposition is not to be explained so much by the measure itself as by the men who were backing it. Henry and his friends were upstarts in Virginia politics, and their introduction of the resolves constituted a challenge to the established leaders of the House of Burgesses.[13]

In any case Randolph and the others who opposed the resolutions were so much upset by their failure to defeat them that they determined, possibly with the advice and approval of the Governor, to get them reversed. On the morning of May 31 when Jefferson went to the House to see what was coming next he found Peter Randolph, a member of the Governor's Council (and a cousin of Peyton's) thumbing through the Journals in search of a precedent for expunging

[11] *Ibid.*, 400.
[12] *An Inquiry into the Rights of the British Colonies* (Williamsburg, 1766).
[13] See Carl Bridenbaugh, *Seat of Empire* (Williamsburg, 1950).

a vote of the House.[14] Though Jefferson stood with him at the clerk's desk for an hour or two till the House bell announced the opening of the meeting, he could not recall whether Randolph found the precedent or not, but when the Burgesses met they did carry a motion to erase the fifth resolution. The Burgesses' Journal is entirely void of any mention of the Stamp Act under May 31. The votes of that day were either not recorded or were erased along with the fifth resolution. But Jefferson's recollection of the expunging is confirmed by Governor Fauquier's letter, which states that on the thirty-first, "there having happened a small alteration in the House there was an attempt to strike all the Resolutions off the Journals. The 5th which was thought the most offensive was accordingly struck off, but it did not succeed as to the other four."[15]

Governor Fauquier does not say how the small alteration in the House occurred, but Jefferson remembered in 1805 that Patrick Henry himself left Williamsburg on the evening of the thirtieth.[16] If Jefferson was right, then Henry himself may be held partly responsible for the rescinding of the fifth resolution, for assuming that no one else changed sides, the loss of his vote would have split the house. Did Henry leave because he thought that the matter had been decided and would not be reconsidered? Did he pair his vote with some other departing legislator from the other side? Or did Peyton Randolph perhaps find a way of spending his five hundred guineas for a single vote?

We will probably never know the answer, but of one thing we can be certain, that though the conservatives were able to get the fifth resolution rescinded before the House dissolved on the first of June, they were not able to keep it out of the newspapers. Word spread to the other colonies, and copies of the resolves were being passed around in Philadelphia by the middle of June.[17] One Philadelphian sent a copy to a friend

[14] *Pa. Mag. of Hist.*, 34 (1910), 399.

[15] *Journals of the House of Burgesses*, lxvii.

[16] *Pa. Mag. of Hist.*, 34 (1910), 389.

[17] Thomas Wharton and Joseph Galloway sent copies to Benjamin Franklin on June 15 and June 18, respectively (Franklin Papers, American Philosophical Society, I, 152, 147).

in Newport, and here on June 24 the *Newport Mercury* gained the distinction of being the first newspaper to print them. Most of the other papers picked up the story from the *Mercury*, but the *Maryland Gazette* ran its own version on July 4, from a source closer to the original.

The puzzling thing about the resolves as printed in the newspapers is that they were not four in number as in the Journals of the Burgesses, or five, as in Patrick Henry's copy, but six in the *Newport Mercury*, and seven in the *Maryland Gazette*. The complete text, as given by the *Gazette*, has a slightly different wording from the five resolves we have considered and includes two new ones.

RESOLVES of the House of Burgesses in VIRGINIA, *June* 1765.

That the first Adventurers & Settlers of this his Majesty's Colony and Dominion of *Virginia*, brought with them, and transmitted to their Posterity, and all other his Majesty's Subjects since inhabiting in this his Majesty's Colony, all the Liberties, Privileges, Franchises, and Immunities, that at any Time have been held, enjoyed, and possessed, by the People of *Great Britain*.

That by Two Royal Charters, granted by King *James* the First, the Colonies aforesaid are Declared Entitled, to all Liberties, Privileges and Immunities, of Denizens and Natural Subjects (to all Intents and Purposes) as if they had been Abiding and Born within the Realm of *England*.

That the Taxation of the People by Themselves, or by Persons Chosen by Themselves to Represent them, who can only know what Taxes the People are able to bear, or the easiest Method of Raising them, and must themselves be affected by every Tax laid upon the People, is the only Security against a Burthensome Taxation; and the Distinguishing Characteristic of *British* FREEDOM; and, without which, the antient Constitution cannot exist.

That his Majesty's Liege People of this his most Ancient and Loyal Colony, have, without Interruption, the inestimable Right of being Governed by such Laws, respecting their internal Polity and Taxation, as are derived from their own Consent, with the Approbation of their Sovereign, or his Substitute; which Right hath never been Forfeited, or Yielded up; but hath been constantly recognized by the Kings and People of *Great Britain.*

Resolved therefore, That the General Assembly of this Colony, with the Consent of his Majesty, or his Substitute, HAVE the Sole Right and Authority to lay Taxes and Impositions upon It's Inhabitants: And, That every Attempt to vest such Authority in any other Person or Persons whatsoever, has a Manifest Tendency to Destroy AMERICAN FREEDOM.

That his Majesty's Liege People, Inhabitants of this Colony, are not bound to yield Obedience to any Law or Ordinance whatsoever, designed to impose any Taxation upon them, other than the Laws or Ordinances of the General Assembly as aforesaid.

That any Person who shall, by Speaking, or Writing, assert or maintain, That any Person or Persons, other than the General Assembly of this Colony, with such Consent as aforesaid, have any Right or Authority to lay or impose any Tax whatever on the Inhabitants thereof, shall be Deemed, AN ENEMY TO THIS HIS MAJESTY'S COLONY.

The *Mercury,* and the papers copying from it, printed six of these in approximately the same form as the *Maryland Gazette*[18] but omitted altogether the third resolve.

The question is where the two extra resolves came from. Possibly they were part of a set of original proposals prepared by Henry and whoever was working with him. The records of the Burgesses indicate that the resolves were amended before their passage, and the amendment may have consisted of striking out the last two as given in the newspaper version. Governor Fauquier, who was not himself present, reported that the initiators of the resolutions had two more "in their pocket, but finding the difficulty they had

[18] The most notable difference is in the fourth resolution where the phrase "internal polity and taxation" as given in the *Maryland Gazette* and in the *Journals of the House of Burgesses* is altered to "taxation and internal police."

in carrying the 5th which was by a single voice, and knowing them to be more virulent and inflammatory; they did not produce them."[19] Fauquier was right in supposing that the extra resolutions were more violent than the others, but he was wrong in supposing that they were not introduced, for the Frenchman, who like Jefferson returned to the Burgesses on the thirty-first, reported:

> *May the 31th.* I returned to the assembly today, and heard very hot Debates stil about the Stamp Dutys. the whole house was for Entering resolves on the records but they Differed much with regard the Contents or purport thereof. some were for shewing their resentment to the highest. one of the resolves that these proposed, was that any person that would offer to sustain that the parlement of Engl'd had a right to impose or lay any tax or Dutys whats'r on the american Colonys, without the Consent of the inhabitants thereof, Should be looked upon as a traitor, and Deemed an Enemy to his Country. there were some others to the same purpose, and the majority was for Entring these resolves, upon which the Governor Disolved the assembly, which hinderd their proceeding.[20]

Unquestionably this refers to the seventh resolution. It is possible that the Frenchman recorded this event under the wrong date. The latter part of the entry for May 31 refers to events of succeeding days, and he may have written the whole entry some days later. In so doing he could have ascribed to the thirty-first what he actually heard on the thirtieth. But there is no reason to doubt that the Burgesses did debate the seventh resolution. If the Frenchman was right in dating the debate on the thirty-first, and if Fauquier was right in asserting that only five resolutions were proposed, then the fact that the seventh resolution was discussed would indicate that it was the one passed on May 30 and rescinded on May 31.

In 1814 Jefferson offered Wirt another theory about the identity of the rescinded resolution: "the 5th has clearly

<hr/>

[19] *Journals of the House of Burgesses,* lxvii–lxviii.
[20] *American Historical Review,* 26 (1920–1921), 745–746.

nothing to justify the debate and proceedings which one of them produced. but the 6th is of that character, and perfectly tallies with the idea impressed on my mind of that which was expunged . . . my hypothesis then is this, that the two disagreed to were the 5th. & 7th. the 5th. because merely tautologous of the 3d. & 4th. and 7th. because leading to individual persecution, for which no mind was then prepared."[21]

If either of the above hypotheses was the case, then the Burgesses were ready on May 30 to go much farther in asserting their rights than has generally been supposed, for both the sixth and the seventh were much more radical than the fifth. But neither of these theories can be considered conclusive: the first rests on slim, albeit entirely contemporary evidence; the second rests on recollection too distant to be trustworthy. On the other hand, the evidence that the fifth resolution was the one rescinded rests solely on the copy found among Henry's papers. The copy is not in Henry's hand and is undated, and Henry's endorsement on the back (which states that these were the resolutions passed) was made many years after the episode. It is certainly not free enough of suspicion to be conclusive evidence.

It would be useful to know which resolution the Burgesses were willing to pass but not to retain after second thought, for it would help us to assess their temper, but unless new evidence appears no positive answer can be given. Of one thing we can nevertheless be certain: they did debate the question of resistance, for the seventh resolution which the Frenchman heard them discuss, presupposed that the Stamp Act would be resisted.

What remains as the indubitable position of the Burgesses with regard to Parliament's authority is the first four resolutions. Fauquier expressed the hope that the House at its next session would reverse these four as it had the fifth.[22] But when the Burgesses met again, he was disappointed. They did

---

[21] *Pa. Mag. of Hist.*, 34 (1910), 398.
[22] Fauquier to Henry Seymour Conway, November 24, 1765, House of Lords Manuscripts, February 6, 1766, Library of Congress transcripts.

not adopt or reaffirm any of the radical extra resolutions, but neither did they revoke the four.

Here then was Virginia's position, and in all essentials it was the same as that defined later in more detail by Daniel Dulany. In phrases borrowed largely from the petitions which had been so fruitlessly delivered to Parliament, the Virginians claimed the rights of Englishmen, and affirmed that one of these was the right to be taxed only by "persons chosen by themselves to represent them" (no room for virtual representation there). The resolutions did not attempt to state what powers Parliament did have in Virginia but only what powers it did not have. As for the action people might take when Parliament went beyond its powers, the resolves said nothing. The unapproved ones had called for resistance, a course which Virginians as private citizens might still adopt, but without the official approval or disapproval of their government.

Although the Burgesses had stopped short of recommending resistance, the resolves were too much for Joseph Royle, the conservative editor of the *Virginia Gazette*. He failed to print them, and consequently the other colonies, instead of obtaining a relatively reliable text from a publication in the colony itself, got news of Virginia's action from the more ardent supporters of the resolutions. Henry and his friends, having failed to secure passage of their most radical items in the House of Burgesses, were able to get them passed unanimously in the newspapers: every newspaper which carried the resolutions printed the fifth, sixth, and seventh as though they had been adopted. When Royle complained that the other papers were stuffed with false news about Virginia, the radicals could reply that "If Mr. *Royle* had been pleased to publish those Resolves, the *Authenticity* of his *Intelligence*, would have been undisputed, and he would not have had any Reason of complaint on that Score."[23]

To the other colonists, then, the Virginia Burgesses appeared much bolder than they had actually been, and their supposed example stirred up other assemblies to a degree of

[23] *Maryland Gazette*, October 3, 1765.

emulation which sometimes surpassed the original. The first colony to imitate Virginia was Rhode Island, where the resolves had first been printed. The Rhode Island Assembly met in May and June, after passage of the Stamp Act had been reported but before news of Virginia's action, and took no notice of the Act. It was not until the September session that the members from Providence, by instruction from their town meeting, moved a series of resolutions copied after those attributed to Virginia.[24] As adopted, the Rhode Island resolutions included the first, second, fourth, fifth, and sixth, all of which had been printed in the *Newport Mercury*; but Rhode Island, not being a royal colony, saw no reason to include the phrase, "together with his Majesty or his Substitutes" contained in Virginia's fifth resolution, and in the sixth resolution, the one calling for resistance, Rhode Island inserted the word "internal" before the word taxation. In the preceding resolutions, which denied Parliament's authority to tax, no distinction was made between kinds of taxation, but the appeal for resistance was directed against "internal taxation." In order to implement the general purpose of this resolution the Rhode Islanders added another and final one, which read:

That all the officers in this colony, appointed by the authority thereof, be, and they are hereby, directed to proceed in the execution of their respective offices in the same manner as usual; and that this Assembly will indemnify and save harmless all the said officers, on account of their conduct, agreeably to this resolution.[25]

Rhode Island alone, by endorsing resistance, dared to speak to Parliament as impudently as everyone supposed that Virginia had spoken, but even Rhode Island did not go so far as to declare that supporters of the Stamp Act were guilty of treason. The other colonies stopped short, as Virginia had in reality, of approving resistance, but every colony which later participated in the Revolution, with the exception of Georgia, North Carolina, Delaware, and New Hampshire, eventually

[24] *Newport Mercury*, August 19, 1765.
[25] *Records of the Colony of Rhode Island*, VI, 451-452. *Prologue to Revolution*, 50-51.

passed declaratory resolutions defining their rights. Most of these denied the authority of Parliament to extend the jurisdiction of admiralty courts; all of them denied its authority to tax the colonies.[26] Those colonies which had made somewhat limited objections to Parliamentary taxation in 1764 now set the matter straight. Rhode Island had been one of these. Connecticut was another, and she clarified her position in a set of resolutions also copied in part from those of Virginia.[27] It was Massachusetts, however, that had been most equivocal the previous year, in omitting all mention of rights in her address to Parliament. And in Massachusetts the effect of the Virginia Resolves was electric.

The House of Representatives in the Bay had never been happy about the address which Lieutenant-Governor Hutchinson had persuaded them to adopt. When they saw the spirited assertion of rights that New York had sent to Parliament shortly after theirs, they were ashamed of their own moderation. Governor Bernard, however, had assured them that their message would be well received and have good effects.[28] When the Stamp Act was passed and the members refused to hear any petitions at all, many of the representatives in the Massachusetts Assembly must have felt that it would have been far better to assert their principles and to hang for a sheep instead of a lamb.[29] Oxenbridge Thacher, who had penned the original assertion of colonial rights, for which Hutchinson's timid plea had been substituted, lay on his deathbed when news of what the Virginians had done reached

---

[26] I have discussed these resolution in "Colonial Ideas of Parliamentary Power," *William and Mary Quarterly,* 3d ser., 5 (1948), 311-341. See pp. 320-325. All the resolves are printed in *Prologue to Revolution,* 47-62. The governor prevented action in North Carolina by keeping the Assembly prorogued. Delaware participated in the Stamp Act Congress, and Georgia and New Hampshire officially approved the proceedings of the Congress.

[27] *Public Records of the Colony of Connecticut,* XII, 421-425.

[28] Alden Bradford, ed., *Speeches of the Governors of Massachusetts from 1765 to 1775* . . . (Boston, 1818), 28; Bernard to John Pownall, November 17, 1764, to Richard Jackson, November 17, 1764, Bernard Papers, III, 260-264, Harvard College Library.

[29] Thomas Hutchinson to Thomas Pownall, March 8, 1766, Massachusetts Archives, XXVI, 200-206.

Boston. "They are men!" he cried.[30] And he or some other patriot quickly penned a column for the *Boston Gazette*, repudiating the shameful work of the previous year, and decrying the imputation of treason which Boston conservatives had pronounced on Virginia's action:

> The People of Virginia have spoke very sensibly, and the frozen Politicians of a more northern Government say they have spoke Treason: Their spirited Resolves do indeed serve as a perfect Contrast for a certain tame, pusillanimous, daub'd insipid Thing, delicately touch'd up and call'd an Address; which was lately sent from this Side the Water, to please the Taste of the Tools of Corruption on the other—Pray Gentlemen, is it Treason for the Deputies of the People to assert their Liberties, or to give them away? . . . We have been told with an Insolence the more intolerable, because disguis'd with a Veil of public Care, that it is not prudence for us to assert our Rights in plain and manly Terms: Nay, we have been told that the word RIGHTS must not be once named among us! Curs'd Prudence of interested designing Politicians![31]

Although Governor Bernard was a believer in this cursed prudence, he was no more pleased with the Stamp Act than the Americans. He had assured the members from Boston the previous summer that the Ministry would much prefer to let the colonies tax themselves. He had even recommended as much himself, and he was convinced that his reorganization of the colonies was necessary before such a measure as this could be successful. He himself had no doubts about Parliament's authority, but he knew that the colonists did. Until that authority was firmly established along the lines he had laid down in his ninety-seven propositions, it was folly to pass an act like the Stamp Act.

These were Bernard's private sentiments, which he uttered

[30] John Adams, *Works,* C. F. Adams, ed. (Boston, 1850–1856), X, 287.
[31] *Boston Gazette,* July 8, 1765.

in bitterness to his friends in England.[32] But since the Ministry chose to ignore his warnings and gave him the Stamp Act to enforce, he felt obliged to do his best by it. In point of fact he had not received a copy of the Act or official notification of it and never did; but he did not doubt the authenticity of the newspaper reports and though the temptation must have been great, he did not attempt to shirk his duty by taking refuge in the technicality of the Ministry's neglect. Trying to put the Act in what he thought the best possible light, he even explained it to the General Assembly as a step in his cherished scheme for reorganizing the colonies. Though the Act was far from fitting into his plans, he told the Assembly: "The general settlement of the American Provinces, which has been long ago proposed, and now probably will be prosecuted to its utmost completion, must necessarily produce some regulations, which, from their novelty only, will appear disagreeable. But I am convinced, and doubt not but experience will confirm it, that they will operate, as they are designed, for the benefit and advantage of the colonies. In the mean time a respectful submission to the decrees of the Parliament, is their interest, as well as their duty."[33]

During the summer of 1765 it became apparent that peaceful submission to the Act, when it should go into effect on November first, was dubious. To assist him in enforcing it, Bernard called together the Assembly on September 25, 1765, and told them frankly that it was not his business to consider the desirability or undesirability of the Stamp Act. "I have only to say," he explained, "that it is an act of the Parliament of Great Britain, and as such ought to be obeyed by the subjects of Great Britain. And I trust that the supremacy of that Parliament over all the members of their wide and diffused empire, never was and never will be denied within these walls. The right of the Parliament of Great Britain to make laws

[32] To John Pownall, August 18, 1765, to Richard Jackson, August 24, 1765, to the Earl of Shelburne, January 4, 1764, Bernard Papers, IV, 11-15, 18-20, 293-296.

[33] Bradford, *Speeches of the Governors,* 34.

for the American colonies, however it has been controverted in America, remains indisputable at Westminster."[34]

The House of Representatives, in answering this exposition of the constitution, showed that they had thrown off the conciliatory mood in which they had been persuaded to appeal for privileges instead of declaring their rights the year before. In a message of considerable dignity they replied:

> You are pleased to say, that the stamp act is an act of Parliament, and as such ought to be observed. This House, sir, has too great a reverence for the supreme legislature of the nation, to question its just authority: It by no means appertains to us to presume to adjust the boundaries of the power of Parliament; but boundaries there undoubtedly are. . . . Furthermore, your Excellency tells us that the right of the Parliament to make laws for the American colonies remains indisputable in Westminster. Without contending this point, we beg leave just to observe that the charter of the province invests the General Assembly with the power of making laws for its internal government and taxation; and that this charter has never yet been forfeited. The Parliament has a right to make all laws within the limits of their own constitution; they claim no more. Your Excellency will acknowledge that there are certain original inherent rights belonging to the people, which the Parliament itself cannot divest them of, consistent with their own constitution: among these is the right of representation in the same body which exercises the power of taxation. There is a necessity that the subjects of America should exercise this power within themselves, otherwise they can have no share in that most essential right, for they are not represented in Parliament, and indeed we think it impracticable.[35]

The Assembly did not proceed to "adjust the boundaries of the power of Parliament" by putting these views into the form of resolutions until a month later. By that time three of their

[34] *Ibid.,* 40.
[35] *Ibid.,* 45.

members had attended a meeting in New York. That meeting, known ever since as the Stamp Act Congress, was suggested by the Massachusetts Assembly, and it established a more definitive statement of colonial rights than the Virginians had furnished in May.

The leading politicians of Massachusetts had long been aware of the advantages which the colonies might gain by collective action. For a single colony to deny the power of Parliament would be futile; for all to deny it together might not be. As early as May 24, 1764, the town of Boston had called for united efforts against the Sugar Act; the town meeting instructed its representatives in the Assembly: "As his Majesty's other Northern American Colonys are embark'd with us in this most important Bottom, we further desire you to use your Endeavors, that their weight may be added to that of this Province; that by the united Applications of all who are Aggrieved, All may happily obtain Redress."[36] Probably as a result of these instructions the House of Representatives had sent a circular letter to the other colonies, urging them to ask their agents in England "to unite in the most serious Remonstrance" against the Sugar Act and the proposed Stamp Act.[37]

This would appear to have been a perfectly unexceptionable proposal, but Governor Bernard sensed that it might have dangerous consequences. He knew that the representatives from Boston were behind it, and he had already come to believe that anything the Boston politicians proposed would end in trouble. "Altho' This may seem at first sight only an Occasional measure for a particular purpose," he wrote to the Lords of Trade, "yet I have reason to believe that the purposes it is to serve are deeper than they now appear. I apprehend that it is intended to take this opportunity . . . to lay a foundation for connecting the demagogues of the several Governments in America to join together in opposition to al

[36] *A Report of the Record Commissioners of the City of Boston, containing the Boston Town Records, 1758 to 1769* (Boston, 1886), 122.
[37] Connecticut Historical Society, *Collections*, 18 (1920), 284–285.

orders from Great Britain which don't square with their notions of the rights of the people. Perhaps I may be too suspicious; a little time will show whether I am or not."[38]

Within a year Bernard saw his suspicions borne out. The proposal had indeed produced no immediate effect: though some colonies had urged their agents to cooperate with each other, neither the agents nor the assemblies had formed a union. But on June 8, 1765, having received news of the Stamp Act, the Massachusetts House of Representatives sent another circular letter to the assemblies of North America inviting them to meet in a congress at New York the following October, "to consider of a general and united, dutiful, loyal and humble Representation of their Condition to His Majesty and the Parliament; and to implore Relief."[39]

Of the thirteen colonies which later took part in the Revolution, nine responded to the invitation. New Hampshire declined but formally approved the proceedings after the congress was over.[40] Virginia, North Carolina, and Georgia were prevented from participating, because their governors refused to convene the assemblies to elect delegates.[41] Delaware and New Jersey met the same obstruction but sent representatives anyhow, chosen when some of the assemblymen defiantly held an informal election of their own. In New York the Assembly's Committee of Correspondence nominated themselves to attend. Twenty-seven delegates in all took part in the congress, and according to one of them they were "an Assembly of the greatest Ability I ever Yet saw."[42]

[38] June 29, 1764, Bernard Papers, III, 157.

[39] *Pennsylvania Archives,* 8th ser., 7 (1935), 5765.

[40] Nathaniel Bouton, ed., *Provincial Papers: Documents and Records Relating to the Province of New Hampshire* (Nashua, 1873), VII, 92.

[41] The North Carolina Assembly later rebuked the governor for preventing their sitting during the crisis. *Colonial Records of North Carolina,* VII, 347. The Georgia Assembly approved the proceedings of the congress and sent copies of the petitions to their agent in London. Allen D. Candler, ed., *The Colonial Records of the State of Georgia* (Atlanta, 1904–1915), XIV, 315-318.

[42] George H. Ryden, ed., *Letters to and from Caesar Rodney, 1756–1784* (Philadelphia, 1933), 26. The delegates were James Otis, Oliver Partridge, and Timothy Ruggles from Massachusetts;

Governor Bernard had watched with misgivings while the Massachusetts Assembly proposed this congress but felt himself helpless to prevent it. He had accordingly made the best of a bad business by taking the lead in it, so as to control the choice of the Massachusetts delegates. He was able to report to the Board of Trade on July 8, 1765, that the Massachusetts delegation, owing to his efforts behind the scenes, contained two "prudent and discreet men such as I am assured will never consent to any undutiful or improper application to the Government of Great Britain."[43] The men were Timothy Ruggles and Oliver Partridge, whom Bernard had gauged correctly. The other member of the delegation—there were three altogether—was James Otis. Otis appears to have been the first to suggest the congress, and may have been sent to it for that reason. His presence might normally have been expected to offset that of the other two members, for he had a great reputation as a rabble-rouser. Fortunately for Bernard, however, Otis had recently changed his tune. In May, even before Otis had proposed the congress, Bernard had been able to report to his friend John Pownall that "the author of the Rights of the Colonies now repents in Sackcloth and ashes for the hand he had in that book. . . . In a pamphlett lately published he has [begged pardon] in humblest Manner of the Ministry and of the Parliament for the liberties he took with them."[44] Bernard's report was correct. When news of the Virginia Resolves reached Boston, Otis is said to have called them treasonable; and though he apparently continued to speak fire in anonymous contributions to the *Boston Gazette*

Metcalf Bowler and Henry Ward from Rhode Island; Eliphalet Dyer, David Rowland, and William Samuel Johnson from Connecticut; Robert R. Livingston, John Cruger, Philip Livingston, William Bayard, and Leonard Lispenard from New York; Robert Ogden, Hendrick Fisher, and Joseph Borden from New Jersey; John Dickinson, John Morton, and George Bryan from Pennsylvania; Thomas McKean and Caesar Rodney from Delaware; William Murdoch, Edward Tilghman, and Thomas Ringgold from Maryland; Thomas Lynch, Christopher Gadsden, and John Rutledge from South Carolina.

[43] Sparks Mss., 43, British Mss., IV, Harvard College Library.
[44] Bernard Papers, III, 289.

his public statements extolled the power of Parliament, and before he left for the congress, he was heard to say that "If the government at home don't very soon send forces to keep the peace of this province they will be cutting one anothers throats from one End, to the other of it."[45]

Otis was always unpredictable, and the insanity that clouded his later years may already have been affecting him, but it would seem that his role at the congress was as subdued as Bernard could have wished. According to John Watts, a New York merchant, he endeavored to get himself elected chairman of the meetings, but failed because the other members thought that "as he had figured much in the popular way, it might give their meeting an ill grace." Watts noted, however, that "it is observed Otis is now a quite different man, and so he seems to be to me, not riotous at all."[46]

The man whom the congress finally chose as chairman instead of Otis was Timothy Ruggles, whose election to the Massachusetts delegation had been engineered by Governor Bernard. As chairman of the meeting Ruggles was in a good position to carry out the instructions Bernard had given him: to get the congress to recommend submission to the Stamp Act until Parliament could be persuaded to repeal it.[47] Had he been successful in dominating the men who made him their chairman, probably the congress would have confined itself to arguing for repeal of the Stamp Act and Sugar Act on the grounds that they would hurt Anglo-colonial trade and bankrupt the colonies. As it turned out, the men who took the lead after the meetings were organized showed a different temper. General Gage exaggerated only a little when he wrote to Secretary of State Conway, "They are of various Characters and opinions, but it's to be feared in general, that the Spirit of Democracy, is strong amongst them." By "Democracy" Gage did not mean a belief in rule by the people

[45] Bernard to John Pownall, October 19, 1765, Sparks Mss., 10, Chalmers, I, Harvard College Library.

[46] John Watts to Governor Monckton, October 12, 1765, Massachusetts Historical Society, *Collections,* 4th ser., 10 (1871), 579-580.

[47] Bernard to Ruggles, September 28, 1765, Bernard Papers, IV, 72.

so much as a belief that the colonists were beyond the control of Parliament, for he went on to inform Conway that the question which the congress was debating was not one "of the inexpediency of the Stamp Act, but that it is unconstitutional, and contrary to their Rights, Supporting the Independency of the Provinces, and not subject to the Legislative Power of Great Britain."[48]

After the members had elected Ruggles as chairman and seated all the delegates, they began drawing up a statement of the "rights and privileges of the British American Colonists." For the next twelve days, excluding Sunday, they argued and scribbled and crossed out and filled in and finally produced the following declarations:

The Members of this Congress, sincerely devoted, with the warmest Sentiments of Affection and Duty to his Majesty's Person and Government, inviolably attached to the present happy Establishment of the Protestant Succession, and with Minds deeply impressed by a Sense of the present and impending Misfortunes of the *British* Colonies on this Continent; having considered as maturely as Time will permit, the Circumstances of the said Colonies, esteem it our indispensable Duty, to make the following Declarations of our humble Opinion, respecting the most Essential Rights and Liberties of the Colonists, and of the Grievances under which they labour, by Reason of several late Acts of Parliament.

I. That his Majesty's Subjects in these Colonies, owe the same Allegiance to the Crown of *Great-Britain,* that is owing from his Subjects born within the Realm, and all due Subordination to that August Body the Parliament of *Great-Britain.*

II. That his Majesty's Liege Subjects in these Colonies, are entitled to all the inherent Rights and Liberties of his Natural born Subjects, within the Kingdom of *Great-Britain.*

III. That it is inseparably essential to the Freedom of

48 October 12, 1765, Clarence E. Carter, ed., *The Correspondence of General Thomas Gage with the Secretaries of State, 1765–1775* (New Haven, 1931), I, 69-70.

a People, and the undoubted Right of *Englishmen,* that no Taxes be imposed on them, but with their own Consent, given personally, or by their Representatives.

IV. That the People of these Colonies are not, and from their local Circumstances cannot be, Represented in the House of Commons in *Great-Britain.*

V. That the only Representatives of the People of these Colonies, are Persons chosen therein by themselves, and that no Taxes ever have been, or can be Constitutionally imposed on them, but by their respective Legislature.

VI. That all Supplies to the Crown, being free Gifts of the People, it is unreasonable and inconsistent with the Principles and Spirit of the *British* Constitution, for the People of *Great-Britain,* to grant to his Majesty the Property of the Colonists.

VII. That Trial by Jury, is the inherent and invaluable Right of every *British* Subject in these Colonies.

VIII. That the late Act of Parliament, entitled, *An Act for granting and applying certain Stamp Duties, and other Duties, in the British Colonies and Plantations in America, &c.* by imposing Taxes on the Inhabitants of these Colonies, and the said Act, and several other Acts, by extending the Jurisdiction of the Courts of Admiralty beyond its ancient Limits, have a manifest Tendency to subvert the Rights and Liberties of the Colonists.

IX. That the Duties imposed by several late Acts of Parliament, from the peculiar Circumstances of these Colonies, will be extremely Burthensome and Grievous; and from the scarcity of Specie, the Payment of them absolutely impracticable.

X. That as the Profits of the Trade of these Colonies ultimately center in *Great-Britain,* to pay for the Manufactures which they are obliged to take from thence, they eventually contribute very largely to all Supplies granted there to the Crown.

XI. That the Restrictions imposed by several late Acts of Parliament, on the Trade of these Colonies, will render them unable to purchase the Manufactures of *Great-Britain.*

XII. That the Increase, Prosperity, and Happiness of these Colonies, depend on the full and free Enjoyment of their Rights and Liberties, and an Intercourse with *Great-Britain* mutually Affectionate and Advantageous.

XIII. That it is the Right of the *British* Subjects in these Colonies, to Petition the King, or either House of Parliament.

Lastly, That it is the indispensable Duty of these Colonies, to the best of Sovereigns, to the Mother Country, and to themselves, to endeavour by a loyal and dutiful Address to his Majesty, and humble Applications to both Houses of Parliament, to procure the Repeal of the Act for granting and applying certain Stamp Duties, of all Clauses of any other Acts of Parliament, whereby the Jurisdiction of the Admiralty is extended as aforesaid, and of the other late Acts for the Restriction of *American* Commerce.[49]

To define these fundamentals was evidently no great problem for the twenty-seven delegates. For that matter it would have been difficult to find an American anywhere who did not believe in them—as far as they went. The principal disagreement which kept the congress arguing for nearly two weeks was whether to balance the denial of Parliament's authority to tax the colonies with an acknowledgment of what authority it did have. But to formulate an acknowledgment which could not be misconstrued to the prejudice of colonial rights proved impossible. According to Robert R. Livingston, one of the New York delegation,

What gave us most trouble was whether we should insist on a Repeal of all acts laying Duties on Trade as well as the Stamp Act all agreed that we ought to obey all acts of trade and that they should regulate our Trade but many were not for making an explicit declaration of and an acknowledgment of such a Power. I thought and many with me that if we did not do it there was not the least hopes

---

[49] *Proceedings of the Congress at New York* (Annapolis, 1766). This was the first printing of the Journals. They are reprinted in Hezekiah Niles, *Principles and Acts of the Revolution* (Baltimore, 1822), 451-461. *Prologue to Revolution*, 62-63.

of success, for except Britain could regulate our Trade her colonies would be of no more use to her than to France or any other power, and that it is impossible to suppose that she would ever give up the point of internal taxes except the other were fully secured and acknowledged. I find all sensible people in town to agree with me in this but we had some who were much too warm to do any good.[50]

From this statement one may gather that all members of the congress accepted the authority of Parliament to regulate the trade of the empire, but that the majority thought it unwise to make any express acknowledgment of such an authority. Undoubtedly what made them unwilling was the double purpose of the Sugar Act. Here was an act which served both to raise revenue and to regulate trade. An admission of Parliament's authority in the regulation of trade might be construed as an admission that the taxes levied under the Sugar Act were constitutional.

It is possible to follow the course of debate in two early drafts of the declarations. Both are in the hand of John Dickinson of Pennsylvania, and it may be that he was the first to formulate a statement for the other members to consider. The first draft is not radically different from the final version except in containing specific acknowledgment of Parliamentary authority in the words: "all Acts of Parliament not inconsistent with the Rights and Liberties of the Colonists are obligatory upon them." In the second draft this was changed to "all Acts of Parliament not inconsistent with the Principles of Freedom are obligatory upon the Colonists." Finally these statements were replaced by the acknowledgment in the first resolution that the colonists owed "all due Subordination to that August Body the Parliament of *Great-Britain*."[51]

The first change probably represents an unsuccessful attempt of the conservative members to satisfy the radicals by

[50] To ———, November 2, 1765, Bancroft Transcripts, New York Public Library.

[51] Both drafts are in the Dickinson Papers, Library Company of Philadelphia. A third draft, printed in Historical Society of Pennsylvania, *Memoirs,* 14 (1895), 183-187, is in the Library of the Historical Society of Pennsylvania.

a more general statement: some colonies could count on "privileges" derived from their charters; others had no charters and wished to base the declaration on a broader principle. Christopher Gadsden of South Carolina seems to have been the leading opponent of any explicit statement. After the congress he wrote, "I have ever been of opinion, that we should all endeavor to stand upon the broad and common ground of those natural and inherent rights that we all feel and know, as men and as descendants of Englishmen, we have a right to, and have always thought this bottom amply sufficient for our future importance. . . . There ought to be no New England men, no New Yorker, &c., known on the Continent, but all of us Americans; a *confirmation* of our essential and common rights as Englishmen may be pleaded from the Charters safely enough, but any further dependence on them may be fatal."[52] Gadsden thought that the desire of the "eastern gentlemen" for the explicit statement of subordination was the result of their placing too much dependence on their charters, and a letter from William Samuel Johnson confirmed this view.[53]

In all probability, then, the second of Dickinson's drafts, with the substitution of "Principles of Freedom" for "Rights and Liberties of the Colonists," was an attempt to meet demands by Gadsden and others that the rights of the colonies be rested on a broader footing than the "privileges" granted in colonial charters. The modification, however, was still unsatisfactory, for it committed the colonists to obedience so long as Parliamentary legislation did not violate the principles of freedom. Since these principles were not clearly defined and were in fact the subject of the dispute between England and America, it would be unwise to make so positive a commitment. The final solution, of course, was to make no mention of Acts of Parliament and to leave colonial subordination undefined except by the weasel-word, "due."

[52] Gadsden to Charles Garth, December 2, 1765, R. W. Gibbes, *Documentary History of the American Revolution* (New York, 1855), I, 8.
[53] Johnson to Gadsden, January 10, 1766, William Samuel Johnson Papers, Connecticut Historical Society.

This solution was evidently resisted by Robert R. Livingston, as we can tell from his letter. It was also resisted by Timothy Ruggles and by Robert Ogden of New Jersey, for both Ruggles and Ogden refused to sign the proceedings of the congress because of the omission of any precise acknowledgment of Parliament's authority.[54] Ruggles and Ogden were probably the strongest supporters of Parliament present. The other members, even those who opposed Gadsden, were so anxious to see a unanimous assertion of colonial rights that they accepted the majority view. William Samuel Johnson, writing to Ogden ten days after the congress broke up, wished that they "had adopted the other Plan of admitting the general superintendance of Parliament and limiting their Power by the Principles and Spirit of the Constitution which sufficiently excludes all Constitutional Right to Tax us, and effectually secures the fundamental Priviledge of Trial by Jury as well as every other Right Essential to British Liberty." But in the interests of unity Johnson had acquiesced in the Declarations.[55]

After the congress had agreed on what their official position should be, they appointed three committees to draw up a petition to the King, a memorial to the House of Lords, and a petition to the House of Commons.[56] At this point Christopher Gadsden objected to the admission of Parliamentary authority that would be implied in petitioning that body. The rights of the colonies, he said, were not derived from Parliament; besides, the House of Commons had shown how

---

[54] Ruggles and Ogden were both rebuked for their stand by their respective assemblies. See Bernard to Board of Trade, March 10, 1766, Chalmers Papers, II, Harvard College Library; *Boston Gazette,* February 17, 1766; Governor Franklin to Board of Trade, December 18, 1765, *Archives of the State of New Jersey,* 1st ser., 9 (1885), 525; Donald L. Kemmerer, *Path to Freedom* (Princeton, 1940), 287-288. The delegates from New York, Connecticut, and South Carolina were not authorized by their assemblies to sign, so that their names also are missing from the documents.

[55] Johnson to Robert Ogden, November 4, 1765, to Eliphalet Dyer, December 31, 1765, William Samuel Johnson Papers, Connecticut Historical Society.

[56] *Prologue to Revolution,* 63-69.

little it cared about petitions from America when it refused even to consider the colonial petitions of the preceding year. The other members of the congress were not ready to join in such a wholesale snub to the supreme legislature of Great Britain. Gadsden could afford to be generous in this question, for he had already won the major battle of the congress in the debate over the Declarations. For the sake of unity he now gave way, and in the short space of four days the two petitions and the memorial were drafted and accepted.[57] The delegates from Connecticut, New York, and South Carolina were not authorized to sign the documents, and official approval by those colonies had to await action by their assemblies, but the other members, with the exception of Ruggles and Ogden, put their signatures to the proceedings, and returned home with copies for transmittal to England.

Although the congress had refused in their official statements to make any specific acknowledgment of Parliament's authority, they left behind, among the waste paper that such a conference begets, one document which suggests what some of them thought about the subject. William Samuel Johnson, having labored over the "Report of the Committee to whom was refer'd the Consideration of the Rights of the British Colonies,"[58] carried it away with him and preserved it among his papers. Its eleven pages had evidently been too wordy to satisfy the congress, but they quarried it for phrases and sentences to incorporate in the Declarations and petitions, and one phrase they took was the crucial "due subordination." Seen in their original context these nebulous words take on greater precision.

Altho the due subordination of the Colonies to the Crown and Parliament and the dependancy of the Colonies on

[57] Gibbes, *Documentary History*, I, 7-9.

[58] There is no record of the appointment of this committee in the journals of the congress. After the adoption of the Declarations, Johnson was appointed to the committee to draw up the petition to the King, but the report referred to here is clearly not the report of that committee. It appears, rather, to be an attempt, probably earlier than any of those in Dickinson's hand, to formulate a declaration of rights. It is now in the William Samuel Johnson Papers, Library of Congress.

Great Britain are what every Intelligent American [wishes] . . . Yet it is most humbly conceived that this subordination and dependency is sufficiently secured by the Common Law, by our Allegiance, by the Negative of the Crown on the Laws of most of the Provinces, but above all by the general superintending power and authority of the whole Empire indisputably lodged in that August Body the Parliament of Great Britain which Authority is clearly admitted here so far as in our Circumstances is Consistent with the Enjoyment of our Essential Rights as Freemen and British Subjects, and we farther humbly Conceive that by the Constitution it is no further admissible in Great Britain itself. It is also submitted whether there is not a vast difference between the Exercise of Parliamentary Jurisdiction in general Acts for the Amendment of the Common Law, or even in general Regulations of Trade and Commerce for the Empire and the Actual Exercise of that Jurisdiction in levying External and Internal Duties and Taxes on the Colonists while they neither are nor can be represented in Parliament. The former may very well consist with a reasonable Measure of Civil Liberty in the Colonies but we must beg leave to say that how the latter is consistent with any degree of Freedom we are wholly at a loss how to Comprehend.

Here the due subordination of the colonies is expressed in terms of Parliament's superintending authority over the whole empire, and it is specified that such authority includes the right to pass legislation regulating trade but does not include the right to tax. This distinction between taxation and legislation was implicit in the abbreviated assertions of the Declarations, particularly in the sixth resolution, "that all Supplies to the Crown, being free Gifts of the People, it is unreasonable and inconsistent with the Principles and Spirit of the *British* Constitution, for the People of *Great-Britain* to grant to his Majesty the Property of the Colonists." The delegates were saying here that acts of taxation, unlike other acts of a legislature, are gifts and that they can be granted only by the representatives of the people who make the gift. The distinction was made explicit in the petition to the House of Commons, where a more extensive borrowing from the Report produced the query, "Whether there be not a material Distinction in Reason and sound Policy, at least, between the necessary Exercise of Parliamentary Jurisdiction in general Acts, for the Amendment of the Common Law, and the Regulation of Trade and Commerce through the whole Empire, and the Exercise of that Jurisdiction by imposing Taxes on the Colonies."[59]

Due subordination, then, meant submission to Parliamentary legislation but not to Parliamentary taxation. The line between the two might be difficult to perceive in Westminster, but it was plain in America. The congress could see it; Daniel Dulany could see it; and the several colonial assemblies could see it, as they showed by endorsing the proceedings of the congress or by resolutions and petitions of their own or by both.[60]

The Americans did not mean that any kind of legislation was allowable. Legislation, for example, which took away the right of trial by jury or any other acknowledged constitutional

[59] *Proceedings of the Congress at New York*, 23. *Prologue to Revolution*, 68. Niles, *Principles and Acts*, 460, has garbled this passage.

[60] The petition from New York to the House of Commons, adopted by the Assembly on December 11, 1765, made the point most sharply by declaring "That all parliamentary Aids in Great-Britain, are the free Gifts of the People by their Representatives, consented to by the Lords and accepted by the Crown, and therefore every Act imposing them, essentially differs from every other Statute, having the Force of a Law in no other respect than the Manner thereby prescribed for levying the gift.

"That agreeable to this Distinction, the House of Commons has always contended for and enjoyed the constitutional Right of originating all Money Bills, as well in aid of the Crown, as for other Purposes.

"That all Supplies to the Crown, being in their Nature free Gifts, it would, as we humbly conceive, be unconstitutional for the People of *Great-Britain,* by their Representatives in Parliament, to dispose of the Property of Millions of his Majesty's Subjects, who are not, and cannot be there represented." *Journal of the Votes and Proceedings of the General Assembly* (New York, 1766), II, 800.

right went beyond the limits of Parliament's authority anywhere, whether in England or in the colonies. There was also the contention made in the Virginia Resolves, and copied from them into the resolves of several other colonies, that Parliament could not interfere with the "internal polity" of the colonies. The meaning of this phrase was not entirely clear in 1765, and because Parliament did not happen at the time to be interfering with whatever was meant by internal polity, it was not clarified. Apparently, however, none of the Parliamentary legislation which was on the books in 1765 came within the scope of this phrase, unless the Stamp Act itself was regarded as doing so, for the constitutional objections raised by the colonists both in the colonial assemblies and in the congress were aimed at the Stamp Act and the Sugar Act. The great distinction, then, which marked off the authority of Parliament in Great Britain from its authority in the colonies was the distinction between legislation and taxation: for Great Britain Parliament might levy taxes as well as make laws; for the colonies it could only make laws.

For the most part the colonial protests argued for the rights of Englishmen on a constitutional basis, but they did mention another kind of rights which Parliament was violating—the rights of man. Although the Americans were confident that the British constitution guaranteed the right to be taxed only by consent, they regarded this right as a product of natural as well as of British law. In the third resolution the congress stated that "it is inseparably essential to the Freedom of a People" as well as "the undoubted Right of *Englishmen*," that they should be taxed only by consent. This appeal to a wider basis for their rights is notably absent in the petitions to King and Parliament, where the congress, like Dulany, asked only for their rights as Englishmen. In two other sets of resolutions, however, those of Massachusetts and Pennsylvania, the colonists grounded their statements on the natural rights of man. Pennsylvania, on September 21, 1765, declared "That the Inhabitants of this Province are entitled to all the Liberties, Rights and Privileges of his Majesty's Subjects in *Great-Britain*, or elsewhere, and that the Constitution of Government in this Province is founded on the natural Rights of Mankind, and the noble Principles of *English* Liberty, and therefore is, or ought to be, perfectly free."[61]

Massachusetts likewise, on October 25, the day that the Stamp Act Congress adjourned, resolved, "That there are certain essential rights of the British constitution of government, which are founded in the law of God and nature, and are the common rights of mankind," and "That the inhabitants of this province are unalienably entitled to those essential rights, in common with all men; and that no law of society can, consistent with the law of God and nature, divest them of those rights."[62] Though their representatives at New York might side with the conservatives, the Massachusetts Assembly was siding with Gadsden.

Thus by the fall of 1765 the colonists had clearly laid down the line where they believed that Parliament should stop, and they had drawn that line not merely as Englishmen but as men. The line was far short of independence, and there was no suggestion in any of the resolutions of the congress or of the assemblies that the colonists wished to cease being Englishmen. Nevertheless, if England chose to force the issue, the colonists would have to decide—and in that winter many were trying to make up their minds—whether they would be men and not English or whether they would be English and not men.

A Note on Internal and External Taxes

It has been argued by Carl Becker in *The Declaration of Independence* that the Stamp Act Congress confined its objections against Parliamentary taxation to internal taxes only. This argument presupposes that the first eight resolutions are based on constitutional principles and apply only to the Stamp Act and that resolutions 9–12 are based on economic considerations and apply only to the Sugar Act. By this reasoning there appears to be no constitutional objection in the resolutions to the "external" taxes levied by the Sugar Act. In all probability this interpretation was influenced by the supposition which was already current in England by 1766

[61] *Pennsylvania Archives*, 8th ser., 7 (1935), 5779.
[62] Bradford, *Speeches of the Governors*, 50.

and which was nurtured and perpetuated, that the colonists in 1765, differentiated between internal and external taxes and had no objections to the latter. I have examined this supposition elsewhere and shown it, I think, to be unfounded.[63] As far as the resolves of the Stamp Act Congress are concerned, it appears to me unlikely for several reasons that the first eight resolutions were intended to apply only to internal taxes and resolutions 9–12 to external. It seems more probable that in the first eight resolutions or at least in the first seven, the congress was stating unqualified constitutional objections to all taxes and that in resolutions 9–12 it merely added the economic objections. This contention is borne out by the petition to the House of Commons and the memorial to the House of Lords. In the petition to the Commons the congress begins by reciting constitutional objections and then proceeds to economic objections with this paragraph:

> But were it ever so clear, that the colonies might in Law, be reasonably deem'd to be Represented in the Honourable House of Commons, yet we conceive, that very good Reasons, from Inconvenience, from the Principles of true Policy, and from the Spirit of the British Constitution, may be adduced to shew, that it would be for the real interest of *Great-Britain*, as well as her Colonies, that the late Regulations should be rescinded, and the several Acts of Parliament imposing Duties and Taxes on the Colonies, and extending the Jurisdiction of the Courts of Admiralty here, beyond their ancient Limits, should be Repeal'd.[64]

Similarly in the memorial to the Lords the economic objections are introduced in this way: "But your Memorialists (not waving their Claim to these Rights, of which with the most becoming Veneration and Deference to the Wisdom and Justice of your Lordships, they apprehend they cannot Reasonably be deprived)."[65]

[63] "Colonial Ideas of Parliamentary Power 1764–1766," *William and Mary Quarterly*, 3d ser., 5 (1948), 311-341; "The Postponement of the Stamp Act," *ibid.*, 7 (1950), 353-392. See the letter by Curtis P. Nettels and my reply, *ibid.*, 6 (1949), 162-170.

[64] *Proceedings of the Congress at New York*, 22.

[65] *Ibid.*, 20.

Another indication that the congress was not confining its constitutional objections to internal taxes lies in the fact that William Samuel Johnson's lengthy statement of principles repeatedly objects to "external and internal duties and taxes." The resolutions themselves make no use of the words "external" or "internal," but shorten Johnson's phrase to the one word "taxes."[66] If there had been an intention to distinguish between internal and external taxes, it is reasonable to suppose that these words would have been used. Since Johnson thought that the resolutions in their final form went too far,[67] it is unlikely that he construed their objections to Parliamentary taxation as more limited than those which he himself had penned. Certainly when the resolutions and petitions reached England, Parliament thought that they made no distinction and refused to consider them partly for that reason. It is perhaps worth noting also that John Dickinson, who drafted the resolutions, did not believe that the constitutional objections were confined to internal taxes. By 1767 the English were already condemning the colonies for inconsistency in abandoning this distinction which in reality they had never held. Dickinson replied in his Farmer's Letters by quoting the resolves of the Stamp Act Congress and then pointing out that there was "no distinction made between *internal* and *external* taxes" in them.[68]

It is difficult, in the face of this evidence, to believe that Carl Becker would have found a distinction between internal and external taxes in the resolves of the Stamp Act Congress if it had not been for the traditional belief that the colonists were making such a distinction at this time.[69]

[66] William Samuel Johnson Papers, Library of Congress.
[67] See letter to Robert Ogden, November 4, 1765, William Samuel Johnson Papers, Connecticut Historical Society.
[68] Historical Society of Pennsylvania, *Memoirs*, 14 (1895), 331–332.
[69] For Carl Becker's argument see *The Declaration of Independence* (New York, 1922), 90. For a more recent statement of the view that the colonists at the time of the Stamp Act objected to internal but not to external taxes, see Lawrence H. Gipson, *The British Empire Before the American Revolution*, vol. 10, *passim*

PART II

ROAD TO REVOLUTION

Chapter VIII

Action: Boston Sets the Pace

THE RESOLUTIONS WHICH the clerks of colonial and inter-colonial assemblies were recording in the summer and fall of 1765 were outspoken denials of Parliament's right to tax the colonies. But only in Rhode Island did the Assembly approve outright resistance. It was one thing to define a right and another to fight for it, particularly if you must fight against a body which you had hitherto accepted as supreme and to which you still acknowledged "all due subordination." Nevertheless, while men like James Otis blew hot and cold, now for colonial rights and now for Parliamentary supremacy, and while others followed Daniel Dulany in affirming colonial rights but wishing only passive resistance, a substantial number of men in every colony recognized that the time had come when more than talk was needed. They had been convinced by Dulany and Otis and by the Virginia Resolves and the declarations of the Stamp Act Congress that Parliament had no right to tax them. They also knew that there was no branch of government higher than Parliament to prevent Parliament's doing what it had no right to do. The burden therefore was left to those whose rights were endangered: they must resist Parliament to preserve their rights, and if that meant an end to Parliamentary supremacy, then that was what it meant.

It would be too much to say that these men wished to throw off the authority of Parliament altogether. Perhaps some of them did, but there is no reason to suppose that they were not content with the constitutional position which their representatives had defined, denying Parliament's right to tax but allowing its right to regulate trade and to pass other general legislation affecting the empire at large. The only point at which they went a step further than the resolutions was in their determination to prevent the supreme legislature from doing what it had no right to do. In this determination they ignored the distinction which Dulany had drawn between propriety and power. But if anyone had told them that in spite of the impropriety of its action, Parliament's power was supreme, they might have answered that supremacy in power cannot be determined by argumentation or declaration. If Parliament lacked the authority to tax America, then its power to do so would have to be tested in American fields and streets. And this was precisely where they proposed to test it.

Although the Virginians had been first to suggest resistance, it was not in Williamsburg but in Boston that argument first gave way to action. The Massachusetts radicals saw that if the colonists were to defeat Parliament's attempt to tax them, they could not rely on their representative assemblies to do the job. The assemblies might resolve, as that of Rhode Island did, that officers of government should carry on business as usual, as though the Act had never been passed. But what if the officers of government who had to use the stamps lay beyond the immediate control of the assemblies? Most of the documents which would require stamps after November first were papers used in legal proceedings. In some colonies the assemblies might withhold the salaries of the judges as a means of bringing them into line, but in others the judges of the superior courts were not appointed by the assemblies, and in all the colonies the independence of the judiciary was regarded as a principle of the British constitution which could be tampered with only at the peril of civil liberty. The assemblies were also powerless to control the royally appointed customs officers who must issue clearances for all ships leaving American harbors. According to the Stamp Act, clearance papers issued after November 1 would have to bear a stamp. If the customs officers chose to comply with the law, and as royal officials they doubtless would comply, what could the assemblies do about it? The duties of customs officers did not fall within their jurisdiction, and royal governors would certainly have vetoed any orders from the assemblies which attempted to regulate matters beyond their authority.

Obviously the radicals who had determined to turn from words to deeds could expect little more than words from their assemblies. For action they must look elsewhere, and where was not hard to guess. In Boston particularly the answer was clear, for in the past the good people of that city had frequently turned from the niceties of theological controversy to achieve some necessary social reform in their own way. Perhaps a few inhabitants could recollect with some amusement how they had laid out a street through Jonathan Loring's barn near Love Street some thirty years before. The selectmen had surveyed the proposed street and found Loring's barn square in the way. There was some doubt whether they had a right to seize the barn, but a gathering of the townspeople resolved the question without argument. Under cover of night and with blackened faces, a technique they had already learned and would employ again in 1773, they levelled the building, and the road went through.[1] In 1747 Boston had demonstrated that even the British Navy must watch its step in Massachusetts. Commodore Knowles in that year anchored his fleet off Nantasket and sent press gangs ashore to fill gaps in his crews. When the Governor and Council would not, as they could not, prevent him, a mob arose in Boston which ruled the city until Commodore Knowles released the men he had seized.[2]

Bostonians sometimes seemed to love violence for its own sake. Over the years there had developed a rivalry between the South End and the North End of the city. On Pope's Day, November 5, when parades were held to celebrate the defeat of Guy Fawkes' famous gunpowder plot, the rivalry between the two sections generally broke out into a free-for-all with stones and barrel staves the principal weapons. The two sides even developed a semi-military organization with recognized leaders, and of late the fighting had become increasingly bloody. In 1764 a child was run over and killed by a wagon

[1] Petition of Jonathan Loring and Jonathan Jackson to Governor Belcher and Council, September, 1732, Curwin Papers, III, 97, American Antiquarian Society.

[2] Thomas Hutchinson, *History of the Colony and Province of Massachusetts Bay*, L. S. Mayo, ed. (Cambridge, 1936), II, 330-333.

bearing an effigy of the pope, but even this had not stopped the battle. Despite the efforts of the militia, the two sides had battered and bruised each other until the South End finally carried the day.[3]

When Boston had to face the problem of nullifying the Stamp Act, it was obvious that men who fought so energetically over the effigy of a pope might be employed in a more worthy cause. The problem was to make them see the threat to their liberties that the Stamp Act presented and to direct their energies accordingly. Sometime in the early summer of 1765 a group of men got together in Boston to prepare for the day when the Stamp Act was supposed to go into effect, November 1. An organization was formed which first called itself The Loyal Nine and later, when its ranks had expanded, the Sons of Liberty. The Nine were John Avery, Thomas Crafts, John Smith, Henry Welles, Thomas Chase, Stephen Cleverly, Henry Bass, Benjamin Edes, and George Trott.[4] They were not the most prominent citizens of Boston, nor were they the men who did most of the talking against the Stamp Act. In general they were artisans and shopkeepers, and they shunned publicity. The names of James Otis and Samuel Adams were conspicuously missing from the list. So was that of John Adams. Perhaps this division of labor was deliberate, in order to keep the radical leaders of the Assembly, who were always conspicuously in the public eye, from bringing too much attention to the group. Or perhaps the effectiveness of the radical leaders in the Assembly might have been impaired if they were openly associated with an organization engaged in the treasonable activities which the Loyal Nine envisaged. Whatever the reason, no conclusive alliance can be proved between the leaders of the

[3] *Massachusetts Gazette and Boston News-Letter,* November 8, 1764; Governor Bernard to John Pownall, November 26, 1765, Bernard Papers, V, 43-46, Harvard College Library.

[4] On the Loyal Nine see John Adams, *Works,* C. F. Adams, ed. (Boston, 1850–1856), II, 178-179; William Gordon, *The History of the Rise, Progress, and Establishment of the Independence of the United States of America* (London, 1788), I, 175; and George P. Anderson, "A Note on Ebenezer Mackintosh," Colonial Society of Massachusetts, *Publications,* 26 (1927), 348-361.

Assembly and the organizers of the popular demonstrations, but it is probable that the Nine maintained close communications with both Otis and Samuel Adams, and on one occasion at least, John Adams spent an evening with them at their headquarters in Chase and Speakman's distillery on Hanover Square.

Only two members of the Loyal Nine enjoyed any local distinction: John Avery, a Harvard graduate, was a distiller and merchant; Benjamin Edes was the printer, along with John Gill, of the *Gazette*, Boston's most enterprising newspaper. Avery's membership lent respectability to the group; Edes's gave it a mouthpiece. Of the two, Edes's contribution was doubtless the more valuable, for his paper published a continuous stream of articles to stir up feeling against the Stamp Act.

By August 14 the Nine felt that Boston was ready for action. They were confident that the well-to-do stood behind the moves which they were contemplating, and that the propaganda published in the *Gazette* had aroused the mass of the people. More important, they had enlisted the services of the man who had led the South End mob to victory over the North Enders the preceding November. Ebenezer McIntosh, a South End shoemaker, was soon to become notorious as a man who could control his two thousand followers with the precision of a general.[5] The Nine had persuaded him that he might do his country a real service by forgetting local quarrels and directing his strength against that hated Act which was designed to rob Americans of their constitutional rights.

On the morning of August 14 the signal for impending action was given by the hanging of an effigy on a tree near Deacon Elliot's house on Newbury Street. It represented Andrew Oliver, the man who, according to reports from England, had been appointed Distributor of Stamps for Massachusetts; alongside hung a piece of symbolism designed to

[5] See George P. Anderson, "Ebenezer Mackintosh: Stamp Act Rioter and Patriot" and "A Note on Ebenezer Mackintosh," Colonial Society of Massachusetts, *Publications,* 26 (1927), 15-64, 348-361.

connect Oliver and the Stamp Act with the most hated man in England. It was a large boot (a pun on the Earl of Bute), with the devil crawling out of it.[6] When Governor Bernard heard of the event he took it seriously. Some members of his council assured him that it was only a boyish prank, not worthy the notice of the government, but in view of the incendiary pieces appearing in the newspapers Bernard thought otherwise. So did Lieutenant-Governor Hutchinson. Hutchinson, as Chief Justice of the Colony, ordered the Sheriff to cut the image down; Bernard took an easier way out: he summoned the Council and turned the problem over to them. Before the Council could gather together in the afternoon, the Sheriff returned with the breathless news that his men could not take down the image without endangering their lives.[7]

Governor Bernard urged upon the Council the seriousness of the situation, but for various reasons they preferred to do nothing about it. Some thought it a trifling matter which would subside by itself if no notice were taken of it. Others admitted its seriousness, but felt that the government was not strong enough to force the issue and had better not risk the attempt. Unwilling, however, to have it go on record that they had done nothing, they passed the problem on to the Sheriff, advising that he be instructed to summon the peace officers. They could scarcely have expected the peace officers to have any effect on the crowd that was gathering about

[6] "Diary of John Rowe," August 14, 1765, Massachusetts Historical Society, *Proceedings,* 2d ser., 10 (1895), 61; Benjamin Hallowell to the Commissioners of the Customs, September 7, 1765, Treasury Papers, Class I, Bundle 442, Library of Congress transcripts.

[7] Governor Bernard to Halifax, August 15, 16, 1765, Bernard Papers, IV, 137-144, and similar letters to the Lords of Trade, same dates, House of Lords Manuscripts, January 14, 1766, Library of Congress transcripts. For the events of August 14 and 15, described in the ensuing five paragraphs see these letters and also *Connecticut Courant,* August 26, 1765; *Boston Gazette,* August 19, 1765, supplement; Hutchinson to ———, August 16, 1765, Massachusetts Archives, XXVI, 145; Cyrus Baldwin to his brother, August 15, 1765, Miscellaneous Manuscripts, XIII, Massachusetts Historical Society. On the location of buildings and streets in Boston see Justin Winsor, ed., *The Memorial History of Boston* (Boston, 1881), II, i-lv.

the tree where the image hung, but some gesture must be made in order to save face. Even as they sat in the Council Chamber the gentlemen could hear the rising voices outside, for the effigy had been cut down from the tree, and taking it with them the mob marched ominously to the Town House, gave three huzzas to let the Council know who was running the town of Boston, and then passed on.

Andrew Oliver had recently constructed a building at his dock on Kilby Street, intending to divide it into shops and rent them. Under the circumstances it was plausible enough to suggest that this was the office where he intended to distribute the stamps. From the Town House then, with McIntosh in the lead, the mob moved on to Kilby Street, and in five minutes Oliver's venture in real estate had gone the way of Jonathan Loring's barn. The next stop was Oliver's house, in the nearby street which bore the family name. Standing in the street the leaders presented those inside with a bit of pantomime, in which Oliver's effigy was beheaded, while the rest of the crowd showered stones through the windows. From here Fort Hill was only a step, and taking what was left of the effigy the mob moved on to the summit where they ceremoniously "stamped" on the figure and burned it in a bonfire, made appropriately of wood which they had carried from the building on Kilby Street.

For the more genteel members of the mob, disguised in the trousers and jackets which marked a workingman, this seems to have been the last stop on the evening's excursion. But McIntosh had not yet completed his work. With his followers he now returned to Oliver's house. Both Oliver and his family had meanwhile retired to a friendly neighbor's, leaving the house in charge of a few trusted friends, who barricaded the doors. Finding the entrance blocked, the mob proceeded to demolish the garden fence and then systematically beat in the doors and windows and entered the house, swearing loudly that they would catch Oliver and kill him. The trusted friends quickly departed, and the mob were preparing to search the neighboring houses when a gentlemen informed them that Oliver had gone to Castle William and thus saved his life.

It was possible to take revenge on his house, and this they did, destroying the furniture, including "a looking glass said to be the largest in North-America," and a large part of the wainscoting. Governor Bernard meanwhile had sent a message to the Colonel of the Militia ordering him to beat an alarm. The Colonel, a realistic man, replied that any drummer sent out would be knocked down and his drum broken before he could strike it—and besides the drummers were probably all up at Oliver's house engaged in what they would consider more worthwhile activities. With this, having made his gesture, Governor Bernard retired to Castle William, safely isolated from mobs by the waters of Boston harbor.

Lieutenant-Governor Hutchinson was more foolhardy. About eleven o'clock, when the tumult seemed to be subsiding, he took the Sheriff with him and went to Oliver's house to persuade the mob to disperse. He had no sooner opened his mouth than one of the ringleaders, perhaps McIntosh, recognized him. "The Governor and the Sheriff!" went the cry, "to your Arms my boys," and a rain of stones descended on the two men as they hurried off into the darkness. The mob was thus left to have its way and continued to make sport of the Stamp Distributor's house until about midnight, when McIntosh evidently decided to call it an evening.

Thus ended the opening move in the program to defeat the Stamp Act. Everyone agreed that it was the most violent riot the town had ever seen. The next day a number of gentlemen called on Andrew Oliver and persuaded him that what had occurred was only the beginning and suggested that he immediately resign his office. Oliver, like other stamp distributors who later followed his example, must have been somewhat confused by the fact that he had not received his commission and thus really had nothing to resign. He promised, however, to write home for leave to resign and in the meantime to do nothing toward executing the Act. This satisfied the Loyal Nine, but their followers could not understand this devious language. In the evening they built another fire on Fort Hill—Governor Bernard, watching from Castle William, knew that the mob was out again—but the leaders who had produced the previous evening's entertainment were able to dissuade their followers from turning the site of Oliver's house into a vacant lot. Instead the mob diverted themselves by surrounding the house of the Lieutenant-Governor. Hutchinson listened to them beating on the doors and shouting for him to come out, until finally a neighbor convinced them that he had fled, and they gradually drifted away.

During the next ten days McIntosh proved his worth by keeping his followers quiet, and the Loyal Nine could rejoice in a job well done. They had obtained the resignation of the Stamp Distributor a good two and a half months before the Act was scheduled to take effect. Moreover they had made plain what would happen to anyone who dared take Oliver's place. When one gentleman let it be known that he would not have been intimidated had he been the stamp master, they gave him a chance to see how Oliver had felt by fixing the date when his house should be pulled down. The gentleman quickly recovered from his courage and retracted his statement.[8] Few people could be found in Boston who would condemn the proceedings of the fourteenth. Even some of the ministers gave their blessing,[9] and the Loyal Nine, feeling their oats, began to think of other grievances that needed redressing. The officers of the customs and of the admiralty court were obvious targets, and during these days there was much talk of the malicious reports they had sent home about the Boston merchants.[10] Then there was Thomas Hutchinson, a man to reckon with.

The conduct of the Lieutenant-Governor, in ordering the images cut down and in attempting to stop the pillage at Oliver's house, marked him as a friend of the Stamp Act and an enemy of colonial rights. It was insinuated that his letters home had encouraged passage of the Act.[11] Still, the Loyal Nine may not have intended to give Hutchinson the

[8] Bernard to Halifax, August 22, 1765, Bernard Papers, IV, 144-148.

[9] *Ibid.*

[10] Hutchinson, *History,* III, 89-90; Bernard to Halifax, August 1, 1765, Bernard Papers, IV, 149-158.

[11] Hutchinson, *History,* III, 88; Hutchinson to ———, August 6, 1765, Hutchinson to Thomas Pownall, August 31, 1765, Massachusetts Archives, XXVI, 145, 149.

treatment they had handed Oliver. On the evening of the twenty-sixth, Hutchinson himself heard the rumor that the mob was to be out that night, and that the officers of the customs and of the admiralty court were to suffer, but that nothing was contemplated against him.[12] On the other hand, Ebenezer Parkman, the minister of Westborough, thirty-five miles from Boston, heard on the twenty-sixth that Governor Bernard, Lieutenant-Governor Hutchinson, and Mr. Story, the Deputy Register of the Admiralty Court would be attacked. The information came in a letter from a friend in Boston, dated the twenty-fourth.[13]

Neither Hutchinson's nor Parkman's information proved entirely correct. On the evening of the twenty-sixth the mob rallied around a bonfire on King Street and then proceeded in two separate bodies.[14] One went to William Story's, and in spite of the fact that Story had published an advertisement in that day's papers denying that he had written home ill reports of the Boston merchants, they destroyed a great part of his public and private papers and damaged his house, office, and furniture. The other group went after the Comptroller of Customs, Benjamin Hallowell. His house was acknowledged to be one of the finest in town—before they got there. Afterwards the windows, sashes, shutters, and doors were gone, the furniture broken, the wainscoting ripped off, the books and papers carried away, and the wine cellar all but empty.

It is possible that the men who originated the program for this evening had intended that it should go no further, but the letter which Parkman received shows that someone at

[12] Hutchinson to Richard Jackson, August 30, 1765, Massachusetts Archives, XXVI, 146.

[13] Diary of Ebenezer Parkman, August 26, 1765, photostat in Massachusetts Historical Society.

[14] On the riot of August 26 see "Diary of Josiah Quincy, Jr.," August 27, 1765, Massachusetts Historical Society, *Proceedings,* 4 (1860), 47-51; Benjamin Hallowell to Commissioners of the Customs, September 7, 1765, Treasury Papers, Class I, Bundle 442; Thomas Hutchinson to Richard Jackson, August 30, 1765, and Thomas Hutchinson, "A Summary of the Disorders in the Massachusetts Province," Massachusetts Archives, XXVI, 146, 180-184; Bernard to Halifax, August 31, 1765, Bernard Papers, IV, 149-158. *Prologue to Revolution,* 108-109.

least had planned what now occurred. McIntosh, who was still master of ceremonies, after the work at Story's and Hallowell's was completed, united his two companies and led them to the Lieutenant-Governor's. Whether he did this on his own initiative or at the request of the Loyal Nine or at the request of some other group will probably never be known. In later years William Gordon, who came to Boston in 1768 and knew most of the persons who were active in the revolutionary movement there, stated that ". . . the mob was led on to the house, by a secret influence, with a view to the destruction of certain papers, known to be there, and which, it is thought, would have proved, that the grant to the New Plymouth Company on Kennebec River, was different from what was contended for by some claimants."[15] The connection between the New Plymouth Company and the riot remains a secret. It may be that McIntosh saw no harm in killing two birds with one mob. He may have attacked the customs and admiralty officers for the Loyal Nine and Hutchinson for someone else.

Certainly in leading the attack on Hutchinson he had an enthusiastic following. Hutchinson was a cool and haughty man, about whom it was easy to believe any evil. McIntosh and company went about the work of wrecking his house with a zeal that far surpassed their previous height of August 14. They destroyed windows, doors, furniture, wainscoting, and paintings, and stole £900 in cash, as well as clothing and silverware. They cut down all the trees in the garden, beat down the partitions in the house and had even begun to remove the slate from the roof when daylight stopped them.

The fury of the attack on Hutchinson alarmed the best people in town. It looked as though the mob had got out of control and was bent upon transforming a commendable hostility to the Stamp Act into a levelling revolution. Rich men began to send their most valuable possessions to the homes of poorer neighbors where they might be safer.[16]

[15] William Gordon, *History*, I, 180.
[16] James Gordon to William Martin, September 10, 1765, Massachusetts Historical Society, *Proceedings*, 2d ser., 13 (1900), 393; Hutchinson to Richard Jackson, September 1765, Massachusetts Archives, XXVI, 150.

The town of Boston held a meeting and disavowed the attack on Hutchinson, though many of the participants in the pillaging must have been present at the meeting.[17] Hutchinson himself concluded that "The encouragers of the first mob never intended matters should go this length, and the people in general express the utmost detestation of this unparalleled outrage."[18] Three companies of militia and a company of cadets were called out to patrol the town and thereafter for many weeks the streets of Boston echoed with the steps of marching men. Even the children were caught up in the excitement. As one harassed parent complained, "the hussa's of the mobbs, the rattleing of drums, the clamour of the soldiers—who comes there—we are all well—and the continual hubub takes up all their attention. . . . As for James, wee cannot keep him from amongst the hurly burly without I would chain him. Thers no getting them kept to their sett times of schooling, eating, goeing to bed, riseing in morning in the midst of this disorder and confusion."[19]

Governor Bernard meanwhile could think of no better way to meet the crisis than by calling a meeting of the Council. Here it came out that McIntosh had led the assault on Hutchinson, and the Council ordered a warrant issued for his arrest. Sheriff Greenleaf found him on King Street and took him up without resistance. McIntosh was evidently so sure of himself that he felt no need to resist. It had already been rumored that the custom-house would be pulled down. Those who felt that the riots had gone far enough were ready to prevent this by use of the militia, but they were not ready to see McIntosh, who could name the instigators of both riots, tried in court. The word accordingly went around that unless McIntosh was released, not a man would appear to defend the custom-house. At this the officers of the customs went to the Sheriff and asked him to release his prisoner. Sheriff Greenleaf agreed and went to the Town House to tell the

[17] *A Report of the Record Commissioners . . . Boston Town Records, 1758 to 1769,* 152; Hutchinson, *History,* III, 91.

[18] Hutchinson to Richard Jackson, August 30, 1765, Massachusetts Archives, XXVI, 146.

[19] James Gordon to William Martin, September 10, 1765, Massachusetts Historical Society, *Proceedings,* 2d ser., 13 (1900), 393.

Governor and Council what he had done. "And did you discharge him?" asked Hutchinson.

"Yes," said Greenleaf.

"Then you have not done your duty."

"And this," Hutchinson wrote later, "was all the notice taken of the discharge."[20]

McIntosh thus went free, and no one was ever punished for the destruction of Hutchinson's property. But from this time forward the persons directing the mob were careful to keep matters more firmly under control, an accomplishment made possible by the willingness of the militia and of McIntosh to cooperate. Further demonstrations of violence were in fact unnecessary, for the Loyal Nine had made it plain that they were not afraid to bring out the mob against anyone who dared oppose them. Governor Bernard, retired in the safety of Castle William, was ready to admit that he did not have the command of ten men and was governor only in name.[21]

By the end of August, then, Boston was ready for the Stamp Act. With both the Stamp Distributor and the mob under control nothing remained to be done until the first of November, when it would be necessary to adopt a more vigilant watch to see that the Act should not be obeyed in any instance. A minor crisis occurred toward the end of September when the stamped papers arrived on a Boston merchantman. Governor Bernard was prepared for this and had announced earlier that he would lodge them in Castle William for safekeeping, since Oliver had disclaimed any responsibility. Fearing that Bernard would make an attempt to distribute them from the Castle, the Loyal Nine hinted that the people would storm the Castle the moment the papers were landed there and destroy them; but the Governor promptly stated in the newspapers that he was not authorized to distribute them and would make no attempt to do so. With this assurance the Loyal Nine were apparently satis-

[20] Peter O. Hutchinson, ed., *The Diary and Letters of Thomas Hutchinson* (London, 1884–1886), I, 70-71.

[21] Governor Bernard to Halifax, August 22, 1765, to Conway, November 25, 1765, Bernard Papers, IV, 144-148, 170-174.

fied, and when the papers arrived they were landed safely at the Castle under cover of two men-of-war in the harbor.[22]

In the ensuing weeks Boston waited uneasily for November first. Governor Bernard, brooding in Castle William over his grand scheme for reorganizing the empire, felt bitter about the mess which George Grenville had made of things. Although he had written to Richard Jackson on August 24, "to send hither Ordinances for Execution which the People have publickly protested against as illegal and not binding upon them, without first providing a power to enforce Obedience, is tempting them to revolt,"[23] yet he could not quite believe that the people of Massachusetts would be so foolish as to prevent the execution of the Act. At first he told himself that the rest of the province would disavow the hotheaded proceedings of the Bostonians. There had always been a split between the coast and the country, and the country had always been more moderate. Bernard had hopes of getting some backing for law and order from the farmers of the interior when the General Assembly should meet. "I depend upon the Assembly to set these Matters to right," he wrote to his friend John Pownall after the first riot, "as I really believe that there is not one out of twenty throughout the Province but what will disapprove the Proceedings of Boston."[24]

When the Assembly came together on September 25, he pointed out to them that the doctrines of the *Boston Gazette*, however appealing in Boston, would never find acceptance in Westminster. Though Parliament may have made a mistake in passing the Stamp Act, it was still an act of Parliament and the General Court of Massachusetts ought to see to its enforcement.[25] When his speech was over, it appeared that the radicals had won over a majority of the farmers in the

[22] Bernard to Lords of Trade, September 7, and September 28, 1765, House of Lords Manuscripts, January 14, 1766.

[23] Bernard Papers, IV, 18-20; cf. Bernard to John Pownall, August 18, 1765, *ibid.*, 11-15.

[24] Bernard to John Pownall, August 18, 1765, Bernard Papers, IV, 11-15.

[25] Alden Bradford, ed., *Speeches of the Governors of Massachusetts . . .* (Boston, 1818), 39-43.

Assembly, and so, as they prepared to draw up an answer to the speech, Bernard adjourned them.[26] Eventually he had to confess that the country people were even more violent in their opposition to the Stamp Act than the Bostonians: "They talk of revolting from Great Britain in the most familiar Manner, and declare that tho' the British Forces should possess themselves of the Coast and Maritime Towns, they never will subdue the inland."[27]

When he became disillusioned about the interior sometime in September, Bernard still clung to the idea that economic necessity would force the people of Massachusetts to accept the Act. He understood well the dependence of Massachusetts on trade. After November first, no ships would be cleared until the Stamp Act was accepted. Then Massachusetts would repent of her folly:

If the Ports and the Courts of Justice are shut up on the first of November, terrible will be the Anarchy and Confusion which will ensue; Necessity will soon oblige and justify an Insurrection of the Poor against the rich, those that want the necessaries of Life against those that have them; But this is not all, it is possible that, when all the Provisions in the Province are divided amongst the People without regard to Property, they may be insufficient to carry them through the Winter, by cutting off the Resources from Pennsylvania and Maryland, upon which this Province has great dependance, a Famine may ensue. Less obvious causes, but very lately, were so near producing one, even with the help of the usual importations, that many perished for want: And who can say that the present internal stock of the Province, is sufficient, without importations to support the Inhabitants through the Winter only?[28]

[26] Bernard to Lords of Trade, September 28, 1765, Bernard Papers, IV, 162-165.
[27] Bernard to Conway, January 25, 1766, Bernard Papers, IV, 201.
[28] Bernard to Lords of Trade, September 7, 1765, Bernard Papers, IV, 158-161.

Bernard was shrewd enough to see that the men directing the opposition to the Stamp Act wanted no insurrection of the poor against the rich. What he did not see was that these men would be able to turn the hatred of the poor against the British government instead of against the rich. It was true that if the ports were closed, famine would be the result in Boston, but before the poor should rise against the rich their fury would be aimed against the men who had closed the ports. In the face of that fury the ports would not stay closed, and neither would the clearances be on stamped paper. Bernard knew how to analyze the difficulties in the British imperial system, but not the immediate political situation. His opponents had taken his measure correctly in the last weeks of August, and they knew that when the crisis came, he would give them little trouble.

As the first of November approached, and word spread that there would be a grand parade and pageant that day, Governor Bernard performed his usual gesture. He called the Council and pointed out the danger that such a parade would end in more violence. To make matters worse, November 5 (Pope's Day) would follow hard after and give fresh occasion for riot. In order to forestall both these outbreaks, Bernard and the Council decided that several companies of militia should guard the town from October 31 to November 6.[29] On the thirty-first the officers of the militia came to the Council Chamber and, as might have been expected, announced that the militia could not be raised. The first drummer sent out had had his drum broken, and the others were bought off.[30] If Bernard had chosen, he could have had 100 regulars on hand. On September 10, General Gage had sent his aide-de-camp to offer that many troops for the maintenance of order. Bernard refused them, because, as he said, things had quieted down then, and because he was afraid that so small a number would only irritate the people without providing adequate protection to the government.[31] When

[29] Bernard to John Pownall, November 1, 1765, Bernard Papers, V, 16-21.
[30] Ibid.
[31] Bernard to Lords of Trade, September 28, 1765, Bernard Papers, IV, 162-165.

November first came, then, Bernard was helpless. He was assured that his image would not be paraded, but nevertheless he retired to Castle William—not that he was afraid, he hastened to assure his correspondents, but he did not wish to be present when insults should be offered to His Majesty's government.[32]

As if to demonstrate how well they had the situation in hand, the Loyal Nine—or the Sons of Liberty, as they now began to call themselves—maintained perfect order in Boston on November first. The day was ushered in by the mournful tolling of church bells. The images of George Grenville and John Huske (whom the Bostonians took to be an instigator of the Stamp Act) were hung on the tree which had held those of Oliver and Bute on August 14. The tree had since been named the Liberty Tree, and a copper plaque commemorating August 14 (but not August 26) hung around the trunk. At two o'clock in the afternoon the images were cut down, and a procession of "innumerable people from the Country as well as the Town," marching in exact order, carried them through the streets to the gallows, hung them again, and then cut them to pieces. On November 5, there was a similar orderly demonstration, in which the union of the South End and the North End was celebrated with all the decorum of a church supper.[33]

No one in Boston supposed for a minute that these polite celebrations were the end of the Stamp Act troubles. The Sons of Liberty had begun to plan for the next step on their program as soon as they had forced Oliver to resign. On August 26, the day when Hutchinson's house was attacked, Benjamin Edes's paper had carried this item:

Since the Resignation of the Stamp Officer, a Question has been thrown out—How shall we carry on Trade without the Stamp'd Papers?—Carry on no Trade at all, say some, for who would desire to increase his Property, at

---

[32] Bernard to Lord Colville, November 1, 1765, Bernard Papers, IV, 84.
[33] Bernard to John Pownall, November 1, 26, 1765, Bernard Papers, V, 16-21, 43-46; *Boston Gazette,* November 11, 1765.

the Expence of Liberty.—Others say, that in Case there shall be no Officer to distribute the Stampt Papers after the first of November, a regular Protest will justify any of his Majesty's Subjects, in any Court of Justice, who shall carry on Business *without* them?[34]

Governor Bernard naively supposed that the colonists would attempt to defeat the Stamp Act by ceasing all activities which required the use of stamps, but the Sons of Liberty had the second alternative in view—to proceed as though the Stamp Act had never been passed. Before attempting to achieve this by direct action, they tried to persuade the Assembly to effect it by law, as the Rhode Island Assembly had done when they resolved to indemnify officials who suffered by disregarding the Act. When the Massachusetts Assembly convened again on October 23, a committee of both houses was appointed to consider a resolution declaring that since the Stamp Distributor had resigned, whereby the people were prevented from obtaining stamps, it should be lawful to do business without stamps, the Act of Parliament to the contrary notwithstanding. Governor Bernard, still underestimating the boldness of the people with whom he was dealing, supposed that this was simply another means of harassing him. "It is true," he wrote to John Pownall, "that they who bring in this Bill know that I cannot and shall not pass it: But what of that? it will answer their purpose; which is to bring upon me all the odium of the inconveniences, losses and miseries which will follow the non-usage of Stamps. The People will be told that all these are owing to me, who refused passing an Act which would have prevented them, and no notice will be taken of my incapacity to pass such an Act: so that I shall be made to appear to bring on these Evils, which I have taken so much pains to prevent."[35]

To Bernard's surprise the resolve did not pass the House, but the reasons for its failure were not calculated to reduce his uneasiness. The representatives rejected it, because they felt that it implied a right in Parliament to levy the tax. If

---

[34] *Boston Gazette,* August 26, 1765.
[35] Bernard to John Pownall, October 26, 1765, Bernard Papers, V, 13-14.

the reason for ignoring the Act was simply that the stamp officer had resigned, the legality of the Act was admitted. If the resolution were adopted and a new Stamp Distributor should be appointed, it would be morally incumbent upon the Assembly to support him. These complex considerations could be avoided only by an open defiance of the Act, and this was more than the Assembly wished to put on its records.[36] The matter was left therefore, for the Sons of Liberty to resolve in their own way.

The most pressing problem would be the opening of the ports so that the trade which was Boston's lifeblood might go on. By putting every possible vessel to sea before November first the merchants gained a little time in which to consider the risks of ignoring an act of Parliament. The risks seemed to diminish in importance as ships returned from voyages to lie idle, accumulating wharf-charges instead of profits; and the conviction that the Stamp Act must be ignored grew stronger.

While the Sons of Liberty waited for public pressure to rise, the customs officers, the Attorney General, and the Governor engaged in an elaborate rigmarole, in which the question of clearing vessels without stamps was tossed from one to the other and back again with graceful and disgraceful gestures, each person trying to shift the unpleasant decision from himself. The whole procedure is only to be understood in the light of the personal feud which had been going on for over a year between the Governor and John Temple, Surveyor General of the Customs.[37] Temple's headquarters were in Boston, but he supervised the collection of the customs in the entire Northern District from Nova Scotia to Connecticut. Bernard was jealous of Temple's power and did all he could to subordinate it to his own inside Massachusetts. Temple, on the other hand, regarded Bernard as a corrupt and grasping politician who had sabotaged the col-

---

[36] Bernard to John Pownall, November 1, 1765, Bernard Papers, V, 16-21.

[37] On this feud see Bernard Papers, III, *passim*, and Public Record Office, Treasury Papers, Class I, Bundles 441, 442. See also Jordan D. Fiore, "The Temple-Bernard Affair," Essex Institute, *Historical Collections*, 90 (1954), 58-83.

lection of the King's revenue (one example was the slowness with which he had moved to the support of John Robinson when Robinson had been put in the Taunton jail at the suit of Job Smith). Knowing that sooner or later either he or Bernard might have to take responsibility for clearing ships without stamps, Temple was anxious, if possible, to put the onus of the decision on Bernard.

The whole situation was further complicated by the fact that the only knowledge of the Stamp Act in Boston was hearsay. Two copies of the Act had come in private letters and from one of these the Act was printed in the newspapers, but Governor Bernard had received no official copy. From the newspapers he discovered that he was obliged by the terms of the Act to take an oath to support it, and accordingly he did so, but he naturally felt somewhat less responsible than he might have, had he known for certain what he was supposed to support. The same was true of Temple, and to a less degree of Oliver himself. Oliver received a notice of his appointment from the Secretary of the Stamp Office in England, but by November first he had not received his official commission as distributor. He surmised that this might be in the packet of stamped papers which was stored in Castle William, but neither he nor anyone else cared to break open the packet and find out.

Although everyone concerned with enforcing the Stamp Act could thus plead ignorance on November first, no one seriously doubted that the Act which had been printed in the newspapers was genuine, and it was plain that the customs officers whose duty it was to grant clearances would have to decide in the near future what course they should take. Accordingly on October 29 Benjamin Hallowell, Comptroller, who had already tasted the fury of the mob, and William Sheaffe, Collector, asked John Temple what they should do.[38] On October 30 he replied that "as I have nothing in Charge from my Superiors concerning the Stamp Act, I can give you no other Advice or direction, for your Conduct than that of strictly observing all Acts of Parliament that

[38] The account of events in this paragraph and the ensuing eight paragraphs is based on the original letters in the House of Lords Manuscripts, March 13, 1766.

have any Relation to the Duty of your Office, and wherein you may be at a loss for the true meaning of any Act of Parliament, I recommend you to the Advocate and Attorney General for their Advice." No help there.

The next day, October 31, Sheaffe and Hallowell went through the formality of asking Oliver for the stamped papers needed in their office. Oliver replied the same day that he had no commission as distributor and even if he did would not be able to handle the stamps. The next step was to ask Governor Bernard what should be done. He replied as quickly as Oliver that he had no authority to appoint a distributor or to distribute them himself. Sheaffe and Hallowell accordingly sent copies of their correspondence with Bernard and Oliver to the Attorney General, Edmund Trowbridge, and to the Advocate General of the Admiralty Court, Robert Auchmuty, and asked for their advice—all this by the evening of October 31.

On November 1, while Boston was diverting itself with the effigies of Grenville and Huske, Trowbridge sent his answer: ask Mr. Temple, the Surveyor General. As Auchmuty did not choose to make any reply at this point, the Collector and Comptroller were now back where they had started from, and here a disturbing thought occurred to them. Suppose they should refuse to grant clearances on the ground that they had no stamped paper. To grant clearances was their job, and no one else could do it. If they refused would they not be liable to suits for damages from every individual who applied for a clearance and was refused? On the other hand, suppose they granted a clearance on unstamped paper, and suppose further that the ship proceeding under this clearance were seized by the British Navy and condemned for proceeding under improper clearance papers. Would they not be liable in such a case to a suit for the value of the ship? Whatever they did were they not thus liable to innumerable suits? And were not the New England merchants notoriously quick to sue customs officers whenever they could?

Hastily they put their questions to the Surveyor General. Without hesitation he replied, "With regard to the Queries you have put to me, as they are mere points of Law, I must refer you to the Advocate and Attorney General." To the

Advocate and the Attorney General they went, and this time obtained a reluctant opinion, that the Comptroller and Collector would not be liable to damages if they cleared ships on unstamped paper, provided they certified that no stamped paper was available. Having received this opinion, which of course was only an opinion and not a guarantee, Sheaffe and Hallowell still hesitated to proceed without some authorization from either the Surveyor General or the Governor. Accordingly they told Temple of the legal advice they had received, and he of course referred them again to the Governor. The Governor gave them the same answer that Temple had previously: "It is the Business of the Attorney General and the Advocate General to advise you in matters of Law and not mine."

It was now the nineteenth of November, and the merchants were becoming restless. Temple still refused to take responsibility. On his advice Sheaffe and Hallowell approached Bernard again on November 22, saying that they were afraid he might not have read Auchmuty's opinion at the time when he told them to go to the Attorney General and Advocate General for advice. Bernard was not to be caught in this trap: "I must again repeat to you that it is not my business to advise you in matter of Law. . . . I have perused the opinion of the Attorney General and Advocate General but desire to be excused giving my opinion upon the case myself."

Sheaffe and Hallowell next pressed the Attorney and Advocate for more explicit instructions, about how the clearances should be drawn up, and whether bonds as well as clearances might be unstamped. The only result was that Trowbridge got cold feet and withdrew his former advice. On November 30 he wrote, "I do not look upon myself as the Proper Person by whose advise You (in an affair of such importance, and which seems to be at present a matter rather of prudence than of Law) are to govern yourselves and therefore must be excused advising you either to grant Cockets or Clearances upon unstamped Papers or to refuse to do it."

On this same day, November 30, Andrew Oliver's commission finally arrived. Sheaffe and Hallowell again hopefully applied for stamps, but Oliver replied quickly enough that though he had received his commission it was still impossible for him to exercise it. Sheaffe and Hallowell therefore went back to plying Auchmuty and Trowbridge with questions. This time Trowbridge folded up completely. They received an answer written by a friend of Trowbridge's who was directed "to inform you that last Monday night he was seized with the Rheumatism in his right Arm and Shoulder to such a degree, as that he hath not ever since been able, either to write as much as his Name or attend to any business, wherefore he must be excused considering or answering those Questions."

By now the pressure was acute, and the Sons of Liberty were almost ready to take action. On December 11 Sheaffe informed the Surveyor General "that the Town was in an uproar and that there was a meeting of the Merchants and that the Mob intended at night to storm the Customhouse." Temple promptly sent the news to Bernard, with the additional intelligence that there was over six thousand pounds sterling of the King's money in the custom-house. As it grew dark, and the King's customs officers listened for the approaching rumble of the mob, Bernard penned his answer: "I will call a Council tomorrow."

But December 17, not December 11, was the day which the Sons of Liberty had scheduled for opening the customhouse, and the night of December 11 passed calmly. On December 13 Sheaffe and Hallowell made one more nervous attempt to get the stamps out of Oliver or to put the blame more squarely upon him. This time they got a categorical response: "In answer to your Letter of this date demanding my determinate and absolute answer to this question, whether I will or will not deliver you any stamp'd papers after having answered it twice already: I say No."

This was plain enough as far as Sheaffe and Hallowell were concerned, but the Sons of Liberty wanted a public statement. Before they put the final pressure on Sheaffe and Hallowell, they wanted to be certain that there would be no stamped papers available. On December 16, therefore, Benjamin Edes published an anonymous letter in the *Gazette*, asking whether Oliver intended to execute the commission he had lately received. Before publishing the letter Edes secured an answer from Oliver, which he also published, stating "that altho' he had now received a Deputation to act as Distributor of the Stamps for the Province of the *Massachusetts*, He had taken no Measures to qualify himself for the Office, nor had he any Thoughts of doing it."

To the Sons of Liberty this did not appear to be a satisfactory answer. They met in their headquarters at the distillery on Hanover Square and wrote another letter to Oliver:

Hanover Square Dec. 16, 1765

Sir,

The respectable Inhabitants of the Town of Boston, observe your Answer to an anonymous Letter published in Messi'rs Edes and Gill's News-Paper of Today, which we don't think satisfactory; therefore desire that you would, To-morrow, appear under Liberty Tree, at 12 o'Clock, to make a public Resignation. Your Non compliance, Sir, will incur the Displeasure of *The True-born Sons of Liberty.* N.B. Provided you comply with the above, you shall be treated with the greatest Politeness and Humanity. If not . . . . .![39]

When a messenger knocked at Oliver's door and handed his servant this letter, it was too late in the evening and the weather too dirty for Oliver to consult the Governor.[40] The next morning, the weather still stormy, notices were found posted up all over town, reading:

St-p! St-p! St-p! No.

Tuesday Morning, Dec. 17th, 1765

The true-born SONS of LIBERTY are desired to meet under Liberty Tree at XII o'Clock This Day, to hear the Public Resignation, under Oath, of Andrew Oliver, Esq; Distributor of Stamps for the Province of the *Massachusetts-Bay.* . .

A Resignation? Yes.[41]

Oliver realized that he had no way out. He sent for his friend John Avery, who was one of the Loyal Nine and

[39] *Boston Gazette,* December 23, 1765.
[40] Andrew Oliver to Governor Bernard, December 17, 1765, House of Lords Manuscripts, February 10, 1766.
[41] *Boston Gazette,* December 23, 1765.

would be able to act as an intermediary between himself and the Sons of Liberty. Avery came to him at nine o'clock and told him that effigies were already prepared as a signal for a riot in case he failed to appear at the Liberty Tree. In a last-minute attempt to save his dignity Oliver offered to make his resignation at the courthouse. This was not acceptable, and so at 12 o'clock noon, escorted by the redoubtable McIntosh himself, Oliver marched through the streets, the rain beating down tempestuously, and read his resignation from an upper window of the house which stood next to the Liberty Tree. In spite of the rain two thousand people had assembled, and when he was finished they gave three huzzas. Oliver replied with a polite, if somewhat bitter, statement that "I shall always think myself very happy when it shall be in my power to serve this people," upon which there were more cheers, and the crowd departed.[42]

Meanwhile messengers had been hurrying back and forth through the rain from Sheaffe and Hallowell to Temple, Trowbridge, Auchmuty, and Bernard. Auchmuty alone seems to have had the courage to advise flatly that the clearances be issued without stamps. Trowbridge still had the rheumatism, and Temple and Bernard refused to offer any advice. Sheaffe and Hallowell were still afraid to take the responsibility themselves. But when two thousand people could assemble on a rainy day to watch Oliver resign for a second time, present danger loomed larger than future damage suits. On the afternoon of the seventeenth the custom-house opened for business, and in the evening the Sons of Liberty sat down in their headquarters to a dinner of celebration, to which they invited their good friend Samuel Adams and spent the evening drinking healths.[43]

[42] Andrew Oliver to Bernard, December 17, 1765, and December 19, 1765, and to the Stamp Office, December 19, 1765, House of Lords Manuscripts, February 10, 1766 and February 14, 1766; *Boston Gazette*, December 23, 1765; Massachusetts Historical Society, *Proceedings*, 12 (1872), 246-247. The *Boston Gazette* gives Oliver's speech as follows: "I shall always think myself very happy to serve this People, when it shall lie in my Power."

[43] House of Lords Manuscripts, March 13, 1766; Henry Bass to Samuel P. Savage, December 19, 1765, Massachusetts Historical Society, *Proceedings*, 44 (1911), 688-689.

With the ports open, the Sons of Liberty wasted no time in arranging for the opening of the courts. On the morning of the eighteenth the town of Boston, by petition of "a number of Inhabitants," held a special meeting in Faneuil Hall, at which a memorial to the Governor was drawn up. The memorial stated that "Law is the great rule of Right, the Security of our Lives and Propertys, and the best Birth right of Englishmen." With the courts closed, the rule of law must cease; therefore the Governor was requested to order the opening of the courts.[44] Since the memorial was addressed to the Governor in Council, Bernard seized upon his customary method of avoiding unpleasant decisions and appointed the next morning, December 19, for a Council meeting. When the Council met, Bernard informed them that he would leave the matter entirely to them. Since most of the members present were no more anxious to face the question than Bernard himself, and since many were absent, the meeting broke up with a decision to call in all the Councillors who lived within twenty miles of Boston for another meeting the following afternoon. As the gentlemen descended from their chamber in the upper story of the Town House, they could find a hint of what was expected of them in a paper hung up in the room below:

> Open your Courts and let Justice prevail
> Open your Offices and let not Trade fail
> For if these men in power will not act,
> We'll get some that will, is actual Fact.[45]

When the Councillors assembled the next day, the lawyers of the town of Boston presented them with a long harangue on the necessity of opening the courts. The arguments were by now familiar. John Adams told them that the Stamp Act was "utterly void, and of no binding Force upon us; for it is against our Rights as Men, and our Priviledges as Englishmen." Parliament, he said, could err, and when it did, need not be obeyed. "A Parliament of Great Britain can have no

44 *Boston Town Records, 1758 to 1769*, p. 159.
45 Bernard to Conway, December 19, 1765, Bernard Papers, IV, 184.

more Right to tax the Colonies than a Parliament of Paris."
James Otis, moved to tears by his own eloquence, argued
that "The shutting up of the Courts is an Abdication, a total
Dissolution of Government," and he too affirmed, as a principle well known to lawyers, "that there are Limits, beyond
which if Parliaments go, their Acts bind not."[46]

Listening to these arguments, Governor Bernard perceived
that the lawyers had given him another loophole. What they
had said, he told them, "would be very pertinent to induce
the Judges of the Superior Court to think the Act of no
Validity, and that therefore they should pay no Regard to
it; . . ." The question at issue was a matter of law, and it
would not do for the executive branch of the government to
determine a matter of law. In short the judges must decide
the question.[47] The Council welcomed this solution, and
adopted a resolution to the effect that the memorial presented
to them was none of their business. In order to appease, as
they hoped, the wrath of Boston, they added a recommenda-
tion that the judges of the several courts determine the
question as soon as possible.[48] When the answer was delivered to the town meeting, on Saturday afternoon, December 21, the meeting considered the extraordinary question of whether the Council's reply was satisfactory, and
came to the unanimous conclusion that it was not.[49]

The Superior Court of the province was not scheduled to
meet until March, so that there was no immediate necessity
for the justices of this court to make a decision, but the
Inferior Court of Common Pleas for Suffolk County was to
meet in Boston during the second week in January, and the
session of the Probate Court of Suffolk County was already

[46] Josiah Quincy, Jr., *Reports of Cases Argued and Adjudged
in the Superior Court of Judicature of the Province of Massachusetts Bay Between 1761 and 1772* (Boston, 1865), 200-209.
[47] *Ibid.*, 206; Bernard to Conway, December 21, 1765, Bernard
Papers, V, 66-68.
[48] Bernard to Conway, December 21, 1765, Bernard Papers, V,
66-68; Thomas Cushing to John Cushing, January 28, 1766, Cushing Papers, Massachusetts Historical Society; *Boston Town Records,
1758 to 1769*, p. 160.
[49] *Boston Town Records, 1758 to 1769*, p. 160.

overdue.[50] In the Probate Court the obstinate figure of Thomas Hutchinson again appeared in the path of the Sons of Liberty. Hutchinson as Chief Justice of the Colony could postpone acting until March. Hutchinson as Judge of the Suffolk County Probate Court, would have to take his stand at once. His friends told him he must choose between four things: "to do business without stamps, to quit the country, to resign my office, or—" Here one may assume the friends supplied a significant gesture.[51]

Hutchinson was not an easy man to scare, but his friends assured him that he had no time to deliberate. His brother, Foster Hutchinson, did not share his unwillingness to do business without stamps. Governor Bernard suggested therefore that Hutchinson deputize his brother to act for him, but Hutchinson could find no precedent for such a proceeding. The Governor then offered to appoint Foster Hutchinson as Judge of the Probate Court for one year only. Such a limited appointment, Governor Bernard persuaded himself, could be made without stamped paper. Hutchinson complied with this arrangement, and so the Probate Court opened.[52]

Meanwhile the Boston town meeting had made inquiries— one suspects that the questions were heavily weighted—and discovered that the judges of the Inferior Court of Common Pleas in Suffolk County were ready to proceed without stamps.[53] When the next town meeting was held on January sixteenth, both the Probate and the Inferior Courts in Suffolk County were open for business as usual, but the courts in

[50] The records of the Inferior Court of Common Pleas of Suffolk County for this period are not preserved, but the summonses are preserved, and they show that this court was scheduled to meet on the second week in January. On the probate court see Thomas E. Atkinson, "The Development of the Massachusetts Probate System," *Michigan Law Review*, 42 (1943), 425-452, and Quincy, *Reports*, 573-579.

[51] Hutchinson to ———, January 15, 1766, Cushing Papers, Massachusetts Historical Society.

[52] Excerpts from Council Records, and from Hutchinson's Correspondence (Massachusetts Archives, XXVI, 193), concerning this episode are in Massachusetts Historical Society, *Proceedings*, 2d ser., 16 (1902), 111 n.

[53] *Boston Town Records, 1758 to 1769*, pp. 160-161.

the other counties of the province were still closed. Since the only way in which the Bostonians could bring pressure upon these courts was through the General Assembly, the town meeting instructed their representatives in the Assembly to use their influence "that Measures may be taken that Justice be also duly Administred in all the County's throughout the Province and that enquiry may be made into the Reasons why the course of Justice in the Province has been in any Measure obstructed."[54]

The House of Representatives was by this time so thoroughly in accord with the town of Boston that on January 24, 1766, a resolution was passed by a vote of 81 to 5, stating that the courts of justice in the colony, and particularly the Superior Court, ought to be opened. When the resolution reached the Council, there again stood Thomas Hutchinson, prepared to block it. He wished the Council to reject it at once, but the other members postponed consideration until January 30.[55] The *Boston Gazette* immediately went to work on Hutchinson with a highly colored story to the effect that he had said that the resolution was "Impertinent and beneath the Notice of the honorable Board, or to that effect."[56] The *Gazette* had attained such a degree of power by this time that the Council thought it necessary to answer the charge. Governor Bernard, recognizing his old enemy Otis as the author, wanted the Council to have him arrested,[57] but the Council was no more ready than Bernard himself to assume responsibility for so dangerous a move, and contented themselves with passing resolutions in which they denied that Hutchinson had ever said anything derogatory to the House of Representatives.[58]

At the same time the Council thought proper to inquire of the judges of the Superior Court whether they would proceed with business when the next scheduled meeting

[54] *Ibid.*, 161.
[55] *Boston Gazette*, January 27, 1766; *Journal of the Honourable House of Representatives* . . . (Boston, 1765 [*i.e.* 1766]), 214-215.
[56] *Boston Gazette*, January 27, 1766.
[57] Quincy, *Reports*, 213; Hutchinson to ――――, February 27, 1766, Massachusetts Archives, XXVI, 199-200.
[58] *Massachusetts Gazette*, January 30, 1766.

should come up on March 11. The judges were as reluctant as everyone else to take a stand on the question but delivered their opinion that if the "Circumstances" of the colony remained in March what they were in January, and the lawyers should wish to proceed, they would be obliged to do so.[59]

This report from the judges was published without any mention of the provision that made opening contingent upon the wishes of the lawyers.[60] Actually the judges were shifting the responsibility back to the lawyers who had pleaded so eloquently before the Council for the opening of the courts. When March 11 rolled around, rumors of the repeal of the Stamp Act had already begun to arrive, and the revolutionary tension had relaxed to the point where the lawyers were dubious about risking their interests in an irregular procedure when a regular one might be obtained by waiting. Hutchinson, the Chief Justice, manufactured an excuse to be absent from the March session—much to the annoyance of John Adams, who found himself as a lawyer in the dilemma which Hutchinson had escaped as a judge.[61] When the judges, perhaps perceiving the hesitation of the lawyers, declared themselves ready to proceed, even James Otis, who had led the movement to force the opening, was unwilling to plead. Finally a case was dug up which had been continued from the previous session, and after disposing of this, the Court postponed other civil business until April and from then successively until June.[62] The newspapers announced that "all the courts of Justice in this Province are now to all Intents and Purposes open."[63] With this token victory, which everyone could hope was the prelude to a real victory in Parliament, the agitation for opening the courts subsided, and Massachusetts waited for the news of repeal.

[59] Quincy, *Reports*, 213.
[60] *Massachusetts Gazette*, February 13, 1766. The whole incident is described by Hutchinson in a letter to Thomas Pownall, not sent, dated March 8, 1766, Massachusetts Archives, XXVI, 200-206.
[61] Quincy, *Reports*, 215; Adams, *Works*, II, 189.
[62] Quincy, *Reports*, 216.
[63] *Massachusetts Gazette*, March 20, 1766.

Chapter IX

Contagion: Riots and Resignations

WHEN THE PEOPLE of Boston began to pull down houses, they transformed the debate over Parliamentary authority into a test of Parliamentary power. What they challenged on Kilby Street, on August 14, was not simply the authority of Parliament—that was a matter for the colonial assemblies and the Stamp Act Congress—but the ability of Parliament to enforce the authority it claimed. For a few days after taking the step, they must have wondered whether they would stand alone. If so, if one colony alone rebelled, the power of Parliament would surely be too much for it. If all rebelled together, it might not be so easy for the English lawmakers to demonstrate their absolute authority.

Boston had to wonder for only a few days. Before two weeks were out, Rhode Island, the pariah of New England, which had helped save Massachusetts from the Pequots a hundred and thirty years before, again came to her rescue. As soon as news of the attack on Andrew Oliver reached Newport, the conservatives there began to hear rumors that their effigies would hang on August 27, as Oliver's had hung on August 14. What would follow the hanging they might guess for themselves. They knew the men who were planning the affair and expostulated with them. They even pleaded with the Governor to prevent it, but all in vain.[1] On August 26, the day before it was to take place, Martin Howard, Jr., appealed to the public, through an advertisement in the *Mercury*, defending his right to speak and publish his opinions and expressing his surprise "at the mistaken notions of those, who, under a Pretence of serving the Cause of Liberty, would take away the Right of private Judgment, and stop the Avenues to Truth, by instigating the Populace, and endeav-

[1] Thomas Moffat, Manuscript account of the Newport riots, Chalmers Papers, Rhode Island, New York Public Library. *Prologue to Revolution*, 109-113.

ouring to point their Fury against the Person and Interest of a Man, meerly because he happens to differ in Opinion from his Countrymen." The advertisement went on to say, "The Writer does not retract any Position contained in the *Halifax Letter;* and therefore does not meanly sollicit any Favour or Exemption from the Abuse intended him, because if his Person and Interests become the Objects of popular Revenge for these Sentiments, he thinks he shall never lament the Cause, whatever may be the Consequences." Howard was nothing if not proud, but his bold defense left his enemies unmoved, except by a desire to see whether he might not, under proper persuasion, lament those sentiments.

On the evening of the day Howard's advertisement appeared, the people of Boston put on their second riot, in which the house of Lieutenant-Governor Hutchinson was attacked. On the following morning, August 27, before news of the Hutchinson riot could have reached Newport, the inhabitants were treated to a parade in which three effigies were carried through the streets with halters about their necks and then suspended from a newly-erected gallows in front of the courthouse, while three leading merchants marched back and forth below the scaffold with clubs on their shoulders. The figures swinging above could be recognized by the labels conspicuously attached to them. One was Augustus Johnston, who had been appointed Distributor of Stamps for Rhode Island. The second was marked "That fawning, insidious, infamous Parricide, Martinus Scriblerus," meaning Martin Howard, Jr., and the third "that mawgazeen of Knowledge, Dr. Murphy," in other words, Dr. Thomas Moffat. The epithets had been drawn from James Otis's scurrilous pamphlet attacking the Newport group, but the artists who constructed the images added one original touch of their own. They connected Howard's neck with Moffat's by a rope bearing another label with their final verdict on the O.Z. letters. Howard and Moffat were supposed to be saying, "We have an hereditary, indefeasible right to an Haltar; besides we encouraged the growth of Hemp you know."[2]

[2] For the events described in this and the ensuing six paragraphs, except as otherwise noted, see the following: *Newport Mercury,*

The gentlemen who had been so suggestively portrayed feared the worst and retired to the safest places they could think of, Moffat to his farm across the Bay in Kingstown, the others to the man-of-war in the harbor. John Robinson went aboard the *Cygnet* too, "well knowing," as he said, "the Disposition of the People towards all Kings Officers, and the Danger to be apprehended from an inflamed Multitude." Evidently, however, the multitude was not as inflamed as the organizers of the show had expected. During the afternoon, therefore, they provided refreshments, with the hope of drawing a larger crowd. According to Doctor Moffat, they sent out runners to invite the people to this free picnic and served "strong drink in plenty with Cheshire cheese and other provocatives to intemperance and riot." When the party was well under way, the effigies were cut down and burned in a bonfire. After this, in spite of the strong drink and the Cheshire cheese, the crowd dispersed, news having been spread that the principal characters required for any further activities had gone aboard the men-of-war. The next morning Moffat, Howard, Johnston, and Robinson returned home and found everything calm, but during this day, in all probability, news of the exciting riot at Boston reached Newport and further aroused the ambition of Newporters to take a more dramatic stand against the conservatives.[3] The events which began around dusk that evening occurred so rapidly that people later found it difficult to trace them in exact order.

As it was growing dark John Robinson and Martin Howard,

September 2, September 9, 1765; *Boston Gazette*, September 2, 1765; *Connecticut Courant*, September 9, 1765; William Almy to Elisha Story, August 29, 1765, Massachusetts Historical Society, *Proceedings*, 55 (1923), 235-237; Chalmers Papers, Rhode Island, New York Public Library; Augustus Johnston to Commissioners of Stamps, August 31, 1765, Treasury Papers, Class I, Bundle 439, Public Record Office, Library of Congress transcripts; John Robinson to Commissioners of Customs, August 28, 1765, Treasury Papers, Class I, Bundle 442. *Prologue to Revolution*, 109-113. See also Lovejoy, *Rhode Island Politics*, 101, 104-110.

[3] A letter in the Stiles Papers, Yale University Library (J. Avery to J. Collins, August 19, 1765), suggests that the instigators of the Newport riot may have been in correspondence with the Loyal Nine in Boston.

Jr., in company with two other gentlemen who may or may not have been Moffat and Johnston, were walking down Queen Street. A man by the name of Samuel Crandall, who bore a private grudge against Robinson—for what reason is not apparent—stepped up at the head of a small party of men and collared the customs officer. Howard and Robinson's other companions succeeded in prying the man loose, and while Robinson hurriedly made his way home, Howard gave the bystanders a lecture on their unseemly behavior. He paid for his daring at once. A mob quickly collected, and with faces painted and broad axes in their hands, they poured down the street to Howard's house and gave it the same treatment that the Boston mob had given Hutchinson's, though Howard himself made his escape.

This was only a beginning. At Doctor Moffat's, where the mob made their next call, they found material worthy of their efforts. Moffat was something of a collector, and the hiss of ripping canvas could be heard in the din as their axes tore through "Venus Sleeping," "Cleopatra," "Polly Peacham," "The Judgment of Hercules," and "The Countess of Coventry." There were also various intricate scientific gadgets of an appealing fragility (known to the times as "philosophical instruments"), such as telescopes, microscopes, barometers, thermometers, compasses, and hydrometers. These and the fine china from the Doctor's cabinet made a satisfying clatter, and there was also a library of valuable books, some of which splashed at the bottom of the well, while others enlarged the libraries of those who themselves had a taste for collecting.[4]

When there was no more fun to be had at the Doctor's, the mob surged on toward John Robinson's. His housemate, Lieutenant Wickham, warned him of their approach in time for him to make his way to safety aboard the *Cygnet*, where Wickham shortly joined him, for Wickham too, by virtue of his associations, was obnoxious. Deprived of the opportunity to manhandle the Collector, the mob spared the house, which did not belong to Robinson anyhow, and went on to the Comptroller, John Nicoll. But he too had fled.

Finally they got around to the Stamp Distributor. Augustus

[4] Treasury Papers, Class I, Bundle 437.

Johnston had already left, but his friends were there, frantically trying to hide his most valuable possessions in neighboring houses. The mob carted off much of what remained; but the house itself was spared, and when his friends promised that he would resign the next morning the crowd departed. By eleven o'clock, still going strong, they had made a full circle and found themselves back at Howard's, where they now tore up floors, hearths, and chimney pieces. Then on to Moffat's once more, to finish the job there in the same way. They finally wound up about 2 A.M. at Howard's again, their broad axes still sharp enough to cut down the tough young locust trees that lined his yard. After triumphantly stuffing the ends of these into the cannons on the Parade, they marched home to the sleep of exhaustion and drink.

As the principal members of Newport's most exclusive club gathered together one by one aboard the *Cygnet*, they found that none of their number had been killed or injured, but their worst forebodings about the mad "Herd" which ruled Rhode Island had been confirmed, and the town of Newport had lost its attraction for them. Moffat and Howard, thinking doubtless of the hostile faces which they had encountered ever since their publication of the O.Z. letters and the Halifax Letter, decided that Newport was not worth saving. Without going ashore they left by the first ship for England. Augustus Johnston, who despite his office was less unpopular than his companions, went back to town and publicly resigned, though he, like Andrew Oliver in Boston, had not yet received his official appointment.

For Robinson the future was not so easy. The riot had begun with an attack on him by Samuel Crandall. And though Crandall was not himself a merchant, Robinson suspected that he had been egged on by the merchants in hope that the customs officers would be intimidated into overlooking smuggling activities. This suspicion was confirmed when, the morning after the riot, a message came to him from Crandall, saying "that if we would agree to receive our Fees agreeable to their Will and Pleasure,[5] and would also deliver up the

[5] This may have meant a proposal that the customs officers should compound with the merchants for a certain annual sum

Sloop Polly and her Cargo, now under Prosecution before Doctor Spry at Halifax, I might come on Shore in Safety, and rely on their Protection."[6] Here was a truly outrageous proposal, to threaten the life of the Collector unless he would disobey an act of Parliament, and unless he would deliver the *Polly*, which had already caused him so much grief. Robinson sued out a warrant for the arrest of Crandall and issued a notice offering a hundred dollars reward for information leading to the conviction of other rioters, but the Sheriff returned the warrant as impossible to execute under peril of his life, and no one appeared to claim the hundred dollars.[7]

The behavior of Governor Ward was almost as disgraceful as that of the mob.[8] He had refused to take action to prevent the display of the effigies, even though he knew all about the plans days in advance. He had left town after the hanging and did not return until the rioting was over. When Robinson applied to him for protection against the men who were trying to intimidate him, he answered with empty assurances, "that everything is perfectly tranquil, and that you may immediately return to town with all the safety imaginable." Robinson and the other customs officers replied that "while one Samuel Crandall, a principal fellow amongst the mob, dares, to this moment, to threaten the collector; and also on

---

in lieu of duties, or it may have meant that the customs officers should allow the merchants or the Rhode Island Assembly to set the fees which the customs officers collected for their services in clearing and entering vessels. In the preceding year acts had been passed regulating the fees which officers of government, including customs officers, could charge for performance of official duties. John R. Bartlett, ed., *Records of the Colony of Rhode Island and Providence Plantations in New England* (Providence, 1856–1865), VI, 413.

[6] John Robinson to Commissioners of Customs, September 5, 1765, Treasury Papers, Class I, Bundle 442.

[7] *Ibid., Newport Mercury*, September 9, 1765.

[8] On Ward's behavior and his exchanges with Robinson and Leslie described below, see Moffat's account in Chalmers Papers, Rhode Island, and *Records of the Colony of Rhode Island*, VI, 453-457.

his and their behalf, prescribe the terms on which he may come on shore, we cannot consider the riot quelled, or that we may attend to the execution of our offices, either with safety to our persons and property, or to the King's revenue." To this communication, which should have resulted in an order for Crandall's arrest, the Governor answered that he had talked with Crandall, and "upon examining him, he assures me, that he has not the least intention of raising any disturbance or riot, or of doing any kind of injury. . . . He says Mr. Robinson has personally used him ill, and he shall insist upon proper satisfaction; but has not even a thought of taking any illegal or riotous method for obtaining it." The Governor again assured the Collector that there was no danger of another riot and that he might safely come ashore, and yet on the same day that he said this, September first, Captain Leslie of the *Cygnet* informed him of a plan in which Crandall was involved, to rescue the *Polly*. Though the case was being tried before Judge Spry at Halifax, the *Polly* was still in Newport harbor, lying under the guns of the *Cygnet*. According to the plan reported to Leslie, the mob was going "to man and arm a number of boats or vessels, and possess themselves of the fort; and in case they find a resistance on my part, when such boats or vessels are endeavoring to take away the said sloop (which will certainly be the case, when we discover any such attempt being made,) that then the guns at the fort are to be fired at His Majesty's ship under my command. This, I own, appears very surprising; but from the repetition of the report, and what happened last year to His Majesty's schooner *St. John*, I must own I think the madness of the mob may carry them to such lengths, without the interposition of the government's authority."

Governor Ward dismissed this communication as he had those from Robinson. But as long as Robinson stayed aboard the *Cygnet*, the customs office in Newport stayed closed, and the merchants were unable to clear vessels for departure. Bold as the merchants might be, they did not at present dare send their ships to sea without clearance papers. The British Navy would seize ships without papers wherever they found them, and there was no mob available on the high seas to force the

Navy to give them back. Consequently as long as Robinson kept the custom-house closed, foreign trade in Newport was at a standstill.

Robinson could afford to wait. He employed his time by writing an account of the riot and also of the *St. John* episode to the Lords of the Treasury in England. The occasion was an appropriate one for supporting his friends' petition for a royal government, and he assured the Lords that all the riots sprang "from the principles of the constitution of the government, which is the most popular that can be formed," and "that the same causes will be the sources of future riots and disturbances."[9] While Robinson was enjoying the hospitality of Captain Leslie and writing his letters, the merchants were clamoring for the custom-house to open. After four days the clamor reached the ears of the Governor, and since Robinson would not come ashore without a bodyguard, the Governor was obliged on September 2 to provide "5 Or 6 civil Officers," to protect him.[10]

With the custom-house open again, business proceeded, but everyone knew that a new crisis was not far away. The people were evidently determined to prevent the use of stamps after November first. The Stamp Distributor had resigned; the Governor had refused to take the oath required of him to assist in enforcing the Act;[11] and the Assembly had passed a resolution directing all officers to ignore the Act.[12] But John Robinson was not an officer of the Colony of Rhode Island; he was an officer of the King. If he refused to disregard the Stamp Act, all trade out of Newport would be at an end. In anticipation of the crisis merchants loaded as many

[9] *Acts of the Privy Council of England, Colonial Series,* VI, 387.

[10] John Robinson to Commissioners of Customs, September 5, 1765, Treasury Papers, Class I, Bundle 442.

[11] According to Ezra Stiles, Governor Ward was upheld in his refusal to take the oath by the Assembly, which voted that he was included in the promise of indemnity in the resolution directing all officers of government to ignore the Act. See above, ch. VII, and Ezra Stiles's Stamp Act Notebook, Stiles Manuscripts, Yale University Library.

[12] *Records of the Colony of Rhode Island,* VI, 452.

of their ships as possible and hurried them out of port before the November first deadline.[13]

The tension increased when news leaked out that the stamped papers for Rhode Island had arrived in Boston and at the direction of Augustus Johnston had been brought to Newport and placed aboard the *Cygnet*—this in spite of his resignation. The stamped papers had of course been shipped before his resignation, and friends in England had given bond for their safety. When he received word of their arrival, he had to do something about them lest they be destroyed and his friends forfeit their bonds. The safest place for stamped papers as well as for stamp distributors, was aboard a man-of-war, and so he had them delivered to the *Cygnet*. Although it is difficult to see how he could honorably have done less, the people of Newport feared that he intended to act in the office he had publicly resigned.[14] During the night of Saturday, October 19, someone posted a paper on the drawbridge at Long Wharf, where Sunday-morning strollers could not fail to notice it. It warned Johnston that his life would not be worth much in Newport, should he attempt to distribute the stamps. It also communicated some resolutions adopted by the "respectable populace," with regard to the Collector of

[13] The listings of clearances in the *Newport Mercury* for the last weeks in October, 1765, are much larger than in previous weeks and much larger than in the corresponding weeks of previous years.

[14] Captain Charles Leslie of the *Cygnet* and Thomas Moffat, both stated that Ezra Stiles, the pastor of the Second Congregational Church at Newport, harangued the crowd after Johnston's original resignation and warned them that it was no resignation at all, that in spite of it Johnston would be able to resume the office whenever he pleased (*Calendar of Home Office Papers of the Reign of George III, 1760–1765,* London, 1878, pp. 610-611; Chalmers Papers, Rhode Island, New York Public Library). Stiles denied that he had anything to do with the violence against Johnston (letter to Benjamin Franklin, November 6, 1765, Stiles Manuscripts), but Johnston's letter to the Commissioners of Stamps, August 31, 1765, suggests that Johnston did intend to carry on the office if popular hostility subsided (Treasury Papers, Class I, Bundle 439; see also *Newport Mercury,* December 30, 1765). See Morgan, *The Gentle Puritan,* ch. 14.

Customs. There was no indication as to who comprised this respectable populace or as to when and where they adopted their resolutions, but the resolutions themselves were not ambiguous:

> That the C---r of N-- shall use none of them [stamps] in his office, upon pain of our highest displeasure.
> That if he will clear no vessels upon paper without Stamps, that he shall be drove out of town with a high hand.
> That any merchant clearing out his vessel upon St--p papers, shall meet with our highest displeasure.[15]

When the fatal day of November first arrived, the merchants had already cleared out all available vessels, so that there was no immediate necessity of facing the issue. However, as more vessels kept coming into port, Robinson realized that he would have to give unstamped clearances or else leave town. On November 21 he went through the formality of applying to Augustus Johnston for the proper stamped papers. Johnston could only answer that it would be dangerous to his life and property to supply them.[16] Faced with the same dilemma as Sheaffe and Hallowell in Boston, Robinson capitulated, and by November 25 was carrying on business as usual at the custom-house.[17]

After Boston and Newport had shown the way, the mere threat of violence was sufficient in most other colonies. In New York James McEvers did not wait to be asked before resigning as Stamp Distributor. He knew that the invitation would probably be similar to that extended to Andrew Oliver. On August 26, while Boston prepared for its second riot and Newport for its first, McEvers publicly announced his resignation, and wrote to a friend in England asking him to secure

---

[15] *Newport Mercury,* October 21, 1765.
[16] *Records of the Colony of Rhode Island,* VI, 476-477.
[17] This fact has been ascertained from evidence in the Aaron Lopez Invoice Book, Newport Historical Society, and from letters of Ezra Stiles to different persons which indicate the sailing dates of ships from Newport, Stiles Manuscripts.

the appointment of someone else. He recounted what had happened to Oliver and expressed his belief that other distributors would receive the same treatment by November first. The consequences for himself, he said, would be disastrous, "as I have a Large Store of Goods and Seldom Less than Twenty thousand Pounds Currency value in it with which the Populace would make sad Havock with Respect to my own Person I am not much Concern'd About it, but I must Confess I am Uneasy about my Store, as a Great Part of What I have Been Labouring hard for, is Center'd there, . . . if it is Practebil Should be Glad to have Some Other Person Appointed in my Place which I Immagen would be Attended with Little Difficulty as there are many who are not in so good a Way of Business and not so Large a Store at Risque that would gladly undertake it, (by the Present Disposition of People here it Appears that a Stranger would be more Agreable than a Native)." If transportation then had been what it is now McEvers might have closed his letter here, but it occurred to him that by the time his letter reached England he might already have suffered the loss of his property; in that event he would be glad to have the income which the office of stamp distributor would provide if the Act should be enforced. "If this Letter Should Come to your hands too Late," he wrote, "and I cannot *Probably* be Releav'd at or about the time the Act is to be in Force in Such Case I Beg you will not make Any Application for my Releasement, as the First month or Six Weeks Service in the Office will be the most Dangerous and Disagreeable Part of it."[18]

McEvers' letter must have made painfully clear in England the folly of a decision which George Grenville had made the preceding March. After he had driven the Stamp Act through Parliament against the objections of the colonial agents, he had determined to make another appeal for colonial goodwill, this one more genuine than his suggestion that the colonies tax themselves. He had summoned the agents and announced that he would appoint native Americans as stamp

[18] James McEvers to Barlow Trecothick, August, 1765, Treasury Papers, Class I, Bundle 439.

distributors.[19] The offices would not be sinecures, but they would be lucrative, and Grenville supposed that the appointment of Americans would be taken as a friendly gesture. Grenville was a politician, and in the world of politicians the distribution of offices is the principal cement of friendship. What he failed to realize was that by making his stamp masters native Americans he was giving the colonists a lever by which to pry them loose from their positions. If the stamp masters had been Englishmen, strangers to the country, with no property or interests invested in it, they could have withstood the pressure of the populace much longer. But the office was not sufficiently valuable in the eyes of most Americans to make it worthwhile sacrificing the property they had accumulated in a lifetime. John Robinson, an Englishman, could have held out indefinitely aboard the *Cygnet* against the Newport mob. Augustus Johnston, though he might come aboard to save his skin, could not bring his house and business with him. And while the mob made off with some of his property, they left enough to work on in case the first night's attack did not produce his resignation. After the Boston mob had shown the way to deal with an American stamp distributor by pulling down Andrew Oliver's new building, the distributors in other colonies, as McEvers' letter reveals, had to weigh the value of their property against the value of the fees they might or might not collect. There were other factors in the equation, a man's honor and dignity for example, and even his life, but no one could neglect to consider the loss in pounds and shillings which accepting the stamp office might entail.

McEvers, by resigning before a mob demanded it, was able to save something of his dignity, and all of his property. William Coxe, his neighbor in New Jersey, did the same. On August 24 he was writing to the Secretary of the Stamp Office in England that "no spirit of undutifulness or disrespect has yet appeared . . . from the People of New Jersey."[20] On September 2 he resigned, though Governor William Franklin

[19] New Haven Colony Historical Society, *Papers*, 9 (1918), 323, 337.
[20] Treasury Papers, Class I, Bundle 455.

maintained that he had received no threats or insults to cause him to do so.[21]

Other distributors, not so far-sighted or not so timid, stuck it out longer and consequently suffered losses or were obliged to eat humble pie. When Zachariah Hood of Maryland refused to resign after his house had been pulled down on September 2, the mob effectively prevented him from acting by forcing him to flee for his life with only the clothes on his back.[22] Lieutenant-Governor Colden of New York gave him refuge in that colony at Fort George, but this was not a very convenient place from which to distribute stamps for Maryland. At first Hood hoped that a man-of-war might be anchored off the Maryland coast from which he could officiate, but by November 10, he had given up this idea as impracticable, and on November 26 the New York mob sought him out and helped their neighbors to the south by forcing his resignation.[23]

George Meserve, Distributor for New Hampshire, owed his appointment to the fact that he was visiting England when the Act was passed. Even before he set foot again in America, he discovered that he had accepted a liability. The pilot who came aboard to guide his ship into Boston harbor on September 8 delivered a letter from the principal gentlemen of Portsmouth, saying that it would not be safe for him to come home until he had first relinquished his office. The rebellious temper of America became even more apparent when the Boston mob forced his ship to lie for two days in the harbor, under protection of the men-of-war there. Not until they were persuaded that the stamped paper for New England was not aboard would they permit her to dock. Awakened to his

[21] William Franklin to Benjamin Franklin, September 7, 1765, Treasury Papers, Class I, Bundle 442.
[22] *Maryland Gazette*, September 5, 1765; Zachary Hood, probably to Captain Kennedy, September 2, 1765, Sedgwick Papers, Massachusetts Historical Society.
[23] *Ibid.*, and Zachariah Hood to Benjamin Franklin, September 23, 1765, to Commissioners of Stamps, November 10, 1765, Treasury Papers, Class I, Bundle 442; *Maryland Gazette,* January 30, 1766; Knollenberg, *Origin of the American Revolution,* 234, 378.

danger, Meserve announced his resignation before going ashore, whereupon the Bostonians received him with acclamations and conducted him to the Exchange Tavern for a celebration.[24] He found his fellow colonists in New Hampshire equally determined but less cordial. Although he agreed to all their demands, he nevertheless slept uneasily, always with arms by his side, and he dared not engage even in private business for fear of having his "Interests destroyed by a mob."[25]

Jared Ingersoll of Connecticut, in spite of being threatened and burned in effigy in various parts of the colony, held his ground for several weeks but was finally obliged to resign on September 15, when a mob accosted him on his way to the meeting of the Assembly and prepared to lynch him.[26]

John Hughes, a proud man with a sharp tongue, was able to avoid bowing to the Philadelphia mobs until October 7, when they wrung from him a promise that he would not execute the Act unless the other colonies did. Since he was Distributor for Delaware as well as Pennsylvania, he was obliged to give an assurance to the people of that colony that his promise included them too.[27]

George Mercer of Virginia, like George Meserve of New Hampshire, had been in England when the Act was passed, and not anticipating opposition, he too had accepted an appointment as Distributor. Mercer did not arrive in Williamsburg until October 30, two days before the Act was to go into effect. Unfortunately for him, his arrival coincided with a meeting of the General Court which had filled the town with people from all over the colony. They met him in the street

[24] *Massachusetts Gazette and Boston News-Letter,* September 12, 1765; George Meserve to Commissioners of Stamps, September 30, 1765, Treasury Papers, Class I, Bundle 442; James Gordon to William Martin, September 10, 1765, Massachusetts Historical Society, *Proceedings,* 2d ser., 13 (1900), 393.

[25] George Meserve to Stamp Office, December 3, 16, 1765, House of Lords Manuscripts, February 14, 1766, Library of Congress transcripts.

[26] *Connecticut Courant,* September 23, 1765. See below, ch. XIV.

[27] *Pennsylvania Gazette,* October 10, 1765. See below, ch. XIII.

even before he had reached his lodgings and demanded his resignation at once. He asked time to consult his friends, and then, followed by the crowd, he walked to the Coffee House, where the Governor and most of the Council were sitting on the porch. These high officials received him warmly, to the chagrin of those below, and when the mob prepared to seize him, Governor Fauquier stepped forward and taking him by the arm, conducted him safely through the awed assembly, to the accompaniment of angry murmurs. The two men walked to the Governor's mansion and there talked the matter over. "He asked me what he should do," Fauquier reported to the Board of Trade. "In return I asked him whether he was afraid for his Life, if he was it was too tender a point for me to advise him; if not his Honor and interest both demanded he should hold the office; and if that should be his resolution he must not regard the reasonings of his Father and Brother two Lawyers attending the Court, who were both frighted out of their senses for him. He left me that night in a State of uncertainty what part he should act."

By the next morning the state of uncertainty was gone. Either from a different view of honor and interest or because his father and brother had communicated their fears on the point too tender for the Governor's advice, George Mercer resigned.[28]

The populace of Charles Town, South Carolina, had two stamp men to take care of, for both Caleb Lloyd, Distributor for the colony, and George Saxby, Inspector of Stamps for North Carolina, South Carolina, and the Bermudas[29] resided in their town. Lloyd fled for his life on October 20 when the arrival of the stamps precipitated a mob bent on destroying both him and the paper. He dared not return to town, and George Saxby, arriving from London on October 27, joined him at Fort Johnson. There, after two days of willing imprisonment, both stamp men agreed to suspend their duties until the petitions of the Stamp Act Congress (which had just

[28] Fauquier to Lords of Trade, November 3, 1765, House of Lords Manuscripts, January 27, 1766; *Pennsylvania Journal*, November 14, 1765.
[29] House of Lords Manuscripts, January 29, 1766.

finished its meetings at New York) had been sent to England
and Parliament's determination on them returned. Hoping to
exonerate themselves in England, they wrote to the British
Stamp Office that they had given in only "after two days being
prisoners in the fort, to prevent Murther and the destruction
of the town which we were well informed by our friends
would certainly have happened the Inspectors house having
been already rendered uninhabitable himself burnt in Effigie
and the Mobs further resolution of pulling the same to the
Ground and putting us to death unless we agreed to sus
pend. . . ."[30]

November first arrived before the people of North Carolina
and Georgia knew who their distributors were to be. Henry
McCulloh, the original appointee for North Carolina, had
declined the office. Dr. William Houston, who had been fixed
on in place of McCulloh, did not hear of his own appointment
until summoned from his home in Duplin County to Wilming
ton, sixty miles distant, to claim a letter from the Stamp Office
The wary citizens of Wilmington, suspecting the contents of
the letter, had intercepted it and turned it over to the Mayor
for delivery. When Houston arrived on November 16 and
opened it, their suspicions were confirmed, and they required
him to resign forthwith.[31]

In Georgia, as November first approached and passed with
out news of stamps or stamp distributor for the colony, nerv
ous radicals conducted their demonstrations with nameless
effigies and sent threatening letters to a number of conserva
tive citizens suspected of secretly holding the office or of
harboring stamps. Finally, on November 7, the Georgia Ga
zette informed its readers that one George Angus was their
man. Angus was not available for threatening, because he had
not yet left England. Furthermore, he was not a native of the
province, the lone exception to Grenville's ruling on this

[30] George Saxby and Caleb Lloyd to Commissioners of Stamps
October 29, 1765, Treasury Papers, Class I, Bundle 455; William
Bull to Lords of Trade, November 3, 1765, House of Lords Manuscripts, February 14, 1766.
[31] New Hampshire Gazette, December 27, 1765; William
Houston to Commissioner of Stamps, November 20, 1765, House
of Lords Manuscripts, February 14, 1766.

point, and hence he was not susceptible to property damage. But it was not property damage that Governor Wright feared for him. To secure him from violence the Governor made elaborate preparations, so that when his ship arrived at Tybee on January 4, he was whisked away to Wright's house before his presence became generally known. There he immediately took the required oaths of office and distributed stamp papers to the customs officers. In spite of this successful beginning George Angus quickly discovered that his new occupation was not a healthy one, and before two weeks were up he had left for parts unknown.[32]

The infection did not spread so alarmingly north of New England or south of Georgia, but in the colonies which later participated in the American Revolution there was no one able or willing on November first to put the Act into execution. And in most of these colonies, or so the royal governors claimed, it was the contagious example of Boston which had set off the troubles.

The royal governors, to be sure, were not the most disinterested observers. Each of them was anxious to exonerate himself and his administration from any blame, and Boston provided a convenient scapegoat; yet the charge probably was justified to a large degree. It may even be true, as Governor William Franklin suggested to his father, that "the Presbyterians of New England have wrote to all their Brethren throughout the Continent, to endeavour to stir up the Inhabitants of each Colony to act as they have done, in hopes of thereby making it appear to the Ministry too difficult a Matter to call them to account for their late outrageous Conduct."[33] Probably, however, it was not necessary to write private letters. The printers of colonial newspapers sent exchange copies to one another, and the news of what had happened in Boston, together with the inflammatory remarks of Boston's patriots, was sent from one end of the continent

---

[32] *Georgia Gazette,* October 31, November 7, 14, 1765; James Wright to Secretary of State Conway, January 31, 1766, in Charles C. Jones, Jr., *The History of Georgia* (Boston, 1883), II, 60-64.
[33] William Franklin to Benjamin Franklin, September 7, 1765, Treasury Papers, Class I, Bundle 442.

to the other in the *Boston Gazette*. The effect of the news in so distant a colony as South Carolina, was described by Governor Bull in a letter to the Lords of Trade on November 3, 1765:

> Accounts had been received from Boston of the Outrages committed there on the 14th and 26th of August last, and also of those at Rhode Island to show their determined Resolutions to prevent or elude the Execution of the Stamp Act in those Provinces, and also of the Intentions, which other Provinces at the Northward had expressed to the like purpose; tho not with so much violence; . . . New England vaunts its Numbers, and arrogates glory to itself in taking the lead of North America. For before those accounts came, the People of this Province, tho' they conceived it too great a burthen, seemed generally disposed to pay a due obedience to the Act, and at the same time in a Dutiful and respectful manner to represent to his Majesty the hardships, which it would lay them under, and to pray relief therein . . . But by the Artifices of some busy Spirits the minds of Men here were so universally poisoned with the principles, which were imbibed and propagated from Boston and Rhode Island, from which Towns, at this time of the year, Vessels very frequently arrive, that after their Example the People of this Town resolved to seize and destroy the Stamp Papers, and to take every means of deterring the Stamp Officers from executing their Duty.[34]

Boston and Rhode Island could take credit for the initial leadership, but people in South Carolina, and for that matter in the other colonies, would scarcely have been ready to follow such distant leaders if the direction of march had not been agreeable.

[34] House of Lords Manuscripts, February 14, 1766. Cf. James Wright to Lords of Trade, November 9, 1765, *ibid.*; Fauquier to Secretary of State Conway, December 11, 1765, House of Lords Manuscripts, February 6, 1766.

Chapter X

Nullification: Ports and Courts

ALTHOUGH MASSACHUSETTS TOOK the lead in violence, several other colonies were putting their ships to sea with clearance papers unstamped before Sheaffe and Hallowell finally opened the Boston custom-house. The speed with which merchants were able to resume business as usual after November first, was measured by their own determination, by the contrary determination of their customs officers and governor, and by the economic needs of their particular colony. In Georgia where, on November first, there were no stamps, no stamp distributor, and indeed no copy of the Stamp Act itself, Governor Wright and his Council felt justified in authorizing the clearance of ships without stamps. The customs officers simply continued to use old forms, with a note to the effect that no stamps were available.[1]

In Georgia this procedure was temporary, and the ports closed on November 30, after Governor Wright and the customs officers received definite notices of the Act;[2] but in Virginia the Act was consistently violated, so far as shipping was concerned, from November second onward. The way was smoothed here by the fact that George Mercer, who brought the stamps for Virginia with him, claimed to have none for the custom-house, so that the necessity of proceeding without them appeared to arise from neglect in England rather than from violence in America.[3] The procedure was facilitated too by the straightforwardness of the Governor and of the Surveyor General of the Western Middle District. The latter, Peter Randolph, when he could not at first persuade the Governor to share the responsibility, did not

[1] *Georgia Gazette*, November 7, 14, 1765; *Colonial Records of Georgia*, IX, 435.

[2] *Colonial Records of Georgia*, IX, 439-440, 454-456.

[3] Certificate by Fauquier, House of Lords Manuscripts, February 14, 1766, Library of Congress transcripts.

wait but on November 2 advised the collectors on his own initiative to clear vessels as usual, and to give a certificate that no stamped paper was available. At the same time, he told them, they should take from the master a waiver of damages in case the vessel should be seized at its destination for lack of a proper clearance. Randolph sensibly concluded that "impossibilities will not be expected of us, and that from the Nature of the Case our Conduct will stand justified."[4] Governor Fauquier quickly saw the reasonableness of Randolph's action, and on November 7 added his sanction to it. Thereafter the certificates testifying to the lack of stamps bore the Governor's signature under the province seal.[5]

Rhode Island followed Virginia by the last week in November, and in the first week of December Pennsylvania, New York, and New Jersey did likewise.[6] In Philadelphia, by an ingenious device not apparently thought of elsewhere, trade had been kept moving throughout November. In all colonial ports merchants had cleared out every ship they could load before November first, but in Philadelphia they cleared ships which were only partially loaded. Although clearances were not supposed to be granted until the entire cargo was declared, all the ships in Philadelphia which had any part of their cargoes aboard obtained clearance papers in the last days of October. When the cargoes had been completed, the owners went to the custom-house and had undated additions entered on their papers. The Collector, John Swift, at first refused to cooperate in this scheme unless the merchants would engage to pay whatever penalties he might undergo as a consequence, but when the Governor failed to back him

[4] Peter Randolph to Collector of Customs at Norfolk, November 2, 1765; *Pa. Mag. of Hist.*, 2 (1878), 298-299.

[5] Fauquier to Lords of Trade, November 11, 1765, House of Lords Manuscripts, February 14, 1766; Andrew Eliot to Charles Stewart, December 6, 1765, Philadelphia Custom House Papers, Historical Society of Pennsylvania.

[6] Abel James and Henry Drinker to John Clitherall, December 3, 1765, James and Drinker Letter Books, Historical Society of Pennsylvania; Collector and Comptroller of New York to Archibald Kennedy, December 10, 1765, and Collector of Perth Amboy to Commissioners of Customs, December 7, 1765, House of Lords Manuscripts, February 14, 1766.

up he gave in.[7] Since it normally took three to four weeks for a ship to complete her cargo, there was relatively little pressure in Philadelphia until the end of November. On November 28 several vessels, with clearance papers dated before the first, were still waiting to finish loading.[8] By this time, however, the number of vessels which had reached port after the first was beginning to mount. On December first the Collector and Comptroller wrote to the Commissioners of Customs describing their troubles:

We have not yet done anything since the first of November, but people who have Vessels loaded begin to be very uneasy and Clamorous, The Winter is near at hand, and We may expect in a short time, that Our Navigation will be stopt by the Ice. The Harbour is full of Vessels, and if We don't begin soon to permit them to depart, they will probably be shut up all the Winter, which will occasion great distress and perhaps Ruin, to many of His Majesty's subjects, and at the same time be a means of lessening the Revenue of Customs.

What we have said above is on a supposition that it is in our power to detain them, but that is not the case, We dare not do it if we would; People will not sit quiet, and see their Interests suffer, and perhaps Ruin brought upon themselves and Famalies, when they have it in their power to redress themselves. . . . So that upon the whole We are of opinion that it will be best to let the business of the Custom house go on as usual, till We receive Instructions to the Contrary: The Surveyor General is of this opinion, but he does not chuse to give Us any Orders, as he cannot

---

[7] Joseph Shippen to Edward Shippen, Jr., November 9, 1765, Shippen Papers, Historical Society of Pennsylvania; Thomas Clifford to Walter and Samuel Franklin, November 12, 1765, Pemberton Papers, Historical Society of Pennsylvania; Samuel and Jonathan Smith to Nathaniel Holmes, November 2, 1765, Samuel and Jonathan Smith Letter Book, Library of Congress; Abel James and Henry Drinker to Parvin and James, November 2, 1765, James and Drinker Letter Books.

[8] Abel James and Henry Drinker to Neate, Pigou, and Booth, November 28, 1765, James and Drinker Letter Books.

undertake to Indemnify Us against the Penalties of an Act of Parliament.[9]

By the next day the Collector and Comptroller accepted the necessities of the situation and began to issue clearances.[10] Before another week went by the Surveyor General, Charles Stewart, also screwed up his courage and sent out orders to all the officers of the Eastern Middle District (New Jersey, Delaware, Pennsylvania, New York, and Quebec) to clear vessels on unstamped paper if they thought it prudent.[11] Though he warned them that his order would not indemnify them in case of suits for damages, they all found it prudent to do as he suggested.

Stewart, in explaining his action to the Commissioners of Customs, pointed out the losses that would be entailed not only in the mainland colonies but in the West Indies, and in England, by keeping the ports closed, but he emphasized the fact that he had really no choice in the matter. One hundred and fifty sail of vessels were rotting in Philadelphia harbor, and if these should remain over the winter the consequences would be appalling: "Nothing is more certain than that so great a Number of Seamen, shut up for that Time in a Town destitute of all Protection to the Inhabitants . . . would commit some terrible Mischief, or rather that they would not suffer themselves to be shut up, but would compel the Officers to clear Vessels without Stamps—This would undoubtedly have been the Consequence of a few days longer Delay, . . ."[12] Idle sailors were a problem in every port, but the bigger the port the bigger the problem. Though the customs officers at New York began to receive threatening letters as soon as the Stamp Distributor resigned, some even demanding that they remit duties which had been collected under the Sugar Act, they were able to hold out until word

[9] Treasury Papers, Class I, Bundle 442, Library of Congress transcripts.

[10] Abel James and Henry Drinker to John Clitherall, December 3, 1765, James and Drinker Letter Books; Philadelphia Custom House Papers, IV; *Pennsylvania Journal*, December 5, 1765.

[11] House of Lords Manuscripts, February 19, 1766.

[12] Charles Stewart to Commissioners of Customs, December 8, 1765, House of Lords Manuscripts, February 19, 1766.

came that the Philadelphia officers had begun to clear ships and that the Surveyor General approved. After they opened the port, on December 4, they wrote to the Commissioners of the Customs: "This step, we thought the more adviseable as we understood the Mob (which are daily increasing and gathering Strength, from the arrival of Seamen, and none going out, and who are the people that are most dangerous on these occasions, as their whole dependance for a subsistence is upon Trade) were soon to have a Meeting."[13] From such a meeting the officers knew what to expect.

Once the Collector and Comptroller began to issue clearances the pressure of the mob in New York slackened, but the situation was complicated by the action of Captain Archibald Kennedy of His Majesty's Ship *Coventry*. Captain Kennedy stopped all vessels he could catch leaving New York, and upon finding the clearance papers unstamped, refused to allow them to proceed. At the same time he allowed vessels to enter unmolested even when their papers, though dated after November first, were unstamped.[14] There continued therefore to be a large floating population of seamen in New York City, who kept the officers of government uneasy.

Duncan Stewart, the Collector of New London, held off the anxious merchants of that port for several weeks, awaiting instructions from John Temple, the Surveyor General of the Northern District in Boston. While Temple, Bernard, and the customs officers in Boston tossed the problem back and forth, Stewart was forced to give way and opened the port on December 14, three days before Boston.[15] Within two weeks New Haven, the only other port of any consequence in Connecticut, had also resumed business.[16]

The custom-house at Portsmouth, New Hampshire, which was also under John Temple's jurisdiction, remained closed

[13] Collector and Comptroller of New York to Commissioners of Customs, November 6, 1765, Treasury Papers, Class I, Bundle 442; same to same, December 20, 1765, House of Lords Manuscripts, February 14, 1766.

[14] *Ibid.*

[15] Duncan Stewart to John Temple, December 19, 1765, House of Lords Manuscripts, March 13, 1766.

[16] *Connecticut Courant*, February 10, 1766.

for a few days after the opening in Boston.[17] But New Hampshire ships had not all been gathering barnacles in port. Somewhere around December fourth Captain John Langdon had put his ship *Hector* out of Portsmouth Harbor for Montserrat, apparently without clearance papers of any kind, and was shortly sending back information about what ports in the West Indies could be safely entered without stamps, so that when officers at Portsmouth began issuing clearances, a fleet of New Hampshire vessels was ready to drive southward to resume the interrupted trade.[18]

Maryland and the Carolinas were last to issue unstamped clearances. On January 30, 1766, the *Maryland Gazette* announced that vessels had cleared last month from Oxford and Pocomoke without stamps and were now clearing from Annapolis in the same way, employing certificates that no stamps were to be had. The issue was not forced until February in the Carolinas. Peter Randolph, as Surveyor General could conceivably have speeded up the opening of these ports the way he did in Virginia. There is some evidence that he attempted to, but was foiled by zealous governors and customs officers. In January Randolph had made a trip to Charles Town and dropped some strong hints to the effect that trade should proceed. These excited the people there, who thought as Henry Laurens acidly observed, that Randolph "had power to annihilate Acts of Parliament." There ensued a verbal battle between the Governor on one side and Randolph and the Assembly on the other, the latter buttressed by petitions from the merchants and the owners and masters of vessels and by the increasing commotions of

[17] Benning Wentworth in a letter to the Lords of Trade, December 16, 1765 (photostat in New Hampshire Historical Society) said that the port was still closed. *New Hampshire Gazette,* December 20, 1765, printed a notice of three ships entered at the Custom House during the preceding week, but none cleared out. Subsequent issues of the *Gazette* omitted the customary Custom House records. The port was probably opened as a result of a popular demonstration on December 26, 1765, described in a letter of that date from George Meserve to the Stamp Office, House of Lords Manuscripts, February 14, 1766.

[18] See shipping agreements and correspondence of John Langdon in the Langdon Papers, New Hampshire Historical Society.

the populace. The Governor capitulated after Caleb Lloyd issued a public notice "that he adhered to his former resolution not to distribute Stamp'd Paper," and on February 4, began issuing certificates to be attached to clearance papers, testifying to the unavailability of stamps. One difficulty remained: the Collector still refused to budge until some superior should give him written orders. Randolph by this time was getting cold feet, and though he repeatedly advised the Collector to proceed, he would not order him to do so, and neither would the Governor. How this impasse was overcome is not apparent from the surviving records, but it was overcome, for by the last week in February vessels from South Carolina were arriving in other colonies.[19]

In North Carolina Governor Tryon at first attempted to secure submission to the Stamp Act by a shrewder strategy than any other governor devised. Sensing that the Assembly might imitate the Virginia Resolves or send delegates to the Congress at New York, he kept them prorogued. At the same time he summoned fifty leading gentlemen from Brunswick, New Hanover, and Bladen counties to meet with him on November 18. After wining and dining them, he explained his own disapproval of the Stamp Act and his particular concern for the people of North Carolina. He would write to England, he said, in terms that would bring a "favorable indulgence and exemption" for North Carolina, whether the Act were repealed or not, provided, of course, that the people did not frustrate his efforts by their own conduct. He recommended that they accept the stamps during the brief period before Parliament repealed the Act or exempted them from it. By so doing they would enjoy unusual opportunities for trade, while the merchants of other colonies twiddled their thumbs. As a further inducement he offered to pay from

[19] Henry Laurens to John Gervais, January 31, 1766, to Rosset and Gervais, February 4, 1766, Laurens Letter Book, Historical Society of Pennsylvania; extracts from the Journals of the Commons House of Assembly of South Carolina, and correspondence between Peter Randolph and Governor Bull, in Colonial Office Papers, Class 5, vol. 649, Library of Congress transcripts; *Virginia Gazette* (Purdie), March 14, 1766; *Maryland Gazette,* March 13, 1766.

his own pocket the cost of the stamps on documents from which he derived a fee as governor, such as deeds, wills, and licenses.

The temptation to break ranks and use the stamps must have been great; yet the gentlemen who dined with Governor Tryon answered him the next day with a firm and dignified refusal. To submit to any part of the Act they said, "would put it out of our Power to refuse with any Propriety, a Submission to the Whole; and as we can never consent to be deprived of the invaluable Privilege of a Trial by Jury, which is one part of that Act, we think it more consistent as well as securer conduct to prevent to the utmost of our Power, the operation of it."

The North Carolinians refused to seek prosperity at the expense of the other colonies. In fact they were still twiddling their own thumbs with the custom-houses closed for several weeks after most other colonies had resumed trade. But by February 12 all ports except Cape Fear were open. The matter did not come to a head there until February 21. Early in January Captain Lobb of His Majesty's Sloop *Viper* had seized three ships entering the Cape Fear River, because their clearance papers, issued in other ports, were unstamped. On February 15 the King's Attorney, Robert Jones, gave his opinion that the seizures were legal and that William Dry, the Collector at Brunswick, should prosecute the vessels in the Admiralty Court at Halifax. As a result the men from Brunswick, New Hanover, and Bladen counties assembled on February 18 in Wilmington where they formed an association to prevent the operation of the Stamp Act. Their organization perfected, they marched on Brunswick a thousand strong and for the next three days were in complete control of the town and port. With the Collector in their power they ransacked his desk for the papers of the seized ships and, having found them, secured from Dry and Lobb not only the release of the vessels but a promise that the port would henceforth be stamp-free. Finally, on February 21, they rounded up all available customs and court officers and forced them to swear an oath not to execute the Stamp Act. Satisfied by this wholesale abjuration, they dispersed, many of them sailing triumphantly back to Wilmington on the liberated sloops.[20]

As previously noted, Georgia, without official notice of the Act, had carried on her shipping as usual until the end of November. When Governor Wright put an end to the unstamped clearances on November 30, neither stamps nor distributor had yet arrived; but Wright, once having learned what England expected of him, adhered strictly to his duty, and Georgia merchants, ship-owners, and captains petitioned in vain for business to proceed as it did in Virginia. When George Angus finally did arrive and under close guard distributed stamps for the customs officers, the latter were able to clear some sixty ships on stamped paper between January 17 and January 30. The Savannah merchants were willing to play the role which those of North Carolina had disdained, and they earned the hatred and contempt of the other colonists for this betrayal of American unity. The country people of Georgia, who were also outraged, gathered in all parts of the province for a march on Savannah. On January 27 Governor Wright heard that there were at least six hundred of them, all armed, and without waiting for them to arrive, he rushed the stamped papers to Fort George on Cockspur Island and from there to His Majesty's Sloop *Speedwell*. By this move he saved the papers from destruction but also saved them from use, for on the island and the warship they were as effectively removed from circulation as the mob could wish.[21] The *Pennsylvania Journal* of February 27, reporting this episode, stated that as a result of it the port was operating without stamps.[22]

The opening of the ports in defiance of the Stamp Act had

[20] *Colonial Records of North Carolina,* VII, 127-130, 168-183.

[21] *Pennsylvania Journal,* February 13, 1766; *Colonial Records of Georgia,* IX, 454-456; James Habersham to Daniel Roubadeau, December 17, 1765, to William Knox, January 29, 1766, Georgia Historical Society, *Collections,* 6 (1904), 56-58; Percy Scott Flippen, "Royal Government in Georgia, 1752-1776," *Georgia Historical Quarterly,* 13 (1929), 142-149; Jones, *History of Georgia,* II, 60-64.

[22] Though newspaper accounts during these days were not wholly reliable, the report seems to be substantiated by records of shipping bonds posted during February, March, and April. See Georgia Historical Society, *Collections,* 8 (1913), 259 ff.

been accomplished in most colonies within less than two months of the date when the Act was supposed to have gone into effect and in all the colonies before the Act was repealed. The interval from November first to the time when officers began to issue clearances, was not a comfortable time for anyone, except perhaps the wheat farmers of the middle colonies. Events which cause trouble for the rest of the population frequently blow their saving good in the direction of the farmers. In the summer of 1765, when it began to appear that New England's ports might be closed on November first, merchants there began to buy heavily in the Philadelphia and New York flour markets. The result was a scarcity of flour and booming prices even before the first of November. In Philadelphia the ships which had obtained their clearance papers with nearly empty holds continued the competition throughout November; and when clearances were issued again in December the prospect of the ice closing the port more effectively than the stamps had, caused the merchants to raise prices again in order to get the farmers to bring their crops to market before it was too late.[23]

This boomtime for farmers was accompanied by high prices and short rations for the rest of the population. In New York the export of flour before November 1 had been so large that there was a shortage of bread, and at the same time the accumulation of ships in the harbor under Captain Kennedy's ban increased the population and the demand for bread. The winter of 1765 was a lean one for New Yorkers and probably for the people of other colonial cities.[24]

The colonial merchants, in spite of their success in resuming trade, were by no means happy about the risks they were running. In most cases they had to waive all claims for damages in case their imperfect clearance papers should result in seizure of their vessels. At first they hardly knew where to

[23] Thomas Clifford to Harper and Hartshorn, October 8, 1765, November 1, 1765, Pemberton Papers; Abel James and Henry Drinker to Lewis Teissier, December 18, 1765, James and Drinker Letter Books.

[24] William Bayard and Co. to John Henniker, December 21, 1765, House of Lords Manuscripts, February 14, 1766.

send their ships. Rumor had it that vessels arriving in the West Indies without stamped papers were being seized, and to send ships to England would be asking for trouble. Many diverted their vessels to the Lisbon trade or the Irish; or to carrying provisions to the northern colonies. Some sent their captains to nose their vessels cautiously into West Indian ports; but all felt the danger of seizure hanging over them and had to choose between that and idle hulls.[25]

In the West Indies the repercussion of the continental opposition to the Stamp Act was felt not merely in similar outbreaks of violence but in a shortage of supplies. The temporary closing of North American continental ports and the reluctance of American merchants to risk their ships in West Indian waters with unstamped clearance papers cut sharply into the flow of provisions and lumber upon which the Islanders depended. A planter in Antigua wrote on December 22, 1765, "Our Crop promises well, but we are likely to be Miserably off for want of Lumber and Northward Provisions, as the North Americans are determined not to submit to the Stamp Act, and of course cannot clear out their Vessells, shou'd this be of any continuance, the Islands (nay the Merchants in England as our Remittances principally center there) will feel the Effects severely, for there is not One tenth part of the Lumber in the Islands that will be required for the next crop . . . when we're deprived of a Trade from the Northward, the Estates here can never be supported."[26]

Meanwhile trade returned to normal. Quebec, Nova Scotia, Florida, Barbados, Grenada, and Jamaica consistently made use of the stamps—to the great disgust of the other colonies

[25] *Maryland Gazette,* January 30, 1766; Abel James and Henry Drinker, letters dated December 7, 27, 28, 1765, January 1, February 8, February 20, May 14, 1766, James and Drinker Letter Books; Thomas Clifford to Captain John Harper, December 16, 1765, Pemberton Papers.

[26] Treasury Papers, Class I, Bundle 452. Part of the shortage in the West Indies was due to resentment by the continental colonies against those of the islands, especially Barbados, which had submitted to the Stamp Act. See *Maryland Gazette,* January 30, 1766; *Georgia Gazette,* June 11, 1766.

—but even in these places ships arriving with unstamped papers from other American ports were unmolested.[27] Before the Act was repealed, American ship captains discovered that they could land in England itself without stamps,[28] and enterprising Philadelphia firms were issuing insurance against seizure at the rate of 2½%, sufficient evidence that the British Navy was not making much effort to enforce the Act.[29] The temporary closing of the ports, besides upsetting the course of trade and causing unexpected scarcities in various regions, had only one important effect, an effect which could scarcely have pleased the authors of the Stamp Act: it caused an increase in smuggling and a corresponding decline in respect for British authority. Though the customs officers finally gave way before the pressure, they waited long enough for the colonists to exhibit their contempt for an unconstitutional law. The officers at New York reported that "vessells were continually going and coming without any regard to the Customhouse or the Laws of trade, and we didn't dare neither would it have been prudent to take any Notice of them";[30] and from Philadelphia the officers wrote plaintively that so long as the Americans were determined not to use stamps, "we must now submit to necessity, and do without

---

[27] *Virginia Gazette* (Purdie), March 7, March 21, April 4, 1766; *Maryland Gazette,* March 13, 1766; *Pennsylvania Journal,* March 6, 1766; Lord Colville to Philip Stephens, February 10, 1766, Admiralty Secretary In Letters 482; Governor of Barbados to Charles Lowndes, February 24, 1766, Treasury Papers, Class I, Bundle 452; Colonial Office Papers, Class 5, LXVI, 273 (the last three are in the Public Record Office, Library of Congress transcripts); Massachusetts Historical Society, *Collections,* 69 (1914), 143; W. B. Kerr, "The Stamp Act in Quebec," *English Historical Review,* 47 (1932), 648-651; W. B. Kerr, "The Stamp Act in Nova Scotia," *New England Quarterly,* 6 (1933), 552-566.

[28] *Pennsylvania Journal,* March 6, 1766; House of Lords Manuscripts, March 5, March 7, 1766.

[29] *North Carolina Gazette,* February 26, 1766, quoted in *Colonial Records of North Carolina,* VII, 168 f.; *Pennsylvania Journal,* April 10, 1766.

[30] Collector and Comptroller of New York to Commissioners of Customs, December 20, 1765, House of Lords Manuscripts, February 14, 1766.

hem, or else in a little time, people will learn to do without either them or us."[31]

In the other colonies, as in Boston, the Sons of Liberty were less successful in opening the courts without stamps than they were in opening the ports. One reason may have been the occupational conservatism of lawyers and judges. This, however, was only one reason, and perhaps not the most important. When the Revolution did come ten years later, the people of Berkshire County, Massachusetts, kept the courts closed for five years, and not because of any lingering loyalty to Great Britain. The temporary closing of the ports benefited only the farmers, and even this benefit would have turned to disaster if the closing had been more than temporary. The closing of the courts, on the other hand, was a decided advantage for a great many people. The proceedings in criminal courts did not require stamps so that the community suffered no interruption in the prosecution of criminals, but the admiralty courts, like the civil courts, could not properly function without stamped papers. The effect of closing the courts, therefore, was to render the opening of the ports less risky, for with the courts closed the means of enforcing both the Stamp Act and the Acts of Trade was removed. The Admiralty Court at Halifax was still open, to be sure, for the stamps were in use there, but there was great inconvenience in carrying cases so far, and the impossibility of trying them in local courts left the naval and customs officers in a quandary. If they seized a vessel, whether for smuggling or for sailing without stamped papers, they could not tell how long it would be before they would be able to have her condemned in court, and they were uncertain how long they were entitled to hold her without trial. In these circumstances they were apt to overlook violations which they might otherwise have stopped.[32]

[31] Collector and Comptroller of Philadelphia to Commissioners of Customs, December 1, 1765, Treasury Papers, Class I, Bundle 42.

[32] See letters from the Deputy Collector at New York to the Attorney General, no date, Philadelphia Custom House Papers, V, and from Captain Sterling of the *Rainbow* to the Lords of the Admiralty, November 5, 1765, House of Lords Manuscripts, January 29, 1766.

Besides facilitating the movement of trade in this way, the closing of the courts benefited everyone who was in debt. Henry Laurens even suspected that the champions of resistance to the Stamp Act intended to "obtain a Credit during their own pleasure by the distruction of the Stamp'd Papers,"[33] for as long as the courts remained closed it was impossible for creditors to bring suit, and if the amount of litigation in colonial courts is any indication, colonial debtors seldom paid until a judge ordered them to.

In colonies where a large number of people were indebted to creditors outside the colony there was a decided advantage in keeping the courts closed. William Samuel Johnson in Fairfield, Connecticut, wrote to his friend Eliphalet Dyer (both were active opponents of the Stamp Act) "Our being so excessively in debt to the Neighbouring Governments seems to be a Reason peculiar to us why we sho'd be less hasty than others in opening the Courts of Law but I am not fully determined what is best in this matter."[34] Even before the passage of the Stamp Act, the indebtedness of Connecticut had caused a shortage of currency and recourse to barter.[35] The closing of the courts gave a temporary respite from the drain of money out of the colony. Although the radicals felt obliged for the sake of political consistency to demand that the courts ignore an unconstitutional law,[36] it is not surprising that Connecticut courts remained closed. When they opened again, after repeal of the Stamp Act, Johnson reported that there were "Riots and Tumults among the People who having so long been loose from the curse

[33] Henry Laurens to Joseph Brown, October 22, 1765, Henry Laurens Letter Book.

[34] December 31, 1765, William Samuel Johnson Papers, Connecticut Historical Society. Cf. Lawrence H. Gipson, *Jared Ingersoll* (New Haven, 1920), 214-216.

[35] *Connecticut Courant*, March 11, May 20, June 10, August 26, September 2, 1765; Oscar Zeichner, *Connecticut's Years of Controversy, 1750-1776* (Chapel Hill, 1949), 46-48.

[36] Sons of Liberty of Norwich, Connecticut, to Sons of Liberty of Portsmouth, New Hampshire, March 3, 1766, Belknap Papers, Massachusetts Historical Society; Resolves of the Meeting at Pomfret, *Boston Gazette*, January 13, 1766.

of the Law unwillingly submit again to its necessary restraints."[37]

The same shortage of currency which Connecticut felt because of her outside indebtedness was created or aggravated in the colonies south of New England by the new Currency Act. Since this was not an act of taxation, the colonists made no attempt to nullify it as a measure beyond the authority of Parliament, but the closing of the courts in some measure helped to ease the problems which it presented. While the Currency Act tended to raise the value of money and thus make the payment of debts more difficult, the closing of the courts prevented the collection of debts and thus tended to reduce the demand for, and the value of, money.

The fact that the creditors of colonial debtors were in many cases English merchants was another reason for keeping the courts closed. If the Stamp Act prevented English merchants from collecting their debts in the colonies they would be all the more anxious to secure repeal of the Act. This line of reasoning operated strongly in Virginia where, as is well known, the tobacco planters were heavily indebted to English creditors. George Washington, anticipating as early as September 20, 1765, that the Stamp Act would close the courts, saw the consequences clearly: "if a stop be put to our judicial proceedings I fancy the Merchants of G. Britain trading to the Colonies will not be among the last to wish for a Repeal of it."[38]

Of course the English merchants were not the only ones to suffer by the suspension of judicial proceedings. No one engaged in commerce on a credit basis was apt to be entirely a creditor or entirely a debtor. If the closing of the courts freed a man from paying one debt, it might also prevent him from collecting another, and, depending upon the exact condition of his current legal obligations, he might be either ahead of the game or far behind. If he had just lost a suit

[37] To Christopher Gadsden, June 25, 1766, William Samuel Johnson Papers, Connecticut Historical Society.

[38] John C. Fitzpatrick, ed., *The Writings of George Washington* (Washington, 1931-1944), II, 426. Cf. the extract of a letter from Philadelphia in *London Chronicle,* December 5-7, 1765.

at law and was thereby obliged to pay, it would be impossible
for him to collect from his own debtors; and it might be
equally impossible for him to borrow money, because the
bond which might be required as security also had to be
stamped. Thus Abel James and Henry Drinker, Philadelphia
business partners, wrote on October 14, 1765, of their melan-
choly thoughts "on the many Mischiefs that will attend us in
that we shall not be able to commence Actions against
Persons who are indebted to us nor proceed legally in many
other Respects, until it is some Way Settled. In Short we know
not whose Lot it may be to be ruin'd. . . ."[39] After the courts
were closed, these lamentations were justified, for another
Philadelphia businessman reported on December 11, 1765,
that "No writs are issued, No land can be Conveyed, No Bonds
can be taken; Some take the Opportunity to walk off without
paying their debts, others dont pay knowing they can't be
sued, thus we are in the utmost confusion."[40]

A few creditors who were shrewd enough to perceive in
advance the exact consequences of the suspension were able
to make a good thing of it. The *Connecticut Courant* reported on February 17, 1766, from Amenia Precinct, New
York, that

> Men of very considerable Interests (having become Surety
> for large Sums of Money, to be paid to Gentlemen in New
> York, barely to oblige a Friend in Connecticut) have un-
> reasonably suffered, by those Gentlemen in New York, who
> were foresighted enough to procure Executions in Season,
> so that they might get their Money, notwithstanding the
> Stamp Act; and those men of Interest are not now in a
> capacity to recover their Dues in Connecticut, or else-
> where, on account of said Act. Four or Five Hundred

[39] To David Barclay and Sons, James and Drinker Letter Books.
[40] Letter Book of John Reynell, Historical Society of Pennsylvania. For similar complaints, see Daniel Roberdeau to John Gill,
November 27, 1765, Roberdeau Letter Book, Historical Society of
Pennsylvania; Abel James and Henry Drinker to Stephen Skinner,
March 10, 1766, James and Drinker Letter Books; William Samuel Johnson, letters to clients, dated November 21, 1765, January
10, February 10, 12, March 11, 1766, William Samuel Johnson
Papers, Connecticut Historical Society.

Pounds worth of Estate, is bid off at Vendue, for just such or such a Sum of Money as the most monied Man there present seems to be possessed of—and that Sum seldom exceeds a Tenth of the real Worth, and the Buyer commonly appears to be the Officer, or Vendue-Master, frequently an Under-Sheriff, or Bum-Bailiff, and made up of the most Trickish of our Species.

It was not the speculators alone who profited from the suspension of justice in New York. According to a writer in the *New York Gazette* on February 20, 1766, "a large Majority of the Inhabitants of the Colony where I live, esteem the present Cessation of Business as a Kind of Jubilee." The farmers of the Hudson Valley, who enjoyed high prices for their produce because of the scarcity caused by closing the ports, seem to have obtained also a brief respite in the payment of their rents. Certainly landlords were unable to evict any who refused to pay, and when the reopening of the courts in the spring of 1766 brought evictions, riots broke out in the Hudson Valley which required troops to suppress.[41]

The economic confusion created by closing the courts echoed the confusion in the minds of lawyers and judges about the reasons for closing them and the extent to which they should be closed. No one suggested that the courts should make use of stamped papers even if they could be had, but opinions varied widely on the question of whether to shut down entirely or to proceed without stamps. Edmund Pendleton, writing to James Madison on December 11, 1765, thought it unwise to close completely, because "the appearance of courts may convince the people that there is not a total end of laws tho' they are disabled to act in some instances, I think they should be held for that purpose and as many things done as can be without stamps, particularly wills, which may be proved and ordered to be recorded, tho' they can't be recorded nor any order made for the appraisement.

[41] William Samuel Johnson to Christopher Gadsden, June 25, 1766, William Samuel Johnson Papers, Connecticut Historical Society.

Administrations can't be granted because the Bond can't be taken. Grand jurys may be sworn and all proceedings had on their presentments and on all criminal matters or breaches of the peace. Justices may issue and trie any warrants or Attachments relative to themselves, but not attachments returnable to Court. . . ."[42]

By February 15, 1766, Pendleton wanted the courts to proceed in all business without stamps but admitted that this might lead the Governor to revoke the commissions of the judges, "and as none that are fit for it will and others dare not succeed them, a total privation of majestracy must follow, and [not] even the peace must be kept, . . ." Pendleton was also bothered by the problem which must arise by the inferior courts opening—as many of them did—without the superior court agreeing to do so: everyone who lost his suit in the inferior court would appeal, and the superior court would disallow the decision because of the lack of stamps on the proceedings. In spite of these difficulties Pendleton thought that the courts should open. He had taken an oath to determine cases according to law, and since he believed that Parliament had had no authority to pass the Stamp Act, he could not regard that Act as a law and felt that it would be a violation of his oath if he refused to proceed because of it.[43] In his own county, as in most counties of Virginia, the other judges were more cautious and thought it best to wait a little longer; but in Accomac County the judges opened court and even warned the lawyers "that any attorney neglecting to carry on his business in court, under pretence of wanting stamps, should have his suits dismissed."[44]

In general it was the lawyers rather than the judges who gave the appearance of being most anxious to open the courts, though it was only an appearance. The lawyers in Boston had argued persuasively for opening on the same

[42] Massachusetts Historical Society, *Proceedings*, 2d ser., 1 (1905), 109.

[43] Pendleton to James Madison, Sr., February 15, 1766, *ibid.* 109-111.

[44] *Pennsylvania Journal*, March 20, 1766. Cf. *Connecticut Courant*, November 1, 1765; *Virginia Gazette* (Purdie), March 21, 1766.

ground that Pendleton urged, that the Stamp Act was ipso facto null and void and that the judges should perform something like judicial review by ignoring it. Other lawyers wanted the courts to proceed without stamps on the ground that none were available, and that plaintiffs should not be denied justice simply because of the action of a mob. Still others pointed out, what in most cases was true on November 1, that the colonial governments had not been officially notified of the Stamp Act and that the distributors, even had they wished to execute their offices, had not received commissions, so that in terms of law the Act was only a rumor and not deserving of recognition. On one ground or another most colonial lawyers agreed that the courts should open without stamps, but when it came to action, their eloquence left them. As we have seen, when the Superior Court of Massachusetts gave way to popular pressure and agreed to do business without stamps, even those who had argued for the opening were unwilling to risk their own future or their clients' interests by trying a case.[45]

The lawyers in other colonies showed much the same vacillation. In Philadelphia they had a meeting on October 16 to decide what they should do after the first of November. According to Edward Shippen, Jr., who was present:

A Variety of sentiments at first appeared, but after some Debate it was carried by a Majority that tho we might perhaps be justified in America in practising in our usual way without stampt paper when none is to be had; Yet if the Parliament of England should determine to force the Act down our Throats, they would immediately set Prosecutions on foot against the principal civil-officers who had ventured to risque the Penalties, in order to strike a Terror into the other Inhabitants; and in that Case they would undoubtedly make Equity and Law give way to Policy, in their Determinations—And what American Fortune could withstand them—So that, upon the whole we determined to do no Act whatsoever after the first of November in our

[45] See above, ch. VIII.

several Offices to hazard the penalties—However we are shortly after that to have another Meeting. . . .[46]

The Philadelphia lawyers had several meetings after the first of November, but in spite of a general agreement that they ought to act without stamps could not quite bring themselves to do so. On November 25, at what was evidently a typical meeting, the only voices against proceeding without stamps were those of John Ross and Joseph Galloway. Ross was too drunk to argue effectively, so that the entire burden fell upon Galloway. His arguments were demolished by the rest of the company, but the meeting nevertheless agreed to desist "till some other Government had sett us the Example."[47] The neighboring governments of Delaware and Maryland did set the example,[48] but the Pennsylvania courts —with a few exceptions among the inferior, county courts— stayed closed.

In New Jersey, as in Pennsylvania, the lawyers made a loud public noise about their opposition to the Act, but they opposed it by ceasing to do business in court, even though the judges declared themselves ready to act. When a promise was finally extracted from the lawyers to proceed after April first, the news of repeal extricated them from their dilemma.[49] In New York the lawyers passed a resolution in December to do business without stamps, but according to William Samuel Johnson, the purpose of this was simply to take the

[46] Edward Shippen, Jr., to Edward Shippen, October 17, 1765, Shippen Papers, XI, Historical Society of Pennsylvania.

[47] Richard Peters, Jr., to Jasper Yeates, November 26, 1765, Yeates Papers, Historical Society of Pennsylvania. Cf. Ernest H. Baldwin, "Joseph Galloway the Loyalist Politician," *Pa. Mag. of Hist.*, 26 (1902), 290-291.

[48] Edward Shippen, Jr., to Edward Shippen, February 22, 1766, Shippen Papers, XI; *Pennsylvania Journal*, February 27, March 20, 1766; *Maryland Gazette*, December 10, 1765, April 3, 1766; Charles A. Barker, *The Background of the Revolution in Maryland* (New Haven, 1940), 308-311.

[49] Richard Smith to the Sons of Liberty in New York, March 15, 1766, William L. Clements Library; *Archives of the State of New Jersey*, 1st ser., 9 (1885), 531-533, 536-548; 24 (1902), 639-640, 660-662; 25 (1903), 30-31, but cf. p. 36.

embarrassing problem from their own hands and pass it on to the judges.[50]

In most cases the judges were no more eager than the lawyers to make the dangerous decision of proceeding without stamps or the increasingly dangerous one of not proceeding at all. Wherever the courts were bent on evading the problem, they did so by successive adjournments until news of repeal arrived. The first news of that event reached the colonies early in April, and the interval of five months was not much longer than the normal interval between sessions.

Where the courts did wish to disregard the Act, they were sometimes prevented by the tactics of the royal governors. In New York some of the judges of the Court of Common Pleas had prepared to take the lawyers at their word and to open in January. They drew up a memorial to justify the action, and since they happened to be members of the Governor's Council as well as judges, proposed to present the memorial to the Governor and have him enter it in the council minutes, "as if," stormed Governor Moore, "so wretched an expedient could be any justification for their disobedience to an Act of Parliament." Moore anticipated this stratagem by collaring the Chief Justice and warning him that any judge who sat upon a case in which the documents were not properly stamped, could expect to lose his seat in the Council as well as his seat on the bench. The threat apparently worked, for on February 20, Moore wrote to Secretary Conway, that "what I then said to the Cheif Justice had the proper effect on him as well as on his bretheren."[51]

In South Carolina the Governor joined with the Clerk of Court to prevent the opening, though not without causing a lively controversy. On November 13, the Court of Common Pleas had met at Charles Town with Chief Justice Shinner alone on the bench. Shinner caused an order to be entered in the books stating that because of the lack of stamped

[50] William Samuel Johnson to Eliphalet Dyer, December 31, 1765, William Samuel Johnson Papers, Connecticut Historical Society.

[51] E. B. O'Callaghan, ed., *Documents Relative to the Colonial History of the State of New York* (Albany, 1856-1887), VII, 806, 811.

papers, which the Distributor had refused to supply, it was necessary to adjourn the Court until December 3. Thereafter adjournment was successively continued until March 4, 1766. On that date three new Associate Justices appeared and after taking their seats prepared to hear cases without the use of stamps. The Attorney General objected to this procedure, and in view of the possibility of a repeal of the Stamp Act in the near future the Court once more adjourned, this time until April 1. On that date, having assembled once more, the Associate Judges determined to proceed in spite of the dissent of the Chief Justice. They would doubtless have succeeded had it not been for the Clerk, Dougal Campbell, who refused to issue a Writ of Venire for the jury. Without the Writ there could be no jury, and without a jury there could be no trial. The judges requested Lieutenant-Governor Bull to suspend Campbell, but Bull stood by the Clerk, and the Court put the matter before the General Assembly. The Assembly was already considering a memorial presented by the merchants and traders of Charles Town, objecting to the closing of the courts. It was not, said the merchants, the business of litigants to provide stamps for the Court, and since the Court did not have the stamps itself, it must go on without them. The Assembly was sympathetic to the merchants, and they too appealed to Bull; but he remained firm, and they were obliged to content themselves with resolutions in favor of the Court's right to make all orders for the regulation of its own practice. The Court itself imposed a fine of £100 sterling on Campbell when they met in May after repeal of the Stamp Act, but Governor Bull had the last word by suspending the punishment.[52]

Rhode Island was the one colony which kept all its courts open without interruption. Fortified by the resolution of the General Assembly which promised indemnity to all officers who disregarded the Stamp Act, the judges both of the in-

[52] Governor Bull to Lords of Trade, May 20, 1766, and Minutes of Inferior Court of Common Pleas, Treasury Papers, Class I, Bundle 445; Henry Laurens to John Lewis Gervais, September 1, 1766, Laurens Letter Book; Edward McCrady, *The History of South Carolina under the Royal Government, 1719-1776* (New York, 1899), 572-575.

ferior courts and the superior court held their sessions according to the regular schedule. The only impediment to the sitting of the courts is recorded laconically in the journal of the Superior Court held at Providence on the third Monday in March: "The Kings Attorney being absent, at this Term the Court appointed Silas Downer to act as Attorney General in his Room."[53] The King's Attorney, as it happened, was Augustus Johnston. It would have been asking too much to expect that the Stamp Distributor should appear in court as attorney, to flout the very law under which he had been appointed. The appointment of Silas Downer in his place was an act of studied irony: Silas Downer was the Corresponding Secretary of the Providence Sons of Liberty.[54]

The only other colonies in which all courts were opened before news of repeal had arrived were New Hampshire, Maryland, and Delaware. The New Hampshire Superior Court was apparently closed until February, but on February 6, it met, with Chief Justice Theodore Atkinson presiding. At this meeting the Clerk behaved precisely as Dougal Campbell later behaved in South Carolina: he refused to issue writs or summonses without stamped paper. But the judges of the New Hampshire Court quickly put him in his place by requiring him to enter the following order on the record in extra large script:

> The Justices considering the Necessity and Expediency for the Preservation of the Peace and good Order of the Province of holding this Court and the having Business done as usuall and No Stampt Paper to be had, in this Province, do order and Command the Clerk of this Court to issue all Writs, Processes and Copies as usual, without Stampt Paper.[55]

[53] Records of the Superior Court, Office of the Clerk of the Supreme Court, Providence.

[54] See documents in his hand in Rhode Island Historical Society Manuscripts, XII, and Peck Manuscripts, III, Rhode Island Historical Society.

[55] Superior Court Records of New Hampshire, New Hampshire Historical Society. On New Hampshire inferior courts see *New Hampshire Gazette*, January 24, 1766; Otis G. Hammond, ed.,

Two days later the Portsmouth Sons of Liberty reported that "Law and Justice go on in their proper course without obstruction."[56]

The Delaware Courts, according to the newspapers at least, were opened in February at the insistence of the Grand Jury. In most colonies there was no interruption in the trial of criminals, for the Stamp Act imposed no tax on the documents used in criminal cases. It was only the civil courts which were closed. The Grand Jury of Delaware, charged with indicting criminals, refused to perform their task until they were assured that the civil courts would be opened.[57]

In Maryland some of the inferior courts began to open as early as November, but the Superior Court held out until the Sons of Liberty from all over the colony staged a meeting at Annapolis on April 1, and demanded its opening. Though the judges at first refused, they changed their minds when the Sons of Liberty repeated the demand with "united Hearts and Voices." Four days later news of repeal arrived to ease the consciences of the judges.[58]

With the exception of scattered inferior courts in the other colonies,[59] these were the only courts which opened in defiance of the Stamp Act. It is apparent, however, that if the Act had continued on the books for a month or two longer, the courts of every colony which later participated in the Revolution, might have been forced to ignore it. Popular demonstrations had already opened many courts, and it is probable that further demonstrations were forestalled by news of repeal.

It is doubtful that the closing of the courts in any colony worked excessive hardships, except perhaps those involved in the foreclosures in Amenia Precinct, New York. Their sus-

---

Probate Records of the Province of New Hampshire, VIII (Concord, 1940), shows several wills proved between November 1, 1765 and May, 1766.

[56] To Sons of Liberty in Boston, Belknap Papers.

[57] *Pennsylvania Journal,* February 27, 1766.

[58] *Maryland Gazette,* December 10, 1765, April 3, 1766; Barker, *Background of the Revolution in Maryland,* 308-311.

[59] I have found evidence of inferior courts being open in North Carolina, Virginia, Pennsylvania, and New Jersey.

pension may have thwarted the colonists' fondness for litigation, but the law's delay has always been one of the facts of life, as inescapable as death and taxes. An additional five months probably meant little to anyone except the radicals. They worried about the tacit admission of Parliamentary authority that was involved. Charles Carroll of Carrollton, for example, argued that "A suspense from business implies a tacit acquaintance of the law, or at least the right of the power of imposing such laws upon us."[60] And Richard Henry Lee wished that the Virginians could let the northern colonies know that the closing of Virginia's courts did not proceed from any regard to the Stamp Act but was simply the best way for Virginians to bring pressure on English merchants to demand repeal.[61] Even had the courts been opened, however, it would have been no great victory for the view which denied the authority of Parliament to tax the colonies, unless the judges had taken advantage of the occasion to declare the Stamp Act null and void. The judges who forced the opening in New Hampshire and those who tried to force it in South Carolina proceeded on the ground that justice should not be stopped simply because no stamps were available. William Samuel Johnson pointed out to his friend, Christopher Gadsden that the South Carolina justices would have played a more worthy part by "demonstrating the unconstitutional nature of the Stamp Act, and thence deducing the Legality of proceeding in Business without taking any Notice of it." But he admitted that "it would have been a very delicate point for a Judge to have Insisted upon in a Court of Law."[62] Marbury vs. Madison was still a long way off.

The closing of the courts and ports was the direct and foreseen result of forcing the stamp distributors to resign. The colonists pried open the ports before the closing had caused serious damage. It seems apparent that they would have

[60] Barker, *Background of the Revolution in Maryland,* 309.

[61] R. H. Lee to Landon Carter, February 24, 1766, James C. Ballagh, ed., *The Letters of Richard Henry Lee* (New York, 1911), I, 15.

[62] June 25, 1766, William Samuel Johnson Papers, Connecticut Historical Society.

forced the opening of the courts also in time to prevent any
very grave consequences. But by the time they had begun to
be irritated by the lack of litigation, they were faced with a
more serious problem, also proceeding from the resignation
of the stamp distributors and also not wholly unforeseen.
Parliament, it appeared, had recognized the challenge to its
authority and might shortly call the unruly children to account.

Chapter XI

Direction: Sons of Liberty

WHEN NEWS OF AMERICAN resistance to the Stamp Act reached England, George Grenville and his friends had been replaced in the government by the men who had opposed the passage of the Stamp Act—though not because they had opposed it. To General Conway, who was now revered all over America, fell the embarrassing task of dealing with the rebellious colonists whose cause he had upheld. Conway, as Secretary of State for the Southern Department, wrote to the colonial governors, deploring the treatment of the stamp distributors. "It is hoped and expected," he said, "that this Want of confidence in the Justice and Tenderness of the Mother Country, and this open Resistance to its Authority, can only have found Place among the lower and more ignorant of the People; the better and wiser Part of the Colonies well know that Decency and Submission may prevail, not only to redress Grievances, but to obtain Grace and Favour; while the Outrage of a publick Violence can expect nothing but Severity and Chastisement."[1]

Conway probably believed that the riots in Boston and those that followed elsewhere were spontaneous outbursts of the rabble. If he read the dispatches which the colonial governors were soon sending to the Lords of Trade, he must have known better by the end of the year.[2] The episodes of violence which defeated the Stamp Act in America were planned and prepared by men who were recognized at the time as

[1] October 24, 1765, Connecticut Historical Society, *Collections*, 18 (1920), 362.

[2] These may be found most conveniently in the House of Lords Manuscripts for the months of January and February, 1766, Library of Congress transcripts. For a somewhat different view of this subject, see Philip Davidson, *Propaganda and the American Revolution* (Chapel Hill, 1941), ch. 4, and "Sons of Liberty and Stamp Men," *North Carolina Historical Review*, 9 (1932), 37-55.

belonging to the "better and wiser part." In every colony there appeared a group who designated themselves as the "Sons of Liberty," and in every colony, the Sons of Liberty, if they were not composed of prominent and well-to-do citizens, at least had their backing. Members of the assembly, who might scruple as assemblymen to call for open rebellion, had no hesitation in planning the nullification of the Stamp Act through mob violence. Merchants, lawyers, and plantation owners may have appeared seldom enough in the actual work of destruction, but that they directed the show from behind the scenes is suggested by every surviving piece of evidence.

Governor Bull of South Carolina, describing the treatment of the Stamp Distributor there, wrote, that "Altho these very numerous Assemblies of the People bore the appearance of common populace; Yet there is great reason to apprehend they were animated and encouraged by some considerable Men, who stood behind the Curtain."[3] Crusty old Henry Laurens, who later became President of the Continental Congress but who disapproved of the violent resistance to the Stamp Act, knew by more than conjecture that the Sons of Liberty came from the higher ranks. At midnight on the twenty-third of October, 1765, he was awakened by a violent thumping and confused roar at his chamber window. Opening it, he heard the cries of "Liberty, Liberty, and Stamp'd Paper." He assured the crowd below that he had no stamps, and when they were not satisfied, "accused them with cruelty to a poor Sick Woman far gone with Child and produced Mrs. Laurens shrieking and wringing her hands." He offered to have it out with any one of them with a brace of pistols, and told them "it was base in such a multitude to attack a single Man." To this he received the answer that they loved and respected him and bore him no grudge, "but that they were sent even by some of my seemingly best friends to search for Stamped Paper which they were certain was in my custody." Perceiving that they were ready to force an entrance, Laurens let them in, and while two of them

[3] To the Lords of Trade, November 3, 1765, House of Lords Manuscripts, February 14, 1766.

held a pair of cutlasses against his chest, he surprised the others by penetrating the "Soot, Sailors habits, slouch hats &c." with which they had disguised themselves, calling nine of his acquaintances by name.[4]

In North Carolina, when the continued paralysis of the port at Cape Fear brought on the crisis already described, the lead was taken by fifty gentlemen of Wilmington, who made no attempt to conceal their identity but signed an open letter to the Collector of Customs, demanding that ships be cleared. When this failed to bring action, they formed an association of "all the principal Gentlemen, Freeholders and other inhabitants of several counties," and forced the issue. Leading the crowd were several prominent citizens: John Ashe, Colonel James Moore, Colonel Hugh Waddell, Alexander Lillington, Colonel Thomas Lloyd, Cornelius Harnett, Moses John De Rosset and others. Most of these men were members of the Assembly, Ashe being the Speaker. De Rosset was Mayor of Wilmington. Two of the number averred that they had been compelled to assume the leadership of the movement, but others were obviously zealous in the cause. Maurice Moore, an Assemblyman and Judge in Salisbury District, was so intemperate in supporting the opposition to the Stamp Act that the Governor suspended him from office. The Governor also found the merchants of the colony "as assiduous in obstructing the reception of the Stamps as any of the Inhabitants."[5]

In Virginia too the better and wiser sort did not bother to hide behind the curtain. Describing the men who forced Mercer to resign, Governor Fauquier said, "This Concourse of People, I should call a Mob, did I not know that it was chiefly if not altogether Composed of Gentlemen of Property in the Colony—some of them at the Head of their respective Counties, and the Merchants of the Country whether English, Scotch or Virginians, for few absented themselves."[6] John

---

[4] Henry Laurens to Joseph Brown, October 28, 1765, Laurens Letter Book, Historical Society of Pennsylvania.
[5] *Colonial Records of North Carolina*, VII, *passim*, especially 43, 168-183, 199.
[6] Fauquier to Lords of Trade, November 3, 1765, House of Lords Manuscripts, January 27, 1766.

Hughes of Pennsylvania carefully pointed out to his superiors in England the true character of the Philadelphia "mob," "as the Great Men here wou'd fain have it Term'd, and believ'd on Your side the Water, and I make no doubt, but it will be so represented by the Proprietary Governor and his Friends."[7] Actually the directors of the Pennsylvania mob were men of standing in Philadelphia: James Tilghman, attorney at law, Robert Morris, Charles Thomson, Archibald McCall, John Cox, and William Richards, all merchants, and William Bradford, the printer.[8] In New Hampshire the Reverend Samuel Langdon, minister of the Congregational Church and later President of Harvard College, was one of the leaders; and after one of the public demonstrations in Portsmouth when the Sons of Liberty had stepped from behind the scenes and shown themselves openly, the *New Hampshire Gazette* reported that they were "no other than the principal Inhabitants of the Town and the Representatives of the Country."[9]

In Boston the Loyal Nine, who directed the activities of Ebenezer McIntosh, were probably themselves subordinate to the merchants and politicians. This at least was the opinion of Thomas Hutchinson, who had a somewhat more than academic interest in the matter. In a letter directed to ex-Governor Pownall on March 8, 1766 he wrote,

It will be some amusement to you to have a more circumstantial account of the present model of government among us. I will begin with the lowest branch partly legislative partly executive. This consists of the rabble of the town of Boston headed by one Mackintosh who I imagine you never heard of. He is a bold fellow and as likely for

[7] To Commissioners of Stamps, November 2, 1765, Treasury Papers, Class I, Bundle 441, Public Record Office, Library of Congress transcripts.

[8] Hughes to Commissioners of Stamps, October 12, 1765, House of Lords Manuscripts, January 14, 1766.

[9] *New Hampshire Gazette,* January 10, 1766. The letters written by the Sons of Liberty in New Hampshire to those in other colonies were written by Langdon, Belknap Papers, Massachusetts Historical Society.

Massianello as you can well conceive. When there is occasion to hang or burn effigies or pull down houses these are employed; but since government has been brought to a system they are somewhat controuled by a superior set consisting of the master-masons carpenters, &c. of the town. . . . When anything of more importance is to be determined as opening the custom house or any matters of trade these are under the direction of a committee of merchants Mr. Rowe at their head then Molyneux Solomon Davis, &c. but all affairs of a general nature opening all the courts of law &c. this is proper for a general meeting of the inhabitants of Boston where Otis with his mobbish eloquence prevails in every motion, and the town first determine what is necessary to be done and then apply either to the Governor and council or resolve that it is necessary the general court should meet and it must be a very extraordinary resolve indeed that is not carried into execution.[10]

There is abundant evidence that the merchants of Boston were at least partly responsible for the riots. Governor Bernard in describing the events of August 14 and 26 to the Secretary of State, told how an old quarrel between the merchants and the admiralty and customs officers had broken out anew just prior to the riots.[11] The attack on Story and Hallowell on August 26 was the payment of a score which the merchants had long held in account against the customhouse. Hallowell's friends, inquiring in town about the reasons for the attack, were told that it stemmed from his strictness in enforcing the Laws of Trade.[12] Hallowell himself wrote to the Lords of Trade on September 7, 1765, that "the leaders or Conductors of the Mob offered to take any Kind of Goods liable to Seizure under their protection and bid defiance to the Officers of the Customs,"[13] and Bernard re-

[10] Massachusetts Archives, XXVI, 207-214.

[11] Bernard to Halifax, August 31, 1765, Bernard Papers, IV, 149-158, Harvard College Library. One of the merchants responsible for reviving the quarrel was Briggs Hallowell, Benjamin's brother.

[12] Treasury Papers, Class I, Bundle 442.

[13] *Ibid.*

ported on November 26, 1765, that people were saying, "let us see now who will seize Merchants Goods, what Judge will condemn them, what Court will dare grant Writs of Assistance now."[14]

In New York Robert Livingston professed to be unacquainted with the "secret party" that conducted the riots, but noted that one of their public posters had evidently been written by a person of education.[15] Actually his brother William and the two other political leaders of the Assembly, John Morin Scott and William Smith, both men of the first rank, must have known more than a little about the secret party and the men who composed it.[16] The documents do not reveal whether or not they had a directing influence in it, but popular opinion gave the Livingstons and their wealthy friends credit for forming it. One Dutch farmer who, like other farmers in the Hudson Valley, felt himself oppressed by the great landlords of the province, complained to the Attorney General that one of the Livingstons (it is not clear who) "has spoke treasonable words against king and parliament we must rase a Rebellion against the damned stamp act and I wil shed the blood against it and turn us sels tu a free republic as Holland this is the vue of Livingstons familie the robbers and murders of common poor people. . . ."[17]

Both Cadwallader Colden, the Lieutenant-Governor of the province, who had reason to hate the Livingstons, and General Gage, who was perhaps a more impartial observer, shared the view that the New York riots were directed by men of standing. Both diagnosed the trouble as coming from the lawyers, who at this time belonged to the wealthiest families in the province. Colden wrote to Conway on November 9 "I have the strongest presumption from numerous Circum

[14] Bernard to John Pownall, November 26, 1765, Bernard Papers, V, 43-46.
[15] To Governor Monckton, November 8, 1765, Massachusetts Historical Society, *Collections,* 4th ser., 10 (1871), 560.
[16] See Dorothy R. Dillon, *The New York Triumvirate* (New York, 1949), 91-99; Davidson, *Propaganda and the American Revolution,* 70.
[17] Howenburgh to J. T. Kemp, Sedgwick Papers, Massachusetts Historical Society.

stances to believe that the Lawyers of this Place are the Authors, Promoters, and Leaders of it. People in general believe it, and many must with certainty know it."[18] Gage went further than Colden and blamed the trouble in every colony on the lawyers. "The Lawyers," he said, "are the Source from whence the Clamors have flowed in every Province. In this Province Nothing Publick is transacted without them, and it is to be wished that even the Bench was free from Blame. The whole Body of Merchants in general, Assembly Men, Magistrates, &c. have been united in this Plan of Riots, and without the Influence and Instigation of these the inferior People would have been quiet. Very great Pains was taken to rouse them before they Stirred. The Sailors who are the only People who may be properly Stiled Mob, are entirely at the Command of the Merchants who employ them."[19]

Gage and Colden were talking about the mob in New York City, but up the river, Albany likewise had its Stamp Act riots, and here too the Sons of Liberty were drawn from the best families in town. They bore the names of the old Dutch mercantile families and many of them were officeholders or relatives of officeholders in the local government.[20]

The most complete information that has been preserved about the Sons of Liberty in any colony is that which Ezra Stiles set down about the group in Newport. Stiles, who had a fortunate penchant for collecting information that would be useful to later historians, not only set down the names of the Newport Sons of Liberty but contributed a biographical sketch of each. His account was written early in 1767 and included only those who were active in the "Committee" at that time, but the members were probably much the same as they had been the year before:

[18] To Secretary Conway, November 9, 1765, O'Callaghan, ed., *Documents Relative to the Colonial History of the State of New York*, VII, 773; New York Historical Society, *Collections for the year 1877* (1878), 61-62.

[19] To Secretary Conway, December 21, 1765, Clarence E. Carter, ed., *The Correspondence of General Thomas Gage with the Secretaries of State, 1763–1775* (New Haven, 1931), I, 79.

[20] Beverly McAnear, "The Albany Stamp Act Riots," *William and Mary Quarterly,* 3d ser., 4 (1947), 486-498.

The Committee contained some Gentlemen of the first Figure in Town for opulence, Sense, and Politeness: and without Question was as respectable as could have been chosen in Newport, and the most respectable Committee of the Sons of Liberty on this Continent. Secretary Ward and Mr. Bowler were deputed by the General Assembly of Rhode Island, and attended the grand Congress of provincial Commissioners at New York in October 1765 which formed the Resolves of the Congress and the Addresses to the King Lords and Commons at that dangerous and memorable Crisis. Colonel Lyndon aetat 65, has been many years Clerk of the General Assembly of the Colony, and of the Inferior Court of common pleas of the County of Newport, a Gentleman of an amiable and respectable reputation, of Politeness and of a good Estate.—Mr. Crook is a Merchant of figure and of good Connexions. He and Mr. Bowler, with two or three more, were the only Sons of Liberty of Consequence among the Churchmen in Town. The Messrs Ellerys were Sons of the late Hon. Dep. Gov. Ellery who possessed an Estate of Twenty Thousand Pounds Sterling. William Ellery Esq. was educated at Harvard College, and for Literature and sound Judgement equal to any Man in Town, and really of the most weight and Firmness of any of the Committee: his Brother Captain Ellery was vigorous, intrepid and bold. Mr. Channing aetat 53 was a Gentleman of the greatest Politeness, a true Friend of Liberty, of free and genteel Elocution, and a Merchant of the largest Business, transacting a Commerce of Four Thousand Sterling a year. Mr. Collins a hearty and zealous and sensible Friend of Liberty—once in the Fall 1765 he had a little Fit of Timidity; but recovered himself intirely and become a glorious Champion in the Cause. Major Otis is a very sensible worthy Man, of a very personable Aspect, a Man of Religion, and an honor to his Country; stedily firmly and immutably attached to Liberty.—He is a Remote Relation to the honorable James Otis of Boston, who first proposed the Congress. Mr. Spooner was from among middling and lower Life, and united in himself the whole Confidence of the plebians—

he was cautious and on his Guard, but his whole soul was in Liberty—he was vigorous and circumspect, safe but enterprizing. a man perhaps aetat 30. He was very necessary, and perhaps as important as any Man of the Committee, as they without him would not have had so intirely the Confidence of the Populace. Mr. Marchant aetat 26 was a judicious sensible and steady and bold Assertor of Liberty, his Intermarriage in a church Family secured him from that Torrent of Church Ribaldry Bellowing and Reproach which they poured forth like a Tempest on the Sons of Liberty, calling them Rebels, Traitors, Republicans, and worthy to be carried home in Chains and tried for their Lives. Of this last number was Maudsley, whom the Sons elected into the Committee for his own Mortification.[21]

Although gentlemen seem to have held the reins among the Sons of Liberty, they could not have succeeded in their ambitions without the support of their social inferiors. Their plans required the use of violence, and violence was not their forte. The wiser and better sort were not accustomed to throwing brickbats or smashing furniture, nor would they have wished to risk their reputations by openly indulging in such uncouth activities. As members of a legislative assembly they might be willing to proclaim the unconstitutionality of Parliamentary taxation, but resistance to Parliament was a larger order, in which the support of the "lower and more ignorant" might be needed.

General Gage testified that the lower and more ignorant had taken a good deal of prodding before they could be brought to act, and Ezra Stiles said that Major Spooner was indispensable to the Newport Sons of Liberty in order to gain the support of these lower ranks. Actually the lower

[21] Ezra Stiles, Stamp Act Notebook, Stiles Papers, Yale University Library. Where Stiles uses the words "church" and "churchmen" he refers to the Anglican Church. One notable leader of the Sons of Liberty whom Stiles does not mention here was Samuel Vernon, another merchant. Moffat listed Vernon and William Ellery as "two of the Chief Ringleaders," Chalmers Papers, Rhode Island, New York Public Library.

classes probably had little to lose directly by the Stamp Act. They might feel some concern over the restriction of trial by jury, but they did not commonly engage in the legal business transactions which required stamped paper. They would not have worried about the extra cost of matriculating at a university or entering a corporation or alienating a piece of land. They might have resented the stamping of dice, playing cards, and newspapers, but they probably read newspapers supplied by the management in their local coffee house, and a pair of dice will last a long time. How then did the Sons of Liberty rouse these people to fury, and more important, how did they control that fury once they had aroused it?

In order to bring the people in general to a sense of the dangers which the Stamp Act held for the colonies, it was necessary to show them the consequences which must inevitably follow if Parliament's right to tax were acknowledged. The Sons of Liberty were farsighted enough to see the issues involved in the Stamp Act, to see that in the long run it would be to Parliament's advantage to draw as large a proportion of revenue as possible from a people who were not close enough at hand to protect themselves through protest or pressure or the ballot box. The more money Parliament could draw from the Americans the less they would have to draw from their own constituents in England. The Americans could thus be bled dry for the benefit of their fellow subjects in England. Although the Stamp Act might cause little immediate distress to most people, they must be made to see it as a prelude to an uncontrolled flood of taxes that would follow as soon as this one gained acceptance. The only way to prevent the gradual enslavement of the colonies was to defeat the Parliamentary tax at its inception, and this is precisely what the Sons of Liberty urged so successfully upon the people of the colonies.

Their method of ringing the alarm was that which their forebears in England had used in the 1630's, the press. But the colonists had a great advantage over the English revolutionists in that they could obtain nearly automatic circulation of their writings through the newspapers. In Boston one of the Sons of Liberty was Benjamin Edes, the printer, with John Gill, of the *Boston Gazette*, which Governor Bernard tagged as "the most factious paper in America."[22] In Providence William Goddard, printer of the *Providence Gazette*, was also a Son of Liberty,[23] and in Philadelphia, William Bradford, printer of the *Pennsylvania Journal*, belonged to the group.[24] Even where the printer of the local paper did not belong he generally cooperated. In Newport Samuel Hall, who had printed the propaganda of the Royalist group there, even including Martin Howard's *Letter from a Gentleman at Halifax*, was wholeheartedly supporting the opposition to the Stamp Act by the summer of 1765.

A printer who refused to cooperate was apt to regret it, for the Sons of Liberty might also be the leaders of the legislative assembly. Many printers relied upon the business of printing the legislative records of the provincial assemblies to keep them going, and those who opposed the Sons of Liberty might lose that source of income. Conversely those who cooperated could expect to be favored. James Parker, a friend of Franklin's, despaired of setting up a press in New York in 1766, because "the Sons of Liberty carry all before them, Mr. Holt [John Holt, printer of the *New York Gazette*] has gained very great Popularity, and being back'd by them, seems to have a Run of Business."[25]

A few newspapers suspended publication after November first, in order to avoid the use of stamps, but most printers ignored the requirement that news sheets be stamped and continued business as usual. Where the Sons of Liberty were well organized, the printers may have thought it safer to continue than to suspend. John Holt, though himself an ardent opponent of the Stamp Act, received a warning on

[22] To John Pownall, July 20, 1765, Bernard Papers, IV, 7-9. On the activities of the press see A. M. Schlesinger, "The Colonial Newspapers and the Stamp Act," *New England Quarterly*, 8 (1935), 63-83, and *Prelude to Independence: The Newspaper War on Britain, 1764-1776* (New York, 1958), 67-84.

[23] Rhode Island Historical Society Manuscripts, XII, 63.

[24] See note 8.

[25] Massachusetts Historical Society, *Proceedings*, 2d ser., 16 (1902), 210.

October 31 saying, "should you at this critical time shut up the press, and basely desert us, depend upon it, your house, person, and effects, will be in imminent danger. We shall therefore expect your paper on Thursday as usual. . . ."[26] Peter Timothy, printer of the *South Carolina Gazette*, who ceased publication during the operation of the Act, was still feeling the loss of business from the hostility of the Sons of Liberty three years later.[27] Andrew Steuart, printer of the *North Carolina Gazette*, had the most trying experience of all. He had suspended publication, allegedly because of illness, before November first. On November 16, the mob which forced the resignation of the Stamp Distributor on that day let him know that he must resume publication—or else. When he did so, and opened his pages to all who wished to contribute, one vigorous upholder of Parliamentary authority sent in a letter. Because he published it, he was threatened with a horse-whipping. He appealed to his readers in bewilderment: "What part is he now to act?—Continue to keep his Press open and free, and be in danger of corporal punishment, or bloque it up and run the risk of having his brains knocked out?" Two weeks later the Governor and Council answered his question by suspending him for printing a letter that was too radical![28]

The printers who cooperated with the Sons of Liberty published many serious articles demonstrating the dangers of the Stamp Act to American rights, but like journalists of later ages they did not stop with appeals to reason. The *Boston Gazette* fed the people a steady diet of incendiary exhortation, directed not only against the local Stamp Distributor, but also against Governor Bernard, Lieutenant-Governor Hutchinson, and even against England itself. As one epigram on the Mother Country put it:

> Spurn the Relation—She's no more a Mother,
> Than Lewis to George a most Christian Brother,

[26] Isaac Q. Leake, *Memoir of the Life and Times of General John Lamb* (Albany, 1850), 13-14.

[27] September 3, 1768, Franklin Papers, II, 139, American Philosophical Society.

[28] *Colonial Records of North Carolina*, VII, 123-124, 168a, 187.

In French Ware and Scotch, grown generous and rich,
She gives her dear Children Pox, Slavery, and Itch.[29]

And to George Grenville the *Gazette* offered this couplet:

To make us all Slaves, now you've lost Sir! the Hope,
You've but to go hang yourself.—We'll find the Rope.[30]

The papers appealed for action in a variety of ways. When the *Boston Gazette* printed a simple quotation labelled as a warning once made to Cardinal Wolsey, "Great Sir, Retreat or you are Ruined," the reader could readily take it as an invitation to help ruin Governor Bernard, in case that harassed official should attempt to prevent nullification of the Stamp Act.[31] When a stamp distributor was advised in the paper to appear before the Liberty Tree at twelve o'clock, every patriotic citizen would take pains to join him there. The *Providence Gazette* suggested the resignation of Augustus Johnston in the strongest possible terms simply by announcing that he had agreed not to execute the Act—five days later he fulfilled the prophecy.[32]

By printing highly colored news of the daring deeds of other colonists, the papers encouraged similar exploits by their own subscribers. The most conspicuously successful example of this type of propaganda was the printing of the Virginia Resolves in a version far different from that which had actually passed the House of Burgesses. By representing the Virginians as more radical than they had actually been, the newspapers succeeded in bringing about resolutions and riots in their own colonies that surpassed what had happened in Virginia. Some papers even extended their exhortations to neighboring colonies. The *Boston Gazette* offered Connecticut good advice about how to deal with Jared Ingersoll,[33] and Governor Franklin of New Jersey complained bit-

[29] *Boston Gazette*, December 2, 1765.
[30] *Ibid.*
[31] *Boston Gazette*, January 6, 1766.
[32] *Providence Gazette Extraordinary*, August 24, 1765.
[33] *Boston Gazette*, August 26, September 9, 1765.

terly that his people had become nearly as much inflamed as those of the other colonies because of the way in which the papers in New York and Pennsylvania had ridiculed them for their moderation, insinuating that he had given them "a Dose of Poppies and Laudanum."[34]

While newspapers served as a constant stimulus to popular indignation, the Sons of Liberty knew that it was not enough simply to stir people up. It was necessary for someone to take the lead in whatever violence was necessary to intimidate the stamp masters and nullify the Act. The Sons of Liberty might in some cases be able to do this themselves, but the social gulf that stood between them and the masses could be a handicap. Ezra Stiles's comments about the importance of Major Spooner to the Newport Sons of Liberty suggests that birth and breeding were already political liabilities. The Boston gentlemen who disguised their rank with trousers when they marched in the mob on August 14, were probably seeking to conceal their part in a disreputable business, but they may also have been making a bid for popularity. It is, at any rate, a fact that in at least two colonies the Sons of Liberty made use of a genuine workingman to lead the mob.

In Boston Ebenezer McIntosh, the shoemaker, already had a reputation as the impresario of the South End mob, when the Stamp Act was passed. McIntosh was evidently willing to work for his betters, for throughout the crucial months from August, 1765, to April, 1766, he followed the orders of the Sons of Liberty, or, as they originally called themselves, the Loyal Nine. It is possible that on the night of August 26 he slipped the reins for a time; but it is evident that the Sons of Liberty, with the assistance of the militia, quickly regained control, and when it became necessary to force Oliver's resignation for a second time on December 17, the affair was carried out under McIntosh's direction without a hitch. Two days later Henry Bass, one of the Sons of Liberty, confided to a friend that "the whole affair transacted by the Loyall Nine, in writing the Letter, getting the advertisements

[34] To Grey Cooper, January 15, 1766, Treasury Papers, Class I, Bundle 452.

Printed, which were all done after 12 o'Clock Monday Night, the Advertisements Pasted up to the amount of a hundred was all done from 9 to 3 oClock." Bass urged his friend to "keep this a profound Secret." "We do every thing," he said, "in order to keep this and the first Affair Private: and are not a little pleas'd to hear that McIntosh has the Credit of the whole Affair."[35]

How the Sons of Liberty in Boston were able to keep Mc-Intosh so well under control is not apparent. He must have known how powerful he really was when the Sheriff did not dare to hold him for more than a few hours on August 27. His submission to the Sons of Liberty, whether willing or unwilling, is rendered the more impressive by the failure of the Newport Sons of Liberty in their experiment with a demagogue.[36] Ezra Stiles mentions Major Spooner as the intermediary between the Newport Sons of Liberty and the lower classes, but he does not mention John Weber who enjoyed a brief but terrifying rule as leader of the Newport mob. Weber was a young Englishman who had been in Newport for only three or four days when the riot of August 29 occurred. He may well have been a sailor with some reputation as a leader among other sailors; and perhaps was employed on a vessel belonging to one of the Sons of Liberty. One account has it that he was a "deserted convict, aged about 20 Or 21 years." In any case, if we are to believe Augustus Johnston, Weber must have been hired by the Sons of Liberty to lead the mob in attacking Robinson, Johnston, Moffat, and Howard. Though his employment was probably supposed to terminate with this exploit, he evidently enjoyed his work too much to stop. As soon as Augustus Johnston had resigned his office on

[35] Massachusetts Historical Society, *Proceedings,* 44 (1911), 688-689.

[36] The account of events in Newport in this and the next three paragraphs is based on *Newport Mercury,* September 2, 1765; Augustus Johnston to Commissioners of Stamps, August 31, 1765, Treasury Papers, Class I, Bundle 439; Charles Leslie to Lord Colville, September 5, 1765, Admiralty Secretary In Letters 482, Public Record Office, Library of Congress transcripts; and *Calendar of Home Office Papers of the Reign of George III, 1760-1765* (London, 1878), 610-611. See also Lovejoy, *Rhode Island Politics,* 108-110.

the morning of August 29, Weber began to grow insolent and insulted several persons, "some of whom," says Johnston, "were the very people concerned in beginning the Riot, by preparing the Effigies, &c. and now began to fear for themselves." These gentlemen, Johnston continues, "were weake enough to immagine, that if they should secure this Fellow, who had exerted himself a good deal in the Disturbances— That it would in some measure attone for the part they had Acted; And accordingly they with the Assistance of the sheriff seized him and carried him on board the Cygnet Man-of-War, he exclaiming that he was betrayed by the very people who first set him to work."

The Sons of Liberty shortly discovered that their problem could not be solved so easily. Weber in his brief night of glory had gained a number of loyal followers. These now gathered together and announced that if Weber were not released forthwith they would give the gentlemen who planned the riot a taste of their own medicine by destroying *their* houses. The threat was effective. A few of the gentlemen went aboard the *Cygnet* and informed Captain Leslie that they had mistakenly apprehended the wrong man. The authorities in town, they said, were now in pursuit of the ringleaders and would bring them aboard as soon as they were taken up. Captain Leslie swallowed the story and released Weber, who was hailed with cheers as he came ashore.

The Sons of Liberty were now in a more desperate position than before. As soon as Weber landed he threatened to pull down their houses. Panic-stricken, the gentlemen offered this monster everything that he wished, gave him money, ordered him clothes, and begged and prayed him to be satisfied. But John Weber with the Newport mob at his back was not to be satisfied by cringing condescension, not even when Sheriff Wanton pleaded "What would you have of me? I will do everything to satisfy you; I will lay myself down, and let you tread on my neck, if that will satisfy you."

Perceiving that appeasement would get them nowhere the gentlemen took a firmer stand and prepared to defend themselves in case the mob should not disperse. The challenge was not accepted, and the crowd were finally persuaded to go quietly to their homes. Nothing happened that night, though the Sons of Liberty must have slept uneasily. The next day Augustus Johnston heaped coals of fire on the heads of his tormenters by rescuing them from the predicament in which their attack upon him had placed them. Johnston had formerly been a popular man in Newport—the town of Johnston, Rhode Island, was named after him—and he had probably regained some measure of his popularity by resigning the stamp office. Moreover he was still Attorney General of the colony. Meeting with Weber alone in the street, he seized him and carried him off to jail. Curiously enough, Weber's followers made no immediate attempt to rescue their hero, and the Sons of Liberty could breathe a sigh of relief. There was of course the danger that Weber, if brought to trial, would reveal the names of his employers, but evidently the Sons of Liberty were able to scare him out of this, for when he was asked for his story, he refused to give it, saying "I shall be tore to Pieces by those who set me on but if my Person can be secured I will say what I know." Charles Leslie, Captain of the *Cygnet*, told Augustus Johnston that he would give Weber protection on the *Cygnet*, if he could be got aboard. But Johnston intended to go on living in Newport and perhaps thought it best to let matters stand for the moment as they were.

The atmosphere remained highly charged. Weber lay in jail, while the Sons of Liberty endeavored to maintain popular feeling against the Stamp Act without touching off another riot. As November approached, everyone sensed the explosiveness of the situation. There must have been a tightening of jaws when the Sons of Liberty learned that Sheriff Wanton had received two letters threatening that unless he released John Weber, his house would be destroyed and the doors of the jail forced.[37] On November first, in order to forestall any possible riot, the Sons of Liberty attempted to divert popular feeling into an orderly demonstration, by staging "a grand funeral of Freedom." A procession of mourners marched through the streets to the burying ground following

[37] *Newport Mercury*, November 4, 1765.

a coffin marked "Old Freedom." Upon arrival at the place of interment, according to the description in the *Mercury,*

A Son of LIBERTY emerging from the horrid Gloom of Despair, addressed himself thus: 'Oh LIBERTY! the Darling of my Soul!—GLORIOUS LIBERTY! admir'd, ador'd, by all true Britons!—LIBERTY dead! it cannot be!'—A groan was then heard, as if coming from the Coffin; and upon closer attention, it proved to be a Trance, for old FREEDOM was not dead—The Goddess Britannia had order'd a guarding Angel to snatch Old FREEDOM from the Jaws of frozen Death, to the Orb of the rising Sun, to remain invulnerable from the attacks of lawless Tyranny and Oppression.[38]

After this agreeable diversion the afternoon was spent in rejoicing, with bells ringing and the courthouse ornamented with flags. In the evening a number of persons patrolled the streets to prevent the gathering of a mob, and the night passed quietly. Weber after two months in jail was reaching the point of despair. When no rescue party attempted to release him on November first, he tried to hang himself in his cell, but was prevented. On the following evening his friends rallied for a last effort. A crowd of twenty or thirty prepared to storm the jail, hoping no doubt to gather reinforcement as they went. But Weber's magnetic personality could not exert its attraction from within the walls of the jail. An alarm was given and the incipient mob dispersed, minus two of their number, "who were seized; and instead of releasing their Associate in Prison, were forced to take up their Residence in the same place."[39] This was the last to be heard of John Weber. Doubtless he was released after the Stamp Act troubles were over, but until then the Sons of Liberty in Newport were careful to direct all opposition to the Stamp Act in person. They celebrated Christmas day by making Augustus Johnston resign his office again, though he had still received no commission from the Treasury Department in

[38] *Ibid.*
[39] *Ibid.*

England.[40] In January they gave warning through the *Mercury* "That no Son of Perdition among us, of what Character in Life soever, shall ever mention that destestable Pamphlet, called a *Stamp Act,* with Applause, nor in any Way, by Word or Writing, Sign or Token, ever aid or assist in the Prosecution of the Contents thereof, without our highest Indignation."[41] When a ship arrived from the West Indies with stamped clearance and bond, the Sons obtained the papers and ceremoniously burnt them, along with two copies of Martin Howard's *Letter from a Gentleman at Halifax.*[42] Never again, however, did the Sons of Liberty in Newport risk a riot. One John Weber was enough.

According to General Gage, the lawyers and merchants who started the mobs in New York also became uneasy about the extraordinary power which they had called into being. Once the violence had begun, a number of demagogues appeared, not distinguished by birth or breeding and only too eager to call out the mob on any pretext. The more conservative merchants and lawyers had to exert themselves continually to prevent a complete breakdown of civil order. Moreover, because of the actions of Captain Kennedy (see above), New York had a large number of unemployed seamen who could attribute their distress at least indirectly to the Stamp Act. At one point the seamen got so far out of hand that it was necessary to enlist the influence of the ship captains in regaining control. Gage thought that the better sort would have preferred to end all riots, but that they would never call in troops to suppress the mob, for fear of losing their main objective, the defeat of the Stamp Act.[43] Like the Newport Sons of Liberty the New Yorkers had to steer a middle course. They must use the power of the mob to defeat the power of Parliament, but they must not allow the mob to escape from their own direction and upset the delicate balance of social classes within the colony.

[40] *Newport Mercury,* December 30, 1765.
[41] *Newport Mercury,* January 6, 1765.
[42] *Newport Mercury,* March 24, 1765.
[43] To Conway, December 21, 1765, January 16, 1766, Carter, ed., *Correspondence of Gage,* I, 78-79, 80-83. Cf. New York Historical Society, *Collections for the year 1881* (1882), 339-371.

How nice a problem this became is well illustrated by the events which occurred when two New York merchants executed a customs bond on stamped paper. The Sons of Liberty could not afford to allow this breach in the opposition to pass unnoticed, and they ordered the two merchants to appear before them at a local coffee house. John Holt, printer of the *New York Gazette*, wrote the following account of what ensued in a private letter to Mrs. Benjamin Franklin:

The Matter was intended to be done privately, but it got wind, and by ten o Clock I suppose 2000 people attended at the Coffee House, among them most of the principal men in Town—The Culprits apologies did not satisfy the people, they were highly blamed and the Sons of Liberty found it necessary to use their Influence to moderate the Resentments of the People. Two Men were dispatch'd to the Collector for the Stamp'd Bonds of which he had 30 in all, he desired Liberty to confer with the Governor, which was granted. The Governor sent Word, if the Stamps were deliver'd to him, he would give his Word and Honour they should not be used; but that if the people were not satisfied with this, they might do as they pleased with them—The message being returnd to the gathering Multitude, they would not agree to the Governors Proposal, but insisted upon the Stamps being deliver'd and burnt, one or two men attended by about a thousand others were then sent for the Stamps, which were brought to the Coffee House, and the Merchant who had used them was order'd himself to kindle the Fire and consume them, those filled in and all, this was accordingly done amidst the Huzza's of the people who were by this Time swell'd to the Number I suppose of about 5000, and in another hour I suppose would have been 10,000—The people pretty quietly dispersed soon After, but their Resentment was not allay'd, Toward the Evening . . . tho' the Sons of Liberty exerted themselves to the utmost, they could not prevent the gathering of the Multitude, who went to Mr Williams's house, broke open the Door and destroyed some of the Furniture, but thro' the Influence of the Sons of Liberty and on his most earnest

Entreaty and promise in the most publick manner to ask pardon next day, or do whatever they should require of him, they were prevail'd on to leave the House, and then went to the Merchants where after huzzaing for some time, they were prevail'd upon to forbear doing any mischief—on Consideration that both the men were well beloved in Town, and bore fair Characters, that the Merchants Wife was not in good Health, and very near her Time and that if the Sons of Liberty undertook under the penalty of £2 [the manuscript is clipped here; the sum was probably at least two figures] that they would both ask the pardon requir'd the next Day mounted on a Scaffold, and do whatever else the people could reasonably desire—Accordingly today about 11 OClock they appear'd in the Fields, and attended by three Clergymen got out of a Window upon a pint House, before many thousand people and declared their Sorrow for what they had done, promised to do so no more and humbly ask'd pardon of the People. It was fear'd they would have been ill used but there was not the least Insult or incivility offer'd them.

The people were generally satisfied and soon dispersed—but many of those of inferior Sort, who delight in mischief merely for its own sake, or for plunder, seem yet to be in such a turbulent Disposition that the two mortified Gentlemen are still in some Danger, but the Sons of Liberty intend to Exert themselves in their Defense.[44]

Even where no large and excitable crowds existed, the Sons of Liberty frequently had to deal with people who tried to turn the existing confusion to their own advantage. Though the term "Sons of Liberty" was claimed in every colony by an organized group seeking to prevent the execution of the Stamp Act, the phrase nevertheless came to have the more general meaning of anyone who opposed the Stamp Act, and

[44] February 15, 1766, Franklin Papers, XLVIII, 92. According to the account in the newspapers the thirty blank forms for bonds and Mediterranean passes had been shipped to Charles Williams, the "naval officer" of New York "without any mention of their being stamped." *Pennsylvania Gazette,* February 27, 1766.

some individuals who perceived that certain kinds of lawlessness had become popular made the mistake of supposing that they could do as they pleased simply by calling themselves Sons of Liberty. Thieves who broke into a house in Maine and stole £700 worth of goods, followed up their crime by sending threatening letters to the victim in the name of the Sons of Liberty;[45] and in South Carolina a group of sailors formed a mob to collect money from people in the streets.[46] The Sons of Liberty in every colony felt obliged to suppress disorders of this kind, especially when carried on in their name, and by the end of the year 1765 they were sometimes referring to themselves as the "true" or the "true-born" Sons of Liberty, to distinguish themselves from those who abused the name.[47] They had no intention of allowing the hatred of the Stamp Act to be diverted into a pretense for criminal or anti-social activities.

In order to keep popular sentiment flowing in the channels they had marked out for it, they took pains to keep themselves constantly in the public eye. In many colonies this purpose was achieved by the clamor for opening the ports and courts. The fact that the British government had been so slow about commissioning the stamp distributors also furnished a suitable occasion for public demonstrations. When the commission reached a distributor after he had resigned, there was a question of whether the first resignation was binding, and the Sons of Liberty usually found it necessary to have a second one, again conducted in public with great ceremony. Many of the activities in which they engaged were harmless enough in themselves. There was, for example, no injury done to anyone in the public burning of occasional stamped papers which arrived on ships from Nova Scotia or Jamaica, nor was anyone harmed by the meeting in Boston on February 20, 1766, when Grenville and Bute were hung in effigy and "Long Life, Health and Prosperity" was drunk to all the Sons

---

[45] *Virginia Gazette* (Purdie), May 9, 1766.
[46] *Pennsylvania Journal*, January 2, 1766.
[47] Cf. Davidson, *Propaganda and the American Revolution*, 69.

of Liberty in America, while the friends of the Stamp Act were toasted with a wish that they might have "a perpetual Itching without the Benefit of Scratching."[48]

These mild diversions did not mask a fact that became increasingly evident to all officers of government during the winter of 1765-66. As the Sons of Liberty perfected their own organization, that of the regular governments was dissolving. Everywhere colonial governors sent home reports of their helplessness. Governor Bernard prepared to flee from his province.[49] Lieutenant-Governor Hutchinson wondered whether authority could be restored even if the Stamp Act were repealed.[50] And from other colonies came the same story. Governor Wright could not rely on the support of more than ten men in Savannah and dared not call the militia for fear of arming his enemies.[51] Governor Wentworth in New Hampshire averred that no governor on the continent could depend upon his militia, "because the Militia are the very People on the other Side the question."[52] Even in Connecticut where all the officers of government were popularly elected, it was reported that "the principal Men are obliged to throw cold water, and to use the utmost Address to extinguish and prevent the Flames breaking out. . . Men of Eighty are ready to gird the sword . . . the very Boys as well as the hardy Rustic are full of fire and at half a Word ready to fight."[53] Governor Colden of New York admitted that he

[48] *Boston Gazette,* February 24, 1766.

[49] Massachusetts Archives, XXVI, 183; Bernard to Lord Colville, November 1, 1765, to Conway, December 19, 1765, Bernard Papers, IV, 84, 184.

[50] Hutchinson to ———, February 27, March 26, 1766, Massachusetts Archives, XXVI, 199, 216.

[51] To Lords of Trade, February 7, 1766, *Georgia Historical Quarterly,* 13 (1929), 148; to Conway, February 7, 1766, Jones, *History of Georgia,* II, 60-64. Wright had seventy Rangers and was promised twenty men from the warship *Speedwell,* but could muster only ten supporters among the inhabitants of Savannah.

[52] To Lords of Trade, October 5, 1765, House of Lords Manuscripts, January 14, 1766.

[53] Ezra Stiles to Benjamin Ellery, October 23, 1765, Stiles Papers.

had no power outside the fort in which he guarded himself.[54] In Pennsylvania Governor Penn thought "we are not more than one degree from open Rebellion."[55]

In this situation wisdom dictated that the nominal authorities should avoid occasions for demonstrating their weakness. A few governors like Franklin of New Jersey and Tryon of North Carolina rode out the storm by openly expressing disapproval of the Stamp Act or at least keeping silent about it.[56] Others like Francis Bernard and Cadwallader Colden invited disaster not only by showing their fear of the mob, but by lecturing the people on the duty of obedience. Colden virtually challenged the New York mob to attack Fort George by ordering extensive preparations for defense, and it was only the coolness of the officers within that prevented the American Revolution from beginning on November 1, 1765, with an attack on it. A milling crowd of several thousand people stood outside and "knocked at the gate, placed their hands on the top of the Ramparts, called out to the guards to fire, threw bricks and stones against the Fort and notwithstanding the highest provocation was given, not a word was returned to the most opprobrious language."[57] Major James, in command at the time, testified before Parliament that if he had fired he could have killed 900 of the mob on that night, but he added that the opposition could thereupon have assembled 50,000 fighting men from New York and New Jersey alone, and that it would have been impossible to hold out against such a force.[58] This opinion was supported by General Gage himself, who wrote to England that fire from the fort could

[54] Collector and Comptroller of New York to Commissioners of Customs, November 4, 1765, Treasury Papers, Class I, Bundle 442.

[55] Richard Penn, Jr., to [Thomas Penn], December 15, 1765, Penn Manuscripts, X, 19, Historical Society of Pennsylvania.

[56] William Franklin to Benjamin Franklin, November 13, 1765, Franklin Papers, I, 168; Colonial Records of North Carolina, VII, 127-128. Cf. Fauquier to Conway, December 11, 1765, House of Lords Manuscripts, February 6, 1766.

[57] Robert R. Livingston to Governor Monckton, November 8, 1765, Massachusetts Historical Society, Collections, 4th ser., 10 (1871), 559-567.

[58] Additional Mss., 33030, British Museum.

have meant the beginning of Civil War.[59] Gage knew that in such a civil war the troops which he commanded would have been all but massacred. Twenty years later, when the fighting that began in 1775 had ended with the Americans victorious, Gage may have looked back and regretted that they had not got it over with in 1765; but at the time there was still hope that British authority might be preserved for the future by suspending it in the present. Men like Gage and Governor Franklin of New Jersey realized that "for any Man to set himself up as an advocate of the Stamp Act in the Colonies is a meer Piece of Quixotism"[60]—even if the man were a colonial governor, sworn to support the authority of Great Britain. Those who do not carry a big stick are well-advised to speak softly, and every colonial governor who understood the smallness of his power, spoke in a whisper or not at all.

With the regular government all but extinguished, the Sons of Liberty steadily tightened their own control. Within their respective colonies, though there may have been uncomfortable moments when a Weber or a McIntosh seemed to be getting out of line, they kept the upper hand. They acted, of course, more arbitrarily than the regular government would have dared to do: they seized private mail, restricted the freedom of the press, and terrorized their enemies without mercy. But this is only to say that they were beginning a revolution. They had seized the power which once belonged to the royal governments, and they were prepared to keep it by fair means or foul until their end, the defeat of the Stamp Act, was accomplished.

How far they were prepared to go became apparent when England responded to the news of American riots. The threats of violence by which the Sons of Liberty exercised authority in America were transformed by three thousand miles of ocean into an impertinence, and Parliament, which had dealt

[59] Quoted in Colden to Conway, November 4, 1765, Treasury Papers, Class I, Bundle 447. Cf. Gage to Conway, November 4, 8, 1765, Carter, ed., *Correspondence of Gage,* I, 70-73.

[60] William Franklin to Benjamin Franklin, Franklin Papers, I, 168.

with mobs before, replied to the challenge with talk of cramming stamps down American throats. When the Sons of Liberty heard this, they knew that they might have to fight for their rights not against a few helpless stamp distributors, but against the British Army. To be sure they probably surmised that the Rockingham government might repeal the Stamp Act before any attempt was made to enforce it. Nevertheless there were already British regulars in America under General Gage, and if repeal should fail, action might come fast. Consequently it was important that they be prepared to fight or give up when the time came and not lose the decision by default. In the winter of 1765–1766, therefore, the Sons of Liberty throughout the colonies sponsored meetings of townspeople in which the citizens put on record their determination to defend their rights.

The Sons of Liberty in Connecticut seem to have taken the lead in holding meetings of this kind. The resolutions adopted show that they appreciated what the defense of their rights might cost. The meeting at New London on December 10, 1765, asserted the natural right of a people to set bounds upon their government and their duty, if lawful methods failed, "to reassume their natural Rights, and the Authority the Laws of Nature and of God have vested them with."[61] The people of Pomfret, Connecticut, asserted on December 25, 1765, "That God and Nature brought us into the world Freemen," and the English constitution confirmed their rights, "nor shall it be in the Power of any to deprive us of them, but with our lives."[62] In Wallingford the Sons of Liberty resolved on January 13, 1766, "That we will oppose the same [Stamp Act] to the last extremity, even to take the field."[63] In the opening months of 1766 the Sons of Liberty in other colonies followed the example of Connecticut with similar resolutions. Meetings were reported at Providence, New York City, Oyster Bay, Huntington, New Brunswick (New Jersey), Cecil County (Maryland), Leedstown and Norfolk (Virginia), and Wilmington (North Carolina), enunciating the

---

61 *Boston Post-Boy*, December 16, 1765.
62 *Boston Gazette*, January 13, 1766.
63 *Connecticut Courant*, February 3, 1766.

readiness of the people to resist the Stamp Act "to the last extremity," "at any Risk whatever," "to the utmost of our power," "with our lives and fortunes," "at every Hazard, paying no Regard to Danger, or to Death."[64]

Such sentiments could be made effective only by a union of the Sons of Liberty, not merely within each colony but among all the colonies. The Americans might cry "liberty or death," but if they preferred the former, they would be most apt to get it by uniting. How early the Sons of Liberty in any colony began to think of intercolonial union is hard to say. The Stamp Act Congress brought together a number of radicals who may have discussed plans for armed resistance in the odd hours when they were not drawing up the declarations of right and the appeals to King and Parliament. The congress was preceded by the issue in New York of a news sheet called the *Constitutional Courant,* which repeated the famous Franklin cartoon of 1754, of the snake cut in pieces, with the motto "Join or die." And the paper itself was filled with articles of an inflammatory nature.[65] But the congress, at least formally, did not consider a union in arms, and even James Otis, in a letter written shortly after to William Samuel Johnson, deplored the violence at Charles Town and New York, and expressed the fear that "Parliament will charge the Colonies with presenting petitions in one hand and a dagger in the other."[66] Nevertheless, even before the delegates could all have returned to their homes, demonstrations of a strikingly similar character were staged in several colonies. The congress broke up on October 24, 1765. On November first, the day when the Stamp Act was to take effect, the Sons of Liberty in Portsmouth, Newport, Baltimore, and Wilmington, North Carolina, all held mock funerals of Liberty, perhaps by

[64] *Newport Mercury,* March 31, 1766; *Maryland Gazette,* January 30, March 20, March 27, April 10, 1766; *Pennsylvania Journal,* January 30, March 6, 13, April 17, 1766. *Prologue to Revolution,* 114-117.

[65] Albert Matthews, "The Snake Devices, 1754–1766, and the Constitutional Courant," Colonial Society of Massachusetts, *Publications,* 11 (1910), 409-453.

[66] November 12, 1765, Bancroft Transcripts, New York Public Library.

coincidence, perhaps as the result of a circularized suggestion.[67]

The first definite move to organize colonial resistance to
the Stamp Act on a continental basis took place in a tavern
in New London on Christmas day of 1765. Two delegates
from the New York Sons of Liberty met there with some of
the Connecticut Sons of Liberty and subscribed an agreement
of mutual aid. They promised each other "to march with the
utmost dispatch, at their own proper costs and expence, on the
first proper notice, (which must be signified to them by at
least six of the sons of liberty) with their whole force if required, and it can be spared, to the relief of those that shall,
are, or may be in danger from the *stamp-act*, or its promoters
and abettors, or any thing relative to it, on account of any
thing that may have been done in opposition to its obtaining."
In addition they promised that they would "endeavour to
bring about, accomplish, and perfect the like *association* with
all the *colonies* on the continent for the like salutary purposes
and no other."[68]

For the next three months the Sons of Liberty all over
North America were sending letters back and forth, perfect-
ing their organization, offering assistance to one another, and
proposing boycotts against any colony that submitted to the
Act. The New Yorkers who had been at New London went
on to Boston and secured the allegiance of the Boston Sons
to the association. Boston in turn wrote to all the towns in
Massachusetts and to Portsmouth, New Hampshire in order
to bring them into the organization.[69] Connecticut likewise
produced a colony-wide organization, with a convention at
Hartford on March 25, which drew up resolutions supporting the intercolonial associations.[70] In March the Providence
Sons of Liberty sent out circular letters to the Sons in other

---

[67] Davidson, *Propaganda and the American Revolution*, 68.

[68] William Gordon, *History of the Rise, Progress, and Establishment of the Independence of the United States of America*
(London, 1788), I, 197-198. Connecticut Historical Society, *Collections*, 18 (1920), 384-386. *Prologue to Revolution*, 117-118.

[69] Belknap Papers.

[70] *Connecticut Courant*, March 10, 1766. See below, ch. XIII,
note 42.

places, proposing correspondence and declaring that "We shall be ready at all Times not only to vindicate ourselves, and the People under our more immediate Inspection, from lawless Might, but as Occasion may require to give aid to the other Colonies, for the rescuing them from every Attempt against their Liberties."[71] There is evidence that the correspondence was carried as far south as South Carolina, and that the South Carolinians offered 500 men to assist the Georgians in getting rid of their stamps.[72] In Maryland a colony-wide organization was effected as a means of forcing open the courts and customs, and New Jersey worked out an organization almost identical with the one which she used for establishing an independent government ten years later.[73]

No central intercolonial organization was established in the three months before the first news of repeal, but plans for a

[71] Rhode Island Historical Society Manuscripts, XII, 64.

[72] Davidson, *Propaganda and the American Revolution,* 69-73; Leake, *John Lamb,* 19; Belknap Papers; Wright to Conway, January 31, 1766, Jones, *History of Georgia,* II, 60-64; Wright to Lords of Trade, February 7, 1766, *Georgia Historical Quarterly,* 13 (1929), 148. The Georgians outside Savannah did stage a march on the town, but found upon arrival that Governor Wright had already put the stamps aboard the sloop *Speedwell* where they could be neither destroyed nor distributed. Consequently there was no need of assistance from South Carolina. Nevertheless, because of Georgia's temporary compliance with the Act the South Carolinians voted to boycott the entire colony. Although there were local Sons of Liberty in Pennsylvania the intercolonial organization seems to have made little headway there. Governor Penn wrote to his uncle on March 21, 1766, "There is a very impudent set of people to the northward who call themselves sons of Liberty, whose business seems to be, to stir up as much discontent and uneasiness as they possibly can. They are not satisfied with the mischief they do at home, but are travelling from one end of the Continent to the other sowing dissention wherever they go. Two of them were here some days ago, but were not received in the manner they expected as the people are determined to wait patiently the Issue of the Stamp Act. They correspond with most of the Colonies from New Hampshire to Georgia and their purpose is to form a general plan of Opposition if ever the stamp act should be attempted to be put in execution, and I am really afraid it would be the Case." Penn Manuscripts, X, 33.

[73] Davidson, *Propaganda and the American Revolution,* 72.

"General Congress" were under discussion,[74] and there can be no doubt that the colonists were getting ready to fight the British Army. It was doubtless easier to get ready than actually to take up arms; but if it came to that, the colonists would at least be clear about what they were fighting for. In their messages to one another expressions of loyalty to the House of Hanover and defiance of Parliament were judiciously mingled on every page. They were assuring themselves, and perhaps protesting a little too much, that they were not rebels, for the resistance they envisaged was resistance only to an unconstitutional enactment of Parliament. The Sons of Liberty in Portsmouth, New Hampshire, expressed the common attitude when they wrote to their companions in Boston, on February 8, that since the Stamp Act violated the fundamental privileges of British subjects, it was "Therefore void of all Lawfull Authority, so that depending upon Meer Force it may Lawfully be oppos'd by Force."[75] The Sons of Liberty, like other revolutionaries, claimed that law and tradition and constitutional precedents were on their side. Ostensibly at least, they had no wish for independence, and they rejected indignantly the accusation commonly made in England that the colonies were scheming for independence. But the wiser among them must have recognized that if it came to war, the House of Hanover would not back them against Parliament, and that independence might be the outcome.

Most Americans would have looked upon such an outcome as undesirable, but many could see that unless Parliament backed down the colonies would be driven to it. John Dickinson, who later withstood the movement for independence until the last moment, could see the direction of events as early as December, 1765. In an appeal to William Pitt, the man who was regarded as most likely to save the empire, Dickinson warned that although independence would be unfortunate for America as well as England, there could be no doubt of the

[74] Leake, *John Lamb,* 19. New York Sons of Liberty to Boston Sons of Liberty, April 2, 1766, Lamb Papers, New York Historical Society.

[75] Belknap Papers.

Americans' ability to achieve it.[76] Intercolonial rivalries and recriminations had hitherto kept them divided, but their quarrels were giving way before their common concern for liberty. "No colony," he pointed out, "apprehends that any other has Designs upon its Liberty. Their Contests are of an inferior Nature, and will vanish when one more dreadful to them commences." Americans would not seek for independence "unless excited by the Treatment they receive from Great Britain," but if once they made the attempt, "The Strength of the Colonies, their Distance, the wealth that would pour into them on opening their Ports to all Nations, the Jealousy entertained of Great Britain by some European Powers, and the peculiar Circumstances of that Kingdome, would insure success."[77] Dickinson anticipated with horror the results of such success: "A multitude of Commonwealths, Crimes & Calamities, Centuries of mutual Jealousies, Hatreds, Wars of Devastation; till at last the exhausted Provinces shall sink into Slavery under the yoke of some fortunate Conqueror."

The only way that such a future could be avoided, in Dickinson's opinion, was for Parliament to give way and repeal the Stamp Act. Dickinson was a lawyer and knew well enough the arguments for and against Parliament's authority to tax the colonies, but he was able to see by December of 1765, that the authority, whatever basis it might or might not have in law and political theory, could not be supported in fact. Rather than put it to the test which the Sons of Liberty were preparing, it would be better for Parliament to abandon it voluntarily. "It may be said," Dickinson wrote to Pitt, "that Great Britain by repealing that Act will tacitly acknowledge, that she has no Right to tax the Colonies. If the Repeal should be construed as such an Acknowledgment, it will only

[76] Dickinson to Pitt, December 21, 1765, Historical Society of Pennsylvania. *Prologue to Revolution*, 118-122.

[77] For similar views of the likelihood of American success in the event of revolution, see John Penn to Thomas Penn, March 21, 1766, Dickinson Papers, Historical Society of Pennsylvania, and a letter from New York, November 8, 1765, Additional Mss., 35911, British Museum.

be renouncing a Right, the Exercise of which can never be repeated without throwing the Colonies into Desperation. This
I hope Great Britain will never do; and therefore she cannot
lose any thing by such a Renunciation. . . . If this shall be
thought by the Parliament too light a Pretence for the repeal, and that their authority may be wounded by such a Condescension, I am afraid they cannot hereafter rely on the
affection of the Colonies."

For three months after Dickinson wrote, the colonies hung
in the balance, hoping for peace, preparing for war. By the
time the news of repeal arrived a great many things had happened, things that might not be remembered in the moment of
jubilation but that could not be easily forgotten in the months
and years that followed. While affection for Great Britain
was being proclaimed on all sides, the Sons of Liberty would
remember with some pride their success in defying Parliament. The unfortunate individuals upon whom they had demonstrated their defiance would remember too, and perhaps
with as much pride, their own behavior during those trying
months.

PART III

PATTERNS OF LOYALTY

Chapter XII

Thomas Hutchinson

IN THE SUMMER OF 1765 there were two courses open to Americans who believed, as most Americans did, that Parliament had no authority to tax them. They could fight, or they could submit and accompany their submission by humble requests for repeal of the Stamp Act and the Sugar Act. The Sons of Liberty chose to fight, and they began to fight so early that their more peaceable countrymen were given no opportunity to try the alternative. Most of those who would have taken the course of submission sat back in silence and helplessly watched the approach of rebellion. A few, because of the offices they held, because of a greater sense of responsibility, or because they had more courage, tried to halt the approach of disaster. The results in every case were ruined lives.

The men who suffered for upholding the authority of Parliament in 1765 were not simply transplanted Englishmen, sighing for love of the mother country. They were Americans, many of them with deep roots in the American past and all of them bound by ties of blood and affection and business and honor to the American life of the day. They had both friends and enemies among their countrymen, for no man who has the character or the wealth or the prominence to influence his fellow men can be without enemies; but in each case their enemies were to be found among the Sons of Liberty and their friends among the peaceable but helpless. Perhaps one reason why they spoke up as they did was that they saw their enemies on the other side, the side of rebellion. And as they saw their enemies, their enemies saw them. When the Sons of Liberty attacked in the summer of 1765, they were attacking not merely the spokesmen of Parliamentary supremacy, but men who, in one way or another, had earned their hatred long before. How else can one account for what happened to men like Thomas Hutchinson, John Hughes, or Jared Ingersoll?

Thomas Hutchinson was not the kind of man who made friends easily. His thin, handsome face, handsome in spite of its long nose, and his tall spare frame held precisely erect, combined to give an impression of remote dignity—a cool man this, who could swallow half the offices in the province and look as though they belonged to him by divine right. And yet he was as free of malice as any man. After the dust had settled on the ruins of his house on the morning of August 27, he must have tried to recall the things he had done to make himself so hated that people wanted to tear his house to pieces. What had made them so angry with him? He had, of course, a few personal enemies. There was James Otis, currently the leader of the Massachusetts House of Representatives. Otis thought that Hutchinson had cheated his father, James Otis, Senior, out of a seat on the Superior Court. Governor Pownall had promised a seat to the elder Otis whenever one should become vacant, but Pownall was no longer in the governor's chair when a vacancy occurred in 1760, and Governor Bernard did not feel bound by his predecessor's commitments. When he offered the position to Hutchinson, the latter remembered the promise and spoke of it, but Bernard for some reason had determined against Otis. He told Hutchinson that whoever received the place it would not be Otis; if Hutchinson refused, it would go to someone else. Under these circumstances he had accepted, but Otis never forgave him. Since then the younger Otis had gone into politics, and as a member of the House of Representatives had taken every opportunity to attack the man who he thought had cheated his father.[1]

James Otis, Jr., was not a man to be nice about his methods, and he used every trick of innuendo and snide suggestion to communicate his own hatred to the people at large. Probably he was partly responsible for the outrage of August

[1] Hutchinson, *History of Massachusetts-Bay*, L. S. Mayo, ed., III, 63–64. The affair is dealt with most extensively in Malcolm Freiberg, Prelude to Purgatory: Thomas Hutchinson in Massachusetts Politics, 1760–1770, Ph.D. dissertation, 1950, Brown University Library.

26 simply by virtue of the feeling against Hutchinson which he had helped to create. Yet he was not solely responsible. Hutchinson could remember occasions, even before Otis turned against him, when he had made himself odious simply by adhering to his convictions in the face of popular opposition. In 1748 he had taken the lead in an action which rendered him extremely unpopular in certain quarters. In that year Massachusetts received reimbursement from the British Treasury for her part in capturing the French fortress of Louisburg in 1745. The capture of Louisburg had been almost entirely the undertaking of Massachusetts and was the only notable success of British arms in the War of the Austrian Succession. A grateful Parliament therefore voted to reimburse Massachusetts for her pains, in the sum of £183,649, 25s. 7d. Heretofore Massachusetts had had to rely on a paper currency which every year depreciated further, to the grief of creditors and delight of debtors. When the British Treasury turned over the sum, all in silver, Hutchinson and other far-sighted individuals saw the opportunity to get rid of paper money in Massachusetts. Hutchinson pressed hard to persuade the Assembly to take this step, and succeeded, with two results: Massachusetts had the soundest currency in North America, and Massachusetts debtors, who lost heavily by the change, hated Hutchinson cordially as the author of their misfortunes.[2]

That had been seventeen years ago. The memory still rankled, but it was not enough to make people suddenly burst out in a wild rage. A more recent event which contributed to the people's dislike was Hutchinson's part in preventing the courts of Massachusetts from violating an act of Parliament. The customs officers in Boston had received strict orders in 1761 from William Pitt to prevent clandestine trade with the enemy. To assist them in discovering such trade they were instructed to apply for writs of assistance (general

[2] Hutchinson to Conway, October 1, 1765, Massachusetts Archives, XXVI, 155; Andrew McF. Davis, *Currency and Banking in the Province of the Massachusetts Bay* (New York, 1901), chs. 10-12. Cf., E. J. Ferguson, *The Power of the Purse: A History of American Public Finance 1776–1790* (Chapel Hill, 1961), 3-24.

warrants) empowering them to break open any building they chose to search for contraband or smuggled goods. Such writs had been authorized by an act of Parliament in 1696 but had never been employed before, and it was doubtful whether the colonial courts had authority to issue them. Some of the other justices of the Superior Court favored a blank refusal, but Hutchinson persuaded the Court to postpone a decision until they obtained more information from England, with the ultimate result that the Court did issue the writs. James Otis, Jr., his new-found enemy, was advocate of the Boston merchants in the case, arguing against the writs of assistance as violations of the natural rights of man. Up to this time Otis had been advocate of the Admiralty Court, a position which would have obliged him to argue in favor of the writs, but he resigned in order to argue against them. As a result Otis gained in popularity what Hutchinson lost.[3]

By his support of hard money in 1748 Hutchinson had earned the dislike of the debtors; by his stand on the writs of assistance he had earned that of the smugglers. According to some estimates, if these two groups were subtracted from the population of Massachusetts, there would be scarcely anyone left. And yet even the episode of the writs of assistance passed without any violent demonstration against him. He had been unpopular, but no one thought of pulling his house down. As a matter of fact, only a year and a half before the riot there had been proof that the people respected his integrity, even though they might not love him. In February, 1764, the House of Representatives with only eight members dissenting asked him to go to England to argue the colony's case against the molasses duty. He had been unable to leave at once, and before he was prepared to go news of the Sugar Act arrived.[4] Yet the vote demonstrated that the people knew

[3] Hutchinson to Conway, October 1, 1765, Massachusetts Archives, XXVI, 155; see Freiberg, Prelude to Purgatory, ch. 1, and O. M. Dickerson, "Writs of Assistance as a Cause of the Revolution," in R. B. Morris, ed., The Era of the American Revolution (New York, 1939), 40-75.

[4] Hutchinson to ———, February 6, 7, 1764, Massachusetts Archives, XXVI, 76-78; Bernard to Jackson, February 2, 1764, Bernard Papers, III, 123-127, Harvard College Library.

him for an honest man. It was what happened in the following year that turned them so bitterly against him.

As Hutchinson considered what he had done during this year to win the reward of August 26 he must have felt some bitterness himself. He was no friend of the Sugar Act or the Stamp Act. When the Massachusetts Assembly voted to send him to London to oppose the Sugar Act, they had not picked the wrong man. Hutchinson was a merchant himself and knew what the Sugar Act would mean to New England commerce. He thought it was a piece of folly which Parliament would repent of. As for the Stamp Act he had been one of the first to see the dangers of that. He had never told the people of Massachusetts of his efforts to prevent it or of his efforts to secure repeal of the Sugar Act. It would not have been fitting for him, as a servant of the Crown, to encourage the people of the colonies in their resistance to acts of Parliament by letting them know he was on their side; yet he was just as convinced as his demagogical enemies that Parliament had had no constitutional right to pass either the Sugar Act or the Stamp Act.

During the spring of 1764, when Governor Bernard was setting down his 97 propositions and James Otis was writing his *Rights of the Colonies*, Hutchinson too was writing about the rights of the colonies.[5] Perhaps he too did some of his writing in Concord, for like Bernard and Otis he was attending the meetings of the Assembly there. Bernard had sent his propositions to Richard Jackson on July 9, suggesting that he get them printed if they were approved in the proper quarters. Hutchinson sent his piece to Jackson too—Jackson knew everybody—on July 23, and enclosed a copy of Otis's pamphlet which had just been rushed into print. It was Hutchinson's intention that Jackson should get his paper printed, provided Jackson thought that it would be helpful in preventing taxation of the colonies, but Hutchinson wanted the authorship kept secret. He wrote the piece in a form common

---

[5] I have published the manuscript, along with some of the observations on Hutchinson made in this chapter, in *New England Quarterly*, 21 (1948), 459-492. All quotations from the manuscript will be found here.

in political writing at the time, as a letter from a gentleman to his friend. At first he wished Jackson to make it appear as coming "from some other colony rather than the Massachusetts, which might prevent fixing upon the author," but upon second thought added that it might be safer if it were made to appear as a production of someone in England. This might be done if "some stroke or other could be inserted having reference to some very late transaction with you of which there could not be time for advice in the colonies."[6]

Hutchinson's uneasiness about having his name connected with the piece may have arisen from the fact that it affirmed the rights—as well as privileges—of the colonies in very explicit terms. In fact there was scarcely any argument used in the later colonial struggle against the Stamp Act that Hutchinson did not anticipate. The only thing that marked him off from the radicals was the calmness with which he stated the case. In the opening paragraph he even apologized for the warmth with which Otis had written: "Before I enter upon the Subject," he wrote, "give me leave to observe to you that the Colonists like all the rest of the human race are of different spirits and dispositions some more calm and moderate others more violent and extravagant. and if now and then some rude and indecent things are thrown out in print in one place and another I hope such things will not be considered as coming from the Colonists in general but from particular persons warmed by the intemperate zeal shall I say of Englishmen in support of what upon a sudden appears to them to be their rights."

Although he thus attempted to undo the damage which he felt would result from Otis's heated phrases, Hutchinson's own position was in every important particular identical with Otis's. Both paid tribute to the standard Whig doctrine of the supremacy of the British Parliament. Hutchinson thought it reasonable that "British Colonies should ever remain subject to the controul of Britain and consequently must be bound by the determinations of the supreme authority there the British Parliament." Otis agreed that "The power of parliament is uncontroulable, but by themselves, and we must obey.

6 Massachusetts Archives, XXVI, 99-100.

They only can repeal their own Acts."[7] Otis, while acknowledging the supremacy of Parliament, argued in terms derived from Locke that Parliament ought not to violate the natural rights of the subject.[8] Hutchinson likewise affirmed that Parliament should have a tender regard for "all rights natural and acquired of every Subject." Hutchinson went on to state that the colonists "claim a power of making Law and a Privilege of exemption from taxes except by their own Representatives." This power, he said, was what they deserved as Englishmen and had been confirmed to them by the charters which stated that the colonists should have the same privileges as natural-born Englishmen. This did not mean that Parliament had resigned all authority over the colonists, but according to Hutchinson Parliament had suspended a part, at least, of the authority which it would have exercised had they remained in England. This authority had been transferred from the home government to the colonial governments, just as in the case of the Roman colonies. And Hutchinson went into the analogy of the Roman colonies in considerable detail, emerging with the conclusion "that it does not seem to be an unreasonable proposition, that the inhabitants of [a] Colony are intitled to all the privileges they enjoyed in their mother Country which will consist with their dependance upon it."

Hutchinson, again like Otis, dismissed the distinction between internal and external taxes favored by some English writers and notably by his friend Richard Jackson. According to this distinction Parliament might levy external taxes, that is, customs duties, on the colonists but not internal or direct taxes. Otis had said: "There is no foundation for the distinction some make in England, between an internal and an external tax on the colonies."[9] Hutchinson put the argument more directly in terms of popular rights. "Is it any difference to me," he asked, "whether I pay three pounds ten shillings duty for a Pipe of wine to an officer of Impost or whether I

[7] *The Rights of the British Colonies Asserted and Proved* (Boston, 1764), 39.
[8] *Ibid., passim,* especially 25-31.
[9] *Ibid.,* 42.

pay the same Sum by an excise of ninepence per Gallon to an excise Officer or would an old Roman have thought his Privileges less affected by the Portorium than by the Stipendium or Decumae?" Hutchinson was more diplomatic than Otis in stating that if there appeared to Parliament to be an essential difference between internal and external taxes, he was willing to accept it; he was willing to take half a loaf as better than none, but, he queried, remembering no doubt that Parliament had already passed the resolution for a stamp tax, "are we sure of retaining even this?" Are we sure in other words, of retaining an exemption even from internal taxes?

Hutchinson next pointed out the weakness of the argument, which apparently had been advanced in England already, that the colonies were as much represented in Parliament as were the nine Englishmen out of ten who had no vote in Parliamentary elections. Hutchinson showed that every important interest in England was represented in Parliament, "but what Member," he asked, "can be said to be the representative of the Colonies more than all the rest?" This passage bears a striking resemblance to General Conway's speech against the Stamp Act on February 15, 1765, when Conway asked, "Will any man in this house get up and say, he is one of the representatives of the colonies; when so far from being an object of their choice, the most sensible man in the colonies scarce knows such a gentleman exists."[10]

In the first part of his manuscript Hutchinson had advanced constitutional arguments against Parliamentary taxation. In the remainder of the paper he dismissed the question of constitutional right and showed the inequity of levying taxes upon colonies which already contributed heavily, through the mercantilist regulations of trade, to the wealth and power of the mother country, and which had been planted, with the exception of Georgia and Halifax, entirely at the expense of the colonists themselves. In this part of the paper Hutchinson anticipated the arguments urged by Colonel Barré in his speech in Parliament on February 6.[11] Hutchinson under-

10 *Georgia Gazette*, August 1, 1765.
11 See above, ch. V.

standably made no charge of corruption against colonial governors, as Barré did, but he did show that the colonies had been planted by the enterprise of the colonists, not by any care on the part of the mother country; and he also showed that for a hundred years the colonists had defended themselves against the Indians without assistance from England and that the late French and Indian War, in which the colonists contributed both men and money, had been fought as much for the benefit of the mother country as for that of the colonies.

The resemblance between Hutchinson's arguments and those used in the House of Commons by General Conway and Colonel Barré was perhaps more than a coincidence. Jackson evidently decided that no good purpose would be served in England by printing the manuscript, but apparently he passed it around discreetly among persons of influence. Arthur Savage of Boston, who arrived in London early in 1765, found that "People seem generally agreed that at the present Junto no Man is so sutable or so likely to Serve the Province as Mr. Hutchinson who is in high Repute here— which is greatly strengthned by a Letter of his to Mr. Jackson . . . which is highly spoken of."[12] The person to whom Jackson finally entrusted the manuscript was His Majesty's new Secretary of State for the Southern Department, General Conway. Exactly when he did so Jackson neglected to say, but he did tell Hutchinson that he had let Conway in on the secret of who the author was. "This was a Piece of Confidence in him," wrote Jackson, "that I thought proper, and have no reason to be sorry I reposed it."[13] Whether Isaac Barré saw the manuscript or not is uncertain but altogether likely, since he along with Conway was known as a friend of the colonies. In November, 1765, after hearing of the assault on Hutchinson's house, Jackson wrote to Governor Bernard: "Nothing can be more unjust than the Treatment of the worthy and unfortunate Lieutenant Governor, nothing can be a greater proof of the Blindness of the

---

[12] To S. P. Savage, January 12, 1765, S. P. Savage Papers, II, Massachusetts Historical Society.

[13] Massachusetts Archives, XXV, 65.

Rabble: I know that He has used the weightiest Arguments against the obnoxious Act, and that they have been used at Home from his Materials."[14] Jackson's testimony that Hutchinson's manuscript had assisted the opponents of the Stamp Act in England was later confirmed by General Conway himself. On May 24, 1776, while his countrymen were preparing to declare their independence, Hutchinson was in England, dining with Sir George Hay, who told him that Conway had observed in a speech in Parliament "that he had received from me in the time of the Stamp Act, such reasons against the passing of it as were irresistible."[15]

In 1765, as he passed the shell of his once handsome house or caught the hostile glances of people on the street, Hutchinson must have reflected with some bitterness on the irony of his situation. He stood in the eyes of his countrymen as a traitor, while Barré and Conway basked in a shower of fulsome tributes. Town-meetings all over America including that of Boston had passed votes of gratitude to these gentlemen.[16] And the only thing that Barré and Conway had done was to urge in Parliament the arguments which he had advanced long before. In fact it was not unlikely that they had derived their arguments from his manuscript.

Hutchinson would certainly have been justified in thinking that he deserved better at the hands of Massachusetts. And yet in a perverse way the mob had been right. Mobs never act reasonably, for they would not be mobs if they did. The people who destroyed Hutchinson's house recognized that he was a man of strength; they had sensed that a showdown was near and that when it came, the strength of Thomas Hutchinson would be against them. Whatever his feelings about the expediency or constitutionality of the Stamp Act, he would be found defending law and order. When the barricades were up, Thomas Hutchinson would be on the other side. And in the summer of 1765 it looked as though the barricades were going up. It was his prudence, his mod-

[14] Massachusetts Archives, XXII, 456.
[15] Peter O. Hutchinson, ed., *The Diary and Letters of Thomas Hutchinson* (London, 1884–1886), II, 58.
[16] *A Report of the Record Commissioners of the City of Boston, containing the Boston Town Records, 1758 to 1769*, p. 157.

eration, his fundamental conservatism that made Hutchinson seem an enemy of the people in 1765, because the time for prudence had suddenly passed. The face of revolution had appeared; he who was not a friend was an enemy; and Hutchinson was an enemy not to be dealt with lightly.

He had demonstrated his moderation in the most positive manner during the year preceding the assault on his house. In the summer of 1765 the people of Massachusetts were thinking of the numerous occasions when he had urged them to submit peacefully to the chains which Parliament was clearly forging for them. The instance in which he had exerted his influence most forcefully was in toning down the petition which Massachusetts sent to the King in November, 1764.[17]

It is interesting that Hutchinson insisted on leaving the word "rights" out of the petition and on confining the objections against taxation to internal taxes. In his own essay he used the word rights and ridiculed the distinction between internal and external taxes. Even more curious is the fact that only a little more than a week after he had finally persuaded the Massachusetts House of Representatives to drop their declaration against the external taxes of the Sugar Act, he wrote to his friend Ebenezer Silliman in Connecticut, chiding him for the fact that Connecticut confined its arguments to internal taxes. Silliman was a member of the committee which worked with Governor Fitch in writing *Reasons why the British Colonies, in America, should not be charged with Internal Taxes, by Authority of Parliament*.[18] "Your distinction between duties upon trade and internal taxes," Hutchinson wrote,

> agrees with the opinion of People in England, particularly your Agent [Richard Jackson]. and with the opinion of most People here Mr. Bernard is full with you in it. I think it imprudent to oppose it and therefore am silent but it is for this reason only. I am for saving as much of our privileges as we can and if the people of England make the distinction I think it tends to strengthen us in our

[17] See the discussion in ch. III, above.
[18] (New Haven, 1764); *Public Records of the Colony of Connecticut*, XII, 256, 651-671.

claim to exemption from internal taxes. Really there is no difference and the fallacy of the argument lies here it is your supposing duties upon trade to be imposed for the sake of regulating trade, whereas the Professed design of the duties by the late Act is to raise a revenue. Can it possibly cause any difference to the subject to impose a duty of £5 on a pipe of wine to be paid as an impost or to impose a duty of excise of 12d a gallon to be paid by the licensed inland vendor. The consumer pays just the same supposing the pipe to be 100 gallons in the one case as the other and the rights of the people are alike affected in both cases. If they will stop where they are I would not dispute their distinction with them, but if they intend to go on there will be a necessity of doing it for they may find duties on trade enough to drain us so thoroughly that it will not be possible to pay internal taxes as a revenue to them or even to support government within ourselves.[19]

In view of Hutchinson's performance in persuading the Massachusetts House of Representatives to adopt an address which objected only to internal taxes, his letter to Silliman is remarkable. He tells Silliman that "most people here" agree with the distinction between "duties upon trade and internal taxes," yet the leader of the House of Representatives had published a pamphlet in which the statement occurred that "there is no foundation for the distinction some make in England, between an internal and an external tax on the colonies,"[20] and in the petition originally approved by the House it was stated with regard to the external duties levied under the Sugar Act, that "we look *upon those Duties as a Tax*, and which we humbly apprehend ought not to be laid without the Representatives of the People affected by them."[21] In the address which Hutchinson had just persuaded the House to accept there was no suggestion that the duties of the Sugar Act were regarded as a tax. The address pleaded

[19] November 9, 1764, Massachusetts Archives, XXVI, 117-118.
[20] Otis, *Rights of the British Colonies*, 42; *Journal of the Honourable House of Representatives* (Boston, 1764), 53, 66.
[21] Massachusetts Archives, XXII, 412-418.

against the Sugar Act solely on economic grounds and confined its constitutional objections to internal taxes. Hutchinson had thus persuaded the Assembly to accept a statement which fell short of what he himself believed to be their due. In the paper he sent to Jackson he declared that all Parliamentary taxation of the colonies, internal or external, violated the rights of the people. In the letter to Silliman he said that the rights of the people were no less affected by external than by internal taxes, and yet he persuaded the House of Representatives not to use the word "rights" and to plead for exemption from internal taxes only. Since the people of Massachusetts knew nothing of Hutchinson's private views, it is no wonder that they thought he was ready to sacrifice their rights. Even if they had known of his efforts to prevent the Stamp Act, they might have continued to think so, though perhaps with less bitterness—and they would not have been wrong.

Until the Stamp Act had become a law Hutchinson had been on the side of the colonists. He had opposed the Act, because he believed that it would violate their rights, not merely their charter rights but their natural rights as men. But he also believed in the supremacy of Parliament, believed in it to the point where defiance of Parliamentary authority, however that authority was exercised, became synonymous with revolution. When Parliament did tax the colonies, Parliament was in the wrong, but that was no reason for the colonies to commit the further wrong of resisting. The only way out of the dilemma, as Hutchinson saw it, was to persuade the members to undo the injustice they had committed. And the most effective means of persuasion was not defiance but prudent submission and humble supplications.[22]

Prudence in the last analysis was Hutchinson's solution for the impasse between Parliamentary supremacy and colonial rights. He prevented the Massachusetts Assembly from asserting their rights, because he did not think it prudent to assert them. He went along with Governor Bernard and Richard Jackson in their distinction between internal and external

[22] Hutchinson to Champion and Hayley, April 9, 1765, *ibid.*, XXVI, 135.

taxes, though he believed it without foundation, because it was prudent to do so. He did not publish his paper on colonial rights, because he did not think it prudent. His was the attitude of honest friends of the colonies in England, who likewise had to reconcile Parliamentary supremacy with colonial rights. Richard Jackson did not think it advisable to publish Hutchinson's manuscript even with the authorship secret. Instead he gave it to Conway, from whom the sentiments expressed in it would come more graciously than from a colonist.

The friends of the colonies in England were distressed by the aggressive declarations of right pouring from America in the summer of 1765,[23] and Hutchinson was distressed by them in Massachusetts. He knew that they would make repeal of the Stamp Act more difficult, and he tried to persuade his countrymen to be more discreet. As he confided to his business correspondents in England, "It can be to no purpose to claim a right of exemption when the whole body of the people of England are against us."[24] It was this attitude which gave Hutchinson his reputation in Massachusetts as an enemy of the people's rights. He thought it foolhardy for people to seek a head-on collision with Parliament by abstract declarations of their rights or by exercising those rights in defiance of an act of Parliament. He even took advantage of his position as chief justice to lecture them on the consequences of such actions. In addresses to the grand juries of the several counties, he let them know, as he put it, "the nature of the offence of opposing by force and violence the execution of an Act of Parliament the supreme legislature of the British Dominions."[25]

Thus as his fellow-countrymen grew more outspoken, more determined to defend their rights, Hutchinson grew more and more prudent. There can be no doubt that his judgment was correct so far as concerned the immediate goal of repealing the Stamp Act. The colonial declarations of right and the

[23] See below, ch. XV.
[24] To Champion and Hayley, April 9, 1765, Massachusetts Archives, XXVI, 135.
[25] Hutchinson to Conway, October 1, 1765, ibid., 155.

violence against the stamp distributors only served to embarrass the men who were attempting to bring about repeal in England. What Hutchinson failed to understand was that the principles he had asserted in his letter to Jackson meant more to his fellow colonists than their attachment to England did. Hitherto they had not been obliged to determine exactly what their rights were. But when Parliament taxed them, they found out where they stood; and having done so, they were unwilling to accept prudence as a solution to their troubles. They did not want privileges; they wanted rights. Hutchinson never understood this. In 1774 he was in England, still seeking to mitigate the harshness of British measures against the colonies, still urging the colonies to forget about their rights and seek accommodation through prudence. When he heard of the Continental Congress, he wrote to a friend in America warning of the ill effects to be expected from such an assembly. "I know it is expected," he wrote, "that the more determined the Colonies appear, the more likely it will be to bring the Government here to their terms. I do not believe it."[26]

Hutchinson of course was right in 1774 as he had been in 1765. The British Parliament would not give way in the face of colonial determination. If the colonists had followed Hutchinson's advice, perhaps they might have preserved their attachment to the mother country without necessarily suffering an unfair burden of taxation. Through humble petitions and silent economic pressure they might have been able to obtain the redress of their immediate grievances. But they would have obtained it as a favor, not as a right. Hutchinson's mistake was in supposing that the colonies were willing to accept favors in place of rights. Fifty years before, they might have been, but never after the passage of the Stamp Act. The colonies had come of age; and Thomas Hutchinson was still trying to play the role of guardian. The price of his mistake in 1765 was a house in ruins; the ultimate price was a life completed in exile.

[26] *Diary and Letters*, I, 217 (August 8, 1774).

Chapter XIII

Jared Ingersoll

WHEN WILLIAM SAMUEL JOHNSON went to England in the fall of 1766, he was shocked at the gulf that separated rich from poor. He wrote about it to his old friend Benjamin Gale, of Killingly, Connecticut, and Gale wrote back like a trueborn Son of Liberty: "the Common people of England are a very different sett of Men from the people of America, otherwise they never would submitt to be taxed in the Manner they are, that a few may be loaded with places and Pensions and riot in Luxury and Excess, while they themselves cannot support themselves and their needy offspring with Bread, I thank God we are not such Jack Asses in America, and I hope in God we never shall be brought to submit to it, . . ."[1]

It is difficult to believe that a man who could denounce British taxation with such zest could curse the Sons of Liberty with equal vigor. Yet in this very letter Benjamin Gale bemoaned the fate of Connecticut under a government in which the Sons of Liberty had the leading hand. He found comfort only in the fact that the governor was very old, and "as age is Honorable," Gale concluded, "I wish he was as old again as he now is."

Benjamin Gale had been no advocate of a stamp tax. For that matter what American had? But for Gale as for many other Americans the Stamp Act had turned the world upside down. In a political and social situation which was precarious at best the Stamp Act had confounded wise and foolish, just and unjust. Connecticut plunged wildly through convulsions of hate, envy, and ambition; and suddenly, senselessly the men against whom Gale and his friends had been fighting for twenty-five years emerged victorious. These men, he was sure, had no claim to be sole champions of liberty or justice

[1] Benjamin Gale to William Samuel Johnson, December 1, 1767, William Samuel Johnson Papers, Connecticut Historical Society.

or reason, and yet the appointment of Jared Ingersoll as Distributor of Stamps had enabled them to appear on the side of the angels while Gale and his friends were forced into the outer darkness. You really had to live in Connecticut to understand what had happened. In fact you had to be a Yale man to understand it properly, for it had all begun at Yale back in the winter of 1741–1742, when Jared Ingersoll was a senior there. Thomas Clap was Rector of Yale in those days.[2] He had been installed in 1740, after serving for fifteen years as pastor of the church in Windham, where he had already outlived one wife and married a second. His first wife had been a niece of Colonel Joseph Whiting of New Haven, and as family relations figured largely in Connecticut, this connection with a prominent New Haven family was of some importance in the events that followed. Clap was a strong-minded man, apt to be pig-headed at times, but always a man to reckon with. He was orthodox in religion, abhorring equally the "Arminian" notions of free will which were beginning to appear in sophisticated quarters and the "enthusiastic" evangelism which was already stirring up thousands in England. The year he became rector enthusiasm crossed the ocean and broke like a tidal wave on his college and his country.

This was the year of the Great Awakening: George Whitefield who had excited so many souls in England, was now cutting a swath through the colonies, and New Haven lay in his path. The students responded as avidly as the rest of the population, and when Whitefield had departed, they sent an invitation to Gilbert Tennent, a native evangelist who was currently splitting the Presbyterian church in Pennsylvania with his denunciations of an unconverted ministry. Tennent came to New Haven and left the students, or some of them at least, in agonies of despair and delight. After him came the wildest enthusiast of them all, James Davenport, who embarrassingly enough was a Yale graduate. Davenport,

[2] On Clap see Clifford K. Shipton, *Biographical Sketches of those who attended Harvard College in the Classes 1722–1725,* (Boston, 1945), 27-50; Louis L. Tucker, *Puritan Protagonist: President Thomas Clap of Yale College* (Chapel Hill, 1962).

whose manners did not comport with President Clap's idea of either a Christian or a Yale man, made himself particularly obnoxious by denouncing the minister of the New Haven church, the Reverend Joseph Noyes.[3]

The effect of all this excitement on the students was what might have been expected. When they attended the New Haven Church, as they regularly did, they found Mr. Noyes's preaching as cold as Davenport had said it was. And from here it was only a step to making the same judgment about the prayers which the President and tutors conducted at college. There is no record that anyone had the audacity to consider Thomas Clap dull, but some of the students who had been most deeply moved by the revivalists could not forbear making invidious comparisons with regard to the religious fervor of the tutors. David Brainerd, who later enjoyed a brief but distinguished career as missionary to the Indians, thought that Tutor Chauncy Whittelsey lacked saving grace. When another student spoke warmly of Whittelsey's performance at prayers. Brainerd retorted that "He has no more Grace than this chair." The statement was overheard by a freshman, who told it to someone in the town, who told it to Rector Clap. Rector Clap had already clamped down on the students' attendance at revival meetings, and he now made an example of Brainerd by expelling him from the college.[4] Three years later, Clap exerted his authority in an even more dictatorial manner by expelling John and Ebenezer

[3] On the Great Awakening in Connecticut see Joseph Tracy, *The Great Awakening; a History of the Revival of Religion* (Boston, 1842); Ellen D. Larned, *History of Windham County, Connecticut* (Worcester, 1874), I, 393-485; Edwin S. Gaustad, The Great Awakening in New England (New York, 1957); Maria L. Greene, *The Development of Religious Liberty in Connecticut* (Boston, 1905), 220-272. The best original accounts of the Awakening at Yale are the following: Samuel Hopkins, *Works* (Boston, 1852), I, 15-18, and Jared Ingersoll, An Historical Account of Some Affairs Relating to the Church, Especially in Connecticut, together with some other Things of a Different Nature, Ms, Library of Congress.

[4] Jonathan Edwards, *An Account of the Life of the Late Reverend Mr. David Brainerd* (Boston, 1749), 20.

Cleaveland. Their only offense was that they had attended the meeting of a "New Light" revivalist church at Canterbury, Connecticut, during the spring vacation.[5]

Although Clap's action was characteristically high-handed, the General Assembly of the colony approved it. The Assembly in 1742, shortly after Brainerd's expulsion from Yale, had passed an act to outlaw itinerant preaching and preaching by any minister not properly ordained. The majority in the Assembly were "Old Lights," hostile to the Awakening, and the following year, in order to prevent the formation of New Light churches, they repealed an act of toleration passed thirty-five years earlier.[6]

With feelings running so high it was not possible for a man to be neutral. Young men in college are not apt to be cautious about forming or disclosing their opinions anyhow, and although Jared Ingersoll was circumspect by nature, that very trait doubtless inclined him toward the Old Lights. During his junior year the students who had been most deeply stirred by the revival were meeting secretly and openly for religious discussions. Samuel Buell, in the class above him, and Brainerd, in the class below, went about visiting the rooms of all the students, inquiring after their spiritual condition, and urging them to repent. Most of the students seem to have borne these visitations patiently and humbly; Samuel Hopkins, who was to become the leading New Light theologian of his generation, was deeply affected by them.[7] But to a man of Ingersoll's temper they were probably distasteful. The kind of life which the New Lights would have had him lead was one in which the pleasures of polite social intercourse would have been all but eliminated. Whitefield on his first visit to New Haven had spoken expressly "against mixed dancing and frolicking of males and females together."[8] Ingersoll was no wanton, but he and his friends doubtless sided with Rector Clap in deploring the misguided zeal of

[5] Larned, *History of Windham County*, I, 417-427.

[6] *Public Records of the Colony of Connecticut*, VIII, 454-457, 521-522.

[7] Hopkins, *Works*, I, 16-18.

[8] *Ibid.*, 15.

the Revival movement.[9] The kind of men whom Ingersoll was friendly with were not the earnest young devotees who were to spread the New Light through America in the ensuing years. Ingersoll preferred the company of men like John Whiting (brother of Colonel Joseph Whiting), and of Nathan Whiting, John's cousin and a brother-in-law of Rector Clap. Later, while the Hopkinses and the Buells were making a name for themselves in the pulpit, Nathan Whiting would be winning fame on the field of battle in the French and Indian War. And at the end of the war Whiting would write to Ingersoll from South Carolina for news of Connecticut, "how is the State? do the Saints Govern, or do some of you Men of the World, take upon you Worldly matters? . . . What for a Commencement had you? was it in the old Stile? were you allowed to dance, kiss the Girls, and drink Wine?"[10] One gathers that Ingersoll and the Whiting boys had had some opportunity to frolic with females during their years at college, and probably without incurring the frowns of Rector Clap. Nathan Whiting had been brought up mainly by his sister Mrs. Clap, and later became Clap's son-in-law as well as his brother-in-law, by marrying the daughter of the Rector's second wife.[11] Family relations were often complicated in New England.

Within a year after he graduated from college Ingersoll himself became a member of the Clap-Whiting clan by marrying Hannah, John Whiting's sister, and eight years later John confirmed the bond by marrying Ingersoll's sister. And to complete the entente which had begun in college, Tutor

[9] Ingersoll's "An historical Account of Some Affairs Relating to the Church, Especially in Connecticut" takes a characteristically objective attitude but is punctuated by parenthetical disclaimers ("as was supposed" or "as they thought it") in stating the position of the New Lights. Indispensable for the study of Ingersoll is Lawrence Gipson's *Jared Ingersoll: A Study of American Loyalism in Relation to British Colonial Government* (New Haven, 1920).

[10] New Haven Colony Historical Society, *Papers*, 9 (1918), 303.

[11] Franklin B. Dexter, *Biographical Sketches of the Graduates of Yale College with Annals of the College History* (New York, 1885), I, 750-751.

Whittelsey, the man whose piety Brainerd had dismissed so harshly, married Elizabeth Whiting, another sister of John.[12]

When Ingersoll settled in New Haven after graduation to study and practice law, it was a foregone conclusion that he would join the church of which Mr. Noyes was then pastor. His wife was already a member; her brother John was to be Deacon for thirty years; and Chauncy Whittelsey was ultimately to succeed Noyes as pastor. In 1742, while Ingersoll was still in college, a separate church had been set up in New Haven by those who agreed with James Davenport's judgment of Mr. Noyes. Similar secession movements had occurred all over the colony, and although the government with its majority of Old Lights had refused to recognize them or to give them official standing as churches, the separations proceeded in defiance of authority. Ingersoll, always on the side of law and order, stood by Mr. Noyes and became a tower of strength to the church in its long-drawn struggle with the New Light group.[13]

Ingersoll was a bright young man. Possessed of the right family connections he moved rapidly upward in his profession, and in 1751, probably through the influence of John Whiting (now clerk of the New Haven County Court), he became King's Attorney for New Haven County.[14] Thus at the age of twenty-nine Ingersoll had become a leading member of the community. He was definitely associated with one side of a continuing religious controversy, but this was nothing against him, for everyone in the colony was associated with one side or the other. The only inauspicious omen for his future lay in the fact that the side which he had chosen was dwindling. The New Lights with their vigorous preaching were steadily growing in numbers and securing more and more strength in the legislature. However, the trend was not

[12] Gipson, *Ingersoll*, 36, 38; Dexter, *Biographical Sketches*, I, 615, 656.

[13] Gipson, *Ingersoll*, 42; Leonard Bacon, *Thirteen Historical Discourses on the Completion of Two Hundred Years, from the Beginning of the First Church in New Haven* (New Haven, 1839), 198-242.

[14] Gipson, *Ingersoll*, 42.

so pronounced that anyone would have dared to predict that the Old Lights were on the way out.

Then in 1753 an upset occurred which strengthened the New Lights immeasurably and embittered the Old Lights. Rector Clap, who had opposed the Awakening so effectively in the 1740's, swung his weight to the side of the New Lights. The shift must have been the more bitter to Ingersoll and to John and Nathan Whiting because they had been in college at the time when the Awakening began and had then formed their judgments and taken their stand under Clap's direction. Nathan had been brought up in Rector Clap's family. Since then he had married Mrs. Clap's daughter and had gone into business in New Haven with Mr. Noyes's son-in-law. To the religious issue was thus added the bitterness of a family quarrel. Clap's desertion may have been consistent with his religious principles, for the New Lights had by this time lost their excessive emotionalism and were probably closer to orthodoxy than the Old Lights; but to the men who had been supporting Mr. Noyes in New Haven, the religious issue was probably overshadowed by what appeared to be personal treachery.

Clap's about-face took the form of a move to establish Yale College as a church with a professor of divinity as pastor. Hitherto there had been no professors at Yale, the president and tutors carrying on all the duties of instruction, and no pastor, the students being required to attend Mr. Noyes's church. What Clap wanted was to establish Naphtali Daggett, a New Light of the class of 1748, as Professor of Divinity, and at the same time to cut off the students from Pastor Noyes's Old Light sermons. Raking up a number of old precedents of the kind that scholars can always find, he proclaimed that a college was an independent ecclesiastical corporation, in short a church, as well as an institution of learning. Jared Ingersoll joined with Benjamin Gale, an Old Light Yale man of the class of 1733, to combat this sophistry; but Clap was able to carry his point, and in 1756 Daggett settled down in New Haven as Professor of Divinity and pastor to the students. One may surmise that he brought with him no love for the New Haven lawyer who opposed his appointment.[15]

The controversy did not cease with Daggett's arrival, but Ingersoll was suddenly removed from it in 1758 by appointment as the colony's London agent. The next three years in London were delightful ones. Though he was far from his family and missed them, he was also removed from the bitter political squabbles that were going on in the colony and was able to indulge in a social life with a glamour unknown to New Haven. The time not engaged by business was agreeably filled with attendance at the Court of St. James's, official balls, plays, operas, and country weekends. In spite of his provincial upbringing, Ingersoll fitted perfectly into the high life. He was a man of grace and dignity, amply built—both in face and figure, attentive to dress and fashion, a man who talked well, who made friends easily. Probably his moments of greatest pleasure came from his nightly "patrole of the Strand" and lingering hours at one of the coffeehouses, where he enjoyed the conversation of men like himself, who appreciated good wine and good company. Ingersoll made many friends in these years, friends who lay beyond the feuds and fights of provincial Connecticut. In fact he had some right to think that the company he kept was rather distinguished. There was Benjamin Franklin, serving as agent for Pennsylvania, with his son William, who would shortly be appointed governor of New Jersey. There was Richard Jackson, who knew everybody and everything, who had corresponded with Benjamin Gale's

[15] Clap's move was defended and attacked in a series of pamphlets: Thomas Clap, *The Religious Constitution of Colleges, Especially of Yale-College in New Haven in the Colony of Connecticut* (New London, 1754); Benjamin Gale, *The Present State of the Colony of Connecticut Considered. In a Letter from a Gentleman in the Eastern Part of said Colony, to his Friend in the Western Part of the same* ([New London], 1755); Clap, *The Answer of the Friend in the West . . .* (New Haven, 1755); Gale, *A Reply to a Pamphlet entitled the Answer of the Friend in the West . . .* ([New London], 1755); Noah Hobart, *A Congratulatory Letter from a Gentleman in the West to His Friend in the East* (New Haven, 1755).

father-in-law Jared Eliot, and for whom Ingersoll secured appointment as his successor in the agency in 1760. John Temple, who became Surveyor General of the New England Customs, was another friend, and so was Thomas Whately, who was to be a secretary to the Treasury when George Grenville took office. Ingersoll used to dine of an evening with Whately and his other friends at the Crown and Anchor Tavern, perhaps rubbing elbows with the famous Samuel Johnson and the men who hung about him.[16]

There were other visiting Americans too, with whom one could talk of home: Joseph Harrison of Newport, at present living with the Marquis of Rockingham but soon to return to America as Collector of Customs for the port of New Haven, and Godfrey Malbone, also of Newport and later the moving spirit in the founding of the Episcopal church in Pomfret, Connecticut. Ingersoll's tastes were catholic. He made friends both with Benjamin Franklin and with Franklin's political opponent, James Hamilton, who had already served in Pennsylvania for five years as the Proprietors' governor and would shortly serve for four years more. He also knew Alexander Wedderburn, who denounced Franklin before the House of Commons in 1774. Ingersoll even made friends with his landlady, Ann Davies, and she later sent him stays of the latest London fashion for Mrs. Ingersoll and wrote him a long description of the coronation of George III, which occurred just after he had left for home. She told him how his friend Harrison rode out in the procession to meet the new Queen when she landed from Germany. Harrison "rode by the side of Coach for half a mile and he says she is very agreable but as not much buety." And Mrs. Davies added, with less restraint, that "Thair was two Gentman of my acquatance as says they wold not gave two pance for her, was she to be had."[17]

It was a pleasant life, but there were times when Ingersoll became homesick, and felt that he would not give twopence for the whole island, let alone its Queen; he used to argue

[16] See Ingersoll's correspondence in New Haven Colony Historical Society, *Papers*, 9 (1918), 234-304.
[17] *Ibid.*, 244, and *passim*.

with Mrs. Bridges, Richard Jackson's sister, about the supe-
riority of America to England, and his preference for New
Haven above all the rest of the world. Even so he stayed in
England for a year after he secured the transfer of the agency
to Richard Jackson, working at business negotiations which
later proved fruitless. It was not until the fall of 1761 that
he returned to New Haven to find the quarrels which he had
left proceeding with increased bitterness.

During his absence the New Lights had made a concerted
effort to gain control of the governor's chair and the upper
house of the Assembly. They had failed, no thanks to Rector
Clap he felt sure, but their strength was still growing, and
the situation at Yale had gone from bad to worse, with Clap
becoming more dictatorial every day. Ingersoll's friends were
now preparing an appeal to the legislature, asking for the
establishment of a committee of visitation to inspect the college regularly and reform abuses there. Ingersoll wrote to
Benjamin Gale for ammunition in the battle and presented
a petition to the Assembly in May, 1763. It was no use. The
New Lights now had a majority in the lower house, and
refused to interfere with Yale. It was remarkable how
the New Lights had developed their political organization.
William Samuel Johnson, himself an Anglican, observed
at this time, that "The N. L. within my short memory
were a small Party merely a religious one, honored within
and restrained by Laws and Decrees of Assembly yet
fresh in everybody's Memory, then looked upon as far
off from the Establishment as the Churchmen, and in
this short period by their continual struggles they have acquired such an Influence as to be nearly the ruling part of
the Government owing to their superior Attention to Civil
Affairs and close union among themselves in Politicks."[18]
This party naturally regarded Ingersoll as their enemy.

[18] To J. Beach, January 4, 1763, William Samuel Johnson Papers,
Connecticut Historical Society. On the Yale College controversy,
see New Haven Colony Historical Society, Papers, 9 (1918), 276-
277; Benjamin Gale, A Calm and Full Vindication of a Letter
. . . (New Haven, 1759); John Graham, An Answer to Mr. Gale's
Pamphlet (New Haven, 1759).

At the same time Ingersoll had become obnoxious to another influential group in the colony. Back in 1754 when Clap was opening his campaign for a professor of divinity at the College, a group of Connecticut speculators had purchased land from the Indians in the Wyoming Valley of Pennsylvania. This group, incorporated as the Susquehannah Company, secured the endorsement of their claims to the region by a resolution of the Connecticut Assembly in 1755. The Assembly overlooked the fact that the land had been purchased from the Iroquois, though the Delawares were in possession of it; they also overlooked the fact that it was in Pennsylvania. According to the theory upon which the Susquehannah Company proceeded, the land was really in Connecticut, because the Connecticut charter of 1662 provided for the extension of the colony westward as far as the Pacific Ocean. Connecticut had not objected when Pennsylvania was chartered in 1681, but the Susquehannah Company thought that it was not too late to object now, and prepared to send settlers to the area.[19]

Jared Ingersoll and Benjamin Gale both owned stock in the company, and when Ingersoll went to England in 1758 he was instructed to promote the Company's interests. But it seems doubtful that either Gale or Ingersoll was a strong supporter of the Company at any time, and when he arrived in England, Ingersoll found that the authorities there thought even less of the project than he did. His friend James Hamilton and the Penn brothers probably argued with him at some length about the unfortunate consequences that might proceed from a disregard of the Pennsylvania charter. Certainly no one thought very highly of a claim that had lain dormant for seventy-five years.

Consequently, when Ingersoll returned to Connecticut, he was not prepared to give the Susquehannah Company much encouragement. The Company had already determined to send a special agent to England to apply for a charter from the King, and Ingersoll, who was now placed on a committee to prepare arguments for the company's rights to the land,

[19] On the Susquehannah Company see Julian Boyd, ed., *The Susquehannah Company Papers* (Wilkes-Barre, Pa., 1930–1933).

evidently distinguished himself by pointing out the various reasons why the company had no rights. He wrote to his friend Hamilton, who was back in Pennsylvania as Governor again, that he thought the Susquehannah project would blow over.[20] This conjecture was supported not only by the eloquence of his own arguments against the project but also by the fact that the Connecticut Assembly, at the insistence of General Amherst (Commander-in-Chief of British forces in America), had issued a proclamation warning the inhabitants of the colony against settling in Pennsylvania, though not actually forbidding them to do so.[21] The Earl of Egremont, then Secretary of State for the Southern Department, soon followed Amherst's demand with a letter to Governor Fitch, requiring him to exert every legal authority against the prosecution of settlements.[22] A delegation of Indians came to Hartford to protest the invasion of their lands, and though many settlers were already on the spot, it began to appear that the project really would fall through. But to the consternation of Ingersoll and other conservatives, opposition only made the speculators more eager to press their claims.[23] Ingersoll attended a meeting of the Company and delivered one final harangue against the project. When the members remained unmoved, he sold out his stock and departed.[24]

With this move Ingersoll became the open enemy of the Susquehannah Company, and by an unfortunate coincidence most of the members of the Company already had reason to dislike him. The Susquehannah Company drew the majority of its members from Windham County, the center of the New Light movement in Connecticut. The Company, of course, had no connection with any church and contained many Old Lights from all over Connecticut, but the bulk of the membership could be found on Sundays in the New Light

---

[20] Thomas Penn to James Hamilton, September 9, 1762, to Richard Peters, September 10, 1762, Boyd, *Susquehannah Papers*, II, 161, 163.

[21] *Ibid.*, xxvii, 135.

[22] *Ibid.*, 194-196.

[23] Ezra Stiles to Pelatiah Webster, May 21, 1763, *ibid.*, 229-230.

[24] *Ibid.*

churches of Windham County, where Ingersoll's name already called up unpleasant memories.

Ingersoll believed his dealings with the Company had been fair and above-board. He had not taken any active measures to injure it, apart from communicating on friendly terms with Governor Hamilton of Pennsylvania, the Company's arch-enemy. Nevertheless he was developing into an unpopular figure: New Lights and members of the Susquehannah Company actively disliked him, and the rest of the population could hardly warm to a man who moved in spheres so remote from their own homely lives. His years abroad, some people said, had given him airs; he was too much a man of the world, too much interested in English affairs above American. To be sure, in a country which still called England "home," it was no great sin to have been in England, and yet there was a certain uneasy distrust of this man, who had fought against the Great Awakening, who dismissed the colony's claims to the West, and who hobnobbed with English politicians. None of these liabilities was enough to sink a man of Ingersoll's undoubted integrity, and had he been able to keep out of public affairs, he might have gone his way unmolested if unloved. But Ingersoll was too big a man and too closely associated with the Old Light party to withdraw entirely from public life, and his enemies had only to wait for the right opportunity to impart to the rest of the population their own violent hatred of the man.

When George Grenville took office in the summer of 1763, events began to occur which ultimately gave Ingersoll's enemies their chance. Grenville appointed Thomas Whately, his friend and Ingersoll's friend, as a secretary to the Treasury Office. Then he turned over to Whately the task of drawing up the Stamp Act, and Whately wrote to Ingersoll for advice. From this innocent beginning Ingersoll was gradually drawn into the snare which time had set for him. Ingersoll liked Whately. Before he heard of Whately's appointment, he had written to him, recalling the many cheerful days they had passed together and assuring him that he would like to dine with him some night at the Crown and Anchor, provided that after dinner he could take a chair to New Haven

Whately answered him with news of their common friends, many of whom had since gone to America, Hamilton for example, who was also writing to Ingersoll, urging a visit to Philadelphia and regretting the want of good company and conversation in America. Whately proposed in jest a tour of the colonies, when he should spend many hours with Ingersoll, and assured him, "I would not disgrace mine Host by English Libertinism; I am a Chip you know of the old Block; my Great Grandfather at the farthest was an Oliverian: and his Posterity is not so degenerated but that I could look as demurely on Sundays, or bundle as merrily on the Week Days, as any the best of the Puritans."[25]

How was Ingersoll to know that this delightful correspondence was paving the way for his disgrace? When Whately asked him about the Sugar Act and the proposed stamp tax, he answered in terms that should have satisfied any American, that the 3d. duty on molasses was more than the trade would bear and that Parliament would better have given a premium than imposed such a duty. As for the imposition of a stamp tax, he could only say that it had caused great alarm in the colonies, that people considered it beyond the authority of Parliament, and that it would be difficult to say how many ways could be invented to avoid the payment of it.[26] Perhaps one of the ways which Ingersoll did not think of was that of threatening to kill the tax collector.

In October of 1764 Ingersoll set sail for England in order to look after a private business venture. Even before he landed, the Connecticut Assembly learning of his trip instructed the Governor to write and ask him to assist Richard Jackson in opposing the Stamp Act. The previous May the Assembly had asked him to serve on the committee which drew up the colony's arguments against the Stamp Act, even though he was not a member of the Assembly. It would appear, then, that the majority of the Assembly still trusted his fidelity to the colony, in spite of the distrust which might

[25] New Haven Colony Historical Society, *Papers*, 9 (1918), 292; Boyd, *Susquehannah Papers*, II, 142-145.
[26] New Haven Colony Historical Society, *Papers*, 9 (1918), 299.

be felt with regard to his religious views or his attitude toward the Susquehannah Company.[27]

Upon arrival in England and even before he heard of the Assembly's action Ingersoll cooperated with the other agents in agitating against the Stamp Act, and was one of the four agents who met with Grenville early in February in a last-minute attempt to stave off the blow. At the same time he resumed his acquaintance with Whately, and at Whately's request wrote a description of the methods of taxation currently in use in Connecticut and calculated the amount which the proposed stamp tax might be expected to produce. According to his figures, the British government might expect to draw £3439. 10s. annually from Connecticut by a stamp tax.[28] When it became apparent that George Grenville was determined to have such a tax, Ingersoll took advantage of his friendship with Whately to get the Act cast in as agreeable a form as possible. He was able to get the duty entirely removed from three items which were included in the original draught of the bill: marriage licenses, commissions of justices of the peace, and notes of hand. On other items he persuaded the Ministry to set the duties at a lower rate than they had intended.[29]

Ingersoll believed with some reason that he had done his country good service. Though he had not succeeded in preventing the stamp tax, he had done more than any other man to reduce the size of it. It was perhaps with a feeling of righteousness produced by this reflection that he accepted from Grenville the office of Stamp Distributor for Connecticut.

The news of the appointment reached Connecticut shortly after news of the Act itself. The first reaction of a number of citizens, some of whom later distinguished themselves for their opposition to the Act, was not unfavorable to Ingersoll. William Samuel Johnson, who was to attend the Stamp Act Congress as one of Connecticut's delegates, wrote to Inger-

[27] Gipson, *Ingersoll*, 124.
[28] Treasury Papers, Class I, Bundle 433, ff. 406, 410, Public Record Office, Library of Congress transcripts.
[29] New Haven Colony Historical Society, *Papers,* 9 (1918), 314.

soll offering to serve as his "subaltern" for the town of Stratford. "Since we are doomed to Stamps and Slavery," he wrote, "and must submit, we hear with pleasure that your gentle hand will fit on our Chains and Shackles, who I know will make them set easie as possible."[30] This was precisely the reaction Ingersoll must have expected from the people of Connecticut when he took the job. But when he returned to New Haven early in August, he found that this attitude of resignation had passed. The change was apparent in Boston, where his ship landed,[31] and his arrival in New Haven was signalized in the *Connecticut Gazette* by a letter which maliciously interpreted his acceptance of the stamp office as treason against his country. With maddening ingenuity the author of the letter discredited in advance whatever defense he could make: "Have three hundred Pounds a Year, or even a more trifling Consideration been found sufficient to debauch from their Interest those who have been entrusted with the most important concerns by the Colonies? . . . *No* you'll say, *I don't delight in the Ruin of my Country, but, since 'tis decreed she must fall, who can blame me for taking a Part in the Plunder?* Tenderly said! why did you not rather say— *If my Father must die, who can accuse me as defective in filial Duty, in becoming his Executioner, that so much of the Estate, at least, as goes to the Hangman, may be retained in the Family?*"[32] The letter was signed "Cato," but Ingersoll doubtless knew who wrote it. It was Naphtali Daggett, the Professor of Divinity at Yale, whose enmity Ingersoll had earned ten years before.[33]

The letter was a signal for Ingersoll's other enemies to close in. Though the newspapers printed his and his friends' letters of explanation and defense, though he announced that he would not execute the Act against the wishes of the people, the tide rose rapidly against him. His effigy—his "virtual representative" the newspapers called it—was hanged in

[30] *Ibid.,* 324. Several other persons also applied to Ingersoll for subordinate positions (*ibid.,* 324-327).

[31] *Boston Gazette,* August 12, 1765.

[32] *Connecticut Gazette,* August 9, 1765, reprinted in *Connecticut Courant,* August 26, 1765.

[33] Gipson, *Ingersoll,* 158.

Lebanon, Windham, New London, and Norwich;[34] and in Windham County and New London County, where the New Lights and the Susquehannah Company were strongest, a movement was set afoot to force his resignation. Ingersoll heard that companies from Windham, Norwich, and New London were planning a march on New Haven. His fellow-townsmen, he knew, whatever their sentiments about the Stamp Act, would resent this interference by the easterners. There would undoubtedly be a clash with a possible loss of life and property, including his own. In order to avert this, he sent messages to his advancing enemies, proposing to meet them at Hartford, where the Governor had called a special session of the Assembly for September 19. Here he hoped to turn over his problems to the legislators. If they wished to nullify the Stamp Act, he would not stand in their way. If they wished to support it, then they could deal with the mob themselves. In either case the responsibility would be off his shoulders. Unfortunately he was able to ride only as far as Weathersfield before meeting an advance contingent of the easterners, about five hundred in number, some in the uniform of militia officers and all armed with staves. Ingersoll was not a timid man, and he held out for some time, arguing, explaining, expostulating, asking "if they thought it was fair that the Counties of Windham and New-London should dictate to all the rest of the Colony?" The only answer he received was "It dont signify to parly—here is a great many People waiting and you must resign." Ingersoll replied with some warmth "that I could Die, and perhaps as well now as another Time; and that I should Die but once." But after all he held no brief for the Stamp Act and decided upon second thought that if he must be a martyr it should be in a better cause.[35] By resigning his office and giving three reluctant cheers Ingersoll was able to send the mob home, though not until he had been conducted to Hartford and obliged to repeat the performance before the Assembly House

[34] *Newport Mercury*, August 26, September 2, 1765; *Connecticut Courant*, September 2, 1765.

[35] New Haven Colony Historical Society, *Papers*, 9 (1918) 341-349.

for the benefit of a larger audience including the assembly-men within.

Jared Ingersoll's troubles were not yet over. The men who organized the march against him and who called themselves the Sons of Liberty had more in view than the defeat of the Stamp Act. They looked toward new lands in Pennsylvania and New Light in religion. With Ingersoll the most unpopular man in Connecticut, they saw the opportunity to unseat a substantial number of those persons in the government who shared his views both on religion and on the Susquehannah Company. For some time now the New Lights had been in control of the Lower House of the Assembly, but the Old Lights still controlled both the governor's council, and the governor's chair itself. Ingersoll's appointment as stamp agent was a disaster for the Old Light party. Only by repudiating him completely and themselves leading the opposition to the Act could they possibly have maintained their position thereafter. Ebenezer Devotion, the Old Light minister in the New Light stronghold of Windham, showed the way by speaking so earnestly for colonial rights that the town sent him to the Assembly as its representative in 1765. But the Old Lights more commonly preferred passive resistance to the Stamp Act, fearing that open resistance would give England the excuse she was looking for to revoke Connecticut's precious charter.[36] Consequently the Sons of Liberty who organized resistance to the Act appear to have been mostly New Lights, and they took such pains to identify their party with the opposition to the Stamp Act, that by January of 1766, it was reported from New Haven that "a Man's religious Principles are made the Test or shall I rather say badge of his political Creed. An Arminian, and a Favourer of the Stamp Act signify the same Man."[37]

Governor Fitch gave the irreparable blow to his own career and to the Old Light party when he complied with the Act

---

[36] Franklin B. Dexter, ed., *The Literary Diary of Ezra Stiles* (New York, 1901), I, 55; Zeichner, *Connecticut's Years of Controversy*, 54-59.

[37] Franklin B. Dexter, ed., *Extracts from the Itineraries and Other Miscellanies of Ezra Stiles* (New Haven, 1916), 509-510.

by swearing to enforce it. Such an oath was required of every governor by the terms of the Act, upon penalty of £1000 sterling. When Fitch called the Council together in order to be sworn in their presence, only four councillors would participate. These four and the Governor himself therefore became the political targets of the Sons of Liberty.[38]

Ingersoll was not a member of the Assembly or the Council, but his association with the Old Lights was so well known that it was advantageous to keep popular feeling against him at a high pitch. His mail was watched and evidently opened, for a rumor spread that he had written to England suggesting that people might submit to the Stamp Act if some of the duties were reduced. Actually his suggestion had been that *if* Parliament did not repeal the Act, they should at least reduce the rates.[39] But it was no use telling this to the Sons of Liberty. A committee of these gentlemen, hailing from Windham County, called upon him and demanded copies of his recent letters. He gave them up when the committee assured him, after reading them, that the populace would be quieted by hearing the true contents. With impudent malice they then held public meetings to which they read excerpts of the correspondence lifted from context in such a way as to make them appear damaging to Ingersoll's character. In response to the reading of such passages the meeting at Litchfield resolved

That if any Person in this Colony has represented that the People in it, might, under any possible Circumstances, become willing to have the aforesaid Act executed upon them, or to have one Farthing of their Property taken from them, except by their own Consent, given as aforesaid; they are perswaded that such Representation must

[38] Ingersoll to Jackson, November 3, 1765, New Haven Colony Historical Society, *Papers,* 9 (1918), 357-360; Zeichner, *Connecticut's Years of Controversy,* 56-59.

[39] Ingersoll to Whately, November 2, 1765, to Jackson, November 3, 1765, New Haven Colony Historical Society, *Papers,* 9 (1918), 353, 357-360.

have been the Result of extreme stupid Ignorance, or dictated by a malignant apostate Spirit.[40]

The ostensible purpose of the meetings sponsored by the Sons of Liberty was to defeat the execution of the Stamp Act, but behind these engineered gatherings of righteously indignant citizens the guiding spirits were preparing for political revolution in the spring elections of 1766. Evidently their plans leaked out a little prematurely, for early in the year it was reported that the New Lights, who controlled the Sons of Liberty, were preparing to take advantage of the excitement against the Stamp Act for their own purposes. A writer in the *Connecticut Courant* on January 13 suggested this and warned the people not to let "blind Enthusiasm, or a low, mean, party Spirit, like a Torrent, sweep all before it." The Old Lights naturally resented the attempt to play politics in the midst of the crisis, for they too abhorred the Stamp Act, and many had joined the Sons of Liberty as a movement which transcended party lines. They were able to get the same meeting at Litchfield which denounced Ingersoll to dissociate itself from political maneuvers by adopting a resolution which expressly denied any intention "to bring about the least alteration in the Legislative Body of the Colony."[41] In spite of such protests, the political organization of the Sons of Liberty went forward, by means of conventions held on an ever-widening basis. Meetings of the people in a particular town or village were succeeded by meetings of a whole county with delegates from each town. Finally, in a convention of representatives from the whole colony at Hartford on March 25, the Sons of Liberty uncovered their plan for getting rid of Old Light control in the council and the governorship.

The meeting had already agreed upon a resolution in favor of corresponding with the Sons of Liberty in other colonies, when a vote was carried requiring all spectators to withdraw. After this order had been carried out, some of the delegates wanted to know why it had been done. The leaders of the

[40] *Connecticut Courant,* February 24, 1766.
[41] *Ibid.*

meeting then stated that they "ment to collect the Minds of the People, for Unity, and by that Means be able to give the Freemen a Lead in the ensuing election, since, should they run upon different Men, the Persons desired might not be elected, by the Freemen." In other words the Sons of Liberty proposed to nominate a slate of candidates for the coming election. When some of the delegates objected strenuously to this plot for a government dominated by New Lights, the political architects of the meeting wisely adjourned it until the following day. They spent the ensuing evening profitably, for the following day without further discussion of the proposal the convention nominated candidates for governor and deputy governor. The delegates from Litchfield, remaining true to the resolves of their convention, four weeks before, voted nine to four against the measure, but a majority of the convention approved it, perhaps because more delegates attended from New London and Windham counties than from any others. Some members would have gone further and named a slate for the Council too, but the opposition was so great that it was finally decided not "to make too great an Alteration in the Body Politick at once."[42]

The scheme was of course successful in spite of everything that Ingersoll and the Old Lights could do. It was useless for Ingersoll to demonstrate his sincerity by publicly urging the courts to open in defiance of the Stamp Act,[43] useless for his friends to protest that "there are a great many brave Hearts in this Colony that hate a stamp-man, but love Mr. Ingersoll."[44] In the eyes of many people Ingersoll's character was ruined and the men with whom he was associated were correspondingly tainted. Guilt by association, as more than one American has learned, cannot be washed away by a mere demonstration of innocence. There might still be many brave hearts that loved Mr. Ingersoll and that loved Governor Fitch, but not enough to win an election, in 1766 or ever after.

[42] Gipson, *Ingersoll*, 218-221; Zeichner, *Connecticut's Years of Controversy*, 70-75.

[43] Emmet Papers, 4897, New York Public Library; New Haven Colony Historical Society, *Papers*, 9 (1918), 376.

[44] Gipson, *Ingersoll*, 189.

Chapter XIV

John Hughes

WHEN THE NEWS reached Philadelphia in the spring of 1763 that France and England had finally made peace, John Hughes, like other Americans, could rejoice. Not only had Great Britain become the greatest power in the western world, but in Pennsylvania the men of good will whom Hughes respected had been able to keep their grip on the reins of government. Politics in Pennsylvania, at all times a tricky business, had been especially difficult during the war, and the formal closing of hostilities brought a welcome lightening of the tension for John Hughes and his friends. Hughes was no longer a young man as he surveyed the prospects opened by the peace. Less than two years later he was to describe himself as "an old Fellow, born and Educated, in the Wilds of America, at a Time, when the Schools were but few."[1] He had watched Pennsylvania grow, watched the German settlers landing on the banks of the Delaware by the thousands, watched the turbulent Scotch-Irish pour into the interior. He had seen the city of Philadelphia mushroom around him, expanding in all directions. Any place which grew as rapidly as Pennsylvania was bound to have growing pains, and if it had not been for the wise and steady leadership of his Quaker friends, Pennsylvania would have felt the pains sharply long before.

Hughes was no Quaker himself. He gave his faith to the Church of England, but he had lived with the Quakers in Pennsylvania long enough to respect them. These Pennsylvania Quakers were not the wild fanatics who had marched naked through the streets of England in Cromwell's time. They were sober men, industrious, thrifty, wise in the ways of the world but still retaining the firmness of conviction

[1] Hughes to Commissioners of Stamps, January 13, 1766, Treasury Papers, Class I, Bundle 452, Public Record Office, Library of Congress transcripts.

that had led their grandfathers to cross the ocean. It was because of their fundamental decency that Pennsylvania had been able to grow up so rapidly and yet so comfortably. In particular their honesty in dealing with the Indians had prevented the bloody clashes which punctuated the advance of the frontier in other colonies. The Quakers, from the time of William Penn, had treated the Indians as human beings, and the Indians had responded in kind. It was only when the Scotch-Irish Presbyterians moved out to the frontier and began to throw their weight about that Indian warfare came to Pennsylvania.

These Presbyterians, Hughes felt, were the principal troublemakers in Pennsylvania politics. Until 1758 the Presbyterians had been relatively easy to handle; until that year they had been split into two factions—the Old Lights and the New Lights—and the two had distrusted each other more than they did outsiders. The split began early in the forties when George Whitefield was storming through the colonies, leaving behind a trail of shrieks and groans and hallelujahs. After the hallelujahs had come dissension and schism to the Presbyterians of Pennsylvania, as to the Congregationalists of Connecticut, and the Presbyterians had consequently been immobilized as a political force. In 1758 when the two sides made peace, with the New Light group in the ascendancy, they became a major force in politics.[2]

Fortunately, as Hughes saw it, the Presbyterians' strength lay in the West; and since the western counties of Pennsylvania did not have as many representatives in the Assembly as the eastern counties, the Presbyterians by themselves, even after the reunion of 1758, did not command anything approaching a majority. Hughes feared, however, a possible coalition between the Presbyterians and some other faction. The largest such group in the colony, the one which might swing the legislature one way or the other, was the Germans. The Germans hitherto had found the rule of the Quakers congenial. Many of them belonged to the Mennonite sect, which

[2] G. S. Klett, *Presbyterians in Colonial Pennsylvania* (Philadelphia, 1937); L. J. Trinterud, *The Forming of an American Tradition* (Philadelphia, 1949).

had religious principles in common with the Quakers. They lived for the most part in the portion of the colony that lay between the Quakers of the East and the Scotch-Irish Presbyterians of the West. Politically, too, they were a middle group. Lacking aggressive leaders of their own, they had hitherto looked to the East for leadership, but what if they should turn in the other direction and ally themselves with the Presbyterians, thereby giving the latter control of a popular, and perhaps a legislative, majority?[3]

Another place where the united Presbyterians could look for support—Hughes sadly faced the fact—was in his own church. Only a year or two after the Presbyterians healed their own division, the Church of England in Pennsylvania was split by precisely the same issue that had troubled the Presbyterians fifteen years earlier. The trouble, as a matter of fact, came from a renegade Presbyterian who had taken orders in the Church of England, a man by the name of MacClenaghan, who appeared in Philadelphia in 1760 and began to preach revival sermons. Though he was strenuously opposed at first, the Philadelphia Anglicans had gradually caught the fever, and by 1763, it had to be admitted, were strongly tainted with New Light ideas. It was characteristic of New Lights to dislike the prudent and rational members of their own denominations and to embrace the wildest fanatics of other denominations. Consequently, though the Anglicans outside Philadelphia did not become illumined by the New Lights and continued to look upon Quaker rule as better at least than Presbyterian, the Philadelphia Anglicans stood ready to join with the Presbyterians.[4]

The great danger to the Quaker regime lay in the combination of the Presbyterians with the Anglicans of Philadelphia

[3] On Pennsylvania politics in this period see C. H. Lincoln, *The Revolutionary Movement in Pennsylvania* (Philadelphia, 1901); W. R. Shepherd, *History of Proprietary Government in Pennsylvania* (New York, 1896); and Theodore Thayer, *Pennsylvania Politics and the Growth of Democracy 1740–1776* (Harrisburg, Pa., 1953).

[4] William S. Perry, ed., *Historical Collections Relating to the American Colonial Church,* vol. II—*Pennsylvania* (Hartford, 1871), 305-311, 319-324, 341, 354-355, 364-365, 392-393, 413-414.

and with the Germans of the middle region. The danger was accentuated by the fact that the Presbyterians had obtained the support of the family which exercised the greatest political and economic power in all Pennsylvania. William Penn, who founded the colony, had been one of the leading Quakers of his time, but his grandchildren, remaining in England, had deserted the faith to become members of the Church of England. If they had adhered faithfully to the interests of that church, Hughes could have found it easier to excuse their other faults. Instead they carried on a flirtation with the Pennsylvania Presbyterians in order to defeat the measures of the Quakers who controlled the Assembly. The Penn family owned all the public land in Pennsylvania and theoretically were entitled to an annual quitrent on all private land. They also appointed the governor of the colony, who had authority to veto any laws passed by the Assembly. This vast power they frequently abused. In particular they consistently refused to make any contribution to the expenses of government by allowing their lands to be taxed, as the lands of all other Pennsylvanians were. This attitude had led to continuous conflict between the Assembly and the governor. Since the Presbyterians were as much at odds with the Quaker-dominated Assembly as the Proprietors were, the two had sought each other as natural allies. As a result the most lucrative offices in the appointment of the proprietary family went to Presbyterians, and William Allen, the political leader of the Presbyterians and perhaps the wealthiest man in the province, was also the Chief Justice of Pennsylvania.[5]

The combination of Proprietors, Presbyterians, and Philadelphia Anglicans with the potential addition of the Germans provided a formidable opposition which had hitherto been unsuccessful. The most trying time had been during the late

[5] See correspondence of William Allen with the proprietors in Penn Papers, Historical Society of Pennsylvania. The alliance between Allen and the Penns was so notorious that Thomas Penn, the Proprietor, advised his nephew, Governor Richard Penn, not to marry Allen's daughter, lest this further evidence of the connection cause criticism. On the other hand he urged his nephew to take Allen's advice in all matters. Penn Correspondence, V, 67, 69; VIII, 78-85.

war. The Quakers, because of their pacifist principles, were not well constituted to run a government at war. They themselves recognized this fact and turned over the actual leadership of the Assembly to well-disposed allies, men like John Hughes and Joseph Galloway and Benjamin Franklin. By this means Pennsylvania had been able to make as great a contribution to the war effort as other colonies. If such a comparison was faint praise, at least the Quakers were not to blame for any deficiencies. The Proprietors and the Presbyterians might scream that the cowardly pacifism of the Quakers was responsible for military failures, but Hughes knew that the greed of the Proprietors in refusing to contribute their share of taxes was at the bottom of the troubles; and he could see that other Pennsylvanians shared his views when they continued to support the Quaker party. Nevertheless, pacifists do not generally win poularity contests in wartime, and all friends of the Quaker regime could breathe a sigh of relief when the war ended with the Quakers and their friends still in the saddle.

Unfortunately the year which opened so auspiciously was to see the most savage Indian attack in history carried out all along the western frontiers of the American colonies, with Pennsylvania hit especially hard. Pontiac's rebellion was a last desperate attempt by the Indians to hold the interior of the American continent against the English. Striking in June, 1763, the Indians by the end of the month had compelled the Pennsylvanians to abandon some of the finest country in America. As always they hit without mercy, killing men, women, and children. No troops were immediately available to stop them, and the survivors pouring eastward brought with them an understandable bitterness against the people who thought that Indians should be treated fairly. With unreasoning rage a group of Presbyterians from Paxton and Donegal townships, unable or afraid to march against the Indians who were ravaging the Western frontier, fell upon a small and thoroughly tame village of twenty Indians near Lancaster, and murdered the six individuals they found at home. The remaining fourteen were rounded up by the Sheriff at Lancaster and placed in the workhouse for their own protection, but the Paxton boys broke into the house and murdered them too. This apparently proved to be so satisfactory a way of expressing their feelings, that the Paxton boys next set their sights on another body of 140 peaceful Indians. In order to protect these from the fate of the others the government moved them to Philadelphia and transferred three companies of Regular troops to Philadelphia to watch over them. In the face of what was going on to the westward, the frontiersmen could only regard this shift of troops as a painful demonstration that the government of Pennsylvania was more interested in protecting the Indians from the frontiersmen than it was in protecting the frontiersmen from the Indians. In wrath some seven hundred men collected and prepared to march on Philadelphia.[6]

This was in February of 1764, two months after the massacre at Lancaster. The governor of the colony, feeling his own inadequacy in the situation, called upon Benjamin Franklin to organize a popular force. Franklin had already published a bitter narrative of the Indian massacres, describing the Paxton boys as "Christian White Savages."[7] The pamphlet had helped to arouse popular feeling against the brutal conduct of the frontiersmen so that Franklin and Hughes found the Philadelphians ready to defend themselves and the Indians who had taken refuge with them.[8] However, Franklin had no desire for civil war; he met the Paxton boys at Germantown and persuaded them to return home. Having done so, he seized the opportunity to aim a blow which he hoped would give the *coup de grâce* to the Proprietary-Presbyterian combination. The Governor in the crisis had been unable to direct the defense of the province. At the same time he was refus-

[6] Carl Van Doren, *Benjamin Franklin* (New York, 1941), 306-311.

[7] *A Narrative of the Late Massacres in Lancaster County* (Philadelphia, 1764), reprinted in Albert H. Smyth, ed., *The Writings of Benjamin Franklin* (New York, 1905–1907), IV, 289-314. See p. 310.

[8] Hugh Neill to the Secretary of the S.P.G., June 25, 1764, Perry, *Historical Collections*, II, 360-361; James Pemberton to Samuel Fothergill, March 7, 1764, Pemberton Papers, XXXIV, 128, Historical Society of Pennsylvania.

ing to sign a bill passed by the Assembly for raising troops, because the bill provided for taxation of proprietary estates in order to help defray the cost. Under Franklin's leadership the Assembly passed a series of resolves and drew up a petition to the King, asking for the establishment of royal government in Pennsylvania.[9]

Franklin had timed the move with a perfect sense of the situation. The Governor's weakness in the crisis and his obstruction to the raising of troops put people out of patience with the proprietary family. The decision to seek a royal government was so generally concurred in that the resolves passed the Assembly with only four dissenting votes. The move was likewise well timed with respect to the situation in England. Franklin, like other well-informed Americans, believed that the mother country was preparing to overhaul the whole imperial system. A group in Rhode Island was petitioning for royal government, as Franklin's friend Martin Howard had informed him. Governor Bernard was advising a revision of all charter governments. Maryland was becoming dissatisfied with proprietary rule. It seemed an auspicious time for getting rid of the baleful influence of the Penn family. And John Hughes was confident that if the Penns were deprived of their governmental privileges, the Presbyterians would be less formidable.

The Presbyterians were not slow to understand the significance of the move. They hurried to the defense of the proprietary charter with counter-petitions and with scurrilous broadsides and pamphlets attacking both Franklin and the Quakers.[10] From the frontier counties they sent in petitions complaining of the fact—and it was a fact—that the three

[9] *Pennsylvania Archives,* 8th ser., 7 (1935), 5591-5607; Carl Van Doren, ed., *Letters and Papers of Benjamin Franklin and Richard Jackson, 1753-1785* (Philadelphia, 1947), 150-152, 211-212.

[10] On the counter-petitions see Penn Correspondence, VIII, *passim,* and Hugh Neill to the Secretary of the S.P.G., October 18, 1764, Perry, *Historical Collections,* II, 364-365. For the voluminous pamphlet literature see Evans, *American Bibliography* (Chicago, 1903-1934), III and IV, items indexed under Pennsylvania, "Tracts in favor of proprietary government."

eastern counties, with a minority of the population, elected a majority of the representatives in the legislature. Hitherto the disproportion had not been great and had not excited jealousy; but the western population was expanding rapidly and now a great furor was raised against the oligarchical rule of the eastern counties, which, the Presbyterians claimed, were seeking to overthrow the foundations of the colony by their petition to the King.[11]

In the Assembly itself the debates were lively. William Allen assured the members that Pennsylvania would find the little finger of the King heavier than the loins of the Proprietor. Allen had no sooner finished than John Hughes was on his feet to cry treason. No one but a rebel, he said, would be guilty of such a statement.[12] But perhaps Hughes did not realize how many Pennsylvanians had misgivings about the petition which he and Franklin were pushing. There was not the same attachment to the charter in Pennsylvania that there was in Rhode Island, where all the charter privileges belonged to the people as a whole. In Pennsylvania the charter was a benefit principally to the proprietary family. Nevertheless the people had gained many rights in the government set up under it; in particular they had gained all the procedures established by William Penn in the famous Charter of Liberties of 1701. If the proprietary charter were revoked, it might be impossible to retain these procedures. No one could tell what form of government the King might provide, especially at a time when Parliament was showing intentions of extending its control over the colonies. In the eyes of many Pennsylvanians, including even some leading Quakers, the petition for royal government was a rash and dangerous move.[13]

[11] Theodore Thayer, "The Quaker Party of Pennsylvania," *Pa. Mag. of Hist.,* 71 (1947), 19-44, and *Pennsylvania Politics,* 7, 103.

[12] Hughes to Commissioners of Stamps, October 12, 1765, House of Lords Manuscripts, January 14, 1766, Library of Congress transcripts. Cf. Allen to Thomas Penn, December 13, 1764, Penn Manuscripts, Official Correspondence, IX, 290.

[13] John Reynell to Mildred and Roberts, November 23, 1764, Letter Book of John Reynell; James Pemberton to Samuel Fothergill, June 13, 1764, Pemberton Papers, XXXIV, 131; and letters of John Griffith and John Churchman, Pemberton Papers, XVII, 63, all in Historical Society of Pennsylvania.

During the summer of 1764 the words flew hot and heavy, and when the elections to the Assembly were held in the first week of October it became apparent that the Presbyterians had scored a minor victory: Franklin and Joseph Galloway, the two principal leaders of the Quaker party, had been defeated for re-election. The campaign against royal government had won enough votes for the Presbyterian-Anglican-Proprietary combination in Philadelphia to defeat the men who had proposed the change. But in the rest of the colony the party of Franklin and Galloway and Hughes held fast. Apparently most westerners were not seriously displeased with their representatives who had favored the petition for royal government, nor were they aroused by the indictment of Pennsylvania's unequal system of representation. Except in Philadelphia the Quakers had been able to discredit the Presbyterian charges as a mere device to distract public attention from the shameful actions of the Paxton boys. Consequently when the Assembly convened, the Quaker party still commanded a large majority, and among that majority was Franklin's old friend John Hughes.[14]

Hughes did not propose to see the talents of the wisest man in Pennsylvania cut off from the services of the Assembly, and it was Hughes who now persuaded the Assembly to send Franklin to England to assist his friend Richard Jackson in prosecuting the appeal to the King for a royal government.[15] However, while the Pennsylvanians had been slaying one another in print, something had occurred in England which could not be overlooked. George Grenville had persuaded Parliament to pass the Sugar Act, and he had announced that a stamp tax might be necessary in the near future.

[14] Thayer, "Quaker Party of Pennsylvania"; Lewis B. Walker, ed., *The Burd Papers: Extracts from Chief Justice William Allen's Letter Book* (n.p., 1897), 62-65; Thomas Balch, ed., *Letters and Papers Relating Chiefly to the Provincial History of Pennsylvania* (Philadelphia, 1855), 204-206; Allen to Thomas Penn, September 25, 1764, Penn Manuscripts, Official Correspondence, IX; Benjamin Marshall to Joseph G. Wanton, October 5, 1764, *Pa. Mag. of Hist.*, 20 (1896), 207.

[15] Hughes to Commissioners of Stamps, October 12, 1765, House of Lords Manuscripts, January 14, 1766; *Pennsylvania Archives*, 8th ser., 7 (1935), 5687-5690.

Though the issue of proprietary vs. royal government in Pennsylvania seemed the more important issue to Hughes, the taxation of the colonies by Parliament was a move which must be resisted vigorously. When he arrived in London Franklin must not only push forward the business of royal government but must also do everything possible to get the Sugar Act repealed and to prevent the passage of the Stamp Act.

After Franklin left on his dual mission, in November, 1764, the factions continued their quarrel with the same virulence. William Allen persuaded one of the Presbyterian propagandists to publish a libelous piece calling Franklin an "inflammatory and virulent man, whose views are not those of peace and reconciliation" and accusing him of misusing public funds, of stirring up political controversies for his own gain, and of taking advantage of his position to win favors for himself and his family.[16] John Hughes came quickly to his friend's defense. On December 20 he published in the *Pennsylvania Gazette* an advertisement in which he offered to pay £10 to the provincial hospital for every accusation against Franklin that could be proved correct, provided that Allen would come out from behind his anonymity and pay £5 for every charge that could be proved false. The challenge was accepted only by another anonymous letter to the newspaper, which Hughes promptly answered with a further attack on the cowardly anonymity of the author.[17]

As Hughes made his bold, defiant gestures the issue which had hitherto seemed a minor irritation beside the major struggle against Proprietor and Presbyterians was rising to overwhelm him. The same torrent that overturned the lives of Francis Bernard, John Robinson, Jared Ingersoll, and Thomas

[16] *An Answer to Mr. Franklin's Remarks on a Late Protest* (Philadelphia, 1764), probably by William Smith. The "late protest" was a protest by the minority in the Assembly against Franklin's appointment as agent, Historical Society of Pennsylvania, *Memoirs,* 14 (1895), 151-154. The *Remarks on a Late Protest* was published by Franklin before leaving for England, Smyth, ed., *Writings,* IV, 273-285.

[17] *Pennsylvania Gazette,* December 27, 1765, January 3, 10, 1766; *Pennsylvania Journal,* same dates.

Hutchinson picked up John Hughes and swept him helpless before the fury of the Presbyterians. Franklin, in London, felt the groundswell of the movement before it reached America. He did everything in his power to prevent passage of the Stamp Act. He pleaded with Grenville and proposed alternatives, but the Minister was adamant.[18] Franklin, ever the realist, fought while the fighting was worthwhile. Even after the Act was passed he worked for its repeal, but meanwhile he made the best of a bad situation. When George Grenville asked him to name a man for stamp distributor in Pennsylvania, he must have seen an opportunity to gain a move in the contest he was simultaneously carrying on with the Proprietors of Pennsylvania. The Penn brothers had also taken an active part in the effort to prevent the stamp tax,[19] but when the campaign had been lost, Grenville did not give them an opportunity to name a candidate for any of the offices which the Act created. Franklin named John Hughes, and Grenville immediately made the appointment. When Thomas Penn later complained to Grenville that this must appear as a reward for Hughes's opposition to the Proprietor, he had to be content with Grenville's promise to write Hughes and warn him that the appointment was not made with any such view in mind.[20] Franklin to all appearances had gained a point in his duel with the Proprietors and the Presbyterians. It was some months before he realized how costly that victory would prove for his friend.

When Hughes received news in May, 1765, that he had been nominated Distributor of Stamps for Pennsylvania, he saw no better than Franklin that this was the end of his political career. He wrote with some satisfaction to his friend

[18] Verner Crane, "Benjamin Franklin and the Stamp Act," Colonial Society of Massachusetts, *Publications*, 32 (1937), 56-77; Verner Crane, ed., *Benjamin Franklin's Letters to the Press* (Chapel Hill, 1950), xxxiii-xlvi, 25-30, 63-73; John Fothergill to James Pemberton, February 27, 1766, Penn Manuscripts, X, 35.

[19] See letters of Thomas Penn, dated February 8, 15, March 9, 1764, Penn Correspondence, VIII, 33, 35, 205, 217.

[20] Thomas Penn to John Penn, April 13, 1765, to Mr. Hockley, September 22, 1765, to William Young, September 28, 1765, Penn Correspondence, VIII, 244, 310, 315-316.

Anthony Wayne that his appointment had given the proprietary party "no small pain."[21] Though his own party had suffered a minor setback in the October election of 1764, they quickly reformed their ranks, and even their opponents admitted that Franklin and Galloway, though no longer members of the Assembly, still ran the show from behind the scenes. In the spring and summer of 1765 the Presbyterians worked furiously to naturalize friendly Germans who agreed to vote for them, but in spite of all their efforts the Quakers held the line and even succeeded in re-electing Galloway that October. Hughes's party was firmly entrenched, and was to remain so until the Revolution, but Hughes himself was already a liability. In his appointment as Distributor of Stamps the Presbyterians had seen an opportunity to attack the Quaker party, and had he not withdrawn his candidacy in this election the Presbyterians might have been successful in crucifying his party along with him.[22]

Early in September Hughes had begun to receive suggestions that he ought to resign. By this time he could perceive the danger in which his appointment had placed him. His position was all the more difficult because the stamps were reported on their way, and yet he had not up to this time received his commission as distributor. In fact he had had no official communication on the subject from the government. On the eighth of the month he wrote to Franklin:

> You are now from Letter to Letter to suppose each may be the last you will receive from your old Friend, as the Spirit or Flame of Rebellion is got to a high Pitch amongst the North Americans; and it seems to me that a sort of

[21] June 1, 1765, Hughes Papers, Historical Society of Pennsylvania.

[22] John Hughes to Lords of the Treasury, February 20, 1766, Treasury Papers, Class I, Bundle 452; William Young to Thomas Penn, December 14, 1765, Penn Manuscripts, Private Correspondence, V; Israel Pemberton to Joseph Pemberton, September 25, 1765, Pemberton Papers, XVIII, 53; Samuel Purviance, Jr., to Colonel Burd, September 20, 1765, Balch, Letters and Papers, 208; John Reynell to James Shirley, May 14, 1765, Letter Book of John Reynell.

Frenzy or Madness has got such hold of the People of all Ranks, that I fancy some Lives will be lost before this Fire is put out. I am at present much perplext what course to steer: For as I have given you Reason to expect I would endeavour to put the Act in Execution, and you no doubt have inform'd the Commissioners; I cannot in point of Honour go back, until something or other is done by the People to render it impossible for me to proceed. But perhaps when a Mob is on foot, my Life and Interest may fall a Sacrifice to an infatuated Multitude.—and I know of no way to prevent it but absolutely declaring off as all the rest have done to the Eastward. But as yet I cannot prevail upon myself, notwithstanding the Threats of some, and the Persuasions of others, to do an Act that appears to me neither loyal nor reputable.

I have hitherto kept matters easy by saying I had nothing to resign, for I have neither received my Commission or any other kind of Writing from the Stamp office. But when it is known I have received my Commission, I fancy I shall not escape the Storm of Presbyterian Rage. And as Captain Friend [who was reported to be bringing the Stamp papers] is expected every day, my Doom will soon be known, but whether I may live to inform you, is yet in the Womb of Futurity.[23]

By the time the Assembly met on September 9, a majority of the members had caught the infection which was sweeping the other colonies. Though they still wanted a royal government, their irritation with the Proprietor was momentarily overshadowed by their resentment against the Stamp Act. On September 10, by a vote of 15 to 14, they resolved to send a delegation to the Stamp Act Congress at New York.[24] Hughes was foolish enough to oppose this move,[25] and the Assembly snubbed him by appointing John Dickinson, George Bryan, and John Morton as delegates. Dickinson was one of the

---

[23] Treasury Papers, Class I, Bundle 442.
[24] *Ibid.; Pennsylvania Archives*, 8th ser., VII (1935), 5767.
[25] Samuel Purviance, Jr., to Colonel Burd, September 20, 1765, Balch, *Letters and Papers*, 208.

four who had voted against the petition for royal government, and Bryan was an up-and-coming Presbyterian politician.

On the same day that the Assembly chose its delegates to the congress, Captain Friend arrived—without the stamp papers.[26] The crisis was thus postponed, but the tension continued. Hughes heard rumors that his house would be pulled down, upon which he announced without hesitation that he would defend it with his life. His friends the Quakers were taking no part in the commotions. As a matter of fact he had many friends in Philadelphia, and if the worst came to the worst, he would not fight alone. The same men who had gathered with him and Franklin to meet the Paxton Presbyterians were ready to stand by him against the Philadelphia Presbyterians. On September 16 the test came. When it was spread about that Hughes's house would be destroyed that night, Joseph Galloway and his other friends, to the number of seven or eight hundred, organized to protect it. As might have been expected the governor, mayor, and other civil officers did nothing. But Hughes's friends posted themselves in different places, prepared to resist the gathering mob. Hughes himself stayed indoors, ready to fight as soon as the house should be entered. From time to time he wrote reports of what was occurring to his friend in London:

I for my Part am well arm'd with Fire-Arms, and am determin'd to stand a Siege. If I live till to-morrow morning I shall give you a further Account, but as it is now about 8 a Clock, I am on my Guard, and only write this between whiles, as every Noise or Bustle of the People calls me off.

9 o Clock.—Severall Friends that patroll between my House and the Coffee House, come in just now, and say, the Collection of Rabble begins to decrease visibly in the Streets,

[26] Except where otherwise noted the events described in this and the ensuing paragraphs are based on letters to and from John Hughes in Treasury Papers, Class I, Bundles 441, 442, 452, and in House of Lords Manuscripts, January 14, 1766. Some of these letters were printed in a supplement to the *Pennsylvania Journal*, September 4, 1766.

and the Appearance of Danger seems a good deal less than it did.

12 a Clock. There are now several Hundreds of our Friends about street, ready to suppress any Mob, if it should attempt to rise, and the Rabble are dispersing.

Sept. 17. 5 in the morning—We are all yet in the Land of the Living, and our Property safe. Thank God.—

There was more trouble to come. Hughes now fell ill and for the next three weeks was confined to his bed. He wrote to the governor the day after his all-night vigil, saying that any reports to the contrary notwithstanding, he had not received a commission from the Stamp Office in England, and that if the stamps should arrive, it would not be his duty to care for them. In Hughes's absence the Assembly adopted their radical resolutions of September 21, against the constitutionality of the Stamp Act,[27] but no popular demonstrations occurred until it was reported that the vessel bearing the stamp papers was beating up the river. On October 5 the stamps arrived and, ominously enough, so did Hughes's commission. Even before he received the document its arrival was announced on the strength of the large packet of mail addressed to him. Accordingly, the gentlemen who had appointed themselves to prevent his execution of the Act, met at the coffee house run by William Bradford, the printer, and sent out orders for muffled drums to be beaten through the streets and for the bells of the churches and state house to be tolled with muffled clappers. At this signal a mob collected, chiefly composed, according to Hughes, of "Presbyterians and proprietary Emissaries with the Chief Justices (Mr. William Allens) Son at their Head animating and encouraging the lower Class." The Governor and Mayor as usual made themselves scarce. The only attempt by any magistrate to interfere with the proceedings was that of Benjamin Shoemaker, an Alderman of the city and a Quaker. Shoemaker, according to Hughes's account, "met with the Drummers, as they were allarming the City and took them to task, requiring to know by what au-

[27] *Pennsylvania Archives*, 8th ser., 7 (1935), 5779-5780.

thority they were endeavouring to raise a Mob, they answered if He would go to the State House, He might know, He then asked who ordered them to beat about Streets, they said they had their orders from the Coffee House. . . Mr. Shoemaker then forbid them to proceed any farther, and said He would go immediately to the Mayor, and have them committed, they answered they could get the Mayor's orders when they pleased; But Mr. Shoemaker could not find the Mayor, nor any Officer to assist him, and therefore was obliged to desist, least He should draw the Mob upon Himself and Family and to have his house pulled down."

By three o'clock in the afternoon a sizeable mob had collected at the state house, and a deputation of seven prominent Philadelphians was sent to ask Hughes for his resignation as Distributor of Stamps. Since Hughes knew that the feeling against him was by no means universal, even though the feeling against the Stamp Act might be, he decided to see how long he could hold out. Lying in bed he told the gentlemen that he had indeed received his commission but that two friends in England had given bond to the sum of £500 for him to perform his duties. He would not resign unless the gentlemen would indemnify his friends. This they of course refused to do. After arguing unsuccessfully with him for an hour the delegation finally told him that he need not resign but only promise not to put the Act into execution until the King's further pleasure was known or until the Act should be executed in the neighboring colonies. Technically this would be only a temporary suspension of office. Hughes could look at it that way if he chose and feel that he had not been derelict in his duty. The delegation who had to deal with this peppery Tory were willing to settle for something less than an outright resignation, partly no doubt because they feared him a little, partly because they knew that popular indignation would prevent use of the stamps anyhow. Hughes agreed to their compromise, perhaps softened a little himself by word from his friends that the mob intended to proceed to the last extremity if he refused. The delegation then withdrew and shortly after sent him a written request for a promise, to be delivered the following Monday (it was then Saturday), that he would not execute the Act. Hughes did not fail to notice that this demand asked for more than he had agreed to. He had merely consented not to execute the Act until the King's further pleasure was known or until it should be executed in the neighboring colonies. Hughes saw Charles Thomson, one of the delegation, in private and called the change to his attention.

On Monday when the group called upon him again, Hughes was prepared with a statement. Fully aware of the rebellious nature of the proceedings against him, he had determined to make his opponents as uncomfortable as possible about what they were doing. He therefore opened his statement with a preamble which said that he was acting under the demand of James Tilghman, Esqr. attorney at law, Messrs. Robert Morris, Charles Thomson, Archibald McCall, John Cox, and William Richards, merchants, and Mr. William Bradford, printer. Moreover in making his promise not to execute the Act he included the conditions of the original agreement. When he presented this statement to the gentlemen, he had the pleasure of watching them squirm over the inclusion of their names: ". . . after some consultation amongst themselves they objected to their names being inserted, I said why come Gentlemen you have not done a thing you are ashamed to own, not in the least they said, but there was no necessity for their names to be inserted, nor would they receive that Resignation, whereupon I said to Mr. Tilghman come Sir take the Pen and please yourself for I see you are determined to be arbitrary."

While Tilghman was drafting a more satisfactory statement, Hughes continued to needle his opponents by asking them what they intended to do with the stamps, now that they had assumed supreme power in the province. "They then look'd at one another for a while, and seemed somewhat confounded." Tilghman at last said, "Let Mr. Hughes take care of them. I answered Gentlemen that cannot be, as you have now fixed matters. For were I to take the Stamps into my Care I should have your Party come about my House to pull it down and destroy both me and them, well says another let the Governor take care of them, another then said perhaps the Governor will call upon Mr. Hughes to put the Act into execution, and when he declines the Governor will perhaps appoint an Officer and the Act may take place, here a general pause ensued, but at last one and all cryed out, let us see who will dare put the Act in execution upon the Governor's Appointment, we will take care of that."

By this time Tilghman had written a statement, and Hughes signed it, promising simply that he would not execute the Act until it was executed in the other colonies. His tormentors were now satisfied, and Hughes himself had at least retained some degree of dignity. He only wished that he knew whether the British government itself would back down before the pressure of the American mobs. If Parliament was going to repeal the Act, it would be foolish for him to risk his life and career by defending it. For the present he still had friends in Pennsylvania who would stand by him, but already the riotous inhabitants of Virginia and Maryland had threatened "that if they ever catch me there, they will make a Sacrifice of me." As time went on he would lose his friends in Pennsylvania too. He was willing to stick by his guns if Britain was prepared to back him, but if Parliament repealed the Stamp Act, he would have suffered for nothing.

There was unfortunately no way of telling what Parliament would do. John Hughes stayed in Philadelphia maintaining his dignity as best he could, and missing no opportunity to let his enemies know the full implications of what they had done. He was a sociable man, quick-tempered but voluble, and he could sometimes be seen in the streets and coffee houses arguing with the men who opposed him. He occasionally confided the contents of his conversations to his superiors in England:

I sometimes tell some of our Warm Blades, that it is a piece of Inconsistency in them to call themselves Englishmen, Because Gentlemen say I, If you are Englishmen you must be bound by Acts of Parliament until that Parliament releases you, from that Obedience, which has not yet been done as I know of,

To this they reply, our Charters have done it,

absolutely no Gentlemen, Your Charters are but the Declaration of the Kings that Granted them, and they cannot be Tortured to mean no more then that the Kings of

Great Britain, would not arbitrarily and without Law raise money on the Subject in America, And this is all our forefathers, seem to have asked, when they left Britain, and Indeed it is all the Kings of Great Britain can legally promise, for the King cannot Bar the Rights of the Lords and Commons, any more then they can his Prerogatives, the Answer then is you are an Enemy to America, and ought to have your brains beat out. . . .

One Reason assign'd for not paying Obedience to this Act of Parliament, is that we have no Representatives in Parliament, I then say let us Petition for Representatives O no we will not agree to that, because we have Representatives of our own, and have always given money when we have been cald upon by the King or his Ministers, and if that will not do let us have a House of Commons in America to settle what shall be the Quota of each Colony when Money is wanted &c.

No Gentlemen you have foreclosed yourselves of that, for you have demonstrated your Proprietary [propensity?] to Rebellion to that Degree that it is my opinion the Ministry never can advise his Majesty to Unite you more than you now are, But if they know'd our Circumstances Rightly they wou'd devide us yet more, by forming New Colinies out of Virginia, and Perhaps some others that are already but too large.

Hughes continued to see the proprietary government as the source of Pennsylvania's troubles, and he did his best to turn the whole episode into an argument for royal government. Knowing that the proprietary governor had been required by instructions from England to assist in the enforcement of the Stamp Act, and knowing also that the governor had failed to give him any protection against the mob, Hughes took pains to place the responsibility for nullification of the Act on the governor's shoulders. When the delegation of October 7 had extracted his promise not to enforce the Act, he wrote the governor a letter, stating what he had done and why he had done it.

Hughes now considered his own responsibility discharged until the government of Pennsylvania should make it possible for him to distribute stamps. When the customs officers on November 4 asked him in writing for the stamped papers on which they were supposed to issue clearances for ships leaving Philadelphia, he took delight in writing them an official account of why he could not deliver the papers. He described first the way in which the mob had assembled to demand his resignation and then went on:

> Secondly altho it was currently reported, thro' the City on the 4th October last that Captain Holland with the stamp papers &c. would be up the next day and that a Mob would be raised to destroy them, Yet neither the Governor, the Supream Judges, the Mayor, Recorder, Aldermen, nor any other Justiciary Officers (Benjamin Shoemaker Esquire excepted) took the least notice therof, nor used any means to preserve the Peace of the City: . . . but as you may be unacquainted with the Situation of the Stamp Papers, I do myself the pleasure of informing you that his Honour the Governor, has committed them to the care of Capt. Hawker Commander of his Majesty's Ship Sardine and I would likewise Gentlemen, beg leave to acquaint you, That he has taken as I am informed, a Solemn Oath "to do his utmost that all and every of the Clauses contained in (the Stamp Act) shall be bona fide observed"—Wherefore I must refer you to him (as I am for the reasons already assigned at *present* incapacitated to supply you with stamp papers &c) for a more full answer if necessary to your letter.

Hughes doubtless wrote this letter with one eye on the officials in England to whom he surmised that it would be transmitted. From time to time he sent reports directly to the stamp commissioners in England, and here he took care to draw the conclusions which he merely implied in his letter to the local customs officers. Thus on November 2, 1765, he wrote, "It is my private Opinion, that if the province of Pennsylvania was changed from Proprietary to a Royal Government and some Person Appointed to Govern it, that had both Interest amongst the People, and a perfect knowledge of them, [Dr. Franklin, for example?] so as to be able to displace the Disloyal, and put into Power and Commission, such only as cou'd be depended on, and have Demonstrated their loyalty to their King, such a Person after the Changes Aforesaid might easily Govern this Province and preserve the Peace of it, and keep it in Subjection to his Majesty which I think we hardly are at this Time."

Besides pointing out the shabby behavior of the proprietary government Hughes kept up a running fire at the Presbyterians. The Proprietors were only interested in maintaining their own selfish interests, but the Presbyterians were downright rebels, if not Republicans. They had become "as averse to Kings, as they were in the Days of Cromwell, and some begin to cry out, *No King but King Jesus.*" The close alliance between these rebels and the proprietary government was a real danger to England's authority in America. This was demonstrated early in January when another consignment of stamped papers arrived in Philadelphia. Hughes reported the incident in a letter to the Stamp Office on January 13, 1766, in which he first told of the republicanism of the Presbyterians and then went on:

And as the Presbyterians, are united with the people in power, and are many of them, in power themselves, in this province, these and the others, countenance, and privately encourage, Riots, so that I really know not, what may be the Consequence, for a few Days ago, the London Ships came up, with some Stamps, and one of the Captains happening, to put a Box of Stamps on Shore, Instantly, the two printers, Messrs Bradford and Hall, got a Drum, and caused it to be beat, about the streets, and raised a Rabble of Boys, Sailors, and Negroes &c. to destroy the Stamps, but they were taken on board again, and the captains notwithstanding, were obliged to take an Oath, that they would not land them in the province, But not one single Magistrate, gave or shewed, the least Disapprobation of this Conduct, Nor is the Justice who swore them, Mr. George Bryan (who is a Red hot presbyterian by the by) any ways blamed by the Governor, for his proceedings on the Occasion, which I think may clearly shew, how far his Honour approves these Measures secretly.

By his waspish defenses of Parliamentary authority Hughes was steadily aggravating the feeling against himself, not only in Pennsylvania but in the neighboring colonies as well. John Holt, an old friend of Franklin's and a leader of the Sons of Liberty in New York (where Hughes's brother was also one of the Sons of Liberty), begged Mrs. Franklin to use her influence on Hughes to make a complete renunciation of his office.[28] He had conceded on November 21 that he would not execute the Act even if the other colonies did, unless the people of Pennsylvania called upon him to do so;[29] but still, to the disgust of the Sons of Liberty in neighboring colonies, he had not made an outright resignation. Every day he received anonymous messages and letters threatening him with "a mob of several thousand people, from the Jerseys, New York, and New England." "I think," he wrote to the Stamp Commissioners, "my Friends, and Relations, and my Credit, and popularity, in this province, will prevent such a step from being taken, but if Presbyterians Schemes succeed, I shall in a little Time fall a Sacrifice, unless I can fly to Britain for Shelter."

Hughes, like Thomas Hutchinson and many others who suffered from the Stamp Act, was far from thinking that the colonies had been justly treated by Great Britain. In letters to his superiors in England he urged a number of reforms in the colonial system. Though he acknowledged the supremacy of the British Parliament, he asked that representation in Parliament be extended to the colonies. He also suggested ways in which England could raise money in America without causing the unnecessary discontent created by the Stamp Act. One method might be to establish an American port to which goods might be shipped, subject to import duty, directly from Europe. Another method was the one favored by his friend Franklin, the establishment of loan offices for the issuance of bills of credit, the interest on which should accrue to the British Treasury.[30] In either of these schemes the advantages received by the colonists would outweigh whatever grievances might be attached to them. In all seriousness he also suggested

[28] February 16, 1766, Franklin Papers, XLVIII, 92, American Philosophical Society.

[29] Pennsylvania Journal, November 21, 1765.

[30] Verner Crane, "Benjamin Franklin and the Stamp Act," Colonial Society of Massachusetts, Publications, 32 (1937), 56-77.

that the Prince of Wales be made Prince of North America as well. This he said, "would naturally attach the Minds of the People to the person of the King of Great Britain, and it would be the Interest, of every King of Great Britain, to make the Tour of North America, whilst prince of Wales, whenever his Circumstances admitted his so doing."

Throughout the Stamp Act troubles Hughes continued to think in terms of local politics. Yet he perceived that the Presbyterians had created or at least caught hold of something bigger than themselves. Somehow or other their attack on the Quaker party and upon himself in particular had been transformed into a broader enveloping movement which threatened to destroy the whole foundation of British authority in America. From his vantage point in Pennsylvania, where everything evil seemed to spell Presbyterianism, Hughes looked at the other colonies and interpreted what he saw as the fruit of one great Presbyterian conspiracy.

By February 20, 1766, he was writing to the Stamp Commissioners that "these Sons of Liberty, who were chiefly composed of Presbyterians at first Onset, aim'd at Sovereignty, and they Dayly succeed in Drawing the weak and unwary amongst other Societies into League and Covenant with them, so that their Numbers begin now to be very formidable and will soon be more so, for they now, in some colonies, have stated Meetings and appoint Committees of Correspondence from one part of the Continent to the other, so that the Spirit of Rebellion (as I call it) is propagated publicly with the Gratest Industry."

As this spirit of rebellion gathered momentum, Hughes saw that his own career had become inseparably attached to the fate of the British Empire. He was content to have it so. He wanted no part of a Presbyterian republic.

In one of his earliest reports to the Stamp Commissioners he had warned of what would happen if Great Britain allowed the Presbyterians to get their own way by mob violence. "If Great Britain can or will suffer such kind of Conduct in her Colonists to pass unpunished," he wrote, "a Man need not be a Prophet or the son of a Prophet to see clearly that her Empire in North America is at an End." When Parliament repealed the Stamp Act in March, 1766, Hughes must have felt that both the British Empire in North America and his own political career were at an end. His party might continue, but henceforth he would be a millstone about its neck, and it was best that he withdraw from the scene. He did not understand this new American world where resistance to Parliament was rewarded by leniency. For the next eight or nine years he wandered through it, wearing his proud red coat, his head high, and proclaiming his loyalty to George III. He died before the Republic he dreaded became an actuality. Had he lived to see it, he would doubtless have said that the Presbyterians had finally got their way.

Hutchinson, Ingersoll, and Hughes were not the only Americans who suffered in 1765 for supporting the supremacy of Parliament, nor were Massachusetts, Connecticut, and Pennsylvania the only colonies where a political faction was able to take advantage of the Stamp Act to belabor its opponents. In every colony the Stamp Act forced men to decide where their final allegiance would be given, to themselves or to Parliament. If the Act had been enforced, there would have been many more to suffer as these three did and as Cadwallader Colden and Zachariah Hood and Thomas Moffat and Martin Howard suffered. There would have been many more too, who would have joined with the Sons of Liberty to uphold their rights at the cost of their subordination to Parliament. Before the Stamp Act was repealed, the men who would have counted most in the struggle that seemed to be approaching must have made up their minds as to which side they would take. But because it was repealed many of them did not have to reveal their decisions and probably most of them thought that the choice they had made could now be forgotten and the whole episode pushed back into oblivion. Unfortunately the question of Parliament's power in the colonies, once raised, could not be dropped, and the way in which Parliament went about repealing the Stamp Act demonstrated clearly to anyone with the heart to look, that the difficult decisions of 1765 would continue to be relevant.

PART IV

REVOLUTION DELAYED

Chapter XV

Repeal

THE PASSAGE OF the Stamp Act had little effect on the tortuous course of British politics in the summer of 1765. While the Americans were cursing George Grenville and planning rebellion, George III was becoming dissatisfied with his Prime Minister for altogether different reasons. The King had never liked Grenville, and shortly after the passage of the Stamp Act the Minister inflicted upon him an insult which was not easy to forgive. Grenville, at the King's request, drew up a bill giving the King the right to appoint a regent in case he should become incapacitated—George had just recovered from a serious illness. Grenville insisted on qualifying the bill to exclude the possibility of the King's appointing his mother as regent. The King's mother was widely believed to be the mistress of the Earl of Bute, who was perhaps the most hated man in British politics. Grenville's insistence on excluding her may have been aimed at excluding the influence of Bute, but it was a direct affront both to her and the King. George was able to secure the insertion of his mother's name in the bill, from the floor of the Commons, and thus to defeat his own Minister. The bill carried in that form with little opposition.[1]

In the absence of any organized party system, the King retained in the 1760's a large share of power in the choice of

[1] On British politics of the period 1765-1766 see W. T. Laprade, "The Stamp Act in British Politics," *American Historical Review*, 35 (1930), 735-757; D. A. Winstanley, *Personal and Party Government* (Cambridge, 1910), 204-275; L. B. Namier, *England in the Age of the American Revolution* (London, 1930), and *The Structure of Politics at the Accession of George III* (London, 1929); L. S. Sutherland, "Edmund Burke and the First Rockingham Ministry," *English Historical Review*, 47 (1932), 46-72. I have relied extensively on these in this account of repeal. On the nature of George III's illness at this time, see Knollenberg, *Origin of the American Revolution*, 275-281.

his ministry. His choice was limited only by the necessity of selecting men who could command a sufficient following in Parliament to get things done. Although Grenville had hitherto encountered no opposition in Parliament worthy of the name, George knew that he could dismiss him any time he chose. When Grenville seemed to regard the influential Duke of Bedford as his master, rather than the King, George knew it was time to be rid of him. The problem was whom to put in his place.

An obvious candidate was William Pitt, but Pitt was not an able politician. He was a colossus, a man to whom everyone had turned in time of crisis, but who could not hold a majority in time of peace. During the Seven-Years War Parliament had had no choice but to obey him. As soon as victory was in sight he lost his grip; yet he still loomed in the House of Commons as the most formidable opponent that any ministry could face. George would have liked to see Pitt at the head of the new ministry, but Pitt's own following in Parliament, while great in talent, was so small in numbers that, even with the support of the King, Pitt would have had to work with others, in particular with the group headed by the Duke of Newcastle and the Marquis of Rockingham. Pitt was, as usual, unwilling to play unless he could make his own rules, and as a result the King had ultimately to devise a ministry headed by the Marquis of Rockingham and including, besides Newcastle, General Henry Seymour Conway and the Duke of Grafton, both of whom were ardent followers of Pitt. Conway indeed had only been induced to enter the ministry, as Secretary of State, on condition that Pitt should be allowed to join it the moment that he expressed a wish to do so.

When the Rockingham Ministry took office early in July, the members of Parliament had retired from the heat of a London summer and would not come together again until December. Until that time Rockingham and his followers would have no opportunity to test their strength, but no one who knew the workings of Parliament had very sanguine hopes for their success. The Duke of Newcastle admitted to a friend "that the administration may have a considerable majority in both houses: but that majority must be made up of their enemies, creatures of the two last administrations, and such as are influenced only by their employments and their interest. Such a majority will last no longer than they find the administration carries everything clearly and roundly. The moment there is the least check, they return to their vomit; . . ."[2] This being the opinion of one of the new ministers it is not surprising that politicians outside the administration, particularly the followers of George Grenville and the Duke of Bedford, should hold it in the utmost contempt. Even before it was formed the Earl of Sandwich had called it "the most rash attempt that ever was made," and by the end of August he was writing to Bedford that "the general language seems turned to ridicule the new ministry, and to pronounce their existence to be of a very short duration."[3] He might have added that his own chaplain, James Scott, under the name of Anti-Sejanus, was writing the most stinging ridicule of the new Ministry in the London newspapers.[4]

By the time Parliament came together in December, the strength of the Ministry had by no means improved, but the need for strength was desperate. The news of the riots in America had turned all talk in that direction, and the Rockingham government was faced with the problem of quieting a rebellion which their opponents had called into being. The absence of Pitt now became more conspicuous than ever. Lord Chesterfield had remarked in the preceding summer that the new Ministry was without a keystone. The keystone, he surmised, would have to be added in the course of the winter, and the keystone would have to be William

[2] Quoted from Additional Mss., 32969, f. 392, British Museum, in Winstanley, *Personal and Party Government*, 242n.

[3] John Russell, ed., *Correspondence of John, Fourth Duke of Bedford* (London, 1846), III, 304, 316. Cf. Thomas Whately to John Temple, July 12, 1765, Stowe Collection, Huntington Library: "The Newcastle Party are now in Office, how long they will continue so is another question. . . ."

[4] Fred J. Hinkhouse, *The Preliminaries of the American Revolution as Seen in the English Press* (New York, 1926), 70-71. *Prologue to Revolution*, 99-100, 131-134.

Pitt.[5] In November the Ministry tried to persuade Pitt to come in. Newcastle even agreed to back out if he would accept a place, but Pitt preferred his solitary glory.

The Ministry, then, must meet the American problem by themselves, supported only by their small following of friends and placeholders. If Rockingham displeased the King, he would fall. If he displeased Pitt, he might also fall, for Pitt's opposition would be a signal not merely for his own followers but for all half-hearted supporters to desert. Feeling himself on such shaky ground, Rockingham took a new step. Since he had no real power in Parliament, he looked for it outside Parliament.

The Old Whigs, as Rockingham's group were called, had some reputation among the people as defenders of freedom. They had supported John Wilkes, in spite of his somewhat shady character, in the fight for freedom of the press. In that fight they had been allied with the merchants of London, who were also generally to be found on the side of freedom and against the government. They were a group of men whom Parliament could neglect only at the expense of the country's prosperity and of the revenues which derived from that prosperity. As Canning later called in the New World to redress the balance of the Old, Rockingham now called in the merchants who traded with the new world to redress the balance of Parliament.[6]

The alliance of Rockingham and the merchants was grounded on a common repugnance to the Stamp Act. Conway, the Secretary of State, had of course been one of the principal speakers against passing it. George Grenville, the father of the measure, would undoubtedly be a leader of the opposition in Parliament, and the best way to discredit him would be to discredit his Act. The merchants had even stronger motives than the Ministry for disliking it. This was one point upon which the merchants trading to North America and those trading to the West Indies could heartily

[5] Bonamy Dobrée, ed., *The Letters of Philip Dormer Stanhope, 4th Earl of Chesterfield* ([London], 1932), VI, 2658.

[6] Sutherland, in *English Historical Review*, 47 (1932), 46-72.

agree. They might be at odds over the Sugar Act, which benefited the islands at the expense of the mainland, but the Stamp Act was pinching them all alike.

The merchants trading to North America, already troubled by the post-war depression, were further vexed by the non-importation agreements which the Americans had adopted as a means of promoting repeal. The Americans had begun to cut down imports and to advocate an increase in home manufactures as soon as the Sugar Act was passed. With the coming of the Stamp Act, they had taken more drastic action. The day before the Act was to go into effect, two hundred New York merchants signed an agreement to import nothing more from Great Britain until the Stamp Act should be repealed. The Philadelphia merchants and retailers subscribed similar agreements the next week, and the Boston merchants in December, to be followed by those of Salem, Marblehead, Plymouth, and Newbury.[7]

The English merchants held no hard feelings toward the Americans for their non-importation agreements but blamed everything on George Grenville's ill-advised schemes. In order, therefore, to force a repeal of the Stamp Act, the London merchants on December 4 organized a committee of twenty-eight to mobilize mercantile sentiment and deluge Parliament with petitions for repeal. Barlow Trecothick, a leading merchant who had been born in Boston, was chairman. Meeting with the Marquis of Rockingham, Trecothick drew up a circular letter which he directed to thirty trading and manufacturing towns throughout the kingdom. As a result petitions came to Parliament not only from the merchants of London but also from the merchants and manufacturers of over twenty other British towns and cities. The petitions made no mention of the rights involved in the Stamp Act but stressed the fact that the North American trade, which suffered under the Grenville measures, was the source of England's prosperity, and that unless Parliament took action, the

[7] Schlesinger, *Colonial Merchants and the American Revolution*, 76-80. The New York agreement is in *Prologue to Revolution*, 106.

merchants and manufacturers and all dependent upon them faced ruin.[8]

This was a language which Parliament was willing to talk, but unfortunately the Ministry could not expect Parliament to judge the Stamp Act simply by its economic effects. Probably one of the principal reasons why George Grenville had pressed the Act was in order to settle once for all the question of right. Certainly that was a principal reason why Parliament passed it. The Americans themselves had raised the question in the summer of 1764 by objecting to Parliament's authority to tax them. Once raised, the question could not easily be ignored, and it had become for many members of Parliament the central issue. They might agree that the Act was ill-advised, they might accept every claim made by the merchants, but they could not afford to give the appearance of backing down before a colonial mob; and they would not abandon the authority which they had claimed in passing the Act.[9]

The dilemma of the Rockingham government, therefore, was to find a way to redress the grievances of the merchants, and at the same time assuage the injured honor of Parliament and maintain at least the semblance of authority. As soon as Parliament met on December 17, though the purpose of the meeting was to issue writs of election to fill vacant seats, George Grenville made it plain that he would not allow the members to forget the colonial affront. In opening the session the King referred to the "matters of importance" which had

[8] *Journals of the House of Commons*, XXX, 462-503. *Prologue to Revolution*, 129-131. Sutherland, in *English Historical Review*, 47 (1932), 62-65; Thomas Penn to William Allen, December 15, 1765, Penn Correspondence, VIII, 338-339, Historical Society of Pennsylvania; *Boston Gazette*, February 24-March 3, 1766 Supplement; Additional Mss., 33030, ff. 208-211, British Museum. Library of Congress transcripts.

[9] This view is supported by a host of letters from the friends of the colonies in England. See those in G. H. Guttridge, ed., *The American Correspondence of a Bristol Merchant, 1766–1776* (Berkeley, California, 1934), 10, 14; *Boston Gazette*, February 24, 1766; Massachusetts Historical Society, *Proceedings*, 2d ser., 11 (1897), 446-448; Massachusetts Archives, XXII, 453-460; Penn Correspondence, VIII, 330.

lately occurred in some of his colonies in America. Grenville immediately wished to know why His Majesty had been advised to speak so leniently on this subject. And the Duke of Bedford called for all papers that had been sent to America since the passage of the Stamp Act to be laid before the House, the purpose being, obviously, to discover some means of embarrassing Conway, the Secretary of State.[10]

Fortunately the House adjourned to January 14, 1766, without agreeing to this motion. The Ministry was thereby given a few more weeks in which to arrive at a formula which would satisfy both merchants and Parliament. At first, apparently, they planned merely to modify the Stamp Act in order to render it less objectionable. As late as January 11, three days before Parliament met, Richard Jackson was writing to Governor Thomas Fitch of Connecticut.

I am informed by the best Intelligence I can procure that the Stamp Act will not be repealed, every other Relief may be, I think, expected, and even this Law will probably be reduced to nothing more, than a Proof of the Power of Parliament to impose Taxes as well as make other Laws for America. Something to Assert this Power is judged necessary by leading Men in both Houses, I wish that some other means of attaining the same End may be thought of rather than this, but I fear no other will.[11]

Rockingham and his followers were considerably handicapped in drawing up a program by the fact that they could not tell what position Pitt would take. They had repeatedly sought his advice and asked him to enter the Ministry, and he as often refused to communicate with them or imposed condi-

[10] *The Parliamentary History of England* . . . (London, 1813), XVI, 83-90; *Maryland Gazette,* March 6, 1766.
[11] Connecticut Historical Society, *Collections,* 18 (1920), 383; Cf. Thomas Penn to William Allen, December 15, 1765, Penn Correspondence, VIII, 338-339; Edmund Pendleton to James Madison, February 15, 1766, Massachusetts Historical Society, *Proceedings,* 2d ser., 19 (1905), 111; Richard and John Samuel to John Yeates, December 4, 1765, Yeates Papers, Historical Society of Pennsylvania.

tions tantamount to dissolving the Ministry. Consequently when Parliament opened on January 14, they still did not know what line he proposed to follow. The King opened the session with a speech which reflected the ministers' intention both of asserting Parliament's constitutional authority and at the same time of pursuing economic measures which would revive colonial trade. The Ministry followed by introducing the usual address of thanks in which they repeated their intention of combining a zeal for the authority of Parliament with "the utmost attention to the important objects of the trade and navigation of these kingdoms." The opposition opened debate on the address by insisting at once that the Stamp Act should be enforced unless repeal were sought simply as a favor. The tenor of the opposition was set by Mr. Robert Nugent's contention that though the Stamp Act might produce little in revenue, "a peppercorn, in acknowledgment of the right, was of more value, than millions without."[12]

Before the Ministry could come to their own defense, William Pitt took the floor for one of his most famous speeches. With relentless eloquence he succeeded in the triple task of supporting the address of thanks, flaying the Ministry, and commending the Americans for their rebellion. The address he said was good, but the Ministry should have called the House together earlier on so important a matter. The Ministry, he made it plain, did not have his confidence. "Pardon me, gentlemen," he said, bowing to them, "confidence is a plant of slow growth in an aged bosom: youth is the season of credulity; by comparing events with each other, reasoning from effects to causes, methinks, I plainly discover the traces of an over-ruling influence." (The last was presumably a reference to Lord Bute, or to the Duke of Newcastle.) On the other hand, his contempt for the preceding ministry was even deeper. Turning to George Grenville, who sat only one seat away from him, he thundered, "as to the late ministry every capital measure they have taken, has been entirely wrong!" With the government

---

[12] *Parliamentary History*, XVI, 90-97; Winstanley, *Personal and Party Government*, 256-259; Laprade, in *American Historical Review*, 35 (1930), 749-750.

and the opposition thus disposed of, Pitt went on to extol the Americans, and before the day was over he had pronounced his famous dictum, "I rejoice that America has resisted." In conclusion the great commoner gave his recommendations. They were:

. . . that the Stamp Act be repealed absolutely, totally, and immediately. That the reason for the repeal be assigned, because it was founded on an erroneous principle. At the same time, let the sovereign authority of this country over the colonies, be asserted in as strong terms as can be devised, and be made to extend to every point of legislation whatsoever. That we may bind their trade, confine their manufactures, and exercise every power whatsoever, except that of taking their money out of their pockets without their consent.[13]

When Pitt had done, the Ministry knew at last where he stood, but the revelation merely added to their difficulties. While they had hoped to minimize the importance of the riots in America, Pitt had glorified them. If he had coupled his encomiums for the Americans with a word of praise for the Ministry, he might have contributed toward effecting the relief of the colonies. As it was, Anti-Sejanus was able to pillory the Ministry in his newspaper columns with a deadly and embarrassing series of questions:

Have they proved that Mr. Pitt, upon whose shoulders they have endeavoured to exalt themselves, will support either them or their system? Has not he more than once hinted at some private influence which they are under, and ridiculed them in the most notorious and public manner? Have they been able by wheedling and fawning, by cringing and crouching, with supple and abject servility, to draw one single drop of comfort from that popular gentleman? Will he espouse their cause and support them in P—t, or leave

[13] *Parliamentary History*, XVI, 97-108; W. S. Taylor and J. H. Pringle, eds., *Correspondence of William Pitt, Earl of Chatham* (London, 1838), II, 363-373. *Prologue to Revolution*, 134-141.

them to shuffle and scramble for themselves? Dare they adopt his idea, or dare they confront it? Will they not rather, lest they should offend the Idol, find out a middle way, and retain the shadow of power over the colonists, while they give up the substance?[14]

In the face of such taunts, the Ministry once again besought the colossus to join them, but the colossus once again laid down impossible terms, demanding among other things that Newcastle should be dismissed and that Lord Temple, who was George Grenville's brother, should be admitted if he chose to come in. The last demand was the most ironical, for at the same time that Pitt in the Commons was rejoicing over the resistance of the Americans, Temple in the Lords had been speaking in favor of continuing the Stamp Act.[15]

Rockingham was thus obliged to carry on unassisted by the prestige which Pitt's support would have brought him, and hampered by the demands of the merchants and the irritation of Parliament. Since Pitt had always been the favorite of the merchants, his speech intensified their zeal against the Stamp Act, while in Parliament it merely shocked the members by its justification of rebellion. The solution Rockingham devised to bridge this gap, though it was perhaps the only one open to him, promised trouble for the future.

On January 17 the leading ministers met at Rockingham's house and came to an agreement. Rockingham described it in a letter to Charles Yorke, the Attorney General: "The ideas we join in are . . . a declaratory act in general terms,—afterwards to proceed to considerations of trade, etc., and finally determination on the stamp act, i.e. a repeal."[16] The formula Rockingham had fixed upon was, except for one particular, the one which Pitt had asked for in his speech of January 14. Pitt had demanded a total repeal of the Stamp Act combined with an assertion of the legislative authority

[14] *London Chronicle*, January 28-30, 1766. *Prologue to Revolution*, 133.
[15] Winstanley, *Personal and Party Government*, 260-262.
[16] Quoted from Additional Mss., 35430, f. 31, British Museum, in Winstanley, *Personal and Party Government*, 262n.

of Parliament. So far Rockingham was ready to oblige. Pitt had also asked "that the reason for the repeal be assigned, because it [the Stamp Act] was founded on an erroneous principle." To have stated the reason that Pitt assigned would have been asking the members of Parliament to display a humility they had never possessed. Rockingham was obliged, in fact, to emphasize the economic reasons for repeal and so far as possible to keep Parliament from considering the question of principle. It was this necessity which made the repeal of the Stamp Act almost as fruitful of evil consequences as the passage.

Rockingham did not introduce the resolution for the Declaratory Act until February 3 and that for repeal of the Stamp Act until February 21.[17] In the interval between the decision of January 17 and the resolution of February 21 the administration did its best to make Parliament feel the great public demand for repeal, while the opposition accused the Ministry of aiding and abetting the colonial rebellion. The Stamp Act had produced more discussion in the press than any other American measure heretofore. Much of the ablest discussion came from the friends of Grenville: the writings of Anti-Sejanus were undoubtedly the cleverest things appearing in the London papers during the winter of 1765–1766. Anti-Sejanus aimed at Parliament more than at the public, and closely followed the proceedings in each House, pouncing upon any bit of testimony or argument that offered an opportunity for ridicule or rebuttal. The failure of the Stamp Act he blamed on the Ministry, alleging that they had not taken proper steps to enforce it. When it came out in Parliament that Governor Moore had been sent to New York without instructions and that Governor Bernard had never received a copy of the Act, he lashed the "inaction and somnolency" of a ministry that would "send off a Governor to one of the principal provinces in America, without any instructions; and let another remain without even a copy of the act, which it was his duty to enforce. A Lieutenant

---

[17] William J. Smith, ed., *The Grenville Papers* (London, 1853), III, 357, 373.

Governor could not act, because he had not proper instructions: and behold, when the Governor himself came—he had no instructions at all."[18] Anti-Sejanus repeatedly warned the members of Parliament of the consequences of appeasing the Americans. "Can it be supposed," he asked, "that the Colonists will ever submit to bear any share in those grievous burdens and taxes, with which we are loaded, when they find that the G--nt will not, or dare not assert its own authority and power? Have we not reason to expect, that they will shake off all dependance and subjection, and neither suffer a limitation of their trade, nor any duty to be imposed upon their commodities? Is not this want of spirit and resolution, a direct encouragement of the mob, to redress every imaginary grievance, by force and violence?"[19] These telling arguments were bolstered by satirical ballads such as "America Triumphant; or Old England's Downfall, to the Tune of There was a jovial Beggar," which contained the verses

Who'd stay in musty England,
And work himself to death,
Where, choaked with debts and taxes,
No man can fetch his breath
                And to America we'll go &c.

Then to America we'll go,
Where we will merry be;
Since there no taxes need be paid,
As wise men all agree.
                And to America we'll go &c.

Then fare thee well, Old England,
Where honesty can't thrive;
Farewell roast-beef, and bread, and beer,
We'll go to yonder hive.
                And to America we'll go &c.[20]

[18] *London Chronicle*, February 22-25, 1766.
[19] *Ibid.*, January 11-14, 1766.
[20] *Ibid.*, February 18-20, 1766. Cf. "The World Turned upside down, or the Old Woman taught Wisdom," *ibid.*, March 8-11, 1766. *Prologue to Revolution*, 156-157.

The Whigs countered with essays on the rights of English-men and with reprints of colonial pamphlets.[21] Throughout the heated debates, from the latter part of 1765 until the final victory of repeal, the *London Chronicle* carried in every issue a notice which read:

TO WHOM IT MAY CONCERN,

MEN OF ENGLAND, THE COLONIES, BRETHREN

Consider well the Reverse of a Dutch medal, struck in their early troubles.

'Two earthen vases, floating on the waters.

Inscription. Frangimur si collidimur.'

By and large the Whigs found their greatest strength not in the press but in the organized petitioning of the merchants and in the actual fact of economic depression. The opposition did their best to discredit the petitions by pointing out, with some reason, that these had been inspired by the government itself in order to bring pressure on Parliament.[22] But whatever the origin of the petitions, there was no denying their exist-ence nor was there any denying the economic power of the merchants who presented them. No government can thrive on hard times, and the members of Parliament could not fail to be impressed by the evidence that times were getting harder. They listened to a series of manufacturers quoting discouraging statistics on unemployment. The Ministry ex-pressed the belief that if the Act were enforced Parliament would have to face 20,000 starving Englishmen petitioning

[21] Hinkhouse, *Preliminaries of the American Revolution as seen in the English Press,* 52-80. The most able newspaper spokesman for the colonists wrote under the name of "Aequus" in *London Chronicle,* November 28-30, December 10-12, 28-30, 1765, Janu-ary 4-7, 9-11, 1766.

[22] *The Annual Register . . . for the Year 1766* (London, 1772), 37; cf. *London Chronicle,* December 3-5, 14-17, 24-26, 1765, January 4-7, 1766.

for its repeal. It was even hinted that 100,000 unemployed workmen would soon march on London.[23]

In addition to these depressing facts and predictions, Parliament had to consider the testimony of military experts that it would be impossible to enforce the Stamp Act unless more troops were sent to America to do the job.[24] With times so hard already, it was appalling to contemplate raising more troops to enforce an act which showed no signs of bringing in large revenue anyhow. Edward Shippen, off in the wilds of Pennsylvania, knew what he was talking about when he told his father that the British would think twice about enforcing the Act when they realized that it would have to be done "by a mighty army raised from among themselves, for the levying of which they must be *forced* to open their own purse-strings, and this, too, before they have recovered themselves, from the last expensive wars with France and Spain."[25] Nor could Parliament any longer dismiss the hostility of the colonies as mere impertinence. The rebellion there was assuming serious proportions, and while no one would wish to countenance rebellion, only a fool would provoke it unnecessarily. The colonies were admittedly an important source of Britain's strength, but colonies in rebellion could strengthen only Britain's enemies. For a variety of reasons, therefore, the Ministry found Parliament ready to give their proposals a careful hearing.

The members did not lack for information. In addition to the petitions from English merchants and manufacturers, they heard petitions from Edward Montague, agent for Virginia and William Knox, agent for Georgia, both carefully phrased so as to avoid any imputation of Parliament's authority and both asking for repeal of the Act. The Ministry paraded some forty merchants, colonial agents, and visiting Americans

---

[23] *Georgia Gazette,* June 4, 1766; Henry Cruger, Jr., to Henry Cruger, February 14, 1766, Massachusetts Historical Society, *Collections,* 69 (1914), 139-142. Cf. Chesterfield to his son, February 11, 1766, *Letters,* Dobrée, ed., VI, 2711-2713.

[24] Additional Mss., 33030, British Museum.

[25] December 25, 1765, Balch, ed., *Letters and Papers Relating Chiefly to the Provincial History of Pennsylvania,* 212-215.

before the bar of the House of Commons. Even Thomas Moffat and Martin Howard, Jr., appeared to give their first-hand accounts of the American riots. So did George Mercer, who assured the Commons that the Act could not be enforced without troops. Barlow Trecothick and Nicholas Ray, both of whom had lived in America and had since become prominent London merchants testified to the need for repeal. The star performer, however, was Benjamin Franklin, whose carefully rehearsed performance, made a great impression and was quickly published.[26] The Board of Trade reported on the revenues which had been derived from the customs service in America in the preceding quarter century year by year, together with the costs of conducting civil government and military defense in America, and the amount of the public debt in each colony. In addition Conway laid before the House all the communications from royal governors and stamp officers describing the troubles in America.[27] A great deal of this information, and the testimony of some of the witnesses, Moffat and Howard for example, must have been far from soothing to the injured dignity of Parliament. The Ministry could not afford, however, to suppress any evidence, for their opponents would have been quick to bring it to light. The most that they could do was to maximize the disastrous economic consequences of the Stamp Act and minimize the colonists' denial of Parliament's authority to tax them.

The picture of colonial views about taxation which the ministers and other friends of the colonies endeavored to paint for Parliament was a good deal less clear and a good deal less radical than the views actually expressed by the colonists through their assemblies and through the Stamp Act Congress. The colonies had distinguished between the power to tax and the power to make laws. The latter, they said, belonged to Parliament for the whole empire, but the power to tax was

[26] *The Examination of Dr. Benjamin Franklin* (London, 1766). *Journals of the House of Commons*, XXX, 455-602; Additional Mss., 33030, British Museum. For a selection from Franklin's testimony see *Prologue to Revolution*, 143-146.

[27] These papers, preserved in the House of Lords, constitute one of the principal sources for the study of the Stamp Act crisis.

the exclusive power of the local representative assembly in each part of the empire. The House of Commons might levy taxes on the people of Great Britain, but only the Massachusetts Assembly could tax the people of Massachusetts. This was the argument not merely of the various colonial assemblies, but also of Daniel Dulany and other colonial pamphleteers. One of Dulany's readers had been William Pitt, and Pitt had argued for the colonial position in his speech of January 14. "It is my opinion," he said, "that this kingdom has no right to lay a tax upon the colonies. At the same time, I assert the authority of this kingdom over the colonies, to be sovereign and supreme, in every circumstance of government and legislation whatsoever. . . . Taxation is no part of the governing or legislative power."[28]

This was the view of Pitt, and this was the view of the Americans, but to most members of Parliament it was a novel idea and a dangerous idea to distinguish between the power to tax and the power to legislate. There was, however, another and slightly less dangerous distinction which had already been proposed, probably on the floor of Parliament, and which it was possible to confuse with the distinction between legislation and taxation: the distinction between internal and external taxes. When it was first suggested that Parliament might tax the colonies externally but not internally is uncertain. Richard Jackson, the agent for Connecticut, expressed his belief in this distinction in a letter to Franklin December 27, 1763, averring that "the Mother Country may prohibit foreign Trade, it may therefore tax it. And the Colonys have a Compensation, in Protection but I dread internal Taxes."[29] At the time when he wrote these words Jackson was a member of Parliament. Governor Bernard made use of the distinction in the plan for reorganizing the colonies which he sent to Halifax; and by the spring of 1764 when James Otis was writing his *Rights of the British Colonies Asserted and Proved* the distinction was sufficiently

[28] *Parliamentary History*, XVI, 99; *Chatham Correspondence*, II, 366. *Prologue to Revolution*, 136.

[29] Van Doren, ed., *Letters and Papers of Benjamin Franklin and Richard Jackson, 1753–1785*, 123–124.

well known so that Otis could disavow it as a "distinction some make in England."[30]

Evidently some of the friends of America, perhaps Richard Jackson, had already rehearsed in Parliament the notion that external taxes on the colonies were constitutional but that internal taxes were not; for when Pitt made his speech in defense of the Americans, the other members of Parliament thought that he was adopting this distinction, or rather they confused this distinction with the one which he did expound, that between taxation and legislation. Pitt actually made two speeches on January 14. In the first, according to the records of the debate, he did not even mention the words external and internal.[31] Yet Grenville, who of course was attacking the Ministry as well as Pitt, said in answer, "I cannot understand the difference between external and internal taxes. They are the same in effect, and only differ in name." Pitt, taking the floor again, clearly dismissed these remarks as not applicable to what he had said. "If the gentleman," cried Pitt, "does not understand the difference between internal and external taxes, I cannot help it; but there is a plain distinction between taxes levied for the purposes of raising revenue, and duties imposed for the regulation of trade, for the accommodation of the subject; although, in the consequences, some revenue might incidentally arise from the latter." Pitt, like the Americans, would admit duties on trade for the purpose of regulation, but not taxes on trade or anything else if for the purpose of revenue.[32]

According to the records, the passage in which he dismissed responsibility for Grenville's failure to understand the difference between internal and external taxes was the only place in his speech where Pitt referred to this distinction or mentioned the words external or internal. Yet some members

[30] *Rights of the British Colonies Asserted and Proved*, 42.

[31] The account of this speech as given in *Chatham Correspondence*, II, 363-373, and *Parliamentary History*, XVI, 97-108, is said to have been "almost verbatim." See Basil Williams, *The Life of William Pitt* (London, 1913), II, 336, 346n. Both speeches are reprinted in *Prologue to Revolution*, 134-141.

[32] *Parliamentary History*, XVI, 101, 105; *Chatham Correspondence*, II, 370. *Prologue to Revolution*, 139-140.

of Parliament came away with the impression that he had differentiated internal and external taxes. Lord George Sackville wrote to his friend General Irwin, on January 17:

> It seems we have all been in a mistake in regard to the Constitution, for Mr. Pitt asserts that the legislature of this country has no right whatever to lay internal taxes upon the colonys; that they are neither actually nor virtually represented, and therfore not subject to our jurisdiction in that particular; but still, as the Mother Country, we may tax and regulate their commerce, prohibit or restrain their manufactures, and do everything but what we have done by the Stamp Act; that in our representative capacity we raise taxes internally and in our legislative capacity we do all the other acts of power. If you understand the difference between representative and legislative capacity it is more than I do, but I assure you it was very fine when I heard it.[33]

Here Sackville has obviously confounded and combined the two distinctions. Perhaps other members of Parliament did the same. In any case it was to the interest of the Rockingham Ministry and of anyone seeking repeal of the Act to foster this confusion, for the distinction between internal and external taxes limited the power of Parliament much less than the wholesale distinction between taxation and legislation. The Ministry therefore made no effort to show what the true position of the Americans was but preferred to let Parliament suppose that the Americans were denying the power merely to levy internal taxes and had no objection to external taxes.

It was evidently for this reason that Rockingham did not make use of the petitions from the Stamp Act Congress. A technical reason was discovered for not hearing them in Parliament, namely, that they were not properly signed. But Charles Garth, one of the special agents appointed to present the one to the House of Commons, told his constituents that a principal reason why the Ministry failed to support the petition was

[33] Historical Manuscripts Commission, *Report on the Manuscripts of Mrs. Stopford-Sackville* (London, 1904), I, 104.

"that it tended to question not only the Right of Parliament to impose internal Taxes, but external Duties. . . ."[34] Pitt, quite consistently, demanded that the petitions be heard, for Pitt had taken precisely the position which the Stamp Act Congress took, but his defense of the Congress only served to embarrass the Ministry in their attempt to keep the radical constitutional theories of the Americans in the background.[35]

The members of the opposition showed some astuteness in pointing out that the Americans actually went farther than merely internal taxes in their denial of Parliament's authority. From Martin Howard they extracted the statement that the colonists "made no Objection while they only Taxed by Customs But now they . . . have in Virginia denied all Taxes." One of the members asked him if they did not also object to the Navigation Acts, but Howard answered fairly enough, "They do not Extend it so far."[36] Hans Stanley, a member of the opposition from Southampton pointed out bluntly that "The Americans have not made the futile Distinction between internal and external taxes."[37] And in the House of Lords, Lord Lyttelton, who had taken the trouble to read Otis's pamphlet, reported that "The Americans themselves make no distinction between external and internal taxes. Mr. Otis, their champion, scouts such a distinction, . . ."[38]

These more accurate delineations of the American position were, fortunately for the proponents of repeal, overshadowed by the spectacular performance of Benjamin Franklin, who managed to convey very forcefully the idea that the Americans objected only to internal taxes. Though Franklin must have known that the American objections to taxation were

[34] Charles Garth to Ringgold, Murdoch, and Tilghman, February 26, 1766, *Maryland Historical Magazine*, 6 (1911), 285. For Garth's extensive account of Parliamentary debates in this letter and another of March 5, 1766, see *Prologue to Revolution*, 147-154.
[35] George Thomas, Earl of Albemarle, *Memoirs of the Marquis of Rockingham* (London, 1852), I, 289-290; Historical Manuscripts Commission, *Stopford-Sackville*, I, 105
[36] Additional Mss., 33030, ff. 133-135, British Museum.
[37] *American Historical Review*, 17 (1912), 566.
[38] *Parliamentary History*, XVI, 167.

more sweeping, he was anxious to assist in the repeal, and he knew that the American claims of exemption were a stumbling block. For that reason, probably, he followed the Rockingham party in minimizing their extent. Much of his testimony had been rehearsed with members friendly to the Ministry, but he gave some of his most effective answers in dealing with questions posed by the opposition. One member asked him if the reasoning by which the colonists objected to internal taxes might not justify them in objecting to external taxes as well. Franklin's answer was so neat that it must have made a lasting impression. "Many arguments have been lately used here to shew them [the colonists], that there is no difference, and that, if you have no right to tax them internally, you have none to tax them externally, or make any other law to bind them. At present they do not reason so; but in time they may possibly be convinced by these arguments." The laughter which must have followed this rather telling blow probably diminished the effect of the next question, asked by a member who had evidently taken the trouble to look at some of the documents which Conway had laid before Parliament: "Do not the resolutions of the Pennsylvania assembly say, all taxes?" To this Franklin could only say, that if the Pennsylvania resolutions said all taxes, they meant only internal taxes. But Franklin had made his point, and somehow the impression remained that the Americans objected only to internal taxes.[39]

How much this misunderstanding of the American position contributed to the repeal of the Stamp Act would be difficult to say. Perhaps very little, for the evidence suggests that pressure from the merchants, rather than consideration for colonial rights, was the force behind repeal. The misunderstanding may even have been a genuine confusion in which the Rockingham Ministry shared, though the Ministry's stand on the petitions of the Stamp Act Congress suggests strongly that they understood the colonial claims better than they were willing to admit. In any case Rockingham was clearly

[39] *Ibid.*, 137-160; see pp. 158-159; Benjamin Franklin, *Writings*, Smyth, ed., IV, 412-448, see pp. 445-446. *Prologue to Revolution*, 146.

responsible for another misunderstanding, the converse of that about internal and external taxes. In drawing up the Declaratory Act, he deliberately phrased it in such a way as to leave the meaning uncertain to those whom it might offend. The result was that the colonists at first misunderstood Parliament's declaration of right, just as Parliament had misunderstood the colonists' declarations.

The idea of a declaratory act, affirming Parliament's authority over the colonies, seems to have occurred to Rockingham fairly early. Such an affirmation of Parliament's authority over Ireland had been made in a Declaratory Act in 1719.[40] With this example before him the Minister had apparently decided as early as December 27 that whatever accommodation he extended to the colonies should be accompanied by a declaration of Parliament's authority.[41] It was not Rockingham, however, but William Pitt who provided the immediate impetus for the act which was finally passed. In asking for repeal of the Stamp Act on January 14 Pitt had said, "At the same time, let the sovereign authority of this country over the colonies, be asserted in as strong terms as can be devised, and be made to extend to every point of legislation whatsoever."[42] Obviously Pitt did not mean that this assertion of sovereign authority should extend to taxation, for his whole speech had been a denial that taxation was a part of the sovereign power, and he demanded at the same time an express recognition that the Stamp Act was unconstitutional. The declaration which he called for was a declaration of Parliament's legislative authority, and Rockingham took care to frame his declaration precisely as Pitt had demanded. The resolution which Rockingham presented to Parliament on February 3 read "That the King's Majesty, by and with the advice and consent of the Lords spiritual and temporal and Commons of Great Britain in parliament assembled, had, hath, and of right ought to have, full power and authority to make laws and statutes of sufficient force and validity to bind the colonies and people

[40] 6 George I, c. 5.
[41] Winstanley, *Personal and Party Government*, 256.
[42] *Parliamentary History*, XVI, 108; *Chatham Correspondence*, II, 373.

of America, subjects of the crown of Great Britain, in all cases whatsoever."[43]

This was the declaration "in general terms" upon which Rockingham and his colleagues had decided on January 17. The fact that the resolution and the act which was framed from it made no mention of taxation was no accident, for the act was designed to satisfy everyone. The members of Parliament, or by far the greater part of them, had derided Pitt's distinction between legislation and taxation. Grenville had expressed the sentiments of the house when he said, "That this kingdom has the sovereign, the supreme legislative power over America, is granted. It cannot be denied; and taxation is a part of that sovereign power."[44] The House should therefore be satisfied by the declaration of Parliament's legislative power even though it did not mention taxation specifically. Pitt and his followers, on the other hand, both in and out of Parliament, in both England and America, could be expected to agree to the declaration, since it merely asserted legislative authority.

Rockingham had taken great pains to keep the act in such general terms. When he sent the resolutions agreed upon by the Ministry to Charles Yorke, his Attorney General, for comments, Yorke noted that the assertion of the right to make laws for the colonies made no specific mention of taxation. Although Yorke doubtless subscribed to the notion that the right to tax was a part of the right to legislate, nevertheless the whole necessity for a declaratory act had arisen from a denial of Parliament's right to tax. Yorke accordingly suggested that the last phrase of the resolution be amended to read "as well in cases of Taxation, as in all other cases whatsoever."[45] This emendation would have left no room for

[43] *Parliamentary History*, XVI, 164.
[44] *Ibid.*, 101.
[45] Albemarle, *Memoirs of Rockingham*, I, 285-287. *Prologue to Revolution*, 141-142. In the Stowe Collection, Huntington Library, there is another draft of the resolution which contains the words "as well in all Cases of Impositions and Taxes, as in all other matters, and for all purposes whatsoever." Additional Mss., 35912, ff. 45-51, British Museum, marked "The within propositions vary in some particulars from those given to Mr. Yorke some time

doubt, but it would have offended Pitt and his followers, and Rockingham shrank from another bout with the Great Commoner. He therefore informed Yorke, in a letter dated January 25, that the word taxation could not appear. "I think I may say," he politely wrote, for his relations with Yorke were not altogether friendly, "that it is our firm Resolution in the House of Lords—I mean among ourselves—that that word must be resisted."[46]

Yorke was not the only Whig dissatisfied with the ambiguous character of the resolution. The Archbishop of Canterbury wrote to the Duke of Newcastle urging that the resolution be "sufficiently vigorous," lest the opposition introduce "extravagant and hurtful" ones and gain "the sole Merit of whatever may be good in those resolutions."[47] Though Rockingham spoke of the firm resolution of his party in the House of Lords, the Earl of Hardwicke, Yorke's brother, to whom Rockingham later offered a seat in the Cabinet, likewise thought that taxation should be specifically mentioned. Hardwicke was so concerned about the matter that when he saw the resolutions which were to be introduced in the House of Lords, he wrote to his brother, observing that "The question about *the right* is in general terms—all cases *whatsoever*. I presume it is the same in your House. Tell me *what you will do*, if taxation is proposed to be inserted. The Ministers desire to flatter North America, not to make it subordinate to this country."[48]

Evidently Hardwicke thought it likely that the opposition would introduce a specific assertion of Parliament's right to

---

ago," proposes a resolution affirming Parliament's power "to make Laws (whether of Taxation, or not) binding upon all the colonies." The origin of these two documents is not indicated.

[46] Additional Mss., 35430, ff. 37-38, British Museum. Albemarle, *Memoirs of Rockingham*, I, 287-288, prints this letter in a slightly different form: the words "must not be inserted" are substituted for "must be resisted." This may be a misreading of the manuscript, or perhaps Albemarle used a different copy of the letter. In either case the meaning is the same. *Prologue to Revolution*, 142.

[47] Additional Mss., 32973, f. 332, British Museum.

[48] January 28, 1766, Albemarle, *Memoirs of Rockingham*, I, 291.

tax and felt tempted to break ranks and vote for such a measure. As the event turned out, it became unnecessary for the
opposition to propose any mention of taxation in the Declaratory Act, because of a move by the man who had all but
dictated the terms of the Act: William Pitt. When Conway
introduced the resolve for the act in the House of Commons,
he implied that it was a wholesale assertion of Parliament's
authority. As a result, Pitt as well as the other members concluded that, although taxation was not mentioned, the words
"in all cases whatsoever" were intended to include it. Colonel Barré, an adherent of Pitt, moved as an amendment, that
the words "in all cases whatsoever" should be struck out.
Barré, in arguing for his amendment, and Pitt in supporting
him, both contended simply that Parliament had no right to
tax the colonies.[49] In the House of Lords Lord Camden
argued the same point.[50] Since the arguments were directed
against the phrase "in all cases whatsoever," the members of
Parliament interpreted the inclusion of this phrase to mean
that the declaration extended to the right of taxation. Why
Pitt and Barré and Camden should have insisted on drawing
out this explicit meaning from the words is not apparent.
Pitt himself had said that the declaration should "extend to
every point of legislation whatsoever." It is difficult to see
how the Act which was passed departed from this prescrip-
tion. The debate over the inclusion of "all cases whatsoever"
only served to accomplish, for the members of Parliament at
least, what Charles Yorke would have accomplished by a specific mention of taxation. If the Act had passed without debate
on this point, it would have been possible for Pitt and other
friends of the colonies to argue later that it did not include
the right to tax. As it was, the meaning was entirely clear to
the men who passed the Act, and the meaning was that Parliament had full authority to tax the colonies.

After passing the Declaratory Act, Parliament reluctantly

[49] *Maryland Historical Magazine*, 6 (1911), 287-305; *American
Historical Review*, 17 (1912), 565-574. *Prologue to Revolution*,
148-154.
[50] *Archives of Maryland*, XIV, 267-268; *Parliamentary History*,
XVI, 177-181.

agreed to repeal the Stamp Act: the issue was in doubt until the end. As one of the merchants put it, "today the Ministry wou'd have the best of it, and things would look well; tomorrow Grenville and his Party wou'd gain the Power, and then of course *no* Repeal."[51] On the evening of February 7 Grenville kept the House of Commons debating until eleven o'clock on a motion he introduced for enforcement.[52] The prospect of civil war, which the members recognized would be the outcome of such a move, was probably responsible in part for the defeat of the motion by 140 votes. But as late as February 8 the *London Chronicle* reported the opinion that the Act would be enforced. The King, after signifying to the Ministry his approval of repeal, let it be known privately that he favored modification.[53] The Ministry, for a desperate moment, even considered resigning. Feelings ran high within Parliament and without. The debates went on night after night till the early hours. After it was all over, one weary merchant wrote to his American friends, "I have been one of those that have attended the House of Commons early and late, or rather late and early, about the American affairs, . . . I am glad this ugly affair is over, for we are heartily tired, and have slaved like horses, sometimes not coming home till two or three o'clock in the morning, and then perhaps fasting."[54] When the crucial debate on the resolution for repeal was held in the committee of the whole on Friday, February 21, the members began arriving at eight o'clock in the morning to reserve their seats. Repeal did not finally carry until two o'clock Saturday morning, by a vote of 275 to 167, with

[51] Henry Cruger, Jr., to Henry Cruger, February 15, 1766, Massachusetts Historical Society, *Collections*, 69 (1914), 139-142.

[52] The debate took place February 7 (Albemarle, *Memoirs of Rockingham*, I, 298). It is described in Henry Cruger, Jr.'s letter, Massachusetts Historical Society, *Collections*, 69 (1914), 139-143; and in notes taken by Nathaniel Ryder, quoted in Gipson, *British Empire before the American Revolution, 10*, 392. The substance of the motion may be found in the papers of the Stowe Collection, Huntington Library.

[53] Massachusetts Historical Society, *Collections*, 69 (1914), 139-142; Albemarle, *Memoirs of Rockingham*, I, 302-303.

[54] *Georgia Gazette*, June 4, 1766.

fifty-two of the King's placeholders voting with the opposition by his permission.[55]

Though the bill had yet to undergo three readings and passage by the Lords, it had survived the critical test, and the people of England did not wait to rejoice. Saturday morning, as soon as the news was abroad, the bells of London's churches began to ring and continued to ring all day. The captains of the West India ships in the Thames broke out their colors, and as the news reached other towns the rejoicing spread all over England. For in spite of the powerful opposition in Parliament, popular opinion had been overwhelmingly for repeal. The economic depression in England was acute and in the minds of the people who suffered most seriously from it, the Stamp Act was to blame. Manufacturers now began rehiring their workers, and ships put out for America with cargoes of British textiles and messages which would spread the rejoicing to America too. "It is repealed, my friend," said one of the messages, "to the universal joy of Britain . . . Had it not been so, there is the strongest reason to think that by this time there would have been more formidable commotions here than any that have been on your side of the Atlantick."[56]

Both Englishmen and Americans had cause to rejoice, for rebellion and civil war had been avoided and the strength of the empire preserved. Unfortunately repeal did not put back into the limbo of ambiguity the words which had been spoken so often in the preceding two years, "the rights of Englishmen" and "the authority of Parliament." Grenville had given a meaning to one phrase, and the colonists to the other, which repeal of the Stamp Act could not erase.

[55] *Virginia Gazette* (Purdie), April 25, 1766. Winstanley, *Personal and Party Government*, 268, 305-306; Chesterfield, *Letters*, VI, 2716.

[56] *Virginia Gazette* (Purdie), April 25, June 13, 1766.

Chapter XVI

Conclusion

ONE OF THE principal arguments which the opposition had used against repeal of the Stamp Act was that the colonies would interpret it as a sign of weakness, that whatever reason Parliament assigned for repeal, the Americans would believe that their own resistance had been the real cause. The friends of the colonies took care to inform their correspondents in America that the violence against the stamp distributors had prolonged the struggle for repeal and had even threatened to prevent it entirely. Letters sent by the committee of merchants in London to the merchants of the principal towns and cities of North America urged the Americans not to exult in the victory as a point gained over Parliamentary authority. Any such attitude would surely strengthen the hand of Grenville and his followers, who might still return to power and undo the great work of reconciliation. The merchants had had a hard fight, in which they had "pawned their words" for the colonies, and "I hope," one of them wrote, "nothing will be done, that may make them ashamed of the assurances they have given, that all would return to quiet and good humour. A contrary behaviour will hurt the present ministry, who are your true friends; and if they fall, your enemies will succeed, from whom you have everything to fear." In order to prevent such a catastrophe, the committee urged the Americans to send over expressions of "filial duty and gratitude to your parent country."[1]

These words were made more pointed by two protests issuing from the minority in the House of Lords against re-

---

[1] Massachusetts Historical Society, *Proceedings*, 55 (1923), 215-223; *ibid.*, 2d ser., 11 (1897), 446-448; *Newport Mercury*, May 12, 1766; *Georgia Gazette*, June 4, 1766. *Prologue to Revolution*, 157-158.

peal of the Stamp Act. Some thirty-three peers published to the country at large, with the sanction of their own illustrious names, the accusations which Anti-Sejanus had been making in the London press. Repeal of the Stamp Act, they said, was a surrender of Parliament's supreme jurisdiction. The reasons the Americans had assigned for disobedience to the Act would extend "to all other laws, of what nature soever, which that Parliament had enacted, or shall enact, to bind them in times to come, and must, if admitted, set them absolutely free from any obedience to the power of the British legislature." By the Declaratory Act, they said, Parliament only "more grievously injured its own dignity and authority by verbally asserting that right which it substantially yields up to its opposition."[2] The total effect would be to push the colonies in the direction toward which they were already verging—independence. In the protests of the Lords the Americans could read the narrowness of their escape as well as their future peril, and they hastened to comply with the advice of the merchants, which had been seconded by Secretary Conway in sending official notice of the repeal. The assemblies of the various colonies drew up addresses of thanks to King and Parliament for their parental solicitude and gave assurance of their loyalty to the King and their submission to the authority of Parliament—though none of them specifically acknowledged that this authority included the right to tax them.[3]

In spite of the loyal sentiments of their addresses, the colonists would have been a little more than human if they had not given themselves some of the credit for repeal. "Had we tamely submitted," they asked themselves, "would the Justice of our Cause have procured us Relief?"[4] Probably few

---

[2] *Parliamentary History of England*, XVI, 181-193.

[3] See note 20 and *Colonial Records of Georgia*, XIV, 380-381; *Colonial Records of North Carolina*, VII, 332-334; *Pennsylvania Archives*, 8th ser., 7 (1935), 5884-5885; J. Almon, ed., *A Collection of Interesting, Authentic Papers, . . .* (London, 1777), 109-110; Nathaniel Bouton, ed., *Provincial Papers: Documents and Records Relating to the Province of New Hampshire*, VII (Nashua, 1873), 106.

[4] *Virginia Gazette* (Rind), May 30, 1766.

could find it in their hearts to say yes. And if any colonists had heard the debates over repeal in Parliament, they would have perceived that some members had indeed shrunk from the difficulty of putting down a rebellion by military force. American resistance, however embarrassing to the merchants, perhaps affected the outcome more favorably than Englishmen liked to admit. Americans went too far, however, when they supposed that they had won acceptance of their view of Parliamentary authority. Thomas Moffat, returning to New England in the latter part of the year, wrote back to a friend in London, "The prevailing notions about the persons, measures, and principles upon which the Stamp Act was repealed would extremely divert you who might not expect so godly a people to be left under so many or so great delusions."[5] Thomas Hutchinson, looking back upon the period some years later, thought that repeal was interpreted throughout the colonies, not as an act of favor, but as a concession to the colonial view that taxation was the power only of a representative body.[6]

The celebrations with which repeal was greeted were decent and orderly, as the committee of merchants had urged. True, the Sheriff of Falmouth (Portland, Maine) was inspired by what he had drunk to ride his horse into the Townhouse and up the stairs, but the rest of the celebrators quietly placed him in the stocks.[7] In Philadelphia, the newspapers reported that "notwithstanding the GREAT and GLORIOUS cause of our present Rejoicings, not one single instance of that Kind of Triumph, so much dreaded by our Friends, and wished for by our Enemies in England, has escaped the warmest Sons of Liberty in this City."[8] Up and down the Atlantic coast, houses were illuminated; paintings and verses composed for the occasion were exhibited; and toasts were drunk publicly to William Pitt and the other men who had cham-

[5] December 12, 1766, Bancroft Transcripts, New York Public Library.

[6] Hutchinson, *History of Massachusetts-Bay,* L. S. Mayo, ed., III, 121.

[7] Joseph Kent to Charles Miller, May 23, 1766, Sullivan Papers, I, Massachusetts Historical Society.

[8] *Pennsylvania Gazette,* May 22, 1766.

pioned the cause of the colonies in Parliament; but the most significant thing about the celebrations was that they were directed by the Sons of Liberty, the men responsible for the violent proceedings which according to the Committee of Merchants had hindered repeal. The Sons of Liberty showed no contrition for their sins. Not only did they direct celebrations of repeal in 1766, but they also staged celebrations upon the anniversary of repeal every year thereafter, until the Revolution began. In Boston they even celebrated the anniversary of August 14, the night of their first riot.[9] Thus the Sons of Liberty kept alive the memory of the glorious days when Americans had risen up against the threat of tyranny and had successfully asserted their rights.

This interpretation of the repeal of the Stamp Act was rendered the more easy by the general terms in which Rockingham had couched the Declaratory Act. After the debate over Barré's motion to omit the words, "in all cases whatsoever," the meaning of the Act was plain to members of Parliament, so plain that one unofficial report of the resolves which formed the basis of the Act summarized it as saying "That the King, Lords, and Commons of this realm have always had, and ought to have the undoubted right to tax the colonies."[10] But the session of Parliament in which the debate took place was a secret one with no visitors allowed. Hugh Hamersley, the secretary to Lord Baltimore, wrote to Governor Sharpe of Maryland that he could give him no report of what had happened in the House of Commons, because "they have throughout the business shut their doors against all strangers."[11] Reports did reach the colonies from members of Parliament who happened to be colonial agents. Charles Garth sent a full report of the debate to the Maryland Assembly.[12] But many colonists, unaware of what had passed in Parliament, were puzzled by the Declaratory Act.

[9] Massachusetts Historical Society, *Proceedings,* 2d ser., 10 (1895), 63, 66; John Adams, *Works,* C. F. Adams, ed., II, 218; *Boston Gazette,* August 21, 1769.

[10] *Newport Mercury,* April 28, 1766.

[11] February 20, 1766, *Archives of Maryland,* XIV, 272.

[12] *Maryland Historical Magazine,* 6 (1911), 287-305.

Though the early reports had said that it asserted Parliament's right to tax, when the actual texts of the resolution and of the Act were reported, it was apparent that Parliament had made no mention of taxation. Ezra Stiles noted that the Act "declared the most absolute parliamentary Authority in Legislation yet with a seeming Ambiguity, as to power of Taxation."[13] John Adams, reading the resolve in the Boston newspapers, observed that it asserted Parliament's right "to make laws for the Colonies in all cases whatever," and wondered "whether they will lay a tax in consequence of that resolution, or what kind of a law they will make."[14] James Otis, on the other hand, assured the Boston town meeting that the Act "had no relation to Taxes," or so at least Governor Bernard was told.[15]

If Otis and others placed such an interpretation on the Act, it was not without reason. Rockingham had deliberately omitted any mention of taxation, and Conway in speaking to Dennys De Berdt, an agent of Massachusetts, told him that the Ministry had been opposed to any Declaratory Act but had been obliged to accept one in order to get a majority for repeal. Conway hoped that the Americans would understand the Act in that light.[16] Richard Jackson, the other agent of Massachusetts, dismissed the Act as a formality. He wrote on March 3, 1766, that repeal "could not have been obtained without another act for declaring the right of Parliament to bind the colonies by laws in all cases whatsoever; which will probably as little prejudice them, as the power we claim in Ireland, the manner of exercising which you are acquainted with."[17] The Massachusetts Assembly was well acquainted with the extent of Parliament's authority in Ireland. They knew, and had stated in an address designed to

---

[13] Stiles to Samuel Langdon, May 24, 1766, Stiles Papers, Yale University Library.

[14] *Works*, II, 192.

[15] Bernard to Shelburne, December 22, 1766, Bernard Papers, IV, 282, Harvard College Library.

[16] De Berdt to Samuel White, February 15, 1766, Colonial Society of Massachusetts, *Publications*, 13 (1912), 312.

[17] Alden Bradford, ed., *Speeches of the Governors of Massachusetts*, 72; Massachusetts Archives, XXII, 458.

be sent to the King in 1764, that Parliament "have never laid any Duty or Tax on the Subjects of Ireland, though that hath ever been deemed, and acknowledgeth it self to be a dependent Kingdom."[18] Daniel Dulany, even though he must have had access to Garth's letter describing the debate over the Act, later argued that the Declaratory Act did not affirm an authority to tax, because if such were the case the Declaratory Act of 6 George I would give a similar authority to Parliament in Ireland. Since it was admitted, he said, that Parliament had no right to tax Ireland, similarly, in spite of the Declaratory Act, Parliament had no right to tax the colonies.[19]

There is no evidence that the Americans, in rejoicing over repeal of the Stamp Act, accepted the right of Parliament to tax them. Many of their loyal addresses of thanks upon the repeal, were phrased so as to reject any such admission. They rejoiced at repeal of the "late unconstitutional Stamp Act," which had "Endanger'd both their Liberty and Property"; they expressed submission to "the rightfull Authority of the British Parliament" or "constitutional subordination" to Parliament, but they maintained that their struggles against the Stamp Act were "not those of Rebellion or Disaffection, But those of Freemen," and were "compatible with the English Constitution."[20] The vague terms of the Declaratory Act enabled them to accept it as a statement of their own position: that Parliament had supreme legislative authority, but that taxation was not a part of legislation.

William Pitt himself had spectacularly supported the American position in Parliament, and the American press like the British press gave to Pitt the credit for carrying the repeal. He had asserted plainly the power of Parliament in all branches of legislation whatsoever, but he had stoutly denied Parliament's right to tax. Upon reading his speech of

[18] Massachusetts Archives, XXII, 415.

[19] Letter to Conway, undated, Sparks Manuscripts, 44, Bundle 7, Harvard College Library.

[20] *Journals of the House of Burgesses of Virginia 1766–1769*, 34; *Archives of the State of New Jersey*, 1st ser., 9 (1885), 560-561; Massachusetts Historical Society, *Proceedings*, 57 (1924), 353-355; Bradford, *Speeches of the Governors of Massachusetts*, 91-92.

January 14, John Adams wrote in his diary: "What has been said in America which Mr. Pitt has not confirmed? Otis, Adams, Hopkins, &c. have said no more."[21] Since they believed that repeal was the work of Pitt many Americans must have found it hard to believe that the Declaratory Act should be interpreted as a denial of everything he had said. George Mason of Virginia observed that the Act asserted the "legislative authority" of Great Britain in all cases whatsoever, but he remembered that "a just and necessary Distinction between Legislation and Taxation hath been made by the greatest and wisest men in the Nation," for surely Pitt was one of the greatest and wisest. Mason noticed, however, that the Act did not specifically disavow the authority to tax, and just as Charles Yorke thought that the Act should have specifically claimed such an authority, Mason thought it should have specifically disclaimed it. Such a disclaimer, he said "wou'd not have impeached or weakened the Vote of Right; on the Contrary it wou'd have strengthened it."[22]

When the Americans did come to realize that the Declaratory Act was intended to affirm the right of taxation, they were by no means ready to accept it. To some this realization came much earlier than is generally supposed. One Virginian apparently saw the Act in this light as soon as he read it. In a letter signed "A British American," which appeared in the *Virginia Gazette* on May 2, 1766, he advised the assemblies of all the American colonies "to take no further notice of the declaration of the British Parliament should it be laid before them than to pay it the respect of ordering it to be laid upon the table for the perusal of the members and without mentioning any thing of the proceedings of parliament to enter upon their journals as strong declarations of their own rights as words can express." This letter was reprinted in the newspapers of other colonies during the summer of 1766, and must have started the inhabitants thinking about the meaning of the Act. The Providence Sons of

[21] *Works*, II, 191.
[22] Kate M. Rowland, *The Life of George Mason, 1725–1792* (New York, 1892), I, 383, original in Library of Congress. *Prologue to Revolution*, 159.

Liberty evidently gave some attention to the matter, for by July 21 their secretary Silas Downer was writing to the Sons of Liberty in New York, urging the necessity of maintaining their organization and their intercolonial connections, because of Parliament's "passing a Law, wherein is affirmed in the strongest Terms a parliamentary Authority and Right to Tax us, to the great prejudice of the Crown, and of the Liberties of America, so that a Way might be ready paved for such Impositions in future, as might coincide with their Systems of Wealth, Power, and Dominion."[23]

In South Carolina Christopher Gadsden pointed out to the local Sons of Liberty that the Declaratory Act was not as harmless as it seemed. He called attention to its preamble, which denied the validity of the colonial resolutions. If Parliament thought these invalid, then Parliament was still claiming the right to tax, and such a claim the colonies must never admit.[24]

Those who perceived the true meaning of the Declaratory Act also perceived that the Americans had small reason to display the gratitude which the merchants had insisted upon, for both Parliament and the merchants had been motivated by a concern for the welfare of England rather than America. A Virginian who signed himself "Algernon Sydney" pointed out that "The Relief they have given is professedly for their own Sakes, not ours."[25] Silas Downer likewise saw that "the Merchants trading to America, whose only Business is the Accumulation of Wealth, solicited the Repeal from Principles of Convenience to themselves; at the same Time holding fast the deleterious Doctrine of a certain Supremacy of the British People over the Americans, and never urging the least Argument in our Favor, founded on the Views whereon the American Opposition was built, but utterly discounting any such."[26] And George Mason ridiculed the merchants for speaking to the colonists like schoolboys, as if to say:

[23] Peck Manuscripts, III, Rhode Island Historical Society.

[24] Edward McCrady, *The History of South Carolina under the Royal Government, 1719–1776* (New York, 1899), 590.

[25] *Virginia Gazette* (Rind), May 30, 1766.

[26] To the New York Sons of Liberty, July 21, 1766, Peck Manuscripts, III.

We have with infinite difficulty and fatigue got you excused this one time; pray be a good boy for the future, do what your papa and mama bid you, and hasten to return them your most grateful acknowledgments for condescending to let you keep what is your own; and then all your acquaintance will love you, and praise you, and give you pretty things; . . . Is not this a little ridiculous, when applied to three millions of as loyal and useful subjects as any in the British dominions, who have been only contending for their birth-right, and have now only gained, or rather kept, what could not, with common justice, or even policy, be denied them?[27]

Not all Americans were able to see as soon as Mason and Downer the implications of what Parliament had done, and even they missed the larger significance of the Declaratory Act. Perhaps even Rockingham failed to understand that his Act assigned a greater authority to Parliament than Grenville had originally claimed with his Stamp Act. Grenville had justified taxing the colonies on the ground that they were represented—virtually—in Parliament. Repeal of the Stamp Act, unaccompanied by the Declaratory Act, could have been utilized as a demonstration that virtual representation worked. Though the Americans did not elect a single member, Parliament had been sufficiently sensitive to their interests, as expressed through the British merchants, to repeal a measure they disliked. What better answer than this to the American claim that virtual representation could not cross the ocean? But the Declaratory Act precluded such an interpretation of repeal, for it rendered unnecessary the pretence of linking taxation and representation, and rested the authority of Parliament on a simple declaration of that body's sovereignty. It was no sooner passed than the *London Gazetteer* announced, "As we are informed it is now decided that the legislature of this Kingdom hath a right to levy taxes on America, we beg leave to inform our correspondents that we can no longer admit any letters in which that right is in any

---

[27] Rowland, *Life of Mason*, I, 382. *Prologue to Revolution*, 159.

wise controverted."[28] In spite of this announcement public discussion of course continued, but officially there was no longer any doubt that Parliament had authority to tax the colonies, and there was no longer any need to justify that authority by the doctrine of virtual representation. The British government had abandoned the constitutional position which linked them with the Americans and had retreated to the heights of arbitrary declaration.

It is possible, of course, that if Rockingham and his friends had stayed in power the Declaratory Act might have remained a harmless gesture. But the mere fact that the Act had been necessary in order to get repeal through Parliament was a sign that Rockingham's desire to avoid the issue which it presented was not generally shared. His control of Parliament had been tenuous at best, and in the summer of 1766 he gave way to a ministry headed at last by Pitt. It was one of the ironies in the career of that ailing and temperamental genius that the next measure for taxing the colonies was passed by an administration in which he was nominally the leader. As the years went by the government fell more and more into the grasp of men who believed with George Grenville that the Stamp Act should have been enforced instead of repealed. In their hands the Declaratory Act became an official permit (presented to them by their opponents), authorizing them to secure from the Americans that "peppercorn in acknowledgement of the right," which they regarded as of more value than millions without. It is not impossible that a ministry disposed to moderation might have obtained money from America without reviving the conflict between colonies and Parliament: in return for the voluntary contributions which the Americans offered to make if called upon in a constitutional manner, Parliament might have been persuaded to leave its avowed authority unexercised. But the men in control after the fall of Rockingham were not interested in voluntary contributions and would not leave the question of right alone.

In the eyes of these men the Americans had been aiming

28 Quoted by W. T. Laprade, *American Historical Review*, 35 (1930), 752. Cf. *London Chronicle*, March 4-6, 1766.

at independence ever since the Peace of Paris. It was a common observation in the mid-eighteenth century that the colonies would not forever remain as dependencies of Great Britain. No one who considered the extent of the North American continent and the rate at which its population was increasing could doubt the truth of the observation, though the separation was scarcely expected to take place in the eighteenth century. Many Englishmen had warned before the Peace of Paris that if Canada were not returned to the French the Americans would no longer feel the need of the British army and navy to protect them and would turn their faces toward independence.[29] When these warnings were ignored and the French menace was ended by the Peace of Paris, the prophets of doom saw their fears justified in the ensuing American resistance to the Stamp Act. Anti-Sejanus told the people of England that "The Americans imbibe notions of independance and liberty with their very milk, and will some time or other shake off all subjection. If we yield to them in this particular, by repealing the Stamp-Act, it is all over; they will from that moment assert their freedom."[30] Rockingham and the merchants by arguing that the Americans objected only to internal taxation had been able to persuade a majority of Parliament that repeal of the Stamp Act would not encourage the movement of the colonies to independence. When the colonies next objected to the external taxes levied by the Townshend duties, many members of Parliament must have been convinced that Anti-Sejanus had been right. The Americans, it appeared, were working their way by gradual stages to the point where they would be completely independent, first freedom from internal taxes, then from external taxes. The Acts of Trade would be next. Little by little the supremacy of the mother country would

[29] See Alvord, *Mississippi Valley in British Politics,* ch. 2.
[30] *London Chronicle,* February 11-13, 1766; cf. *ibid.,* March 22-25, 1766; *Parliamentary History,* XVI, 181-193; Thomas Penn to John Penn, January 11, 1766, Penn Correspondence, Historical Society of Pennsylvania; Thomas Martin to Daniel Rindge, December 24, 1765, Wentworth Papers, New Hampshire Historical Society.

be whittled away until the last bond was severed. The movement must be halted or at least retarded before it went any farther. Granted that America would one day become independent, there was no reason why that event should take place while the American population was little more than a quarter of Great Britain's.

As the English thought that they saw the Americans inching their way toward independence, the Americans thought that they saw a sinister party in England seeking by gradual degrees to enslave them. There had been rumors of a plan to reorganize the colonies ever since the fall of Quebec, and Governor Bernard had intimated that the Stamp Act was a part of that plan. But to Americans a plan that included taxation of an unrepresented people could have been engineered only by men intending them evil. Moreover, the act had been more than a tax: it had extended the jurisdiction of the admiralty courts in such a way as to eliminate the right of Americans to trial by jury in cases where Englishmen had jealously preserved it for themselves. Moreover, the act had envisaged taxes on documents used in ecclesiastical courts, thus implying that such courts would be established in the colonies. Ezra Stiles believed that if the act had succeeded, the revenue from it would have been used to support Anglican bishops in America. Even William Samuel Johnson, who would have welcomed the establishment of bishops, thought that the ministry must have had a "formal design" constantly in view for several years. "Fortunately," he wrote in January, 1766, "they have of late precipitated their Measures and by that means opened our Eyes. Had they proceeded by slow and insensible degrees as they have been wont to do perhaps in a course of years they might have effected their baneful purpose. But by pressing it too much and making more haste than good speed they have defeated the whole design and given such an Alarm as will forever keep America upon her guard."[31]

[31] To Christopher Gadsden, January 10, 1766, William Samuel Johnson Papers, Connecticut Historical Society. Stiles to Samuel Langdon, May 24, 1766, Stiles Papers, Yale University Library. On the colonial fear of Anglican bishops in relation to the Stamp Act, see Bridenbaugh, *Mitre and Sceptre*, ch. 9.

With the repeal of the Stamp Act many Americans, misinterpreting the meaning of the Declaratory Act, believed that the plot had been foiled, and when Rockingham was replaced by Pitt, they rejoiced that their fastest friend was now in control. When the attempt to tax them was renewed under a ministry with Pitt at the head, they could see that the repeal was only a pause in the relentless advance of the plot to enslave them, and the vagueness of the Declaratory Act an effort to lull them into delusions of security, while stronger chains were fastened about them.

Thus while Rockingham had been able to hide from Parliament the full extent of the Americans' objection to its authority and from the Americans the full extent of Parliament's assertion of it, he had actually heightened the incompatibility of the two positions. When this incompatibility became evident, as it soon did, the happy misunderstanding he had fostered served only to exaggerate the difference. The English were encouraged to believe that the Americans were seeking independence in easy stages and the Americans to think that the English were trying to enslave them by slow and insensible degrees. The situation was not irretrievable, but to retrieve it would have required an understanding on each side of the exact limits of the other's claims. Such an understanding was rendered difficult at best by the illusions that now existed on both sides of the water as a result of the Stamp Act. But even if an understanding could have been achieved, reconciliation would have required also a willingness to compromise, for while neither side had such extravagant aims as the other supposed, there was nevertheless a genuine and irreconcilable conflict between Parliament's insistence on its authority to tax the colonies and the Americans' denial of that authority.

Unfortunately the Stamp Act period had not merely created illusions about the aims of both Englishmen and Americans but had also impaired the disposition to compromise in both countries and had in some cases discredited the men who would have been willing to do so. The circumstances that enabled Lord North to retain power from 1770 to 1782 were complex, but undoubtedly one reason was the conviction of most members of Parliament after 1768 that the repeal of the Stamp Act had been a mistake. Certainly this conviction was expressed again and again on the floor of the House of Commons, and the Whigs felt obliged to apologize for the measure which had staved off revolution in 1766.

In America too the Stamp Act had discredited moderates and enabled extremists to gain greater influence than they had ever enjoyed before. To be sure there must have been many Americans who would have taken the side of England if worst had come to worst in 1766, and some of these, not having been obliged to declare themselves, retained whatever influence in colonial politics they may have had before. In some cases a man's political career might even survive an open opposition to the riots of 1765. Joseph Galloway continued to sit in the Pennsylvania Assembly and to play an important part in public life in spite of the aid and comfort he had given to John Hughes. But there can be no doubt that the Stamp Act destroyed the popular prestige of many men who might have kept a restraining hand on their countrymen in the years that followed. In Rhode Island those who had sought a royal government were flushed into the open and disgraced. In Massachusetts Governor Bernard could no longer account himself a popular governor, and Thomas Hutchinson, though people might think that the resentment against him had gone too far, could never again claim the prestige which his long public career had formerly assured him. John Hughes was no longer a factor in Pennsylvania. Jared Ingersoll and Thomas Fitch were politically dead in Connecticut.

The withdrawal of men such as these from public life was accompanied by the rise of bolder and more aggressive politicians who had made their reputation in resistance to the Stamp Act. The part that a man had played in 1765 was not the criterion of his political success in every colony; and it would be wrong to suggest that the American Revolution was brought about entirely by the men who led the resistance to the Stamp Act. By 1776 some of the leaders of 1765 had died and some, for example Daniel Dulany, had gone over to the other side. Nevertheless, of the twenty-seven members of the

Stamp Act Congress, only John Cruger, William Bayard, William Samuel Johnson, and Timothy Ruggles are known to have been loyalist or neutral in 1776,[32] and Ruggles had refused to approve the proceedings of the congress. On the other hand several of the members: Gadsden, Rutledge, Dickinson, Bryan, Rodney, R. R. Livingston, Eliphalet Dyer, and Otis took leading roles in the subsequent pre-revolutionary agitation. Others who took no part in the congress but led the resistance to the Stamp Act within their own colonies were likewise conspicuous in the revolutionary movement. It seems particularly significant that the men who brought on the revolution in the two leading colonies, Massachusetts and Virginia, gained their ascendancy at the time of the Stamp Act.

In Virginia the Stamp Act provided the opportunity for Patrick Henry's spectacular entry into politics. Perhaps the most significant thing about the conflicting stories of Henry's speech for the Stamp Act Resolves is the fact that it was later remembered as more violent than it actually was. Henry had a long and fiery career in Virginia politics, and when men looked back upon it after it was over, they remembered the Stamp Act as the time when he had first assumed the leadership of the House of Burgesses. Richard Henry Lee, Henry's right-hand man in the revolutionary movement, likewise stepped into political prominence at the time of the Stamp Act. Lee, like Henry, saw the Act as a threat to the rights of Englishmen, and like Henry also, he saw it as an opportunity to break his way into a position of greater influence. When he first heard of it, he was so oblivious to the principle involved that he applied for the position of Stamp Distributor, but soon—within a few days, he claimed—recognized his mistake and withdrew the request. Instead he took upon himself the leadership of the Sons of Liberty in Virginia, and organized riots to force the resignation of Mercer and to punish a merchant who expressed a wish to clear ships with stamped papers. In vain did the Mercers later reveal to the public that Lee had applied for the position of Distributor. In the course of the resistance he had demonstrated his opposi-

[32] I am indebted to an unpublished study of the subsequent careers of the members by David S. Lovejoy.

tion to the Act so consistently that he remained a popular hero and finally offered the resolution at Philadelphia with which American independence began.[33]

In Massachusetts the men who had followed Otis's fitful leadership in the Stamp Act crisis made unequivocal use of the episode to crush their opponents after repeal. On April 14 and May 5, 1766, they inserted in the *Boston Gazette* a warning to the freemen not to vote for anyone in the coming elections who was known to be a supporter of the Stamp Act, and lest there be any doubt as to whom they meant, they explained that a supporter of the Stamp Act was anyone who had opposed vigorous measures against it.

James Otis continued to be the leading spirit in the Massachusetts Assembly until he lost his sanity in 1769. Then his lieutenant, Samuel Adams, took over. Otis's political career had begun before the Stamp Act, but it was the Stamp Act which had given him the greatest power and notoriety in spite of his occasional lapses into a legalistic and obscure sort of loyalism. Samuel Adams, on the other hand, seems to have first come into view as a political leader at the time of the Stamp Act, with the drafting of the Massachusetts Resolves of October 25, 1765. Between them Otis and Adams called the tune for the Massachusetts Assembly from the time of the Stamp Act to the final dissolution of that body by General Gage. During this time they made life miserable for both Bernard and Hutchinson as well as for John Robinson, who came to Boston as Commissioner of the Customs in 1768. Probably no American did more than Samuel Adams to bring on the revolutionary crisis.[34]

Besides disposing the colonies to accept radical leadership the Stamp Act period furnished those leaders with a method for bringing pressure to bear in England. Hitherto the colonies had never been able to unite for any purpose, not even

[33] Ballagh, ed., *Letters of Richard Henry Lee,* I, 16; *Virginia Gazette* (Purdie and Dixon), October 3, 1766. See also Thad W. Tate, "The Coming of the Revolution in Virginia," *William and Mary Quarterly,* 3d ser. 19 (1962), 323-343.

[34] John C. Miller, *Sam Adams, Pioneer in Propaganda* (Boston, 1936), 48-81.

for their own defense against the French and Indians. The Stamp Act, much to their own surprise, enabled them to act together. "The Ministry never Imagined we would or could so generally Unite in opposition to their measures," William Samuel Johnson wrote exultantly, "nor I confess till I saw the Experiment made did I. . . ."[35] The most spectacular achievement in unity was of course the Stamp Act Congress, but the non-importation agreements adopted by the merchants of Boston, New York, and Philadelphia were equally surprising and more effective. If the merchants in any of these cities had chosen to continue importations, they would have profited heavily from the abstinence of the others. Their unanimity affected British exports sufficiently to give the British merchants an urgent reason to wish for repeal. Still further unity had been achieved among the Sons of Liberty in preventing the use of stamps in any colony from Maine to Georgia and in beginning the intercolonial union which was projected at New London on December 25 and which was making rapid progress when the Act was repealed. Observing all these signs of the united strength of the colonies, Joseph Warren in March of 1766 wrote to his friend Edmund Dana that Grenville's measures had brought about "what the most zealous Colonist never could have expected! The Colonies until now were ever at variance and foolishly jealous of each other, they are now . . . united . . . nor will they soon forget the weight which this close union gives them."[36]

The colonies remembered the strength of union well enough, as they demonstrated later in their non-importation agreements against the Townshend Duties, in their continental congresses, and finally in their formation of a continental army. Yet in the last analysis the significance of the Stamp Act crisis lies in the emergence, not of leaders and methods and organizations, but of well-defined constitutional principles. The resolutions of the colonial and intercolonial assemblies in

[35] William Samuel Johnson to Christopher Gadsden, January 10, June 25, 1766, William Samuel Johnson Papers, Connecticut Historical Society.

[36] Miscellaneous Manuscripts, 1765–1767, Massachusetts Historical Society.

1765 laid down the line on which Americans stood until they cut their connections with England. Consistently from 1765 to 1776 they denied the authority of Parliament to tax them externally or internally; consistently they affirmed their willingness to submit to whatever legislation Parliament should enact for the supervision of the empire as a whole. To be sure, by the time when the First Continental Congress was called in 1774 they had become convinced that Parliament had no more authority to legislate for them than to tax them (this had been the position of the most radical Americans in 1765). But even while thus extending their objections to Parliamentary authority, they agreed not to exercise their full rights but to consent voluntarily to Parliament's supervisory legislation.[37]

In spite of the radical temper of the colonial leaders the position taken in 1765 would have served as a basis for reconciliation at any time until the Declaration of Independence. There was, however, no middle ground, no intermediate line to which the colonists were willing to retreat in the face of British efforts to tax them. They "stood Bluff" in 1776 on the line they had drawn in 1765, and when the Ministry this time refused to recede from its demands, they fought.

[37] W. C. Ford and Gaillard Hunt, eds., *Journals of the Continental Congress* (Washington, 1904–1937), I, 68-69.

Chapter XVII
Epilogue

WHAT, THEN, OF the men who had urged submission and faith in the ultimate justice and wisdom of the mother country? These were the loyalists of '65 and this study would not be complete without a final reckoning of the price of their loyalty. England did what she could for them as she later did for the loyalists of '76. Parliament first recommended that the various assemblies reimburse anyone who had lost property in the riots. When it became apparent that the colonial governments would not comply, George Grenville was able to shame his fellow members into a resolution that the King should "bestow some mark of his favor upon those Governors and Officers in America who had suffered by their Loyalty."[1]

In accordance with this resolution, England conferred honors and offices upon the men who had tried to uphold her authority during the time of the Stamp Act. What England could do for them was a poor enough compensation for what they had lost. For nearly a lifetime they had dreamt their different dreams of power, prestige, and success and had suddenly found not only their dreams but their whole world gone up in the smoke of their burning effigies. England could not restore their dreams nor, try as she might, their world. But England could at least enable them to stay alive and wherever feasible help them to a new start in a different place.

Of those who appear in this book old John Hughes probably fared the best. After the riots and the threats had ceased, he retired to his country home, Walnut Grove, where he could be seen playing the farmer, an old man with a hoe hacking away at the weeds in his fields. Bewildered but unbowed, he would occasionally visit his Quaker neighbors, who still knew him for a friend if not a Friend, and enjoy the kind of bantering conversation in which he excelled. His reward came in 1769 when he was made Collector of Customs

[1] William Samuel Johnson to Samuel Johnson, May 18, 1767, Bancroft Transcripts, New York Public Library; to Jared Ingersoll, May 16, 1767, New Haven Colony Historical Society, *Papers*, 9 (1918), 405-408.

at Portsmouth, New Hampshire. He sold his house (where later the British troops would enjoy their last entertainment from the local loyalists before evacuating Philadelphia), and rode by coach to Portsmouth, enjoying as he passed the salutations of the gentry. "In going this long Journey," he wrote back to one of his old neighbors, "I often thought of ovids Metamorphosese and could hardly forbear Laughing when I recollected the old Gray headed fellow that used to be troting up and Down a meadow at Walnut Grove with the Resemblance of a Grubing hoe on his shoulder and his feet wet and Dirty and often times his Legs also but now Riding in Great State in a Coach and four pinked off like a Beau—and treated as a person of Consequence—with your most Humble Servant Mr Collector—you are heartily wilcome to our Town &c &c—then comes a Card—with the Compliments to the Collector &c &c to Request the favour of his Dining or supping with him as the time admitted—and as to see the old fellow sent to his lodgings in a chariot with a postilion behind and sometimes a Servant into the bargain—I say, when I considered these things Seriously I could not help Reflecting upon the folly and vanity of those persons who upon such a change (which is but Temporary) forget not only their former Acquaintance but themselves also and thereby Render themselves Ridiculous and Contemptible."[2]

John Hughes was not the man to forget his friends, and he had been more than a little hurt by the way in which his political party in Pennsylvania dropped him after the Stamp Act troubles, when they discovered that he was a liability. However, his engaging personality made him new friends quickly. In Portsmouth he was soon on the best of terms with Governor Wentworth, and when he left early in 1771 to become Collector at Charles Town, South Carolina, he carried Wentworth's introduction to the best families there. Though he wrote to his old neighbors in Pennsylvania that South Carolina in the winter was certainly the worst place in the world "for it Rains almost without Intermission, and there is a kind of raw Moist Cold in the air," he was nevertheless very happy there. So at least he persuaded himself. There was just

[2] To Jonathan Roberts, September 7, 1769, Hughes Papers, Historical Society of Pennsylvania.

a touch of homesickness in one of his last letters to his son, saying "Whatever may be the Sentiments of Pennsylvanians Relative to me, I have now the pleasure to say, that in the greatest of my popular Credit in that province, I was not by any Means as happy as I am now, it is true whilst I sacrificed my time and consequently my fortune to support a party I was a clever fellow, But when it became me to Discharge my Duty to my Sovereign, I was then with both parties a very bad man, here I have the pleasure to know, that from the Governor to the Meanest Merchant I am highly esteemed, nor is there a single man in the province but heartily wish me to Remain Amongst them." Hughes remained amongst them for more than a year, nursing his pride and indulging his love for conversation, but by the spring of 1772 he had died, hoping to gain "an acquaintance with, Innumerable other beings, of much superior knowledge, abilities and Sincerity," superior certainly to the men who had persecuted him for doing his duty to his sovereign.[3]

Jared Ingersoll received a commission in 1769 as Judge of the Vice-Admiralty Court at Philadelphia, but did not go there till 1771. When he did, the newspapers in Connecticut accused him of giving assistance to the enemies of the Susquehannah Company. The Philadelphians in turn could develop no great love for the Judge of an Admiralty Court. When the fighting began he hardly knew which way to turn. "I am Conscious," he wrote to his nephew in New Haven, "of having done no wrong to my Country and so I am inclined to fear none from it, . . . at the same time I consider myself like a Saint of old, as a Pilgrim and Stranger in the Earth having no Abiding City." In the end he sent his family back to New Haven but remained in Philadelphia himself, until Pennsylvania decided that she did not want him and shipped him off to Connecticut. He died there in 1781, having preserved, as his epitaph said, "a graceful and majestic Dignity," but still a man without a country.[4]

---

[3] John Hughes to Jonathan Roberts, February 1, April 13, September 25, 1771; to Isaac Hughes, July 25, 1771, Hughes Papers. Cf. *Pa. Mag. of Hist.*, 61 (1937), 468.
[4] Gipson, *Jared Ingersoll*, 294-295, 323-326. New Haven Colony Historical Society, *Papers*, 9 (1918), 418, 456, 472.

Governor Bernard stayed on in Massachusetts until 1770 trying to recover his lost popularity and succeeding only in sinking it further. James Otis and his crowd seized every opportunity to magnify the hatred against him. When Richard Jackson wrote that Bernard had helped materially in securing the repeal of the Stamp Act, the *Boston Gazette* sneered its disbelief,[5] and Otis maintained in public that he could name the very room in Bernard's house where the Stamp Act had been drafted.[6] The Assembly sent letters to England asking for his recall, and when he finally departed, the people of Boston demonstrated their joy by a celebration which he could watch from the harbor.[7] Bernard was rewarded for his pains by a knighthood, a satisfactory compensation perhaps for the chorus of hatred he had endured in Boston, but scarcely the fulfillment of his dream of serving as the architect for a new empire. The final blow to this vision came when Parliament adopted one of his recommendations as a means of punishing Massachusetts for the Boston Tea Party. The Massachusetts Government Act, by giving to the King the authority to appoint the Governor's Council, put the Council at last out of the power of the House of Representatives. It was a measure which Bernard had urged for years, but coming when it did, as a punishment instead of a reform, it helped to bring on the Revolution it was designed to prevent.

When Bernard left Boston, Thomas Hutchinson stepped into his place, first as acting governor, finally as governor. He had coveted the place since 1766, when his son, seeking compensation for his losses in England, had first received hints that the governorship might be his reward.[8] Hutchinson felt that his own understanding of the people of Massachusetts and the accumulated prestige of his long career might enable him to succeed where Bernard had failed. But he was indulg-

---

[5] *Boston Gazette*, April 28, May 5, 19, 1766.

[6] Bernard to Shelburne, December 22, 1766, Chalmers Papers, II, Harvard College Library.

[7] *Boston Gazette*, August 7, 1769; Thomas Young to John Wilkes, August 3, 1769, Massachusetts Historical Society, *Proceedings*, 47 (1914), 207.

[8] Thomas Hutchinson, Jr., to Thomas Hutchinson, July, 1766, Massachusetts Archives, XXV, 86.

ing in wishful thinking. Otis had not been satisfied with Hutchinson's losses in the riots and fought him as consistently as he fought Bernard, blocking him from a seat in the Council, and blaming him, along with Bernard, for everything unpleasant that happened in Massachusetts. Hutchinson's career as governor was as unhappy as Samuel Adams, who took up where Otis left off, could make it. When he finally had to go to England to defend himself against the charges which his enemies kept bringing against him, he found himself trapped there by the Revolution, obliged to sit helplessly in London, as news poured in of distressing events in America. He might console himself with finishing the History of Massachusetts, writing a volume to cover the years which he could remember too well, but he had to do without the letter books which might have assisted him in setting details straight. These were back in Massachusetts in the hands of his enemies, and would be used by another historian, of inferior talent, to help in writing the first history of the Revolution. Hutchinson was at least fortunate enough to die before it appeared.[9]

The victims of the Newport mob all received appropriate rewards: Thomas Moffat returned from London in 1766 to become Collector of Customs at New London;[10] Martin Howard, Jr., became Chief Justice of North Carolina, where he later handed out severe sentences to the rebels who fought at Alamance in 1771;[11] Augustus Johnston received a commission as Judge of the Admiralty Court at Charles Town;[12] and John Robinson was named to the newly formed American Board of Commissioners of the Customs, which sat in Boston and supervised the collection of His Majesty's revenue in the

[9] William Gordon, a Boston clergyman sympathetic to the Revolution, had access to Hutchinson's seized letters in writing his *History of the Rise, Progress, and Establishment of the Independence of the United States of America* (London, 1788). See vol. I.

[10] Frances M. Caulkins, *History of New London, Connecticut* (New London, 1852), 478; *Gentleman's Magazine*, 57 (1787), 277; Diary of Thomas Moffat, Library of Congress.

[11] *Colonial Records of North Carolina*, VII, 427-428; VIII, 642-643.

[12] New Haven Colony Historical Society, *Papers*, 9 (1918), 423, 432.

whole of North America.[13] It was John Robinson who settled in blood a debt which was owed not merely to himself but to his friends in Rhode Island and to Bernard and Hutchinson as well. When Robinson came to Boston, James Otis added his name to his blacklist and filled the newspapers with insulting accusations against the customs commissioners in general and against Robinson in particular. Robinson bore the attacks for a time; he found a few congenial men of his own sentiments in Boston, men who knew what loyalty to Great Britain meant. He even found a wife in the daughter of one of them. But in the face of Otis's vile attacks, he scarcely lived a happy or peaceful life. He finally took to going about armed and made no secret of his intentions to give Otis what he deserved when the occasion offered.

On the night of September fifth in the year 1769, Robinson and a number of other gentlemen were sitting in the British Coffee House, enjoying the fare and the conversation, when in walked Otis. As he saw the man, Robinson must have thought not only of his own recent experiences, but also of what had happened to his old friends in Newport. It was Otis's epithets that the mob had attached to the effigies of Dr. Moffat and Martin Howard; it was Otis's pamphlets which had helped to excite the rage against them. Robinson marched up to the man and seized him by the nose. In the scuffle that followed the lights went out, but it was not too dark for Robinson to give his enemy a crushing blow on the head. Though Otis later sued him, the damage which Robinson had done could no more be compensated than the damage which his victim had done to Moffat, and Howard, and Hutchinson, and Bernard, and indirectly to every loyalist in America. Otis recovered physically, but Robinson's blow had destroyed his mind, and he would never again serve as the leader of Boston's violent men. It was a piece of poetic justice, a token revenge in behalf of those who had in their own way "stood Bluff," though not on their constitutional rights. Having completed his part, John Robinson sailed for England with his bride and drifted out of the stream of history.

[13] William Tudor, *The Life of James Otis* (Boston, 1823), 362-366; John Robinson to Joseph Harrison, October 5, 1769, Chalmers Papers, III, 38, Harvard College Library.

Index